THE PARTY: THE SOCI
1960-

VOLUME 2: INTERREGNUM, DECLINE AND COLLAPSE, 1973-1988

A POLITICAL MEMOIR
Barry Sheppard

Resistance Books would be glad to have readers' opinions of this book, and any suggestions you may have for future publications or wider distribution.

Our books are available at special quantity discounts to educational and non-profit organizations, and to bookstores.

To contact us, please write to:

Resistance Books

PO Box 62732, London, SW2 9CQ

Email at contact@socialistresistance.org

Graphic design © Resistance Books.

Front cover photo: Sandinista fighters entering Managua July 19, 1979 greeted by mass outpouring. © Corbis.

Back cover photo: Caroline Lund working at her automobile factory. Photo by co-worker.

ISBN: 978-0-902869-59-2

Printed in Britain by Lightning Source

THE PARTY: THE SOCIALIST WORKERS PARTY
1960-1988

VOLUME 2: INTERREGNUM, DECLINE AND COLLAPSE, 1973-1988

A POLITICAL MEMOIR
Barry Sheppard

Resistance Books

Contents

INTRODUCTION

This is the second volume of a two-volume book. The first volume, which covered the period of the radicalization of "The Sixties," 1960-1973, should be read in conjunction with the present volume.* My main conclusion here is that the Socialist Workers Party (SWP) was transformed into its opposite in many essential ways from what I describe in the first volume.

The present volume is divided into two parts. The first part I call an "interregnum," because it forms a bridge from the first volume to the second part of this one, and covers the period from 1973 through the end of 1979. In these years the SWP remained active in the broader class struggle at home and abroad. We took important initiatives, including launching a lawsuit against the government for its undemocratic "dirty tricks" against us and by implication against the wider movements for social justice. There was also an important intervention in a struggle to desegregate the public school system in Boston.

The SWP, together with other parties and leaders in the Fourth International, put a great deal of energy into a struggle to reverse the ultraleft course adopted by the International in 1969. This was described in Volume One. For a time the resulting factional struggle intensified, and then was resolved. The initiative for this resolution came from the other side, the leaders of the International Majority Tendency, through a "self-criticism" of the 1969 turn. Our position was vindicated, and opened the way for a rebuilding of the Fourth International, which my companion Caroline Lund and I were intimately involved with.

In 1978-1979, the SWP projected a course to widen its field of activity through a reorientation to the industrial work force and to embrace the revolutions in Nicaragua and Grenada, which we saw as extensions of the Cuban Revolution. In addition, we were deeply involved in the debates concerning the Portuguese revolution of 1974-1975 and the Afghani revolution that began in 1978. During the 1978-1979 revolution in Iran we worked with Iranian comrades to try to build a socialist alternative, a project I was involved with.

But also from the mid-1970s on, there were negative developments in the party leadership, which began to take shape in an incremental fashion. In the period covered by the second part of this volume, 1980-1988, these negative developments came to dominate. The result was an accelerating decline of the SWP both politically and organizationally. From the vibrant interventionist party of "The Sixties," the SWP degenerated into an abstentionist sect, walling itself off from the wider class struggle and the rest of the left, shrinking by 1988 to less than 50 percent in size from its high point in 1976-1978. This trend has continued in the decades since.

The first chapter in Part Two concerns U.S. politics, and is a continuation of similar chapters in Part One. The second chapter discusses what I mean when I say the SWP became a cult. There is what may appear to be a digression, a discussion of defeats of revolutions in Afghanistan, Iran, Nicaragua, Grenada, and Poland. But these defeats weighed heavily on the SWP, and form part of the objective situation the party faced in the 1980s.

This book in two volumes is a political memoir about my time in the SWP beginning in November 1959. In July 1988, my companion Caroline Lund and I resigned from the SWP. I call it a political memoir of this nearly 30-year period for two reasons. One is that it is not a personal memoir. My personal life wasn't much different from the hundreds of thousands of my generation radicalized in "The Sixties," and doesn't shed much light on what we were like as members of that generation that hasn't been written about extensively elsewhere. I only refer to my personal life insofar as it affected my political life. The second reason is that these volumes don't purport to be a comprehensive history of the SWP from 1960 through 1988, nor of the broader political context domestically or internationally. But because I was a central leader of the SWP for most of this time, and of the Fourth International for much of it, my political memoir touches on much of this history.

One theme of this volume is that the collapse of the SWP was not inevitable. As the radicalization of "The Sixties" receded, the objective situation made it increasingly difficult for a small Marxist organization to grow. But with a more correct orientation the SWP could have survived and remained an important force on the left. It would have been able to play a role in building a revolutionary alternative in the wake of the greatest crisis of the capitalist system since the Great Depression, beginning in 2007. Without the SWP, rebuilding the socialist movement in the United States has been made more difficult. The decline of the left in general following the collapse of the Soviet bloc and the restoration of capitalism in China has meant no other organization has been up to the task. The discredited Communist Party is no longer the obstacle it once was, clearing the field. There are other revolutionary socialist groups and individuals, and perhaps a new beginning can come out of them.

I believe the worldwide crisis of the capitalist system that began in 2007 represents a massive attack on the working class. The drive by the government and the corporations to make the working people bear the burden of this crisis will impel new forms of struggle and organizations to emerge. The rebuilding of a revolutionary socialist party is an urgent necessity to help lead this process as it unfolds. A new radicalization will develop, and we must coalesce a conscious Marxist party out of it and to lead it to victory.

I hope this political memoir will help in this process, both by preserving positive lessons and pointing to some things to avoid in the experience of the SWP. People from other traditions, new and old ones, will also contribute to this necessary rebirth.

Various people have read all or parts of this manuscript and made suggestions. For this volume, I would like to thank Jan Arnold, Steve Bloom, Bob Capistrano, Cliff Conner, Richard Fidler, Lynn Henderson, Paul LeBlanc, Linda Loew, Doug Lorimer, Malik Miah, John Percy, Jose Perez, John Riddell, Kateh Vafadari, David Walters, and Babak Zahraie. Gus Horowitz made especially helpful suggestions.

From their suggestions and criticisms I have made my own selection for incorporation into the book.

Special thanks to my editor, Mark Harris. Thanks also to the Holt Labor Library, and its librarians, Shannon Sheppard and David Walters.

The political views expressed here are mine, as are any errors. I expect that others, including those listed above, will present different experiences, express criticisms and alternative views. I hope my book will stimulate such discussion, and I welcome all such, however sharp. This too will be part of the process of rebuilding a revolutionary socialist party.

There has been a delay between the publication of the first volume and this one. The illness and death of my companion Caroline Lund (1944-2006) diverted my energy into caregiving and then grief for a period of years. This volume is weaker than it would otherwise have been if she had been able to participate in discussions with me about it, and help edit it. It is dedicated to her memory.

---

* Barry Sheppard, *The Party: The Socialist Workers Party 1960-1988, Vol. 1: The Sixties, A Political Memoir* (Resistance Books, 2005). 354 pages.

Part One:
Interregnum, 1973 - 1979

CHAPTER ONE: THE EBBING OF THE RADICALIZATION

In January 1973, the United States signed a "peace" agreement with North Vietnam and the National Liberation Front (NLF) of South Vietnam, which provided for the withdrawal of most U.S. troops. The war, however, was not over. The agreement carved up South Vietnam into areas under the control of the North Vietnamese/NLF and the U.S. puppet regime in South Vietnam. Washington continued to massively supply its regime in Saigon, and kept U.S. military personnel in the country as advisors.

But the subsequent withdrawal of the bulk of U.S. troops led to the end of the antiwar movement. The war itself didn't end until two years later, when the South Vietnamese regime was overthrown and the country reunited under what had been "North" Vietnam, winning Vietnamese self-determination. The antiwar movement was one factor in this great victory.

There had been two major forces behind the development of the radicalization of "The Sixties," the antiwar movement and the fight for Black freedom. The later had won a historic victory with the overthrow of the Jim Crow system of legal racial segregation and oppression in the South. The spread of the movement to include the North's *de facto* segregation was most sharply expressed in Black rebellions across the country in the mid- to-late 1960s.

The ruling capitalist class was not only forced into dismantling Jim Crow, but to granting further rights to Blacks such as affirmative action. There were real openings for change for African Americans after the end of legal segregation.

However, no sector of the Black movement proved capable of projecting what to do next in this context. Related to this was the fact that the radicalization had not spurred the working class as a whole into massive political action in its own interests, which would have signaled a new stage for all social movements.

This is not to say that the victories of the 1960-73 period for Black, Latino, Native American and other people's rights were overturned. Nor were those of the women's movement that emerged in the late1960s out of the radicalization. Increased rights for gays and lesbians also grew out of the women's movement and the broader radicalization. Attitudes among the American people were fundamentally changed on these and other issues, and gains continued to be made. But the ebb of the radicalization provided an opening for a gradual ruling class counter-offensive in the 1970-

2000 decades. An example of this is the whittling away at affirmative action for oppressed minorities and women. This was evident even as additional victories were won.

In January 1973, the U.S. Supreme Court declared that abortion was legal, striking down laws against it in 46 states. This victory for women's rights came after the new and growing women's liberation movement had waged a four-year struggle. It was the first major victory for the new movement.

In March 1972, Congress passed the Equal Rights Amendment (ERA) to the Constitution. The amendment then had to be ratified by 38 states within seven years. The ERA read, "Equality of rights under the law shall not be denied on account of sex." But by the summer of 1973, Caroline Lund wrote in *The Militant*, "After a spurt of quick approvals in [30] states, the ratification process has ground almost to a halt earlier this year in the face of an organized, well-financed campaign to defeat it.

"This campaign has been spearheaded by such right-wing forces as the [racist pro-segregation] American Independent Party, the [virulent anticommunist] John Birch Society, members of the Catholic Church hierarchy, Goldwater [of the Republican Party's right wing] supporter Phyllis Schlafly, and anti-feminist women's groups such as 'Happiness of Womanhood' (HOW)."

Caroline also reported that "unfortunately this struggle for citizenship for women has not won the support of all sections of the women's movement, the labor movement, or groups that consider themselves socialist.

"Opponents of the ERA include the AFL-CIO officialdom, the Communist Party, a California-based organization called Union Women's Alliance to Gain Equality (Union WAGE), and the Maoist-oriented Revolutionary Union."

The main argument of these groups was that the ERA would gut existing laws for the protection of working class women. This was a bogus position. As Caroline wrote, "Some state laws are beneficial to women workers, such as those requiring rest breaks, adequate ventilation, etc. Others are clearly detrimental to women in the guise of 'protection,' such as those prohibiting women from doing night work or from entering certain occupations such as bartending, metal molding, mining, working in blast furnaces or smelters, and many others."

Such forces "have lost sight of the significance of the principle of equal rights for women, especially working women. They in essence tell women workers to settle for the few 'protections' they have rather than fight for equal rights across the board and extension of good protective laws to men also."[1]

The Socialist Workers Party (SWP) itself had adopted this reactionary position when the subject of the ERA came up after the Second World War. We changed our position with the rise of the new women's liberation movement in the late 1960s.

The setback Caroline noted marked a retreat for the movement for the ERA, which as I write in 2011 still has not been adopted. The retreat was not only on this issue. As the radicalization ebbed, the National Organization for Women (NOW) increasingly looked to the Democratic Party as opposed to the mobilization of women to fight for their rights.

•••

The war in Vietnam and the mass movement in opposition to the war had a major impact, called the "Vietnam syndrome." The big majority of the American people became very distrustful of going to war for a whole period. In fact, it took the terrorist attacks of September 11, 2001 to give the ruling class new hope that the Vietnam syndrome was at last over, and it appeared to be as the United States had the support of the great majority to go to war in Afghanistan and Iraq. But the failure of the war in Iraq has shown that this support was not as deep as first appeared, and as I write this, the Vietnam syndrome is making a comeback, indicating how deep the changes in attitudes from "The Sixties" continues to be.*

While the general radicalization eventually went into a retreat in the 1970s, the changes in social attitudes meant continued growth for the SWP in this decade. Some who had rejected us earlier or were repelled by the disintegration of Students for a Democratic Society (SDS) into the terrorist Weather Underground and Maoist sects, took a closer look and decided to join the SWP or Young Socialist Alliance (YSA). Others were attracted to initiatives we took. One of these was our civil liberties lawsuit against the government.

This lawsuit came out of the political crisis of the Nixon administration in 1973-74. Republican Richard Nixon was reelected in 1972, in part because he promised to get the United States out of Vietnam. He also appealed to the "silent majority" that was uneasy about aspects of the radicalization, especially rights for Blacks and women. His Vice President, Spiro Agnew, was exposed as a crook shortly after being reelected, and resigned in disgrace in 1973. Agnew was a vehement anti-communist and viciously red-baited the antiwar movement. He was a living example of the adage that "Patriotism is the last refuge of a scoundrel."

Then Nixon himself came under suspicion, in what became known as the Watergate scandal. It arose out of a break-in by a group of thugs who were captured while in the Democratic National

Campaign Committee's offices in the Watergate apartment complex in Washington, D.C. during the 1972 presidential election campaign. Nixon was eventually proven to have ordered the break-in, looking for anything that could be used against the Democrats in the elections. Nixon, under threat of impeachment in Congress, resigned in disgrace, another scoundrel and crook who wrapped himself in the flag.

There were more far-reaching results of the investigation of the scandal. The government's dirty tricks against the Black and antiwar movements came to light, such as FBI director J. Edgar Hoover's campaign to discredit Martin Luther King. "Cointelpro" (Counter-Intelligence Program) was exposed as a many-year FBI campaign to infiltrate, disrupt, discredit, and victimize dissident groups. Coupled with the government's lying about the Vietnam War, documented by Daniel Ellsberg's release of the Pentagon Papers, the Watergate revelations raised public distrust of the government to an unprecedented high.

We, of course, knew that the SWP was one of the targeted groups, not only of the FBI, but a whole number of agencies from the CIA on down. In my own experience, I found out by accident that I was fired from a job because of the FBI a few months after I joined the SWP in November 1959. Every time I entered the country from abroad I was pulled out of line at immigration and all my papers were photocopied.

Government attacks on the SWP had a long history. Party leaders had been convicted in 1940 under the Smith Act, and members were framed or denied their rights since then, resulting in many defense cases the party was compelled to wage. For many years during the McCarthyite witchhunt in the 1950s, party leaders were denied passports. Our members in the maritime industry were blackballed. The government attack on the party was far-reaching and broad.

In the political atmosphere of the unfolding Watergate scandal, the SWP Political Committee decided to launch a lawsuit against the government. The suit, which was filed in July 1973, charged Nixon and others with "illegal acts of blacklisting, harassment, electronic surveillance, burglary, mail tampering, and terrorism" against the SWP and YSA, and their members and supporters. Leonard Boudin, the foremost constitutional lawyer in the country, filed the suit. In addition to the SWP and YSA as organizations, there were named plaintiffs, including me.

It would take 13 more years of "discovery" proceedings (in which the various political police agencies were forced to turn over thousands of pages of documents), motions and counter-motions, and a lengthy trial before the suit was concluded in our favor.

The Political Rights Defense Fund (PRDF) was formed to support the suit and raise money to fund it. PRDF would eventually garner wide support on the left and among supporters of civil and democratic rights generally. As the suit progressed, we uncovered wide-ranging violations of our democratic rights as alleged. While it took over a decade, we eventually won the suit in an outstanding decision defending civil liberties.

The judge in the case, Thomas Griesa, issued a lengthy decision.

He wrote that the government's investigation of the party began in 1936 with a "series of directives issued by President Roosevelt to J. Edgar Hoover, Director of the FBI."

On the FBI alone, the judge's decision detailed 57 disruption operations. These included 20,000 days of listening to wiretaps and 12,000 days of listening to "bugs" planted in SWP offices and members' homes, 208 burglaries resulting in the theft or photocopying of 9,864 private documents. Our initial charges were confirmed in spades.

In December 1972 we had won an important victory that helped set the stage for our confidence in filing the PRDF suit. A federal judge ordered the reinstatement of Morris Starsky, a professor at Arizona State University, fired by the ASU regents for his socialist and antiwar views.

When Starsky came to ASU in the philosophy department in 1964 he became one of the initiators of the antiwar movement there. In subsequent years he was known on campus and in Tempe, Arizona, where ASU is located, as a fighter for Black and Chicano students and for student rights in general, as well as for his support for striking workers. He played a key role in organizing the YSA on the campus. He joined the SWP.

When the regents began the process that would lead to his firing, Starsky, with the help of the party, set up a defense committee based on support for his democratic rights. As was always our practice in such cases, no one who came to his defense was asked to endorse his political views—only his rights. It was this defense committee that filed the successful suit for his reinstatement.

Starsky was a very personable and likeable fellow. He was a favorite among the party and YSA membership. Unfortunately, he had a heart condition that led to his early death in 1989.

•••

The SWP held a convention in August 1973. It was our largest convention to date, with over 1,400 in attendance. Most were observers. The delegates elected from the branches, who held the decisive votes, were a smaller group. I gave the political report to the convention for the outgoing Political Committee. At the time, I had moved to Los Angeles and was part of the L.A. branch, although I remained on the Political Committee.**

At the 1973 convention, a disturbing development was brought to the attention of the leadership. Two comrades, a man who went by the name of "Geb," and a women comrade who called herself "Sudie," authored a few written contributions to the preconvention discussion that went pretty far in the counter-cultural direction, including advocating repeal of our policy of prohibiting the use of illegal drugs by party members. They won few supporters, not enough to obtain a delegate.

However, we learned that Geb and Sudie had brought illegal drugs to the convention, including "hard" drugs like the one known as PCP. That is, having failed to win the party to their position concerning illegal drugs, they flouted the party's policy unilaterally.

We had adopted a strict policy against any members using any illegal drugs. This was not done for moralistic reasons, but for security. We did not have any such policy regarding alcohol, for example, the use of which can be just as dangerous as many illegal drugs.

The key for us was that certain drugs were *illegal*. Since they were illegal, the political police could victimize any of our members using such drugs, and go after the party itself. In fact, this happened many times to other organizations and activists. One that stuck in my mind occurred in 1966 in Texas. A Black activist was sitting on a park bench, when two plainclothes undercover cops sat down on each side of him. One asked him to pass a cigarette to the other. It turned out to be marijuana. The activist was arrested and sentenced to 10 years.

Our blanket ban on illegal drugs was well known in the whole radical movement. This made it much more difficult for the political police to victimize us on these grounds, including by planting drugs on our members, and I can't recall any instance.

So what Sudie and Geb did by bringing such drugs to a convention endangered the whole organization as well as invited guests. We knew the FBI had sent informants into the party (and later proved this through our suit). Luckily, the discovery of Sudie and Geb's drugs was limited to a few people.

Since they were members of the L.A. branch, Wendy Lyons, who was the branch organizer, brought charges against them when the branch members had returned from the convention. I stayed at Oberlin after the convention to attend a brief meeting of the newly elected National Committee, and to help edit the transcribed reports given to the convention for publication. When I returned to L.A., the trial, which was held over a few weekly branch meetings, was still going on. There was no question of whether or not Sudie and Geb were guilty, as they admitted as much when presented with the evidence. But there was a disagreement in the branch about whether they should be expelled or sanctioned in some lesser fashion such as a censure or suspension for a time.

There were over 100 members of the branch, so the discussion about the penalty was lengthy and necessarily thorough. My participation in the discussion was mainly educational, centering on the danger that illegal drugs posed for the party. No one referred to the political positions of Sudie and Geb—the party jealously defended the rights of members to present their positions, however little support they had in the membership. Eventually, the branch majority came to the considered decision that Sudie and Geb should be expelled.

The large size of the L.A. branch and the fact that it contained some virtually inactive members made it hard to organize. I remember before a branch meeting some members called Wendy at our apartment to ask if the meeting was cancelled because it was raining. What was involved were not violent thunderstorms or a hurricane. Wendy looked at me with a smile and said, "Do they think they'll melt?"

Wendy and I had the full support of two old-timers in the branch, Oscar Coover and Leo Frumpkin, in working to turn the branch around. Oscar worked as a carpenter on movie sets in Hollywood. He grew up in the party—his father of the same name was a founding member of the SWP in 1938 and was a central person in the leadership of the great 1934 Teamster strikes in Minneapolis. Leo had joined the SWP in L.A. as a teenager involved in a local battle of Jewish high school students against a fascist anti-Semite. This was at the end of the Second World War.

The L.A. headquarters was in a seedy part of town off Sunset Boulevard. Prostitutes patrolled the nearby streets at night, and sometimes our women members were accosted on their way to branch meetings. We decided to move, and also to divide the branch in two. We established new headquarters near California State University, Los Angeles (CSLA) and the University of California, Los Angeles (UCLA). The branch near CSLA was also near East Los Angeles, a largely Chicano small city that was a center of Chicano political activity. East L.A. was an unincorporated area of mostly white sprawling Los Angeles County, and thus denied self-government—one of the political issues roiling the city. "Cheech and Chong" would later pay homage to East L.A. in their hilarious film/song, "Born in East L.A." The other branch was in Santa Monica, west of L.A. proper, and near UCLA.

We elected a city committee, and I became the city organizer, while Wendy became the organizer of the branch near Cal State, and Stu Singer organizer of the branch near UCLA. I was out of town a lot, either to New York to attend meetings of the Political Committee and, once in the fall, to the Far East. While in L.A. I helped in constructing the new headquarters while participating in regular branch activities, including sales of *The Militant* and attending the weekly forums of one of the two branches. In addition, I organized meetings of the city committee, which would consider citywide initiatives that both branches would participate in. In the main, the branches discussed and decided most of our activity.

We were still recruiting, and literature and *Militant* sales were good in neighborhoods and campuses. The two branches were over 20 miles apart. As city organizer I needed a car, which the city organization bought—a clunker of a second-hand Nissan. This was before Japanese companies like Nissan, Toyota and Honda began to build really good cars. While returning from nearby Santa Barbara (nearby by California standards) to sell subscriptions at the University of California, Santa Barbara (UCSB) campus, my car's engine blew up. We were stranded for some hours miles from L.A.

At that time the United Farm Workers (UFW) had been waging a bitter struggle against agribusiness in California, particularly lettuce and grape growers and Gallo wines. After winning some contracts, the largely Chicano and Filipino union faced a new offensive by the bosses aided by the corrupt and right-wing officialdom of the Teamsters union. Ostensibly what was involved was a jurisdictional dispute between the Teamsters and the UFW. Companies that previously had contracts with the UFW, and others the UFW was seeking to organize, signed "sweetheart" deals with the Teamsters that guaranteed the owners a stranglehold over these especially oppressed and exploited workers.

The UFW had launched a strike against these companies on April 15, 1973. Right away, in an obviously coordinated action with the bosses, the Teamsters hired squadrons of goons at $50 a day (a tidy sum at the time) to physically assault the UFW picket lines. It was only through such intimidation that the fake Teamster contracts were signed.

Millions of people who were radicalized in "The Sixties" had adopted the struggle of the farm workers as their own. It combined a labor fight with the broader Chicano movement, and became a cause célèbre of the times. As a result, there was widespread knowledge of the despicable role of the Teamsters, and condemnation even among union officials. Finally, the AFL-CIO tops told the Teamster officials to back off, which they did in July. A center of the strike was in

Coachella Valley. Writing from the Valley, *Militant* reporter Andrea Baron wrote, "The striking United Farm Workers Union scored a major victory ... with the withdrawal of the Teamster-hired goons from all the agricultural areas being picketed by the UFW."

After the thugs were withdrawn, Baron reported that "this week was the first time since the grape strike began April 15 that there were no violent incidents here. The absence of the Teamster goons is clearly the reason why."[2] The UFW had a policy of avoiding confrontations with the thugs, but strikers were forced at times to defend themselves. The corporate press had tried to blame "both sides," but now this was exposed as a lie.

The victory was the backdrop to the September convention of the UFW held in Fresno, California. From Los Angeles, we sent a large delegation to the convention, to report, talk and mingle with the delegates and otherwise show our support, and to distribute *The Militant* and other literature. Sales were brisk.···

Miguel Pendas and Harry Ring reported on the convention for *The Militant*. "The United Farm workers convention ... confirmed the determination of the members of this beleaguered union to continue their fight until they defeat the profit-hungry agribusiness interests that are out to destroy them," they wrote.

There were about 400 elected delegates to the convention, and over 1,000 additional supporters. "The character of the UFW as a movement of the most exploited and oppressed workers was apparent. For the established unions ... a convention often means a gathering at a comfortable hotel in a major city or resort. Delegates receive generous expense allowances and food, drink, and entertainment sometimes become a principal preoccupation.

"At this convention the sessions were held in a public arena. Delegates were provided bag lunches at their tables and hot meals in the evenings. They relied on mass housing or the homes of local members and supporters of the union."

With the withdrawal of the Teamster-hired thugs, the union still faced the fact that many growers had already signed "sweetheart" contracts with the Teamsters. "In its fight to void the fake Teamster pacts and win genuine representation for field hands, the UFW will now officially direct its major energies to promoting the boycott of scab grapes, lettuce and Gallo wines," wrote Pendas and Ring. Millions of people got behind the boycott and the UFW, including every radical tendency. I myself didn't eat grapes for some years—like every member of the SWP and YSA.[3]

The Los Angeles branch was larger than most, and had its own political opportunities, but in general, SWP branches were continuing to grow. We noted an upturn in union struggles, and hoped this would lead to a renewal of the radicalization. Thus at the time we did not fully understand that we were entering a new period of gradual decline of social struggles. This is not surprising, since it is often only in retrospect that such changes can become clear.

---

* The wars in Iraq and Afghanistan are unpopular, even though they have not resulted in a mass movement against them, except for the few months leading up to the invasion of Iraq in 2003. Once the shooting started, the movement sharply contracted. One reason for this is the fact that the ruling class does not dare to reinstitute the draft for fear of provoking a new youth radicalization. The wars are being funded by borrowing, not through taxes, which raises problems for the rulers down the road.

** This book is not a personal memoir. I do not discuss my personal life except when it is necessary to the political content of the book, and such references are bare-boned. As I explained in Volume One of this work, "In the spring of 1972 I worked closely with Wendy Lyons, who was our national antiwar director. We made a number of trips together to talk to leaders of NPAC [National Peace Action Coalition, the broad antiwar coalition we worked in and helped lead] as well as to branches. We became close.

"In the summer, the triangle of me, Wendy and Caroline [Lund] caused considerable emotional turmoil for the three of us...." The SWP leadership decided "to send Wendy and myself to Los Angeles, where the branch was in need of leadership strengthening. I also needed some R&R. So the triangle was settled—for a time." I had lived with Caroline since 1966. In autumn of 1974, Caroline and I got back together, and remained together until her death in 2006.

*** I was in one of the cars that drove to Fresno for the UFW convention. While driving, on September 20, we listened on the radio to a famous tennis match between Billie Jean King, winner of five Wimbledon women's tennis titles, and Bobby Riggs, a former tennis champion himself. Linda Jenness wrote in The Militant (Sept. 21, 1973), "Riggs is a loudmouth hustler proud of his image as male chauvinist of the year.... Riggs spends his time today attacking women's tennis. According to Riggs, 'a woman's place is in the bedroom and kitchen, in that order.'" Riggs apparently thought his maleness would trump King even though he was much older. The match became a kind of symbol for women, and we cheered in the car as King beat him.

1 The Militant, June 1, 1973.

2 Ibid., July 20, 1973.
3 Ibid., Oct. 5, 1973.

CHAPTER TWO: THE MILITARY COUP IN CHILE

International events were still a major backdrop to our work in the United States. The war in Vietnam raged on. In the fall of 1973, there were two big interventions by U.S. imperialism through surrogates—the military coup in Chile ushering in a brutal dictatorship that lasted decades, and the Israel-Arab war. The coup happened on September 11, 1973—a "9/11" conveniently forgotten in the capitalist media.

This chapter is a summary of the position the SWP developed on the situation in Chile as reflected in reports in *The Militant* and *Intercontinental Press*, contained in *Disaster in Chile*, edited by Les Evans, Pathfinder Press (New York, 1974). I recommend reading this book for a complete overview of the SWP's analysis. In the early 1980s, Jack Barnes, the SWP National Secretary, claimed that we had been wrong at the time about the Allende government, but his comments were vague. In 1981, the SWP reprinted a speech Fidel Castro had made on Allende's overthrow, together with an introduction by Betsy Stone, but there was nothing in either that amounted to an argument that we had in fact been wrong. I believe our original analysis of events as they unfolded was correct.

•••

In September 1970, Salvador Allende, a leader of the Chilean Socialist Party (SP), in a bloc called Popular Unity (UP in its Spanish initials) that included the Communist Party (CP) and four other small capitalist parties, won election as the country's president with a 36 percent plurality. The candidate of the right-wing National Party came in second with 35 percent, and the Christian Democratic Party candidate won 28 percent. The Nixon administration, not wanting to appear as backing the far right, openly supported the candidate of the Christian Democrats and poured money into his campaign.

The Chilean SP differed from other Socialist parties in Latin America and around the world in that it did not line up with Washington in the Cold War. A left wing had developed in the SP, which Allende was associated with. One of his campaign promises that particularly irked Washington was to restore diplomatic and trade relations with Cuba, which Allende promptly did upon taking office. Most Latin American governments had broken relations with

Cuba following its revolution, under intense pressure from the colossus to the north.

Allende's election indicated a new shift to the left by a significant section of the working class and lower middle class. By April 1971, the UP bloc increased its vote in municipal elections to 50 percent, with the SP making the biggest gains within the bloc. This reflected popular support for reforms by the new government that helped the most disadvantaged sections of the population. These reforms included a freeze on the prices of consumer goods while the lowest category of wages was raised by 50 percent and the rest by 25 to 30 percent. Family allowances were doubled, and school supplies were provided free.

By the end of its first year in office, the UP government had nationalized the copper mines owned largely by U.S. firms, and begun to implement an agrarian reform that had been promised but not carried out by the previous Christian Democrat regime. Washington's hostility intensified and it began to mobilize client states in Latin America to isolate the Allende government. It also began to limit credit as well as trade. These measures to squeeze the Chilean economy would intensify over the following years.

The SP and the CP were dominant in the UP coalition, but there were also smaller capitalist parties, including the Radical Party, which had a history as one of the important capitalist parties in the past. The significance of the inclusion of these small bourgeois parties wasn't in their electoral following, which was negligible. What their inclusion did signify was that the UP coalition would not step beyond the bounds of capitalism, even as it pledged reforms in the interests of the workers and peasants. Such a coalition, which sought to bring together the working people and the "enlightened" sectors of the bourgeoisie, is inherently unstable, as it looks to reconcile two opposing classes with opposite interests.

SWP leader Peter Camejo wrote in *The Militant*:

"With the blessings of outgoing [Christian Democrat] President Frei, the army, and the church, Allende took office and promised to lead Chile to socialism by obeying the constitution based on capitalist property relations and upholding the primary defenders of capitalist private property, the army and police.

"Thus, in order to remain in power, Allende must constantly demonstrate to the ruling class that he can contain the masses. Most crucial in this respect is keeping the mass organizations disarmed. On the other hand, if he losses his mass support, the ruling class would no longer need to tolerate him. Therefore, Allende must bend sufficiently to mass pressure to maintain his mass support.

"The politics of the Allende regime are by nature forced into a balancing act between the oppressed and the oppressor classes."[1]

This dynamic played itself out up to the moment of the military coup.

In the wake of Allende's election, workers and peasants began to take things into their own hands. A December 1971 statement by the United Secretariat of the Fourth International pointed out "in the period since the election, the workers and peasants have not at all limited themselves to supporting Allende and waiting for the government to act. They have often taken the initiative, obliging the government to approve the things that have been done. More importantly, the practical actions undertaken by the masses have often gone beyond the program of the Popular Unity. Peasants have taken over land without waiting for formal decisions and have even seized properties that could not be touched according to the [agrarian reform] law. Workers have undertaken actions along the same lines, accelerating the process of [nationalization] and hitting enterprises that in principle were to be left in the sector of privately owned property."

The bourgeoisie and U.S. imperialism reacted with increasing alarm at the masses breaking out in such a fashion. In 1972 the class struggle further heated up. The capitalists and shopkeepers were sabotaging the economy to stir up unrest. Inflation began to gallop. The reactionary press began to openly agitate against the government, and fomented demonstrations by right-wing gangs armed with clubs and iron bars. The fascist *Patria y Libertad* [Homeland and Liberty] began to show its face in these actions. The fight was rapidly shifting from parliament, where the main capitalist opposition parties, the Christian Democrats and the National Party, held a majority, to the streets.

In October 1972 a "bosses strike" was organized that aimed to weaken popular support for the government. In response, millions of workers mobilized to keep the country going. Factories abandoned by the bosses were occupied and reopened. In the face of a strike by trucking companies designed to halt distribution of food and other necessities, other means of transportation were sequestered and trade was kept open. As the organ of the SP's left wing, *Ahora de Chile*, described, the workers "were there, producing, transporting, guarding, distributing, organizing so that the country wouldn't shut down. We were there for the twenty-seven days of the crisis. If this isn't true, let our compañero presidente say so. It was the physical presence of millions of workers that kept him in power." The result was a setback for the capitalists, and a strengthening of the confidence of the working class. The poor in the shantytowns surrounding the big cities were drawn onto the side of the more organized and stable workers who were the backbone of the counter-offensive. Large sections of the middle class were also drawn away from the bourgeoisie.

The Chilean capitalist class in its majority initially backed the Allende regime. Since Allende had won the presidency with a bare plurality but not a majority in 1970, the election was thrown into parliament. The Christian Democrats pledged their support to Allende, which insured his election, and then even the National Party representatives voted for him.

What the main sectors of the capitalist class were counting on was that Allende could contain the workers and peasants because of his authority among them. There was also the hope that the Allende coalition could help modernize the economy, which the previous Christian Democrat regime had tried to do but was blocked by the National Party and its base among the landlords and traditional oligarchy. Likewise, the main capitalist sectors viewed the UP as a potential counter-weight to these more reactionary sectors. For the time being, the capitalist class as a whole sought to carry out such modernization through maintaining bourgeois democracy and the constitution. In so doing, the bosses were continuing a long tradition of bourgeois democracy in Chile, which had served them well.

Both the SP and the CP adhered to a class collaborationist strategy. The SP was to the left of the CP, and as the class struggle intensified, a left wing within it emerged, as indicated by the above quotation from *Ahora de Chile*. However, this left wing remained committed to the SP's collaborationist strategy with the capitalist class to the catastrophic end.

The CP was the best organized force in the UP bloc, in contrast to the heterogeneous and loose SP. It consistently sought to apply the breaks on the mobilizations of the workers and peasants, and to keep them within the bounds of bourgeois legality. Allende had promised that his reforms would someday open the road to socialism, and he undoubtedly believed this. The CP, however, held rigidly to the Stalinist dogma that in underdeveloped countries like Chile, there could not be a socialist revolution until there was a prolonged period of capitalism. The UP coalition, in this view, could help win reforms for the working people while helping to modernize Chilean capitalism, but must remain subordinate to the capitalist class. Socialism was put off to a distant future.

Stalin had developed this "theory" for the countries exploited by imperialism in the 1930s. His objective was to placate the imperialist countries in the (vain) hope that they would leave the Soviet Union alone to develop "socialism in one country." Even though it was compelled to adapt to the Cuban Revolution after the fact, the Kremlin sought to reassure Washington that it would derail any further extension of the socialist revolution in U.S. imperialism's "backyard." Soviet pressure on the Chilean CP to toe this line became acute in the period of the UP government as the Kremlin sought "détente" with the United States.

Another organization that would emerge to play a role was the Movement of the Revolutionary Left (MIR in its Spanish initials). The MIR was a guerrilla grouping, among many that had sprung up in Latin America after the Cuban Revolution. It had a small base in the peasantry and in the shantytowns before Allende's election, but in the main ignored the organized working class. It was completely taken aback by the election of Allende, which it had dismissed as unlikely.

The MIR was for a socialist revolution, and stood to the left of both the SP and CP, but had nowhere near their influence in the working class or among the peasantry or shantytowns. In the wake of the UP victory, the MIR reoriented itself in the new situation. As a voice to the left of the SP and CP, it began to grow. Its criticisms of the UP government were often trenchant, and it began to take important initiatives in the mass movement. As a consequence, the MIR became the target of the SP's right wing and especially of the CP, both of whom accused it of "ultraleftism." These attacks were not only aimed at combating the ideas and actions initiated or supported by the MIR, but also at the "ultraleftism" of workers and peasants who were going "too far" for the reformists controlling the UP government.

The left wing of the SP and the MIR were enthusiastic supporters of the workers who kept the economy running during the bosses' strike of October 1972. Both the MIR and the left wing of the SP wanted to build upon the workers' takeover of factories and means of distribution to deepen workers' control of the economy. The CP and SP right wing had to formally support the workers' actions, too, to keep their base. But the CP and SP leadership resisted the workers' initiatives.

Allende himself moved to the right. His response to the crisis was not to turn to the workers, peasants and urban poor, but, with the full support of the CP, to seek to placate the armed forces, loyal to the capitalists and their imperialist masters, in the hope they would not overthrow the government. Following the defeat of the bosses' strike, Allende appointed a new cabinet with chief of the armed forces, General Carlos Prats, in charge of the Ministry of the Interior. The appointment gave General Prats authority over the police and local governments. Further, Admiral Ismael Huerta was appointed minister of the Ministry of Public Works and Transport, and General Claudio Sepulveda was put in charge of the Ministry of Mines. The latter two ministries were vital to the economy. The real levers of power were now in the military's hands. For the moment the armed forces did not advance a military coup.

Incorporating these leaders of the armed forces into the cabinet was an attempt by the UP leadership to reassure the capitalists, in the wake of the defeat of their strike, that the new government was one of "national unity" and stability. This worked at first, but soon unraveled as the polarization between the two major classes deepened.

The ruling class sabotage of the economy continued. Basic goods were becoming scarce. The efforts to subvert the economy were backed by the U.S. boycott of Chilean copper and other export goods, and denial of credit to the UP regime. Prices, speculation and hording were rising. Denunciations of the government in the opposition press blamed shortages on the UP. The masses began to organize committees to take over direct distribution of scarce items.

It was in this atmosphere that the election campaigns of both the right and left were waged leading up to the March 4, 1973 legislative vote. The Christian Democrats put up a common electoral bloc with the National Party called the Democratic Confederation. The right was expecting to win more seats in both the Senate and Chamber of Deputies, enough to have a two-thirds majority. Such a margin would enable the opposition to veto government initiatives and even impeach Allende. The right expected to win 60 percent of the vote. But it lost seats in both houses, as the UP won in important working class districts. The UP gained an additional six seats in the Chamber and three in the Senate. The overall vote for the Democratic Confederation was 54.7 percent, a disappointment for them. The UP won 43.4 percent overall, which they expected.

The National Party gained seats at the expense of the Christian Democrats. It proclaimed in its campaign it would get "Allende's head" and eliminate the CP. The Christian Democrats on the other hand claimed they didn't want to overthrow Allende, just force him to correct his "errors."

There were differences on the left, too. The MIR and the left wing of the SP, and some smaller groups including the Trotskyists, warned against the danger of a military coup. They advocated the arming of the workers and helped set up armed units. The CP denounced such "ultraleftism" as not having faith in the armed forces. Allende was opposed to arming the workers, too, but used softer language than the CP, while lauding the armed forces as a bulwark of democracy.

The CP also urged that the "social sector" of the economy be restricted and that some enterprises nationalized under pressure of the workers during the bosses strike be returned to their former owners. Allende also supported this orientation, but played down its scope. The far left on the other hand advocated more nationalizations and support to the new class organizations forged in the heat of the class struggle. These included the various committees set up to oversee distribution of goods, municipal councils, factory committees and the cordones industriales, organizations embracing workers in a number of factories grouped together in the industrial belts surrounding the capital, Santiago.

On March 27, 1973, the generals in the cabinet resigned. This was not what it appeared on the surface, a concession to the left. It served to defuse widening suspicion that their presence in the government was a prelude to a military takeover. Moreover, as long as they were part of the cabinet, their participation made the right's criticism of the government more difficult, lest it be seen as a criticism of the armed forces, too.

From November 1972 through March 1973, the military had blocked with Allende against the far right. Its departure opened the way for a renewed offensive by the right, which began to organize street protests. The fascist Homeland and Liberty was growing stronger, and joined these actions to attack left newspapers, parties and individuals.

The UP parties and the far left held large counter-demonstrations. Jack Barnes and Mary-Alice Waters went to Chile for the SWP and saw these large mobilizations. At the same time, Allende retreated from further reforms and sought to put the brakes on popular struggles. In Allende's SP the right wing was gaining, and the left wing itself was being pulled in its wake. Increasingly, the CP dominated the UP with its more blatant class collaboration strategy.

On the morning of June 29 a minority grouping in the army attempted a coup d'etat. The coup was rapidly put down by troops still loyal to the "democratic order," but with the workers playing the decisive role. The United Workers Confederation (CUT in its Spanish initials), called for the workers to seize the factories as a preventative measure against the attempted putsch. The CP leaders of the CUT were forced to take this drastic measure because of the seriousness of the situation, and the workers responded. The plotters were isolated.

The right was for the time being set back politically as a result of the attempted coup. But a fresh rightist offensive began on July 25 with a new bosses' and professionals' strike. The far right was emboldened and carried out terrorist attacks, including the assassination of Allende's aide, Captain Araya, on July 27. The army began operations against the armed groups of workers, peasants and shantytown residents that had formed in spite of the UP government's opposition. These groups were a "parallel army" that had to be crushed, according to one Christian Democrat leader. However, these armed groups encompassed a minority of the working people.

Rightist officers were haranguing troops that the only solution was to overthrow the government. The first steps would be to destroy the mass organizations of the left, especially the cordones industriales and the municipal committees.

In August the Navy brass began arresting hundreds of "extremist" sailors and naval yard workers, and subjecting them to brutal torture. These were sailors and workers who were beginning to oppose the danger of a military coup.

The MIR and the left Socialists had done some political work in the armed forces to win over the ranks, but the UP government rejected any such attempts, claiming that the army stood above the class struggle.

In the face of the bosses' strike, Allende once again turned not to the workers to launch a revolutionary counter-offensive, but to the military. General Prats was again appointed to the cabinet. But under pressure from both the left and the right, this government soon collapsed. Allende then appointed General Pinochet as commander of the armed forces.

In early September, the economic crisis caused by the bosses' strike and the failure of the UP to counter it led to catastrophic shortages. The middle classes were driven to a frenzy. The bourgeoisie, with the full backing and guidance of Washington, sensed that the time was ripe for a decisive blow. On September 11, the Navy seized the port of Valparaiso, and the army under General Pinochet took power in Santiago, murdering Allende and unleashing one of the most brutal dictatorships in Latin American history. In the next few years Argentina and Uruguay would also follow the Chilean example. (There is some dispute whether Allende committed suicide or was shot by soldiers. In either case, however, it was the army's storming of the Presidential Palace and trapping Allende that directly led to his death. This is why I use the term murder.)

Allende was able to make a final radio broadcast before he was killed, declaring, "I am not going to resign! I will pay for loyalty to the people with my life."

He reiterated his loyalty to the Constitution and denounced the coup leaders for trampling on it. He singled out "foreign capital, imperialism," who "together with the reaction, created the climate in which the Armed Forces broke their tradition [of staying out of politics]" to further the "social sector who today are hoping, with foreign assistance, to re-conquer the power to continue defending their profits and their privileges." He concluded, "Long live Chile! Long live the people! Long live the workers!"

The army and the air force began an all-out attack on the mass organizations with bombings and artillery bombardments of factories and shantytowns. The members of the SP, CP, MIR and mass organizations including not only the various popular committees, but also the trade unions were hunted down, their organizations declared illegal. Tens of thousands were arrested, tortured, executed and "disappeared" in a reign of terror that ushered in a totalitarian military regime that lasted decades.

One of the military's first targets was non-citizens. It initially justified its coup with a heavy propaganda campaign charging that "foreigners" were attempting to establish a "communist dictatorship." It called on people to turn in non-Chileans. Under the Allende regime Chile was a refuge for many Latin Americans fleeing repressive regimes. In addition there were many people from around the world, including Americans, who came to Chile to observe and help the government and the mass organizations. Others were there as students, reporters, and so forth. All were targeted.

General Prats, who did not support the coup, fled to Argentina. Pinochet's secret police hunted him down and killed him.

•••

Our response in the United States was to immediately call for united protest actions against the suppression of democratic rights, the pogrom of non-citizens, and the terror unleashed against the left. Other organizations, socialist political parties, Latin American solidarity groups and defenders of civil liberties made similar appeals. This was our immediate duty as U.S. citizens because of the role Washington played in supporting the coup. The full extent of the U.S. role remains shrouded in classified documents, but some facts have been declassified and summarized by Peter Kornbluth, a senior analyst for the National Security Archive at George Washington University.

According to Kornbluth, the documents include cables "written by U.S. Ambassador Edward Korry after Allende's election, detailing conversations with President Eduardo Frei on how to block the president-elect from being inaugurated. The cables contain detailed descriptions and opinions on the various political forces in Chile, including the Chilean military, the Christian Democrat Party, and the U.S. business community. CIA memoranda and reports on 'Project FUBELT'—the codename for covert operations to promote a military coup and undermine Allende's government. The documents, CIA cables to its Santiago station, and summaries of covert action in 1970, provide a clear paper trail to the decisions and operations against Allende's government. National Security Council Strategy papers which record efforts to 'destabilize' Chile economically, and isolate Allende's government diplomatically, between 1970 and 1973. State Department and NSC memoranda and cables after the coup, providing evidence of human rights atrocities under the new military regime led by General Pinochet. FBI documents on Operation Condor—the state-sponsored terrorism of the Chilean secret police, DINA. The documents ... provide evidence on the carbombing assassination of Orlando Letelier and Ronnie Mofitt [opponents of Pinochet] in Washington D.C., and the murder of Chilean General Carlos Pratts [Prats] and his wife in Buenos Aires, among other operations."[2]

There were a number of united protest actions around the country. In Los Angeles, the SWP members including myself threw ourselves into doing what we could. More protests continued in the months ahead. The SWP also explained, in *The Militant* and in public forums, the course of events in Chile, beginning with the election of Allende up through the coup.

This defeat was not inevitable. What was lacking was a mass revolutionary socialist party, even starting out as a minority party, that could have won the leadership of the workers, peasants and the semi-proletarians of the shantytowns. Such a party would have supported every progressive move made by the UP government, but would have warned that the SP's and CP's class collaborationist approach would have to be replaced with a class struggle perspective. That perspective could have won over the best of the rank and file of these reformist parties, as well as the bulk of the MIR, as the class struggle deepened and the bankruptcy of the SP and CP leadership's approach became more and more exposed.

The MIR was small at the beginning of the UP government. It grew as it presented a socialist alternative. But it was hampered by aspects of its former guerrillaist orientation. One of which was that while it advocated the arming of the workers, in its practical work it organized small armed groups only under its own control. Combined with this ultraleftism and elitism, the MIR wasn't consistent in exposing the bourgeois character of the UP government. These weaknesses diminished its ability to win over the best of the workers and peasants who supported the SP and the CP.

The defeat in Chile demoralized workers and peasants and the left throughout Latin America. We felt the impact of the defeat in the

United States, too. It was another factor in the decline of the radicalization.

1 *The Militant*, Aug. 6, 1971.
2 Peter Kornbluth, "Declassified Documents Relating to the Military Coup, Sept. 11, 1973." The National Security Archive. The George Washington University.
http://www.gwu.edu/~nsarchiv/NSAEBB/NSAEBB8/nsaebb8i.htm. See also "Chile and the United States: Declassified Documents relating to the Military Coup, 1970-1976.
http://www.gwu.edu/~nsarchiv/NSAEBB/NSAEBB8/nsaebb8.htm.

CHAPTER THREE: ARAB-ISRAEL WAR

In October 1973 war broke out once again in the Middle East. Egyptian military forces crossed the Suez Canal to attack Israeli forces occupying the Sinai Peninsula, land that Israel had seized from Egypt in the 1967 war. Syria crossed into the Golan Heights, which Israel had likewise seized in 1967.

The Sinai Peninsula was internationally recognized as part of Egypt. The Golan Heights was also recognized as part of Syria. This did not prevent the mainstream U.S. press from loudly proclaiming that "the Arabs" had invaded Israel. Democratic and Republican politicians tried to outdo each other in denouncing Egypt and Syria in warmongering support to Israel.

The Wall Street Journal, which is not usually read by ordinary working people, admitted in its October 8 issue, "The many battle communiqués may have obscured the fact that to outsiders [outside the United States and Israel] ... the war isn't being fought in Israel itself but on occupied Arab territories.... The attack by the Arabs Saturday is viewed by them not as an assault on a foreign land but as an attempt to return lost lands."

Writing in *The Militant,* Tony Thomas described Israel's strategic goals:

"There is ample evidence that the Israelis have long desired a new war as an excuse to further their expansionist designs against the Arab states.

"The Oct. 9 *New York Post* reported that months ago Israeli military experts had told its correspondents that 'the Israeli military was hoping for a full scale invasion' to give them reason to cross Suez and 'destroy the Egyptian Army.'

"Moreover, statements by Israeli leaders since the current conflict began make clear that their aim in the war is not only to hold on to the territories occupied in 1967, but to grab even more territory.

"Major General Aharon Yariv, special adviser to the Israeli chief of staff, declared Oct. 9 that the Israeli troops would take whatever they can get away with: 'I would emphasize to the enemy that violation of the cease-fire lines [from the 1967 war] is not a one-sided game.'"[1]

But Israel and the United States were stunned when the Egyptian military pushed the occupier's forces back into Sinai. This was in spite of the fact that Israel had been armed to the teeth by the United

States to make it by far the most powerful military in the region, stronger, in fact, than the combined forces of all the Arab states.

In a front-page editorial calling for protests, *The Militant* stated:

"The imperialist rulers of the United States, who have armed and financed the Zionist state of Israel, have alerted the Sixth Fleet, and moved marines closer to the battle zones.

"If Israel needs more than arms, money, and diplomatic backing already provided by Washington, the U.S. government stands ready to intervene directly. Such a move would raise to a new height the ever-present danger of a world nuclear conflagration.

"Already the U.S. is rushing arms and warplanes to Israel. According to the Oct. 11 *New York Times*, the Pentagon 'has refused to confirm or deny reports that Israel is flying military supplies from the United States and from U.S. bases in Britain and West Germany.'

"The government has also declined comment on a report in a Virginia newspaper that witnesses saw a plane with Israeli markings loading missiles and bombs at the Ocean Naval Air Station in Virginia. According to the eyewitnesses, the Israeli markings were covered over as the plane was being loaded."[2]

Writing in *The Militant* a week later, Dick Roberts reported, "Testimony to the preliminary military success of the Egyptian and Syrian forces came in the massive U.S. military supply operation and Sixth Fleet mobilization.... *Time* magazine called it history's biggest airlift. Reporting from Pease Air Force Base in New Hampshire, *Time* stated, 'During the day, half a dozen blue-and-white [Israeli] Boeing 747s had shuttled in and out of the base. The frenetic activity at Pease A.F.B. was part of a mammoth airlift to resupply the Israeli army.'"[3]

Nixon asked for and got from Congress $2.2 billion to finance the operation.

The Militant's warning of the danger of a nuclear war wasn't idle. In fact, Israel had secret nuclear weapons. Golda Meir, Israel's prime minister, later admitted that Israel had been poised to use nuclear weapons against Cairo and Damascus if the war had continued to go badly for Israel.

The massive influx of additional arms did allow Israel to stop the Egyptian army in Sinai. As a result, the Egyptian Third Army was surrounded and threatened with annihilation. In response, the Soviet Union declared it was ready to intervene in Egypt's defense.

Washington claimed every right to intervene militarily, but it also claimed that Moscow had no such right. The crisis led to a secret emergency meeting in Moscow between the two superpowers on October 20-21. At the meeting, U.S. Secretary of State Henry Kissinger told Soviet Premier Leonid Brezhnev that the United States would go on hair-trigger nuclear alert against the Soviet Union if it helped Egypt. This threat of nuclear war put the world on the brink. It was another demonstration, like the 1962 Cuban missile crisis, that Washington was ready to unleash a nuclear holocaust to further its aims, however irrational that would be.

Under this threat, Moscow backed down. The settlement that was imposed gave the Sinai and Golan Heights back to Israel. Zionist forces were now once again on the east bank of the Egyptian Suez Canal. Together with the West Bank (of the Jordan river), Israel got to keep the spoils of its 1967 war against Egypt, Syria, and Jordan. However, the Egyptian Third Army was spared. Years later, Israel returned much of the Sinai to Egypt in an agreement that made Egypt an ally of Israel.

The war was an attempt by Egypt and Syria to regain land occupied by Israel in the 1967 war. But the Zionist state itself was created by occupying Palestinian land long before 1967. During the First World War, the Turkish-based Ottoman Empire was destroyed. The imperialist powers of Britain and France carved up those Arab countries that had been under the Ottomans. Britain got Palestine. This was later made "legal" by the League of Nations, itself a tool of the imperialist West, through recognizing a "British mandate" over Palestine. Consequently, the British declared that a Jewish state would be established on Palestinian soil.

After the Second World War, European Jews, survivors of the Holocaust unleashed by German imperialism under the Nazis, were encouraged by the victors to emigrate to Palestine. The United States and Britain had blocked Jewish refugees from Nazi oppression from their own borders before the war, and wanted to limit emigration after. In 1948, the United Nations (U.N.) declared a portion of Palestine a Jewish state. Faced with this land grab, Arab countries attempted to prevent it, and the first Israeli-Arab war occurred. Backed by the West, especially Britain, Israel won and expanded its territory beyond the original U.N. mandate.

Thus occurred one of the greatest tragedies and ironies of history. The Jewish people, long oppressed in Europe, had been decimated during the Second World War by the murderous Nazi regime. Now, in the war's aftermath, many Jews became tools of the imperialist interests of Britain, France, and increasingly the United States in setting up on Palestinian land an illegitimate state, Israel, as a Jewish state that denied not only the lands of the Palestinians, but also their fundamental national rights. Of course, many Jewish socialists were anti-Zionist and opposed this. Some who supported the foundation of Israel, most notably Albert Einstein, sought to ensure that this not result in the oppression of the Palestinians—a vain hope. Other Jews who did emigrate to Israel did so in the hope of establishing a socialist society. In the years since, they too were betrayed, and their socialist experiments were abandoned.

Following the initial influx of Jews from Europe, there were further waves of Jewish immigration, from Arab lands, and then the former Soviet bloc. These Jews, fleeing oppression in their own countries, also became a part of the oppressor state of Israel.

From the beginning, the new state was completely beholden to Western imperialism for its very existence. Israel has been in a state of hostility, now open, now muted, with its neighbors since 1948. Over the years, Israel has more and more become a garrison state, an outpost of imperialism in the Middle East, especially U.S. imperialism in recent decades. Without this support, Israel would collapse.

After the 1967 war, Al Fatah, the most important organization in the formation of the Palestine Liberation Organization (PLO), recognized that however illegitimate the formation of Israel was, it was a fact that Jewish people had now immigrated to historic Palestine. The PLO put forward as a solution the creation of a single, democratic and secular state incorporating both the Jewish and Palestinian peoples as equals.

This proposal remains the only realistic solution for both the Palestinians and the Israeli Jews. Israeli reliance on Washington for its very existence cannot last forever. U.S. imperialism, even if not overthrown, will be pushed back in the Middle East sooner or later by the peoples of the region.

As a nation, Israeli Jews will be compelled for their survival to turn away from the West, and toward their Palestinian brothers and sisters, and the countries of the Middle East, as their equals and partners in bringing peace to the region. Even more, this path will lead Jewish workers and farmers, including Jewish émigrés from Third World countries who face discrimination within Israel, to reject the Israeli ruling class for new bonds of *class solidarity* with workers and farmers in the Arab world, with whom they share a common struggle against capitalist exploitation.

---

1 *The Militant,* Oct. 19, 1973.
2 Ibid.
3 Ibid., Oct. 26, 1973.

CHAPTER FOUR: THE FACTION STRUGGLE IN THE FOURTH INTERNATIONAL DEEPENS

The World Congress of the Fourth International in 1969 marked a sharp turn in orientation by a majority of delegates. This turn was first expressed in the majority resolution on Latin America, which predicted a long period of rural guerrilla war throughout the continent. The resolution precluded mass working class upsurges in the urban centers, arguing that any such upsurges would be quickly smashed by the military, which had come to power in many countries. Consequently, it projected that our sections in Latin America should begin preparations for, or start engaging in, rural guerrilla war.

Bolivia was projected to be the most ripe for guerrilla war. Some at the World Congress even proclaimed that the next World Congress would take place in La Paz, the capital. It was ironic that the majority of the Fourth International would make this turn after the defeat in 1967 of the attempt by Che Guevara to launch a guerrilla movement in Bolivia. After Che's murder, ordered by the CIA, the Cuban leadership began to abandon the guerrilla orientation it had championed for most of the decade following the triumph of the Cuban Revolution in 1959. Thus, a key element for any attempt to launch guerrilla war, the backing of the Cuban leadership, was already fading away.

A minority at the World Congress opposed this turn. Our delegation was part of this minority, and in fact led it. SWP leader Joe Hansen gave the report for the minority opposing the guerrilla turn. There were other sections, and comrades in other sections, which supported the minority, the largest of which was one wing of the Argentine section, which had split over the question of guerrilla war before the World Congress. The two organizations that emerged from the split each kept the name of the party, Revolutionary Workers Party (PRT in its Spanish initials). They were distinguished by the names of their respected newspapers: one was the PRT (Combatiente) (Fighter) and the other the PRT (Verdad) (Truth). The delegates from the PRT (Combatiente) were strongly in favor of the guerrilla turn, while the PRT (Verdad) led by Hugo Moreno, supported the minority.

The minority argued that the majority had elevated a tactic, rural guerrilla war based on the peasantry, to a generalized strategy.

Moreover, this was done without regard to the concrete situation in each country in Latin America, the size of our sections or their political maturity. Guerrilla war based on the peasantry can be a tactic in certain concrete circumstances, the minority said, in the context of building a party based in the working class, both rural and urban.

The error of the majority was to deduce from a general abstract evaluation of the supposed overall political situation in the whole of Latin America a strategy for each of our national organizations there. The Congress adopted the guerrilla turn by majority vote.

Soon after the World Congress, the Bolivian comrades, together with some other forces, launched a guerrilla front. This attempt was quickly smashed by the government, which launched a witchhunt in which some were killed, many tortured, and hundreds imprisoned. But instead of reconsidering their line, the majority instead backed a new guerrilla attempt in Argentina launched by the PRT (Combatiente).

In both Bolivia and Argentina there were mass working class uprisings in 1969-71. Yet the guerrilla orientation in both countries disoriented our comrades, and they were not able to effectively participate in these mass uprisings. (It was only the existence of the mass movement in Bolivia that saved many of our comrades and others they worked with from execution.)

In Argentina, the only adaptation the PRT (Combatiente) comrades made was to switch from rural guerrilla warfare to urban guerrilla warfare. They formed the Revolutionary Army of the People (ERP in its Spanish initials) to carry out this orientation. The ERP carried out some spectacular actions, such as commandeering shipments of food and distributing it in poor neighborhoods and attempting to aid workers' struggles with armed actions. But these actions were undertaken from outside the mass movement, in the spirit of what the Maoists called "serving the people."

Tragically, the Argentine guerrilla attempt also ended in defeat with the murder by the government of its key leaders. Sometime before the defeat these comrades had left the Fourth International, looking toward Maoism and the guerrilla strategy of Che Guevara.[1]

The Argentine PRT (Verdad), by contrast, was able to be part of the mass upsurge through their work in the trade unions, and consequently made important organizational progress. It was soon apparent that the turn of the 1969 World Congress concerning Latin America was not limited to that continent. In 1971, the majority adopted a line on Western Europe that extended and broadened the ultraleft turn projected in the guerrilla orientation to Latin America. Again, the majority made an analysis of the situation throughout the continent, and came to the conclusion that socialist revolution was around the corner in at least some countries in Europe. Some projected revolutions would take place in the next half decade or so, while a few enthusiasts said in two years.

While this evaluation was overly optimistic, it is true there was a youth radicalization that did have an impact on many workers. The youth radicalization, which was part of the same phenomenon in the United States, spanned much of the globe, driven by the opposition to the Vietnam War. In addition, in many countries of Europe, the May-June 1968 student-worker uprising in France had an important impact.[2]

On the basis of this continent-wide evaluation a strategy for our Western European sections was deduced. It was called winning the "new mass vanguard." By the "new mass vanguard" the majority meant the organizations that had grown out of the youth radicalization. Besides the Fourth International groups, there were Maoists, anarchists, and a variety of organizations that stood somewhere between ourselves and the Communist and Socialist parties.

In the United States, perhaps the most important equivalent of the European "new mass vanguard" was the Students for a Democratic Society (SDS). Indeed, leading figures in the majority faction began to look to SDS as superior to the SWP and YSA. It was ironic that by 1969, SDS had already broken up into competing Maoist groups and the terrorist Weathermen.[3]

The majority idea was to seek "initiatives in action" that "correspond to the concerns of the vanguard." In reality, this meant political adaptation to these other forces, which generally had an ultraleft bent. "Initiatives in action" in practice turned out to mean initiating confrontations with the police. The turn to guerrilla war in Latin America was having its echo in Europe.

In Latin America, the formula sought to influence and lead the peasantry through guerrilla groups formed in the main by urban intellectuals and other sections of the petty bourgeoisie, although involving some workers. In Argentina, this idea became transformed into mainly urban intellectuals waging urban guerrilla warfare. This orientation would supposedly spark the working class into action. Accordingly, in this first stage of guerrilla war, work in the mass workers' organizations was downplayed.

There was a similar concept being applied in Europe. Our sections sought to initiate their own versions of actions that "correspond to the concerns of the vanguard." It was hoped that this approach would unite the "vanguard" behind these actions, which would be so spectacular that they would spark the working class into action. Our little wheel would set in motion the larger wheel of the new mass vanguard that would bring into action the mass of radicalized youth, finally setting the big wheel of the working class turning. It was telling that the majority resolution on Western Europe had little to say about work in the trade unions.

I believe that underneath this orientation was a misreading of the May-June 1968 revolutionary upsurge in France. In that situation, our French comrades had correctly called for a united front of what would be later called the "new mass vanguard" in a defensive battle against a police assault on student demonstrations that initially grew out of actions against the Vietnam War.

The context was the decade-old authoritarian and repressive regime of Charles De Gaulle. The workers, peasants and sections of the petty bourgeoisie had suffered greatly under De Gaulle. When the students joined by other young people fought against the police assault, the workers were galvanized into what became the greatest general strike in French history.[4]

What I think was underpinning the majority's "new mass vanguard" approach was hope for a repetition of the French events, but forgetting the specific situation of the students and workers that made those events possible. In the aftermath, not even in France were those conditions duplicated, and certainly not in most of the countries of Western Europe. Portugal and Spain did both explode in the mid-1970s, although not in the way envisioned in the "new mass vanguard" orientation.

The majority orientation in Europe was to the largely student youth that made up the far left organizations. Work in the mass organizations of the working class was viewed as secondary, and in any case not very important since the wheels within wheels would do the job.

What was being rejected in both Latin America and Europe was the necessity of building a revolutionary socialist party based in the working class. Impatient for a breakthrough, a shortcut around the hard work of building such a party became the orientation.

In December 1972, a meeting of the International Executive Committee (IEC) of the Fourth International was held. This was after the debacles in Bolivia and Argentina had become abundantly clear. The majority leadership in the International could have pulled back from the guerrilla turn based on the test of events. Instead, the majority reaffirmed the essential correctness of the 1969 turn, laying the basis for a generalization of the "strategy of armed struggle" for Latin America that was adopted by majority vote at the January 1974 World Congress. In addition, the new orientation for Europe projected by the United Secretariat was adopted.

The failure of the majority to pull back from the 1969 turn at the 1972 IEC, led the international minority and the SWP representatives including me, to declare the formation of the Leninist Trotskyist Tendency (LTT), an organized grouping to fight for the rejection of the 1969 turn and its extension to Europe. The majority organized itself as the International Majority Tendency (IMT).

The French Communist League was the most important and by far the largest section of the Fourth International in Western Europe. Consequently, it set the tone for the other European sections. Its growth in numbers and in prestige was the result of the exemplary role the French comrades had played in the May-June 1968 events.

In an internal discussion bulletin in June 1972, leading comrades of the League proposed an orientation in France toward "minority violence," clarifying "initiatives in action" that even included a proposal for farmer-based guerrilla warfare in France. While the majority of the League's leaders rejected that specific proposal, the thrust of the general orientation toward minority violence was accepted.

The concept was put into action the following year on June 21, 1973 when the League sought a deliberate confrontation with the police. The issue was a publicly advertised attempt to prevent a meeting of the fascist New Order. The League called for a counter-demonstration against the fascists, a perfectly correct position. But the counter-demonstration consisted mainly of League marshals, who came prepared to fight.*

The mass organizations of the working class, the Social Democratic and Communist parties, and the trade unions, did not participate. In fact, there was no danger of a fascist attempt to attack the mass workers' organizations, or to stage a violent attack on anyone, including the police. The small New Order was merely holding a meeting.

The result was that the League's marshals clashed not with the fascists, but with the police. The police were badly beaten, which the government used as a pretext to ban the League and arrest two of its leaders, Pierre Rousset and Alain Krivine. In a press conference after the action, Krivine said, "We carried out the June 21 action as a test, as a warning to the nation [of the fascist threat]. We have shown the way."[5]

But the action did not galvanize the organizations of the "new mass vanguard," let alone the mass organizations of the working class. It did not "show the way."

Fortunately, the League and the Fourth International, in an about face, organized a mass campaign in France and internationally, based on support for the democratic right of the League to exist. This campaign did include the other organizations of the "far left," and even the Socialist and Communist parties as well as supporters of civil liberties and democratic rights in France. We in the SWP vigorously participated in this international campaign. The campaign gained so much support that the French government was forced to lift the ban on the League and release Rousset and Krivine.

In England, the International Marxist Group (IMG) led a demonstration that was publicized as a challenge to the police. Consequently, the police used the IMG's ultraleft rhetoric to portray the demonstration as violent. The police were well prepared and responded with a massive and violent attack. One demonstrator, Peter Graham, was murdered. The IMG was not prepared to physically defend the demonstration, which was disbursed.

In should be noted that not all European sections attempted some form of minority violence. The terms "initiatives in action" that "correspond to the concerns of the vanguard" were sufficiently vague as to give all sorts of interpretations. But the political disorientation was signaled when the British, Belgian, French and Spanish sections hailed the assassination by Basque nationalists of Spanish dictator Francisco Franco's hated Prime Minister Carrero Blanco in December 1973. It was claimed that the assassination "gave an impulse" to the class struggle, as a leader of the Spanish section of the Fourth International put it.

This response went directly against the long-held Marxist position that such acts of individual terrorism were ineffective and ended up hurting the workers' movement. The assassination of Carrero Blanco was no exception.[6]

The differences in the Fourth International were becoming quite sharp. Minorities that supported the LTT in majority-IMT sections came under great pressure. Expulsions and splits occurred. Before the 1969 World Congress, the Argentine section had already split over the question of guerrilla war. There were important splits also in Spain, Mexico and Canada with the separate organizations lining up on each side of the political divide in the International. In the British IMG, a minority that supported the minority position internationally was almost driven out (The situation got so bad that majority comrades had put up pictures of Joe Hansen to throw darts at). A special commission, composed of supporters of both the majority and minority of the International, was set up to investigate. The commission reached a common conclusion against such factionalism, which helped restore more comradely methods of functioning on the part of the British majority.

Factionalism against the Argentine Socialist Labor Party (PST in its Spanish initials), as the wing of the former section that opposed the 1969 turn was now called, and the U.S. SWP was especially pronounced. At the January 1974 World Congress the atmosphere was so poisoned that the LTT decided it had to transform itself into a tightly-knit faction to fight any further attempts to expel groupings such as the Argentine PST, and to fight to change the leadership of the Fourth International in view of the generalization of the error of the 1969 World Congress by the majority. It was clear to us that there was a wing in the IMT which favored a split in the International.

Another difference emerged. The majority leadership began to accuse the minority, especially the SWP, of violating "international democratic centralism." It's true that we put forth publicly our own positions (while always publishing for our membership and publicly the positions of the IMT majority). The SWP had a long tradition of rejecting any concept of an international "center" that dictated to the sections. Our view of internationalism on the organizational level was one of international collaboration. This point will become important as I discuss the degeneration of the SWP in Part Two of this volume.

---

* Sometimes socialists, trade unions and other mass organizations are compelled to organize armed self-defense when attacked by the police, racist or fascist organizations. This has been true in many strikes and demonstrations, attacks by groups like the Ku Klux Klan on Blacks, etc. When and how to organize such self-defense is a concrete problem to be decided in the context of the given situation.

1 For a full account of the implementation of the guerrilla turn, see "Argentina and Bolivia—the Balance Sheet," in *The Leninist Strategy of Party Building*, Joseph Hansen (Pathfinder Press, 1979) pp. 208-311. See also Volume One of this work, pp. 261-265.

2 See Volume One of this work, pp. 191-198.

3 Tariq Ali, *Street Fighting Years: An Autobiography of the Sixties*, (Fontana/Collins, 1987) pp. 245-246. While this book was written after Ali had left the Fourth International, Ali still retained his prejudices about the SWP and YSA, and lauds SDS. In the early 1970s, Ali was a leading figure in the British International Marxist Group (IMG) and the majority faction in the Fourth International.

4 See Volume One of this work, pp. 191-198.

5 Joseph Hansen, op. cit. (Pathfinder Press, 1979) pp. 419-428.

6 Ibid., pp. 440-441.

CHAPTER FIVE: THE EXPULSION OF THE INTERNATIONALIST TENDENCY

It was in this international context that a grouping formed inside the SWP that supported the International Majority Tendency (IMT). This grouping called itself the Internationalist Tendency (IT).

The roots of the IT went back to the 1971 convention of the SWP, where a tendency calling itself the Proletarian Orientation Tendency (POT) challenged the SWP majority's orientation. At first glance, it appeared that the POT was only calling for the party to emphasize work in the trade unions, and to encourage more comrades to get union jobs. But it soon became apparent that the POT was really challenging our antiwar work, which had an important center on the campuses, our identification with and enthusiastic support of Black and Chicano nationalism and the new women's liberation movement. They belittled these movements as "petty bourgeois," counterposing them to what they saw as the real class struggle of the workers.

In contrast, the SWP majority saw these movements as part of the broader class struggle, which the workers movement should champion.[1]

Their central resolution, *For a Proletarian Orientation* rooted the SWP's errors in the supposed adaptations by the party to the views of one of the leaders of the Cochranite minority tendency in 1953, Mike Bartell. At that time, the minority in the SWP had the backing of the International Secretary of the Fourth International, Michel Pablo. The resolution also charged that the SWP had adopted the analysis of the changes in the working class and among students that had been developed by Ernest Mandel in the 1960s, which they said led us astray. (We did in fact agree with Ernest.) How did this tendency later link up with the International majority? It might seem that the POT line would run counter to the IMT's approach in Latin America and Europe. Moreover, Ernest Mandel was one of the leaders of the IMT.

However, there was another aspect of the IMT that had emerged from the turn of the 1969 World Congress, the downplaying of democratic demands and struggles. These were seen by some in the IMT as diversions from the short-term fight for power through guerrilla war in Latin America or the wheels within wheels of the "new mass vanguard" orientation in Europe.

Most day-to-day workers' struggles focus around immediate and democratic demands, such as for better wages and working conditions, or for democratic rights against government repression. The Black, Chicano and women's movements were largely organized around democratic demands. To immerse ourselves in these struggles was seen by many in the IMT as not facing up to the burning question of conquering power.

Some younger leaders of the IMT thus began to raise objections to the SWP's vigorous support of Black and Chicano nationalism, the women's movement, and our work in the antiwar movement among students. These movements were organized largely around democratic demands. Such criticisms, often made not openly but in scuttlebutt, dovetailed with the positions put forward by the POT.

By the time leading up to the 1973 SWP convention, the former supporters of the POT had found common ground with others in the party who supported the IMT line. They coalesced into the IT, which put forward a counter-position to the party leadership in the discussion leading up to the 1973 convention. They stated that they were in agreement with the IMT resolution putting forward the "new mass vanguard" line for Europe. Apparently, they could not all agree to support the "armed struggle" strategy in Latin America, which wasn't played up in the IT resolution.

In attacking the position of the majority of the SWP, the IT resolution said, "The ideologies of nationalism and feminism are characterized [by the SWP majority] as thoroughly progressive because they are held by oppressed layers. The formation of independent parties by Blacks, Chicanos, [and] women is seen not as a lesser evil to complete passivity, but as a superior form of organization. Separate transitional programs stressing the autonomy of each 'sector' are put forward to encourage the formation of these parties." Accordingly, another section of their resolution was titled, "Tail-ending 'Consistent' Nationalism and Feminism," which further developed their position that instead of leading the SWP leadership was opportunistically adapting to these social movements.[2]

This is not the place to answer this old resolution. I'll merely note that the SWP never said that Black and Chicano nationalism were "thoroughly" progressive, nor did we ever advocate a women's party. Most of the SWP positions that the IT attacked dated from well before the 1969 World Congress, and were, in fact, supported by a big majority of the leadership of the Fourth International at the time. The exception was the position the SWP developed after 1969 on the new women's liberation movement. Many IMT leaders in sections in Europe rejected the SWP position on the new women's movement.

As the new women's movement spread internationally, the IMT leaders at first took a sectarian attitude toward it in their own countries. This dovetailed with the POT and later the IT position. However, women comrades in the European sections chaffed under this sectarian attitude, and were attracted to the new women's movement. They eventually revolted, leading to a change in attitude on the part of the European sections.

I should also add that because of their internal differences the IT resolution was so filled with caveats and exceptions that it was hard to pin down their real positions. There was a very thorough discussion before the 1973 SWP convention, both written and oral. It was the most voluminous discussion in the history of the SWP and of any other party in the International, for that matter. I drafted the majority resolution and gave the report for the majority at the convention. The vote of the delegates was overwhelmingly in favor.

The internal atmosphere in the SWP during this political fight had become rather hot, especially in those branches where the IT had some support. That was unfortunate, but not necessarily unusual. As the factionalism heated up in the International, however, before and especially after the 1974 World Congress, the IT became transformed not just into a tightly organized faction, but into something quite different. They began acting and defining themselves as if they were independent of the SWP, for the time being still a part of the SWP, but seeing themselves as the nucleus of a separate party that would eventually split from the SWP. We were not aware of this at first.

In the spring of 1974, Jose Perez, a YSA leader, made a national speaking tour and one of his stops was at a campus chapter of the YSA (we had many such chapters by that time, not only city chapters). He was put up at the apartment of a YSA comrade who happened to support the IT. By accident, he came across what looked like an internal discussion bulletin leading up to a secret convention of the IT.

He brought the existence of the document to the attention of the party leadership. I questioned him thoroughly to make sure he had found the document by accident and had not rummaged around in the apartment.*

The party leadership turned the matter over to the Control Commission to investigate. The Control Commission is elected by the party convention, and is composed of people who are not part of the National Committee. The criteria for election are that these comrades be known to the party membership as fair-minded, trustworthy individuals. For specific investigations the National Committee (or Political Committee acting for the NC) appoints one person. Most of the cases the Control Commission took up through the years concerned allegations of misconduct by individual members, or by branch leaderships against individual members.

The Political Committee appointed Gus Horowitz to be the National Committee representative on the Control Commission. The first step the Commission took was to obtain most of the IT documents, including the report on its secret convention.

These documents revealed that the IT was already beginning to act on its own in the wider mass movements, almost as if it were a separate organization in its own right. The IT comrades were performing such work under the discipline of the IT and not of the SWP, although they were counseled to do such work surreptitiously.**

The Control Commission twice interviewed representatives of the IT concerning these acts of indiscipline. The first interview was with Bill Massey on June 20, 1974. Comrade Michaloux from the international IMT leadership was also present. In a letter dated June 9 to the SWP Political Committee, Massey admitted that the IT had indeed carried out these actions, and "we promise to do it again when the need arises." A second meeting was held June 23 with Massey and John Barzman, also a central representative of the IT leadership. At this meeting they again reiterated that they would defy SWP decisions when they so chose. Their argument was that they should not be bound by SWP decisions they believed ran counter to positions of the majority in the Fourth International.

This position flew in the face of an agreement by both sides at the January 1974 World congress, formally adopted by the Congress. Among other things this agreement reiterated a stipulation in the Statutes of the Fourth International that in no case can the United Secretariat or the International Executive Committee or even the World Congress dictate tactics to any section.

At the June 23 meeting, Barzman and Massey said that IT members would also continue to boycott SWP finances, because, in their opinion the SWP was violating "international democratic centralism" by not paying its fair share of dues to the International.

This assertion was part of the campaign by the IMT charging that the SWP was violating international democratic centralism in general.***

The secret IT documents referred to bodies of the IMT that had been kept secret from the rest of the International. In effect, the IMT had constructed a parallel international with its own centralized discipline. The IMT did announce to the International that its members on the International Executive Committee comprised an IMT Steering Committee. But under the Steering Committee was a secret Enlarged Bureau, which paralleled the United Secretariat;

under that was the administrative IMT Bureau, which paralleled the Bureau of the United Secretariat. There was at least one regional organ of the IMT, the North American Bureau.

Much of the discussion in the IT bulletins revolved around whether to split from the SWP, with many of the leading comrades of the IT favoring immediate split. Bill Massey drafted the main document from its leadership for the IT convention. In it he characterized the SWP as "deadly sick" and stated it is "an objective fact that the cadre of this party are politically incapable of either understanding or putting into practice a revolutionary line." An amendment was accepted that the IT is "the nucleus of the future section of the Fourth International in the United States."

The Massey resolution concludes, "the result of these theoretical deviations [which the resolution had previously explained at length], when considered as the foundation of the overall practice of the SWP, and seen in relation to the less subtle secondary aspects of crass opportunism and adaptationism, combine to define the SWP as a sect."

Right before the IT convention, a group of nine comrades resigned from the IT. These included Berta and Robert Langston, who wrote a lengthy document for the secret IT discussion bulletin explaining that they did so because of the split orientation of the Massey resolution. They wrote, "the logic of the ITPC's [IT Political Committee] position is that the IT, defining itself as the nucleus of a section in the U.S., would begin to combine the exercise of political leadership of groupings outside the SWP and YSA with an entry tactic inside the SWP and YSA."

They summarized, "the comrades of the ITPC are projecting a line the logic of which is precisely to build a rival organization to the SWP." The comrades who resigned from the IT reiterated their support to the IMT internationally.

There was another document in the secret IT discussion bulletin, in which a grouping in Los Angeles firmly stated their disagreement with the IMT line on Latin America. However, when these comrades voted in the Los Angeles SWP branch on resolutions before the special SWP pre-World Congress convention in late 1973, they voted *for* the IMT position on Latin America, under discipline of the IT to do so. A faction that places its members under discipline to vote against their own positions is in violation of the most elementary principles of democracy in a revolutionary organization. Without honesty about one's views in the party no democratic discussion is possible. This action demonstrated that the IT was an unprincipled combination.

From the perspective of already viewing themselves as the nucleus of a rival organization to the SWP, the political differences within the IT would seem normal. Unlike a tendency or faction, united around a consistent political point of view, a separate party organization, or the nucleus of such, could indeed encompass conflicting political viewpoints or tendencies.

The IT leadership faced an obstacle to their split orientation. That was the opposition of the IMT leadership internationally.

One IT document cited by the Control Commission was an official report on the IT conference by Alec. The conference was held May 25-27 in Chicago. At the conference Massey gave a report "on the most recent session of the Enlarged IMT Bureau meeting and on the meeting of the NAB [North American Bureau of the IMT] which preceded the IMT Bureau meeting." These meetings were held prior to the IT conference.

The North American Bureau was composed of representatives of the Canadian Revolutionary Marxist Group (RMG), which had split from the Canadian section of the FI, and the IT. At its meeting was a representative of the IMT Bureau, Charles Michaloux. As Alec reported, "At the NAB the comrades from the North American Sections [sic] disagreed very firmly with the representative of the IMT Bureau on perspectives for the building of a section in the United States. The request to cancel the IT conference was rejected...." Then an Enlarged IMT Bureau meeting was held.

Alec summarizes the IMT Enlarged Bureau report, which "argued that the [Massey] document posed problems, in that it incorrectly viewed the degenerative process of the SWP as completed and in that context seemed to set in motion a series of events leading to the expulsion of the IT and the establishment of the IT as a flimsy group outside of the SWP. It called for a hard political fight inside the SWP and proposed rejection of the [Massey] document, cancellation of the conference and the opening of a discussion within the IMT." According to Alec's report, the Enlarged Bureau also decided that the IT should "recruit people politically to the FI [Fourth International] and organizationally to the SWP." Such "double recruiting"—first to the IT's political viewpoints, and then to the SWP but only "organizationally"—was outside the bounds of the normal functioning of a faction in the SWP. If this proposal had been made by the IMT to the SWP openly, it would certainly have been rejected. That's why it was secret.

The IT went ahead with its conference in spite of the Enlarged Bureau's objection. But faced with the Enlarged Bureau's opposition to their split perspective, and wishing to retain their connection to the IMT internationally, the delegates to the IT conference adopted the following contorted motion:

"1. Stating agreement with the NAB in rejecting the position of the IMT Bureau.

2. Rejection of the motion of the Enlarged IMT Bureau.

3. Accepting the authority of the Enlarged IMT Bureau but pledging to seek to reverse the decision.

4. The opening of an immediate discussion in the IMT on North America."

The conference also voted to adopt the report given to the conference by Barzman supporting the Massey resolution. The Barzman report was not published by the IT. From the context, however, it is clear that this report defended the split perspective of the Massey resolution, but also proposed the above motion in light of the opposition by the Enlarged Bureau.

Thus the IT conference voted both agreement with the split perspective of the Massey resolution and to remain in the SWP for a time, seeking a reversal of the IMT Enlarged Bureau position. Clearly, the decision to stay in the SWP for the time being was merely a tactical expedient.

The Control Commission found that the material contained in the secret IT documents gave "proof positive that the IT is operating as a separate party organization operating both within the SWP and outside the SWP." Further, the Control Commission concluded that "the IT party has its own, secret highly organized and centralized independent party structure functioning on all levels, nationally and internationally. It has its own party discipline that supercedes SWP discipline. It determines its own areas of external activity and establishes its own relations with opponent groups. Persons who are not members of the SWP, the YSA, or the Fourth International are allowed to participate in its internal deliberations and are given access to its internal bulletins attacking the SWP...."

The SWP's organizational principles in effect at the time recognized the right of formation of tendencies and factions. A tendency was defined as a grouping of comrades holding a set of views, documented in the regular party discussions, as opposed to those adopted by the majority of the party. A tendency was not a disciplined organization, but a group of like-minded comrades who sought to change the party's political positions through the normal democratic procedures of the party. Members of a tendency had the right to collaborate in working out their positions, which were presented in writing to the party as a whole. After leadership bodies decided disputed questions, however, the majority view was the position of the party unless and until it was changed in subsequent discussions. After a party convention, for example, the majority positions as registered by the votes of delegates became the party positions and all members were expected to carry them out. Tendencies weren't required to dissolve following decisions of party bodies.

A faction was defined as a disciplined grouping of supporters of minority positions who not only sought to change the party's positions, but also believed it necessary to change the party's leadership. Factions had the same rights as tendencies such as being under no obligation to dissolve after party decisions are made. In addition to collaboration among faction members in working out their positions, factions discipline their members in tactics in fighting for leadership.

Factions do have aspects of a party within the party. But they are expected to be loyal to the party as they carry out their fight to change party positions and leadership. Loyalty to the party is the bedrock of democratic centralism, which is democracy in decision-making and unity in action in carrying out decisions.

Loyalty to the party is the concept that the SWP is the party you build and defend whatever your criticisms. It is the bedrock of party organization. Without loyalty to the party there can be no common ground for either democratic discussion or unity in action.

The SWP organizational principles also gave to the party as a whole the right to regulate its internal affairs, including the functioning of tendencies or factions. For example, the elected leadership decided when preconvention discussion was opened in the discussion bulletin and the branches. Some later day critics of the SWP's organizational principles claim that this right of the party as a whole meant that the majority had the right to interfere in the internal affairs of tendencies or factions. This claim is false and there were no instances of this happening up to this time.

However, factions were expected to explain to the party as a whole the extent of their internal discipline and their organizational structure. The IT did neither.

While having the unconditional right to circulate, discuss and modify their resolutions to be presented to the party as a whole, factions do not have the right to have their own discussion bulletin unless that is approved by the party. Of course, in the case of the IT their secret discussion bulletin was not created for the purpose of preparing resolutions to be put forward during the SWP's preconvention discussion. No such resolutions were in the IT discussion bulletin or discussed at their secret convention.

There were no a priori limits on tendencies or factions. For example, the elected leadership could decide to authorize minority views to be expressed in public in the party's publications. This had happened in the past, one contemporary example being the publication of the two contending positions in the 1971 discussion on Israel and the Arab Revolution.

Factions had the right of internal discussion. But they had no right to recruit to themselves and then bring their recruits into the party "organizationally." Tendencies or factions could not take it upon themselves to express their views publicly, including under the guise of presenting the positions of the majority of the Fourth International as they interpreted them, without authorization from the party. Moreover, all the views of the majority of the Fourth International were publicly published by the SWP.

Most important, tendencies or factions had no right to discuss when or how to split from the party. People holding the view that the party should be split and a rival organization set up to replace it had no right to membership. This idea goes beyond the SWP. Any organization that took itself seriously would not tolerate people with a split orientation within its ranks.

Once decisions were reached, the discussion was closed, unless the party as a whole decided otherwise. Accordingly, we sought a balance between periods of discussion and periods of united action, although the party didn't come to a halt during periods of discussion, but continued to operate on previously adopted decisions.

The IT was clearly not a tendency in the usual sense of the term, but a highly centralized organization. Nor was it even a faction in the usual sense, as allowed by the SWP statutes or organizational principles. Loyal factions do not characterize the party as "deadly sick" and as a "sect" whose members "are politically incapable of either understanding or putting into practice a revolutionary line." They do not hold secret discussions on when and how to split from the SWP. They do not boycott party finances and activities or justify such by unilaterally deciding that the SWP was violating "international democratic centralism."

It is my opinion that the IT was counting on a split in the International, with the IMT recognizing the IT as its sympathizing section in the United States. Neither of these things came to pass, and it was clear that the IMT was not going to back a split from the SWP by the IT.

The Control Commission wrote a lengthy political report that took up the organizational questions involved, as well as the documentation of the facts. The report was based entirely on the IT documents themselves and included as appendices the main IT documents that proved the case.

So strong was the Control Commission report that the IT could not even attempt to answer it directly. They did write a subsequent document for the International entitled, "The Myth of the IT Split—Purge Politics of the LTF." But this document consisted mostly of a recital of the IT version of various incidents, almost impossible to judge by anyone who was not on the spot. They pretty much ignored the secret IT documents, which all could read, and on which the Control Commission had based its case.

The Control Commission report recommended that the IT be removed from the party, which the Political Committee did. What was involved was the recognition that the IT had already split in spirit and was acting as if it had already split in fact.

Formally, the IT was not expelled. The party membership was re-registered excluding the IT members. The members of the IT were characterized as members of a separate and rival organization. Those supporters of the IMT, like Berta and Robert Langston, who had resigned from the IT, remained members of the SWP (although they later voluntarily left the SWP and joined the IT after it was out of the party).

There is no doubt the removal of the IT was justified. Whatever questions or criticisms might be raised about the procedures, methods and terminology used by the SWP leadership in this matter, it is hard for me to see how anyone could argue seriously that the IT deserved to remain as members.

Nevertheless, certain aspects of procedure should be addressed.

Was the SWP leadership in error because of the method we used in removing the IT? Should there instead have been a trial and a formal motion for expulsion or some other disciplinary proposal?

First of all, I repeat, the method used, re-registering the party, is secondary to the main issue, which is that for the reasons already explained we were justified in throwing them out. However, there can be legitimate discussion about the method we chose, re-registering the party, as it precluded those expelled being able to appeal the action to the convention.

In my opinion, the right to a trial and an appeal is not an absolute in cases of political splits. Trials and appeals are generally meant for individual cases where infraction of the rules is at issue. These are not really meant for splits or expulsions of political groups. It had been extremely rare for any group on the left, including the SWP, to hold trials in the case of political splits.

The method chosen in the IT case was in the context of the deepening factionalism in the International. If we had put the IT members on trial and expelled them, it would have opened the door to the IMT leadership to assert its right to intervene in the trial. We rejected implicitly any right of the Fourth International leadership bodies to intervene in our internal affairs in any way. But to add an argument over this point would have detracted from the main issue. We felt that it was better to lop off the IT with a swift blow, avoiding a situation in which the IMT leadership demanded to participate in our internal affairs.

We also delayed carrying out the re-registration until after a meeting of the United Secretariat was over. Strictly speaking, the Control Commission's conclusions were ready a little earlier, but the Political Committee held off making its decision for a few days. We did so because we feared that the split wing of the IMT would inflame the situation during that United Secretariat meeting. This also gave us the opportunity to prepare publication of the documents in very swift fashion.

Could we have simply published the IT documents before the whole International, and given the IT a "cease and desist order," putting the ball in the IT's court? That would have given fair-minded people in the Fourth International the evidence beforehand. But this course would also have entailed the IMT split wing intervening in our affairs. Again, this would have exacerbated tensions in the International and diverted the political discussion. Moreover, while we could guarantee the publication in English of the IT documents, non-English-speaking sections of the International where the IMT had a majority were notorious for delaying translation and publication of the internal discussion. Furthermore, our experience gave us no confidence in the probity of the IT. We felt certain that they would continue functioning as usual, and would defy any "cease and desist" instruction, just delaying the whole affair to no avail.

From the advantage of hindsight, however, I think we did make three errors.

The first was to have the Control Commission exceed its mandate to investigate and report the facts and its recommendations to the Political Committee. The Control Commission went much further and wrote a lengthy political report on the organizational principles involved. The political analysis and conclusions should more properly have been drawn up by the Political Committee. The latter certainly could have written the report based on the Control Commission's findings of fact, and agreed with its recommendation that the IT be removed from the party.

In effect, there was a blurring of the distinction between the functions of the Control Commission and the political leadership of the party. This compromised the moral standing of the Control Commission as an objective and impartial body distinct from the

National Committee and the Political Committee. This marked an early step in the corruption of the internal standards of the party.

Another error was not to have allowed either the POT or the IT representation on the National Committee at the 1971 and 1973 conventions. If we had done so, these representatives would have participated in NC meetings. They would have been under pressure to present their views openly in the discussion. If they had done so it would have strengthened the party as a whole. It's possible that either side would have influenced the other in some way, although it is my opinion that was unlikely, given the factional situation in the International. I don't think that giving them representation on the National Committee would have prevented a split, but not doing so certainly embittered the IT rank and file, who were more open to the split perspective as a result.

A third error was a lack of temperance in some of the language we employed, both nationally and on a branch level. This sharpened the atmosphere and hardened positions, and was not necessary. The IT itself was certainly not free of such intemperance. But as the party leadership we bore a responsibility in this regard.

In particular, calling the IT a "party" went a bit too far, and gave our critics a handle on which they could hang their briefs. The IT stated that they saw themselves as the *nucleus* of a party in opposition to the SWP. In fact, that self-characterization would have been sufficient to describe them fully and to justify their expulsion.

As it turned out, once the IT was outside the SWP, it quickly became a "flimsy group" as the Enlarged Bureau of the IMT had warned. Once the IMT and LTF were dissolved less than three years later, IT members went their separate ways. I will discuss the subsequent evolution of the IMT and LTF in a later chapter.

---

* Many in the IT thought that the party majority had placed a spy inside the IT who had access to the document. The majority would never do such a thing. Such a spy would have to lie and declare his or her agreement with the political positions of the IT. It was deeply ingrained in the culture of the SWP that all comrades had the obligation to register their political positions openly, either orally in branch discussions, or in a written form, or by their votes on political resolutions. To pretend to have political positions not held in order to spy on a minority in the party was unthinkable.

** There was a major exception in which the IT carried out its own activity publicly. At demonstrations around the country in May 1974 to protest the September 1973 U.S.-backed military coup in Chile, the

IT members broke party discipline concerning what we were saying to other demonstrators and the public.

IT members had, before the demonstration, put forward in branches where they had members the proposal that we distribute a statement on the coup that the United Secretariat had unanimously adopted (with SWP approval) in September 1973. This statement called for support to the armed resistance in Chile to the coup. But by May of 1974, it had become clear the massive repression unleashed by the military around General Pinochet had crushed the resistance. The trade unions and all socialist organizations and other opponents of the coup were outlawed and their members hunted down. The September 1973 statement had become outdated. The IT proposal was voted down in the branches.

The party leadership nationally and in the branches proposed in light of the circumstances on the ground in Chile to instead support the campaign being waged by the U.S. Committee in Defense of Latin American Political Prisoners (USLA) to come to the aid of those victimized by the dictatorship. USLA called for the humane treatment of those imprisoned and their release, and to stop the mass arrests, torture, executions and "disappearing" of opponents of the Pinochet dictatorship.

The IT members, clearly under order of their national leaders, went ahead and distributed the September 1973 statement at the demonstrations. They also concentrated on selling not *The Militant*, but the paper of the Canadian RMG, the *Old Mole*.

*** Reactionary legislation passed in the 1940s barred the SWP from formal membership in the Fourth International. Among other things, this meant that we did not pay dues. Our votes in Fourth International bodies were not formally counted, although they carried great moral weight. However, the SWP continued to make its financial contribution as we always had. What we did was pay all of the costs of our members living in Europe who were elected as consultative members of the United Secretariat, and the travel and living expenses of our members who attended meetings of the various bodies of the Fourth International. These expenses were considerable. All of these meetings were held in Europe, in part because many of the International leaders were barred from entering the United States. Another reason was that travel costs for representatives from the European sections to the United States would be a considerable burden to the Fourth International itself, since such expenses were paid for out of the International's treasury, i.e. from dues and individual contributions.

We also were responsible for covering the costs of the writing staff and the printing and distributing of *Intercontinental Press*, which originated as a press service with articles by Fourth International leaders and other material the sections could use as they saw fit. Joe Hansen was its editor since its early days in Paris following the reunification of the International in 1963, and when it moved to New York after an illness made it difficult for Joe to remain abroad. We also covered the costs of translating, printing and mailing of the English language International Discussion and Information Bulletins.

As the faction struggle in the International deepened, *Intercontinental Press* carried articles that reflected the views of the minority. The IMT leadership saw this as a violation of international democratic centralism. But every majority resolution was printed in *Intercontinental Press*, as were all articles submitted by leaders of the IMT. What the IMT leaders wanted to suppress was public expression of minority views.

1 See Volume One of this work, pp. 299-303.
2 "The Building of a Revolutionary Party in Capitalist America, Political Counter Resolution Submitted by the Internationalist Tendency," SWP Discussion Bulletin, Vol. 31 No. 18, July 1973. p. 7.

CHAPTER SIX: TWO VIEWS OF INTERNATIONALISM

Concerning the charge by some leaders of the International Majority Tendency (IMT) and the International Tendency (IT) that the SWP was violating international democratic centralism, what was at stake were two different conceptions of the Fourth International. The view of the IMT leaders is revealed in how they acted in the IT case. It has already been noted that the Enlarged Bureau of the IMT imposed discipline on the IT preventing it from immediately leaving the SWP. According to Alec's report, the Enlarged Bureau also decided that the IT should "recruit people politically to the FI [Fourth International] and organizationally to the SWP." Moreover, instructing the IT to act in this fashion went against the spirit of the Statutes of the Fourth International, which forbade international leadership bodies from dictating tactics to sections or sympathizing groups.

Alec also reported that the Enlarged Bureau had instructed that "members of the SWP and YSA who support the IMT must join or rejoin (in the case of 9 comrades who recently resigned) the IT."

Two things should be noted about this instruction. The first is that the Enlarged Bureau's discipline over its supporters in a group of the Fourth International extends to telling them which internal faction they "must" be part of. This is another instance of dictating tactics to members of sections by an "international center" and expresses clearly the IMT leadership's concept of international democratic centralism.

Second, it endorses the IT practice (openly adopted in the Massey resolution at its convention) of recruiting to its faction YSA members who were not members of the SWP. This was another violation of the organizational norms of the SWP, which had been codified and adopted by convention of the SWP.

Neither the IMT Steering Committee nor any of its other bodies or the IT itself informed the SWP of the IT's split course. Instead, the IMT leadership acted behind the back of the party and directly intervened in the internal affairs of the SWP. This ran counter to the agreements reached and adopted by the January 1974 World Congress, the Statutes and other resolutions of the Fourth International including even the IMT's own political resolution adopted by majority vote at the World Congress!

Our conception of the International was diametrically opposed to that of the IMT. We categorically rejected any leadership bodies of the Fourth International acting behind the backs of any sections or sympathizing groups in any way whatsoever. Relations between leadership bodies and any group of the International must be open and clearly stated. As well, leadership bodies that differ with groups in the International must state so openly.

It is especially egregious for leadership bodies to connive with internal groupings bent on splitting with a section or sympathizing organization. This had happened once before, in 1953. The International leadership at the time around Michel Pablo, who was International Secretary of the Fourth International, had secretly conspired with an internal faction inside the SWP with the goal of splitting the SWP. This connivance was discovered by the SWP leadership. When this faction, known as the Cochran faction for its leading spokesman, carried out an action against a party decision, they were promptly expelled with the exception of the National Committee members of the minority, who were suspended—only the convention could expel NC members. The minority faction had withdrawn from organized party activity, culminating in a boycott of a celebration of the 25th anniversary of the publication of *The Militant*. This expulsion was done by the introduction into each branch of a motion to repudiate the boycott. Those who voted for the repudiation were re-registered as members; those who did not were dropped.

Moreover, it came to light that the Pablo cabal had engineered splits in other sections. In light of this intolerable situation, the SWP leadership in conjunction with leaderships in other Fourth International sections broke with Pablo, with the result that the International was split into two groups, the International Committee, which we supported, and the International Secretariat led by Pablo. When this split was healed in 1963, one of our conditions was that leadership bodies were prohibited from such interference in the internal life of the sections, and that Michel Pablo could not be an officer of the International.

It was the founding leader of the SWP, James P. Cannon, who led the party majority in the 1953 split. We younger leaders had been well educated along these lines, and we bridled at what we found to be the IMT secret interference in the SWP. We got the idea of re-registering the party membership from the action of the party majority in 1953.

Cannon had learned from bitter experience the evils of what he termed "Cominternism" in the early years of the U.S. Communist Party (CP). He was a founding member of one of the two Communist parties that emerged from the left wing of the U.S. Socialist Party that supported the Russian Revolution, and the subsequent formation of the Communist International. These groups eventually succeeded in fusing to form a united Communist Party. This fusion was helped along by the leaders of the Communist International, who also had some sharp disagreements politically with the newly won comrades in the United States. But at no time did the leadership of the International at the time of Lenin and Trotsky ever order the U.S. groups what to do organizationally, or impose a political line upon them. In those days, it was understood that such methods ran counter to the goal of building real revolutionary parties with self-confident leaderships. Patient explanation and discussion was the rule.

It was under the growing counter-revolution in the USSR led by Joseph Stalin that the Communist International over a period of years was turned into its opposite. From an international organization of democratic parties that largely decided their own affairs in pursuit of a worldwide socialist revolution, the parties of the Comintern were turned into lickspittle groups run by Moscow in pursuit of the current political line of the rising Soviet bureaucracy. Stalin's new theory of promoting "socialism in one country" provided the justification for this transformation. More and more, the Kremlin dictated the policies and even the selection of leaders in every country.

This was the situation in the American CP when Cannon and a small group of like-minded individuals were expelled from the party as "Trotskyists" in 1928. The new group they formed, which would go on to found the SWP ten years later, was inoculated against such dictates from the "leading center," as Moscow began referring to itself.

In his book, *The First Ten Years of American Trotskyism*, Cannon relates an incident concerning Trotsky himself. At issue was a member who had been expelled from the New York branch, who, it was later learned, had made his way to Turkey where Trotsky was living in exile. He apparently was working with Trotsky. Cannon wrote to Trotsky, informing him of the expulsion of this individual. Cannon writes that the leadership waited with some consternation for Trotsky's reply, ready to break with the Old Man over the question. Trotsky wrote back that he never intended to go behind the back of the New York branch and would certainly abide by its decision, much to the relief of the party leadership. In *Speeches to the Party*, a compilation of Cannon's speeches during the 1953 split, he explained this position further. I and the other younger leaders of the party had been educated in this and other examples, and would tolerate no breach of this key principle of internationalism by the IMT or anyone else.

The Communist International had been formed by splits in the old Social Democratic International after the Russian Revolution. The new International rejected the violation of socialist internationalism of the Social Democratic leaderships when they endorsed "their own" bourgeoisies in the West in their struggle over colonial spoils in the slaughter of the First World War. While relatively small, the new Communist parties in general had roots in the working class and followers in the thousands and tens of thousands. The International itself had a leadership that had stood at the head of the victorious Russian Revolution.

The Fourth International from its founding in 1938 against the degeneration of the Third (Communist) International, up through the period discussed in this chapter, was largely marginalized by the Stalinists. While many sections, including in the United States, had participated and even led important mass struggles, they were basically propaganda groups. The Communist International in its early years was able to have more centralism (although not of a bureaucratic or "commandist" type) than the much weaker Fourth International.

The SWP leadership worked hard to help build up a "center" for the Fourth International, first around Trotsky, especially when he was in Mexico. The Second World War separated the Trotskyist groups from one another. After the war, the SWP helped build up a new center in Europe, around Pablo, Ernest Mandel, Pierre Frank and then others. The SWP had some comrades in Europe to further this process until the 1953 split. In the period of the witchhunt, many SWP leaders couldn't get passports, and we were isolated from our co-thinkers. This changed in the late 1950s and with the reunification in 1963, Joe and Reba Hansen lived in Paris and were part of the new leadership.

We were for strengthening the International center. We were for more political leadership from the center, with more articles contributed from the center for our press internationally, and with more discussion between the center and the sections and between the sections, and for more international travel to facilitate greater collaboration.

At the same time, in our view all the sections had to be responsible for deciding their own positions not only concerning their own countries, but also big world events. Each section had the obligation to defend its views through its press. Foreign to the SWP's conception of internationalism was the idea that an "international center" would work out positions on all questions, which would then be parroted in the press of the sections. Building self-confident parties capable of effective intervention in the class struggle cannot be decreed from afar.

"International democratic centralism" is something of a misnomer. It is not like the "democratic centralism" practiced by sections of the International in their own organizations. Revolutions are not made in all or many countries at once. Socialist revolutions are international in content, but occur only on a national basis in particular countries as the result of class struggles in those countries. To help such revolutions succeed requires the formation of centralized combat parties over time, growing out of the real situations each party faces in its own country.

The situation facing the Fourth International since its foundation up through the early 1970s makes the idea that it could impose the same discipline on sections as the sections themselves expected of their members, absurd. To the extent it was tried such impositions stunted the growth and maturity of the sections.

It is ironic, but the SWP itself later in the 1980s would impose on groupings around the world that supported the SWP politically an even more grotesque version of international centralization than the IMT ever dreamed of. A chapter in Part Two will describe the disastrous results.

CHAPTER SEVEN: POLITICAL FERMENT

The lawsuit against government spying, disruption and harassment filed by the SWP and YSA in the summer of 1973 began to bear fruit. In January 1974, the Political Rights Defense Fund (PRDF), which was formed to mobilize support for the suit, held a press conference to publicize the initial response of the government.

U.S. Attorney Paul Curran admitted that the government had conducted a broad spy operation against the SWP dating back to 1945. (The suit would later uncover that the operation actually dated back to the 1930s, and was initiated by then President Roosevelt.) In carefully worded statements, the government admitted it had a specific "SWP Disruption Program" in place since 1961. This included electronic surveillance, and singling out SWP members and supporters for special victimization, including intimidation from FBI agents and visits to families and employers.

In July 1974 an FBI informer, James Nilson, was discovered in the Bloomington, Indiana YSA. Bloomington is the site of Indiana University. Two YSA members interviewed him, and he admitted that in addition to informing, his FBI handler instructed him to try to start fights in the organization and disrupt in other ways. He was also told to find out everything he could about the local PRDF. It was clear that the FBI was continuing its "Disruption Program."

Later in the year we scored an important victory. "In a far-reaching decision Dec. 13, [U.S. District court Judge Thomas Griesa] granted a motion of the Young Socialist Alliance for an injunction against FBI plans to spy on the five-day YSA national convention scheduled to begin in St. Louis on December 28," *The Militant* reported. Griesa was the judge handling our suit.[1]

Other revelations of government dirty tricks came to light. NBC news reporter Carl Stern had sued under the Freedom Of Information Act for materials about the FBI and COINTELPRO (counterintelligence program) dating back to 1961. Although names, sentences and entire portions of the documents were deleted, they nevertheless revealed a massive campaign of disruption aimed at the SWP, Communist Party (CP) and other socialist groups, the Black Panther Party and other Black nationalist organizations. These documents were memorandums from FBI Director J. Edgar Hoover.

"The purpose of this new counterintelliegence endeavor," Hoover says, "is to expose, disrupt, misdirect, discredit and otherwise neutralize the activities of black nationalist, hate-type organizations and groupings, their leadership, spokesmen, membership and supporters...."

One document dated March 4, 1968, one month before Dr. Martin Luther King was assassinated, had projected the goal to "Prevent the rise of a black 'messiah' who could unify, and electrify, the militant black nationalist movement."

While his name was blacked out, it was clear King was a target. The name blacked out was four typewriter spaces long. Putting his name back in, the memo would continue, "King could be a very real contender for this position should he abandon his supposed 'obedience' to 'white', liberal doctrines (nonviolence) and embrace black nationalism." Another blacked out name had the same number of letters as "Malcolm X" and in addition the top right part of the "X" was still visible. The sentence would read, "Malcolm X might have been such a 'messiah,' he is the martyr of the movement today."[2] This memo is another piece in the case that it was some government agency (or agencies) that was involved in the assassinations of both leaders.

In the coming months and years, our lawsuit uncovered more and more documents concerning the illegal campaign the various political police agencies conducted over the decades against the SWP and YSA. These documents often disclosed information about other organizations and persons, such as attempts to foment strife between the CP and the SWP, between us and various Black, Chicano and women's groups—through the planting of false information, fake leaflets, and so on. PRDF began to be seen as playing a key role in fighting for civil rights and liberties, and began to win wider and wider support.

•••

In 1974 the SWP and YSA continued to grow, and were active to the best of their abilities as small organizations in the broader social movements and issues. One campaign we were involved in was a national strike by truck drivers who owned their own trucks. The drivers were rebelling against high fuel costs, increasing taxes and other onerous government regulations, and poor remuneration from the big companies that contracted them out. In reality, many such owner-operators' trucks were largely owned by the banks on long-term loans—another burden.

While we had no members who were truck owner-operators, we were able to join their demonstrations and rallies. We had launched some 100 election campaigns across the country in 1974, and our candidates and other members would come down to picket lines to show their support. *The Militant* gave the battle extensive coverage and we had good sales to truckers.

These actions were very militant. Truckers closed down diesel pumps through truck blockades of recalcitrant station owners. Decisions on how to conduct the strike were made in large democratic meetings.

One such meeting in Minneapolis was reported in *The Militant* by Greg Cornell:

"The truckers' shutdown in Minnesota has to be one of the most militant, massive, democratic and innovative labor struggles to hit this state in 25 years. 'We're going to strike along with the rest of the country,' Denny Hollgren of Duluth told a cheering strike meeting of 1,000 truckers in St. Paul Feb. 10. 'We're going to stick it out until we win.'

"'It seems like the only way to get anything in this country is to protest,' one Minnesota trucker organizer told me.... Several organizing centers have sprung up in key cities across the state to maintain and spread the strike." The government attempted to intervene and force the truckers back to work. "In the St. Paul meeting, which lasted nearly three hours, everyone was allowed to speak. Dozens of drivers took the floor, including two independent truck owners who favored returning to work. The two were roundly booed but were nevertheless allowed to present their case.

"The strikers listened and then repudiated any proposal to accept the government's settlement. They voted without a single nay to continue the shutdown. [A strike leader] pledged to truckers at the meeting that 'before the trucks roll again,' it would take a majority vote to end the strike."[3]

A weakness in the battle was the hostility of the corrupt bureaucrats at the top of the Teamsters' union, which sought to drive a wedge between the owner-operators and the Teamster truckers employed directly by the shipping companies. *The Militant* ran an interview with SWP leader Farrell Dobbs about how the Teamsters handled the issue when he was on the staff of the union's general organizers, which successfully organized the long-haul drivers in the last half of the 1930s. This campaign followed the successful 1934 Teamsters strikes and mass battles in 1934, of which Dobbs was a young leader, and which were organized by the Trotskyists.

The Militant asked Dobbs, "Some people have questioned whether these drivers should be viewed as workers or as a variety of small businessmen." Dobbs replied, "Basically the independent owner-operators must be seen as workers who are required to provide their own tools as a condition of employment. In their case, this means that working drivers have to provide their own trucks.

This practice has long been pushed by the employers and the trucking industry. Their object is to foist off on the worker part of the overhead of the trucking operation, and at the same time try to give the worker the mistaken impression that he is an integral part of the trucking industry, as distinguished from drivers who simply work for companies that own fleets of trucks."

During the upsurge of the Teamster union, Dobbs recalled, the independent truckers were brought into the union. They had their own organization within the union to discuss their particular issues, but then met with the rest of the membership in general meetings. The power of the union was thus brought to bear behind them, and they were able to win significant gains. Dobbs was able to help clarify the issues before the current independent strikers as well as for other younger class struggle militants, including our own members.4

•••

One of our important election campaigns in 1974 was to run Olga Rodriguez for Governor of California and Dan Styron for U.S. Senator from the state. Early in the year I helped write the campaign platform and from Los Angeles worked with party units in the San Francisco Bay Area and San Diego in launching the campaign. It became a flagship for our election campaigns around the county.

Running a young Chicana for governor in a state with a large Latino population dovetailed with efforts by the independent La Raza Unida Party to run Chicano candidates in the Southwest, especially in Texas. We also ran Mariana Hernandez and Manuel Barrera for city council in heavily Latino East Los Angeles, an area that was a center of the Chicano movement in the county.

I made many trips to San Diego and the Bay Area to help with the campaign and as a de facto state organizer. I would stay with Farrell Dobbs and Marvel Scholl when in the Bay Area. When Farrell moved to the Bay Area a few years earlier to retire from the central party leadership, Jack Barnes had informed the Political Committee that Farrell had requested that only Jack be his contact with the new leadership, and that the rest of us should refrain from engaging him in discussions about what was happening in the party. I scrupulously went along with this, believing it was Farrell's way of not trying to interfere with the young leadership in guiding party affairs. Much later, after I had resigned from the party in 1988, I found out that Jack had lied, and that Farrell had wondered why I had refrained from talking to him about party politics. This little maneuver of Jack's was a forewarning of what was to develop.

•••

In the turbulent years of "The Sixties" many different kinds of small organizations developed. Some of these attempted to set up "communes" of like-minded youth that would exist outside of mainstream society and offer an example of non-capitalist relations within the communes. These were usually short-lived as they came into conflict with capitalist society and its many blandishments. Many became cults around charismatic individuals, suffered internal personality conflicts, and as the case with many cults often became sexual harems for the (male) cult leader.

Other cults appeared which had no connection whatever with the left or radical politics at all. The group the sadist Charles Manson organized comes to mind. They carried out spectacular murders of Hollywood stars just for the hell of it.

One small terrorist group did claim to be on the left, the weirdly named Symbionese Liberation Army (SLA). One of the SLA's first actions was the murder of a Black education official in Oakland, California, because, they said, he was a "sellout." In early 1974 they made their most spectacular action by kidnapping Patricia Hearst, an heiress to the vast Hearst fortune. The SLA carried out some robberies and had some money. In the wake of the Hearst kidnapping, which received national attention in the daily media, the SLA tried the gimmick of distributing food to poor people.

Angered that some poor Black people accepted some of this food, then California Governor and future President Ronald Reagan declared on March 6, "It's just too bad we can't have an epidemic of botulism." In a public statement, SWP candidate Olga Rodriguez replied, "While Reagan may be cruder than most capitalist politicians, his comment clearly expressed the disgusting racism and inhumanity of the rulers of this country. Questioned later by the press, Reagan refused to deny his statement. He claims that those who took the food were 'aiding and abetting lawlessness'.... What arrogance! It is capitalist politicians like Reagan, Nixon and Agnew who have been proved to be the biggest criminals in the country."

In the same issue of *The Militant* that carried Rodriguez' statement, an article by Cindy Burke noted:

"Terrorist acts by isolated groups like the SLA give the ruling class a handle for repression under circumstances in which the masses are not involved, but instead are confused and passive.

"Already the prison authorities have been able to close down the Black Cultural Association at Vacaville prison. On the pretext that alleged SLA members participated in the program, authorities claimed the BCA was a front for infiltrating terrorists into the prisons.

"When the masses are regulated to the role of passive observer and recipients of bounty from the SLA, even the distribution of free food can be turned to the capitalists' advantage. The most glaring example of this was the distribution in [mostly Black] East Oakland, which culminated in the arrest of almost 50 Blacks. Dozens were injured in confrontations caused when food was literally thrown from trucks at the 5,000 Blacks who had assembled.

"Black community leaders have charged that the event was set up by the police. The community, angered by the racist and inhuman conduct of the distribution, was later invaded by the police, who blocked off East 14th Street for 10 blocks and marched through the streets harassing and beating Blacks at random.

"The FBI has sent in two additional SWAT teams to investigate the [Hearst] kidnapping in the Bay Area. SWAT means 'Special Weapons Attack Team.' There can be no doubt that one task of these teams will be to infiltrate and disrupt left-wing groups under the guise of investigating the Hearst kidnapping. Defense against such attacks is hampered by the confusion and disorientation caused by the SLA kidnapping."5

The SLA was reveling in its national notoriety, and its seeming ability to stay one step ahead of the cops and FBI, who were fully mobilized especially in California. The SLA then released a spectacular video of a bank robbery by SLA members accompanied by Patty Hearst, renamed "Tanya," armed with a rifle. The video was shown over and over on national TV. Apparently Patty Hearst was either traumatized, weak-minded and easily manipulated by the cult, or was won over by them. The video amounted to a taunting of the authorities, who went berserk.

The Los Angeles police soon discovered that six SLA members were living in a small bungalow in the Black community. The cops amassed a force of 500, surrounding the house on May 17, 1974. They then opened fire of such intensity that the home was engulfed in flames. The police made no attempt to evacuate people in the surrounding area, and held back the arrival of the fire department. All six inside the house were incinerated. Of course there was damage to the surrounding homes.

At a press conference on May 21 held by the American Civil Liberties Union, representatives of the Black community denounced the police attack. "The police must not be allowed to act as prosecuting attorney, jury of peers, sentencing judge, and executioner, all in one," said the Reverend Edgar Edwards, pastor at the Emmanuel Church of Christ, located near the holocaust. With a ratio of about 100 cops to one suspect, he said, "We believe a more human solution could have been found than burning people to death...." Compounding the cold-blooded killing of the entrapped suspects, Edwards said, was "the vast destruction of property. As you travel through that block you see many, many houses showing the marks of fire and violence." One reporter on the scene said that to him the thing that stood out was the stark terror in the eyes of children and fear in the faces of the adults.[6]

It turned out that one of the incinerated SLA victims had been the wife of a member of the YSA at Indiana University in Bloomington, Indiana. I flew to Bloomington to demonstrate the solidarity of the national movement with the local YSA, whose members were understandably shook up, and especially with Gary Attwood, whose wife, Angela, had been burned to death in the police assault. He still loved Angela, and was devastated by the tragedy.

I interviewed Gary, which was printed in *The Militant*. He explained how he and Angela had become radicalized at Indiana U. in the aftermath of the demonstrations at the 1968 Democratic Party national convention, and the massive student strike in 1970. While Gary eventually gravitated toward the YSA, he and Angela became increasingly politically estranged as she was drawn toward Maoism and then toward terrorism, as their mutual friends Bill and Emily Harris evolved in that direction. She and Gary broke up and she and the Harrises left for California to join the SLA. Gary meanwhile had become an opponent of individual terrorism and a Marxist.

•••

In the early 1970s, there had been a number of important strikes. This trend continued in 1974. "In mid-July, government mediators announced, the number of strikes in progress hit 588, the highest total since they began keeping count 15 years ago," Andy Rose wrote in *The Militant*. "Almost a quarter of a million workers were on strike." Rose reported that most of these strikes were local, in enterprises of less than 1,000 workers. Most of these strikes were about workers' efforts to increase wages to keep up with soaring inflation.[7]

A strike by Retail Clerks Local 1100 at the Sears department store in San Francisco had been going on for six months by February 1974. The Local was led by Walter Johnson, a militant unionist with some vision, who came out against the war in Vietnam early when most labor leaders didn't. Local 1100 was known for mobilizing its members in support of other labor struggles. The San Francisco SWP branch had worked closely with Johnson, who was open to suggestions for sensible militant action. SWP leader Nat Weinstein led the branch's work in support of Local 1100's activities. The SWP had two members who worked at Sears, and they became part of the

Local's leadership. In 1973, the Local spearheaded the formation of the United Labor Action Committee, which worked to mobilize support in the city and wider Bay Area for all labor struggles.

Sears was out to crush the union. The company refused to even make a counter-offer to the union's demands. It had the backing of the National Labor Relations Board, which sat on the many grievances the union had filed citing multiple violations of labor law by Sears. Mass picketing was organized by Local 1100, but with the support of the cops scabs got through. In one instance, a scab attacked a striker and used his head to break the striker's bullhorn.

A united meeting of the Bay Area labor movement was called for February 3 to support the strike. In preparation for the meeting, Local 1100 representatives spoke to union and community meetings. SWP members in other unions were organizing support in their locals. A march was called for February 9 that culminated in a rally and mass picketing at the main Sears store. The rally was addressed by various Bay Area labor leaders and even some politicians. The picketers surrounded the store, closing it down. Then in a surprise move, hundreds of picketers stormed into the store from two entrances on opposite sides of the store and engaged in a sit-in. It was such militant mass actions combined with reaching out to the rest of the labor movement and the community that led to a union victory.

•••

While there were a number of small, local strikes in the first part of the year, there was an important national strike by the United Mine Workers of America (UMWA) in November 1974. The UMWA had undergone an important change when the Miners for Democracy, a caucus within the union, succeeded in overthrowing the corrupt dictatorial regime of Tony Boyle after a long and bitter struggle. Boyle had ordered the murder of Miners for Democracy leader Jacob Jablonski and his family. Boyle was convicted of the murders. The new leadership made sweeping changes, democratizing the union. Arnold Miller became the new president.

The strike began November 12, when 120,000 miners walked off the job. A tentative settlement was reached the very next day. The proposed agreement was put before the full elected bargaining council, and some members expressed reservations. Then it was presented to 830 local union delegates, who took it back to the membership. Each member was given the full written proposed contract. Then it was discussed in each local and after that the membership voted. This was the first time in the history of the

UMWA that the membership got to vote on the document establishing the conditions they have to labor under every day.

The capitalist press expressed the owning class' fear of the union giving the ultimate power to the membership. The *New York Times* editorialized against giving the ranks of the UMWA—or any other union—control over all union affairs, in spite of the *Times'* rhetoric about democracy. The bosses fear the mobilized power of the membership.

Union democracy and rank and file control greatly strengthened the union, bringing the power of an informed and sovereign membership to bear. The coal barons knew that behind the union negotiators was the power of the mobilized membership. There were important gains in the tentative agreement on wages, mine safety, and pensions. For the first time there was a cost of living clause to increase wages to compensate for inflation, and other gains.

Many members felt, however, that they could have gotten more if they had continued the strike. On December 5, Miller announced that the agreement was approved by 56 to 44 percent. Moreover, the mobilized rank and file felt their strength, and would enforce the contract against the bosses' attempts to weaken it.

The price of oil had risen, making coal more profitable, and the bosses expanded production, bringing in young workers. These workers were influenced by the radicalization of "The Sixties," as were most young people. This influx of feisty youth had proven to be an important factor in the overthrow of the Boyle machine.

However, the deep worldwide recession that developed in the second half of 1974 and into 1975 began to put a damper on union struggles.

•••

"The Sixties" continued to have an impact throughout the 1970s (and to this day, in fact). One important feature was the rise of national and racial consciousness among oppressed and discriminated-against people in the wake of the Black struggle. An aspect of this in New York City were attempts by local school boards representing areas composed largely of people of color to take control of their schools.

Opposing these attempts was Albert Shanker, president of the United Federation of Teachers (UFT). In 1968 he led a racist teachers' strike in Brooklyn against Black parents seeking control over their schools. The teachers union was overwhelmingly white, and one of the parents' demands was for more Black teachers. SWP and other anti-racist teachers crossed the picket lines.

In the early 1970s, parents in the largely Puerto Rican, Asian and Black community in Manhattan's Lower East Side sought to correct the deplorable education their children were getting by taking control over their schools. Again, the Shankerites whipped up white teachers against the community with crude racist appeals. The New York City SWP actively participated in the parents' struggle and earned their respect.

At the American Federation of Teachers (AFT) convention in August 1974 (the AFT was the national federation that grew out of the UFT), a resolution was introduced to support the Political Rights Defense Fund. As The Militant reported, "The resolution's call for support to this civil liberties effort was well received by several delegates on the resolutions committee, who saw it as a way of responding to the Nixon administration's attacks on its political opponents.

"Shanker's hacks on the committee, however, set their sights on defeating the resolution. Abe Levine of the UFT declared that while he supported civil liberties, that wasn't the real issue. He denounced the SWP and YSA's role in school District 1 in Lower Manhattan and said such people could not be supported…. Another Shankerite assailed the SWP for opposing the racist 1968 teachers' strike."[8]

The SWP ran Katherine Sojourner for Congress for the Lower East Side. Sojourner was a tireless worker in the parents' struggle, and was well liked by the activists. We opened a storefront campaign office in the Lower East Side, which became a center of activity for the struggle. A sixth grader taped the following note at the storefront office: "My name is Lillian Mojica. Every day we come to work at Socialist Workers '74. My brother and sister and me come at 10 on Saturday. On other days we come at three or four because we go to school. All I can say is we love Socialist Workers '74."

The SWP and YSA organized classes on socialism every Saturday afternoon after the day's campaigning. "The growing support for Sojourner's candidacy was reflected at an Oct. 19 campaign banquet," wrote Craig Gannon for The Militant. "A crowd of 215 people attended, including 40 District 1 parents, bilingual teachers and paraprofessionals, and parent-supported school board members and candidates." Leaders of the battle spoke.[9]

•••

In 1973, Duncan Ferguson, an American artist and member of the SWP, died. "Duncan joined the Socialist Workers Party back in 1941, and he was 41 years of age at the time," Harry Ring wrote in his obituary. "He was already an established sculptor. His work was on exhibit in the [New York] Metropolitan Museum, the Whitney, the

Museum of Modern Art, and numerous others.... Duncan left a professorship at Louisiana State University. He was head of the fine arts department there. He had decided that he wanted to be an active member of the party, and he packed his bags and came to New York.... He came into the movement as a full-time revolutionary, and he remained one until his death."

By "full time" or "professional" revolutionary we meant those who devoted their lives to the struggle for socialism, not only those who worked directly for the party. Duncan continued his sculpting while working in various industrial jobs. When his health began to fail in the 1950s, he got a job at a large community center in Cleveland, where he taught sculpture. That is where I met him and his companion Cleo in 1962 while I was on a speaking tour for the YSA. I would visit him whenever I was in Cleveland in the following years.

---

1 *The Militant,* Dec. 27, 1974.
2 Ibid., Jan. 25 and March 24, 1974.
3 Ibid., Feb. 24, 1974.
4 Ibid.
5 Ibid., March 15, 1974.
6 Ibid., May 29, 1974.
7 Ibid., Aug. 2, 1974.
8 Ibid., Sept. 23, 1974.
9 Ibid., Nov. 8, 1974.

CHAPTER EIGHT: THE BOSTON BUSING WAR

The 1954 U.S. Supreme Court decision that segregated schools were inherently unequal dealt a legal blow to the Jim Crow system in the South. Under this system, segregation and the oppression of Blacks were codified in law. However, it took the rise of the civil rights and Black liberation movements of the 1950s and 1960s to smash Jim Crow.

While there was *de jure* (by law) school segregation in the South, there was *de facto* (in fact) segregation in the North, which continued even after the overthrow of Jim Crow. Boston was one of the major cities where this was true. What set Boston apart was the decision by powerful forces in the city to organize a legal and extra-legal campaign to defend school segregation against a legal victory, initiated by Black community organizations, ordering the desegregation of Boston's schools. What the suit brought by community organizations proved was that the *de facto* segregation in the Boston schools was in fact *de jure* segregation carried out in a deliberate campaign by city and school leaders over decades.

Boston was divided into ethnically defined sub-cities, created in the course of different waves of immigration. South Boston, East Boston, Hyde Park, and Charleston were white enclaves. Most Blacks lived in Roxbury and Dorchester. The Boston School Committee had blatantly under-funded Black schools and made them substantially inferior to white schools.[1]

In 1965, the Massachusetts state legislature made *de facto* school segregation illegal, but the law was not enforced. In 1972, the National Association for the Advancement of Colored People (NAACP) and other groups in Boston's Black community filed a lawsuit against Boston's system of school segregation. In 1974, Federal Judge Wendell Garrity found in favor of the lawsuit, and issued an order that desegregation would begin in the fall school term by busing Black students into white schools and vice-versa. The first phase of the desegregation plan would pair Roxbury with South Boston.

The racists had been organizing throughout the summer to meet the fall's desegregation plan with violence. Egged on by the racist Boston School Committee, the city administration and the Democratic Party machine, the white and largely Irish South Boston community was mobilized to physically attack Black students being bused into formerly all-white schools there. On the first day of school, white racist mobs attacked the Black children. They threw beer cans, rocks, and bottles, and pounded the buses with their fists and clubs. Racist graffiti was everywhere: "Niggers suck," "No niggers in South Boston," "niggers eat shit," "Bus 'em back to Africa," "Boneheads beware," "French fried niggers for sale."[2] While the racists' leaders used euphemisms, on the street it was crystal clear what the war was about.

This was the first battle in a two-year war between the Black community and the mobilized racists and their leaders, most prominently in the Boston School Committee.

In this war, the SWP and YSA were to play an increasingly important role as an integral part of the struggle of the Black community and its supporters.

The public face of the racists was ROAR (Restore Our Alienated Rights), led by Louise Day Hicks. She was part of the Democratic Party machine, had been elected to Congress, and as a City Council member was the foremost racist on the School Committee. Her close ties with the city administration enabled her to obtain City Hall rooms for meetings of ROAR.

ROAR called for a white student boycott of the Black schools targeted for desegregation.

A few weeks after school began in the fall of 1974, a Black man, Andre Yvon Jean Louis, drove as usual after work from Roxbury to South Boston to pick up his wife who worked in a laundry. He encountered the anti-busing mob by chance, and was pulled from his car and nearly beaten to death. Shouts of "Get the nigger!" and "Lynch him!"[3] riled the crowd. Finally police, who had been reluctantly protecting the Black students, saved him from near certain death. Such random attacks on Blacks throughout the city would mark the whole period of the busing war.

Black community organizations formed the Freedom House Coalition to defend desegregation. The coalition and the Boston NAACP became the principle supporters for the Black community.

The Boston SWP and YSA threw their forces into the fight. The national SWP and YSA sent leading people, including myself, to Boston to advise. I would make many such trips as the liaison between the Political Committee and the Boston Branch in the first phase of the struggle. We also began to transfer comrades, including young Blacks, to beef up the SWP branch and the YSA chapter. Our political thrust was that the Black community and its supporters should counter-mobilize against the racists. There were important grass roots leaders in the Black community who shared this approach.

The first significant public protest was a meeting called on short notice by the YSA and the Ujima Society, a Black student organization, at the University of Massachusetts in Boston. Five hundred people, including high school students being bused to South Boston, showed up on September 26, 1974 and heard first-hand reports from students and others about the racist violence, reports which were not getting into the mainstream press. The YSA initiated other "teach-ins" at the many campuses in the Boston area.

The SWP was running Don Gurewitz for governor, and Ollie Bivins, a Black student at Boston University, for lieutenant governor. They made the busing fight the center of their campaign. Their antiracist message received wide coverage. The Democratic and Republican candidates avoided the issue so as not to alienate the anti-busing vote. The Democrat was Michael Dukakis, who would later run for president against George Bush the Elder, who, ironically, would use anti-Black fears to smear him. Dukakis won the election for governor, with the backing of the racist Boston Democratic Party machine.

The city was boiling. Black students who had been bused into Hyde Park High were also met with rocks and bottles. Fights between Black and white students in the schools were common, with the violence being organized by white student thugs against the outnumbered Blacks. Meanwhile, President Ford issued a statement against Judge Garrity's court order. The prestige of the White House was thrown into the fight on the side of the racists, further emboldening them.

On October 6, there was a rally against the racist violence at the State House. It was largely white, and included many radicals. Youth Against War and Fascism (YAWF), the youth group of Workers World initiated the action.

YAWF saw the need for a counter-mobilization against the racists, and began to privately circulate a letter to prominent Black leaders urging a march. They set up an Emergency Committee for a National Mobilization, but with little publicity. On November 14, State Senator William Owens, flanked by members of the staff of the Emergency Committee, publicly called for a mass action for December 14, 1974. Owens, who was Black, opposed busing as did YAWF, but, like YAWF, saw the need for action against the racists and for "the elementary democratic right of these [Black] children to go to any school in safety."[4] The proposal for the December 14 march now had hundreds of endorsers.

In addition, another demonstration was called for November 30. This was initiated by the liberal wing of the Democratic Party, reflecting a rift with the racist Boston Democratic machine. The

November 30 demonstration had the endorsement of prominent members of the clergy, and was designed to reach out to whites. Thomas Atkins, the young head of the Boston NAACP, became involved in the planning. Atkins had been a leader in the desegregation fight, and would emerge as a central leader as the war intensified. The party and YSA worked to build the action.

On November 29, Coretta Scott King, Martin Luther King's widow, came to Boston to address a news conference, together with Atkins, to promote the next day's action. The march, lead by Mrs. King, was the first protest in the streets against the racists, who had thought the streets were theirs. Flanking Mrs. King were community leaders Atkins and Owens. Drawing some 2,500, it was a building block for the December 14 march.

But there were signs of problems emerging with the Emergency Committee. As *Militant* reporter Jon Hillson wrote in *The Battle of Boston*:

"Something, however, was not going right with the plans for the December 14 march called by State Senator Owens. When supporters went to the Emergency Committee's office to sign up as volunteers or inquire about citywide and campus meetings to publicize the demonstration, they got vague answers at best. The logistical and political preparation required for an ambitious undertaking such as a national demonstration was great....

"A small staff occupying a tiny office had been set up, hardly sufficient to meet the needs of a large action. No public meetings to discuss plans were set. Further, the staff members appeared to have an ambivalent attitude toward the November 30 march, as if it were a threat to December 14. They were not sure they supported it. December 14 appeared stalled....

"Moreover, the staff was entirely new to Boston. Because they all shared the political perspective of Youth Against War and Fascism, they viewed the Emergency Committee as their private preserve," Hillson explained.[5]

There was another development on the Boston area campuses, where committees in support of December 14 appeared. In many cases, members of the YSA initiated these committees. The Boston area committees called for a meeting at Boston University on November 24, which was attended by activists from 18 New England campuses. This working gathering launched the Student Committee for the December 14 March, to organize student participation as well as to reach out beyond the campuses. Among the leaders of the new organization were Ray Sherbill, President of the Boston University Student Union; Willie McKinney, president of the Roxbury Community College Student Government; Paul Mailhot, a student at

Boston State College and a YSA member; and Maceo Dixon, a national officer of the YSA who moved to Boston together with his companion Reba Williams. Dixon and Williams were part of a layer of young Blacks who had been recruited to the YSA. They had been active in Detroit in the movement to abolish an elite police unit that was notorious for brutalizing and killing Blacks.

This new organization was built on principles the SWP and YSA had developed in the Vietnam antiwar movement. It sought to involve all that wanted to build the action, regardless of their political affiliation or lack thereof. Decisions were made democratically at meetings open to all activists.

Meanwhile, the racists were again mobilizing, attacking buses bringing Black students to formerly all-white schools, and organizing white students to attack Black students. The Black students who were on the front lines were the real heroes of the struggle. "I ain't gonna run. We got a right to go there," was the mood of stubborn pride among them.[6]

Adult organizations began openly joining and leading the racist mobs. Wearing purple berets with blue pom-poms, the uniform of the Mullins gang of toughs in South Boston, this gang was the most important. On December 11, the racist mobilizations climaxed in a battle outside South Boston High. Groups of white students left the school to join the growing racist mob. Black students were waiting for buses to take them home under police protection. At first the police were outnumbered by the racists. They became the targets of the mob. Reinforcements were brought in, and there was a pitched battle between the bigots and the police.

Many Boston cops came from the same all-white neighborhoods as the racist mobs. Their sympathies lay with them. But the attacks on their own forces enraged the police who smashed the mob and got the Black children out.

It should be noted that not all whites, including white students, in the white conclaves joined in the racist attacks, whether they supported busing or not. Communities like South Boston were increasingly terrorized by the organized racists, who ostracized and threatened whites that opposed the violence. White parents that didn't go along with the ROAR-organized school boycotts and sent their children to schools in Roxbury were especially targeted. In the schools it was a minority of white thugs who organized attacks on Blacks, and intimidated white students who didn't go along.

The Student Committee had called for a national teach-in at Harvard for December 13, on the eve of the march. The staff of the Committee continued to grow and included veterans of the antiwar and women's liberation movements, and others who were new to organizing a mass protest. They were working 12 to 14-hour days, for a pittance. The racist intimidation and threats in South Boston High and other schools transformed the December 14 march into an emergency mobilization. In response, the Committee reached out beyond the Boston area to mobilize people to come to the march.

The Student Committee had called a press conference on December 12. The media jammed the pressroom at the State House for the conference. Maceo Dixon, speaking for the Committee, was joined by Robert Harper, a Black student leader from Harvard; John Boone, who lost his job as commissioner of the State Department of Corrections for his defense of Black prisoners; Rev. Vernon Carter, a leader of the Black community and a long-time foe of segregated schools in Boston, and best-selling author and teacher Jonathan Kozol.

The teach-in at Harvard the next day drew 1,200 students. The highlight of the meeting was the appearance of three Black high school students who described the white violence in the schools. Dixon read out statements to the conference from prominent Black leaders across the country, including Rosa Parks, the heroine of the Montgomery bus boycott. Rev. Ralph D. Abernathy, of the Southern Christian Leadership Conference, spoke, as did Rev. Carter and Kozol.

•••

State Senator Owens came late to the teach-in, but told Dixon in private that the march route, which had been negotiated with the police, would be secretly changed, so as to lead to a confrontation with the police.

The march had been advertised as a peaceful mass action. Owens and YAWF were attempting to dupe the great majority of those coming to the march into a fight with the police, without their knowledge or consent. This secret plan was contemptuous of the demonstrators. YAWF knew it could never get approval of the overwhelming majority of protesters for such a confrontation, so it plotted to trick them into it. This would be a serious blow to the anti-racist struggle, enabling the press, the Boston establishment, and even the national government under President Ford to portray the movement as violent, shifting the blame for the violence from the racist mobs and their supporters to the antiracist movement and the Black community itself. This manipulative scheme would also create deep suspicion among anti-racist activists concerning any future actions.

Dixon alerted the party and YSA nationally. We would do what we could, in concert with other leaders of the Student Committee and the Black community, to head off YAWF's plans.

The Emergency Committee had its own marshals for the demonstration, drawn in the main from out-of-towners sympathetic to YAWF. The Student Committee had organized 500 marshals, including activists from other areas involved in building the march, but mostly from the Boston area, including Black students on the buses. These marshals included veterans of the antiwar movement as well as first-time organizers who were given extensive and intense training in organizing a peaceful march.

On December 14, the Student Committee marshals, briefed on the problem of YAWF's plans, arrived at the march's starting point early in the day, and set up a big, rectangular phalanx of monitors. They distributed flyers to the march participants as they arrived with the original march route. The Emergency Committee marshals tore up the flyers (those they got their hands on) with the original march route, and falsely told people that their new route had been secured. In fact, the cops, learning of the Emergency Committee's plans, massed at the point the new route would diverge from the original one. Tensions were high between the Emergency Committee and the Student Committee.

The march was scheduled to step off at noon. But by one o'clock Owens, who was supposed to lead the march, hadn't arrived. Confusion about the march route was building among the assembled demonstrators. The party had a leadership committee present, including myself and Fred Halstead, a veteran of many antiwar and trade union marches and strikes. We decided we had to act. The Student Committee leaders and marshals, who were aware of YAWF's plans, agreed that they would start the march immediately, taking it over in fact from the Emergency Committee.

Because its marshals had arrived early, the Student Committee contingent was in the front. It began the march, much to the consternation of the Emergency Committee, which tried in vain to hold back demonstrators. The marchers simply overwhelmed the Emergency Committee marshals attempting to hold them back, and joined the march that had already taken off.

I saw one Emergency Committee marshal become so frustrated that he reached up and punched Fred (who was big and tall) in the face. Fred, who always had a cool head in such confrontations, ignored his attacker and continued to urge the demonstrators forward into the march.

A line of Student Committee marshals stood between the march and the massed cops, and diverted the march to the original route.

Owens, who had shown up by that time, and a handful of YAWF supporters, tried to confront the police and were arrested, but the march went on successfully. For a time, marchers behind the Emergency Committee contingent were held up, but soon were on the original march route, with the Student Committee marshals helped by Rev. Abernathy guiding them. When this second contingent arrived at the rally point on the Boston Common, a huge cheer went up.

Some 12,000 people were at the rally. There were banners from all kinds of organizations in the crowd. A wide range of speakers, including Black high school students, Nobel laureate George Wald, the poet Amiri Baraka of the Congress of Afrikan People, William Lucy of the Coalition of Black Trade Unionists, comedian Dick Gregory, and Owens himself, who decided to join the march following his pathetic stunt. The march was front-page news in Boston and the lead story on the evening television news. There were sympathy rallies in other cities, initiated by us.

As Hillson wrote, the action's "greatest success would be in what grew out of it, for it inspired a process of education and action to continue the struggle. Two hundred and fifty Black, Puerto Rican and white students who packed a classroom at the University of Massachusetts in downtown Boston on the night of December 14 sensed that. They were physically exhausted, some already wheezing from the chill, but the room was alive with energy. Something big had happened that day, something new and powerful....

"At the teach-in and march they had been urged by the Student Committee to attend this meeting.... The proposal put before them was for a national student gathering in Boston on February 14 and 15 to map strategy to meet the racist offensive. After discussion, the vote was unanimous."[7]

The next day 3,000 people came to a march organized by the racists, much smaller than it could have been. Infighting among the bigots' leadership took its toll. The antiracist mobilizations were having an effect even in the ranks of the racists. They had lost a battle, but still had their machine intact and would continue the war.

Thomas Atkins, the young Black lawyer who led the Boston NAACP, had not endorsed the December 14 action, out of suspicion of the role of the Emergency Committee. He did endorse the December 13 teach-in, and was impressed by how the Student Committee handled December 14. He began to work with the Student Committee, and especially with Don Gurewitz.

Atkins had a firm belief that the struggle would be won in the courts, which was the basic strategy of the national NAACP. However, he saw the value of mass action to back up that legal strategy. Atkins was right on both counts. He came up with the idea of a mass march on May 17, the anniversary of the 1954 Supreme Court decision outlawing school segregation. By opposing desegregation the School Committee, the Mayor, and the City Council were seeking to undermine the Supreme Court decision.

Over the Christmas holiday, Atkins called Gurewitz to discuss the idea of a May 17 march. He didn't reach Gurewitz because the latter was attending the YSA convention in St. Louis. The convention mobilized the YSA nationally for the desegregation fight. Malik Miah, the newly elected National Chairman of the YSA, gave the key report. A "victory for the racists [in Boston]," the young Black leader said, "would set in motion other racists across the country to try do what [former President] Nixon's rhetoric about law and order couldn't—beat back gains won by Blacks over the last two decades."

Miah continued, "The struggle in Boston is around a simple, basic democratic right: the right to an equal education...around whether or not the buses keep rolling to South Boston schools. If the racist boycott is victorious and the court desegregation order rescinded—that is, the buses stop rolling—that would be a defeat for Black rights.... The issue in Boston is *equal* education for Blacks. That's it—plain and simple. The racists say no! We say yes! The racists say no buses. We say the buses must roll. The line is drawn: for or against busing."[8]

At the invitation of the convention, I spoke about the anti-racist struggles the YSA had engaged in during the 1960s, from the lunch counter sit-ins, the interview Jack Barnes and I held with Malcolm X, and other struggles (see Volume One of this work). Since the majority of YSA members and delegates were relatively new recruits, my talk helped establish continuity between the current battle the YSA was immersing itself in and past struggles.

Upon his return to Boston, Gurewitz met with Atkins about the May 17 idea. More discussions were held with the leaders of the Student Committee, which had changed its name to the National Student Committee Against Racism (NSCAR), reflecting its expansion across the country. NSCAR leader Maceo Dixon then met with Atkins. They saw eye to eye on the May 17 march. NSCAR leaders proposed that there be a teach-in the first day of the February 14-15, 1975 conference, at which the May 17 action would be announced. The next day would be for discussion and debate.

Meanwhile, the racists hooked up with new forces. A Black doctor, Kenneth Edelin, was indicted for manslaughter for having performed a legal abortion. The "right to life" movement joined hands with the anti-busing movement to attack Dr. Edelin as well as busing. The two forces joined in subsequent actions against desegregation, abortion rights, and the women's Equal Rights Amendment.

Some 2,000 students, representing 113 different organizations, including 50 Black student groups, came from 147 colleges and 58 high schools to the NSCAR-initiated conference. It was the largest gathering of student activists since the antiwar movement. Atkins spoke to the evening rally and received a standing ovation. The gathering voted overwhelmingly to support the May 17 Boston march, as well as building national actions on April 4, the anniversary of the assassination of Martin Luther King.

There were some sharp debates at the conference, with various Maoists and others attempting to disrupt it on the grounds that they opposed desegregation by busing. They claimed to be for Black control of schools in the Black communities. The counterposition of desegregation and Black community control was a false one. The SWP and the YSA supported both concepts, as tools in the fight for equal education. But the situation in Boston at the time was the fight for desegregation by busing, and the lines had been drawn in blood. The Maoists had talked themselves into being opponents of desegregation, whatever reasons they tried to give for it.[9] In fact, these Maoists were implicitly challenging the whole civil rights struggle of the 1960s in the South for desegregation. They were joined by some ultra-Black-nationalists. But, as Malcolm X came to realize, it was our view that the fight for Black Power and Black control of the Black communities and the fight against segregation were not contradictory, but two sides of the same fight for Black equality.

The Maoists were decisively defeated at the conference after a full and democratic discussion. There were other minor differences at the conference. As participants in the discussion, the leaders of NSCAR and our own fraction were faced with many challenges in helping to clarify the issues. In the beginning of the fight, in the fall of 1974, we had reinforced the Boston branch of the SWP and the YSA chapter with seasoned leaders of the antiwar movement, to help build the Student Committee and the December 14 march. Many of these fighters were white. In the lead-up to the NSCAR conference, we decided to shift gears, and make a transition in the leadership of our forces in Boston to younger Black comrades. To this end, we sent in a layer of such comrades, including Maceo Dixon, Mac Warren, Reba Williams, Hattie McCutcheon, Norman Oliver, and others. Newly elected YSA National Chairman Malik Miah also moved to Boston. I was at the conference as an advisor. Our decision to make a transition in the leadership was explained to the comrades involved in the work, and a committee of our young Black leaders led our fraction at the conference.

Maceo Dixon soon became the most prominent spokesperson for NSCAR. Mac Warren was the on-the-ground organizer, and he became the head of organizing the marshals, not only for NSCAR, but for the broader movement, including for the May 17 demonstration. Malik Miah soon took over the running of the NSCAR office, in addition to his responsibilities as a YSA leader (which also put him on the Political Committee of the SWP). He had to make many trips between New York and Boston as a result. My role faded away, as Malik became the liaison between the party center and Boston.

On May 3, the Progressive Labor Party, a Maoist formation, brought 2,500 people from around the country for an anti-racist march into South Boston. Some carried clubs and chains. They were met by a racist mob, which had at its core the South Boston Defense League, as the Mulligan gang now called itself. A battle ensued. The antiracist demonstrators were completely unprepared for such a confrontation and were routed. The police utilized the fracas to attack the antiracists, while leaving the racists alone.

The provocative tactics of Progressive Labor and the broader group it dominated, the Committee Against Racism (CAR), was used by the press to attempt to discredit the entire antiracist movement and the upcoming May 17 march as violent. As such, rumors spread through South Boston that there was a "communist invasion." ROAR used the debacle to build for its first national convention, set for the same weekend as the May 17 march. The bulk of the antiracist forces repudiated CAR and Atkins made it clear they were not welcome at any future actions.

Support for the May 17 march was building. The national NAACP endorsed, as did many other established civil rights groups. At the march itself there were people from many different organizations, including the Urban League; Southern Christian Leadership Conference; Americans for Democratic Action; the National Organization for Women and a contingent of supporters of Dr. Edelin (who had been convicted); members of the American Federation of State, County Municipal Employees; and many others. There were banners of Pan-Africanists, gays, clergy and various socialist groups.

Hillson says, "It was that kind of mix, the tradition and history of the civil rights movement blending with the energy of Black and radical minded militants in a spirit of good nature and camaraderie. NSCAR marshals, some of them young Blacks knowledgeable about Africa and students of socialist politics, wearing dashikis and Afro cuts, teamed up with conservatively dressed Black workers, members of the Roxbury lodges of the Masons and the Elks."[10]

As the marchers came into the Boston Commons, the NAACP's Atkins greeted them. There was a wide range of speakers, including Roy Wilkins, the elder statesman of the NAACP. "If Wilkins personified the traditional and conservative at the rally, NSCAR Coordinator Maceo Dixon personified the rebel," observed Hillson. "His speech drew the warmest response."[11]

There was an attempt by Progressive Labor to take over the march, but it was quickly dealt with, and most people on the march were unaware of it. Cliff Conner, a member of the SWP and YSA at the time and who was one of the marshals, remembers the incident:

"A well organized contingent of Progressive Labor [PL] people with a couple of huge loudspeakers mounted on mobile platforms was planning to divert the march from its planned route and lead it toward the ROAR convention, to create a confrontation. Some of our rank and filers (not including me) who were unknown to PL, had infiltrated the PL group, pretending to support their plan. Two of them armed with bolt-cutters cut the wires to the mobile loudspeakers at the moment that they began to try to take over the march. Then they ran like hell. I remember it as a hilarious scene, with the PLers impotently huffing and puffing and hurling threats at us (our marshals in the meantime surrounded them and prevented them from catching the wire-snippers). It seemed to me a good lesson in how to deal with unscrupulous people: you can't always 'play fair.'"

Our tactics of building peaceful mass actions were aimed at bringing in all forces ready to support the desegregation struggle, including the NAACP and other liberal groups. We were attacked by ultraleft groups for doing so. SWP and YSA members at the time were attending the conventions of all the traditional civil rights groups, especially the NAACP, because of their support of busing in Boston. We were seeking to ally with young people in these groups who were drawn into struggle by the Boston battle.

The march was evenly divided between Black and white. It became especially loud as it passed the hall where ROAR was holding its conference. The NAACP estimated the crowd at 50,000, NSCAR said 15,000, and the police said 15,000 to 20,000. In many other cities across the country there were NAACP/NSCAR events in solidarity with the Boston march.

ROAR elected Louise Day Hicks as its president at its convention. The ROAR rally on May 18 drew some 2,000 and featured a parade of racist speakers, including local Democrats, members of the School Committee, City Council, and Massachusetts state legislature, and the head of the Boston Police Patrolmen's Association. Other speakers included diehard segregationists from the South. Klansmen, John Birchers and Nazis mingled with the crowd. A minister from Charlestown, West Virginia, bragged about how "atheistic, communist, anti-white" books were burned in Charlestown.

The day of the ROAR rally, a Black student from Utah and some white students who had marched the day before decided to go to the beach. They ended up at Carson Beach in South Boston, which the racists considered "theirs" and were beaten up. In June, the bigots devised new tactics, waiting on an overpass to drop rocks, bottles and bricks on Black motorists the thugs thought were trying to go to Carson Beach. Black homes in "white" areas were firebombed and stoned. The May 17 march had dealt the racists a big blow, but had not defeated them. Gangs of roving whites randomly attacked cars with Blacks in them with baseball bats—there were hundreds of such incidents over the summer.

During the previous school year Mac Warren had trained crisis team marshals to ride the school buses, monitor bus departure and arrival centers, serve as intermediaries with the cops and sometimes enter the schools. SWP and YSA members participated in the crisis teams. The teams instilled a sense of discipline among the Black students, to urge them to refuse to be drawn into no-win fights. The teams continued to meet over the summer amid the escalating violence.

On July 27 a group of Black Bible salespeople from South Carolina decided to call it a day after going door to door, and started looking for a beach to cool off in the sweltering heat. Being from out-of-town, they stumbled upon Carson Beach. No sooner had they stretched out on the sand they were set upon by a white mob, and were chased with pipes and clubs back toward their car. Before they could unlock the car the racists reached them. One victim was hospitalized with head, rib and leg injuries, while the rest managed to flee. Two days later, Boston SCAR called a news conference. Mac Warren was joined by NAACP youth leader Leon Rock. They blasted police inaction in this and other incidents, laying the blame on Mayor Kevin White. SCAR announced the formation of a commission of inquiry for August 2. The commission heard high school students, parents and members of the community angrily document the racist terror.

Meanwhile, racist mobs organized by the South Boston Defense League occupied Carson Beach to keep Blacks out. The beach had become the symbol of the war. Momentum built for a picnic at the beach for August 10. Dixon and Warren had organized a well-disciplined force of marshals. Thomas Atkins led off a motorcade from Roxbury to the beach, under heavy police guard as the racists made known that they would have snipers along the route to murder Atkins. Stern rules were announced to the picnickers—non-violence was the order of the day.

However, Progressive Labor and CAR, who were not part of the protest, showed up with clubs and rocks. Fights broke out. The marshals succeeded in disarming the mostly white CAR members, but the damage had been done. The cops seized on the provocation to wade into the crowd of Blacks and white supporters, clubs swinging. In retaliation, white motorists began to be attacked by Black youth in Black areas. The cops responded by mass arrests and beatings of Blacks.

•••

Phase Two of Judge Garrity's desegregation plan was scheduled to begin in September. This time there were many reporters on hand, as well as hundreds of police and federal marshals. Again the racist mobs came out. The reporters were stunned by the virulence of the open racism. Noted Hillson, "For many of the reporters the violence and the rage of the bigots was mind-boggling. At the same time, the Black students had carried themselves with singular dignity, braving taunts and insults, occasionally smiling at the huge gatherings of reporters as they made their way through police lines. The contrast between them (in hostile territory, outnumbered by the whites, ordered about by nervous police) and the racist students (who blithely told the media, 'We just don't like niggers') was striking. That difference would be communicated on television news across the country."[12]

Racists battled the police night and day. The situation at South Boston High became a "madhouse," according to Maceo Dixon. It was becoming unsafe for the Black students to go to that school. Black community leaders began to call for the school to be shut down. Charleston High was also boiling. Hearings on the situation were held by Judge Garrity. Mac Warren met with Eric Van Loon, attorney for the Black plaintiffs, and provided him with the names of Black students willing to testify. Their testimony was so powerful that Garrity issued a sweeping order placing South Boston High under direct federal control, and stripping the School Committee of authority over administering the desegregation plan and over school security.

In October NSCAR held its second national conference of 1,300 supporters. While the need for another mass action was great, the mood among the Black community leadership was to shy away. One reason for this hesitation was that 1976 was a presidential election year, and soon the primary elections would be held. The Democrats put great pressure on the Black leadership to back away from any mass action. In this situation the NSCAR conference realized that it was not strong enough to call an action itself, and instead proposed a campaign of education.

The racists were emboldened by the lack of an antiracist mobilization, and soon escalated the violence to new levels. They were also angry that the courts had rebuffed legal attempts to scuttle Phase Two. They were emboldened when the Senate passed two amendments to other bills attacking "forced busing"—the polite term for opposition to desegregation. One, sponsored by liberal Democrat Joseph Biden of Delaware (later U.S. Vice President under Barack Obama, the first Black U.S. President), prohibited the U.S. Department of Health, Welfare and Education (HEW) from withholding funds from school districts refusing to implement desegregation plans. The other, sponsored by racist Democrat Robert Byrd of West Virginia, prohibited HEW from funding for busing for purposes of desegregation.

The racists were becoming better organized, and fought pitched battles with the police, often inflicting serious casualties. Democratic Mayor White demagogically blamed desegregation for a fiscal crisis that hit the school system. As 1976 opened violence against Blacks increased dramatically. One incident hit close to home for Maceo Dixon. His companion, Reba Williams, also a member of the SWP who worked on the NSCAR staff, was jumped by three white thugs as she walked home.

The more militant grass roots leaders in the Black community, many of them women, began to see the need for a counter-mobilization, no matter that it was an election year. Local leaders Ellen Jackson, Ruth Batson, and Maceo Dixon sent a letter to Black leaders across the country, urging support for a national demonstration in Boston. "We have come to the conclusion," they wrote, "that what is critically needed today is a broad and massive movement to respond to violent attacks of ROAR and other opponents of Black rights." They went on to explain that Boston had become the center of the desegregation struggle, and a defeat there would embolden racists to smash desegregation efforts nationally.

Other key Black leaders and NSCAR became the nucleus of the effort to build another mass march. NSCAR called an emergency meeting of its steering committee, at which some 300 attended. The out-of-towners were shocked to hear first hand accounts of the racist terror, and of the boldness of the organized bigots in physically taking on the police. Ruth Batson told the meeting, "NSCAR has filled a void in this city. I speak for many people with whom I work." The NSCAR steering committee members went back to their cities around the country to begin to build support for a national march.

On March 9, the April 24 demonstration was announced as the date for a national march for desegregation in Boston. It was supported by key Black leaders in Boston and in the state legislature, as well as over 100 prominent people nationally. However, the national and local NAACP did not endorse, under pressure from the national Democratic Party not to "rock the boat" in an election year, a bad sign. That same day, the Massachusetts House of Representatives overwhelmingly backed an anti-busing Constitutional amendment. Earlier in the month, the Democratic Presidential primaries were held. Ellen Jackson termed them "deadly—there is no one for us."

Candidates Henry Jackson and George Wallace courted the anti-busing vote. Wallace, notorious for his fight against Black rights in the 1960s as Governor of Alabama, won the vote in Boston and Henry Jackson won statewide. Jackson, a senator from Washington, was known for his hawkish stance as a supporter of the Vietnam War and was on the right wing of the Democratic Party. The Democratic liberals in the race avoided the issue. Jimmy Carter, who said he was against "forced busing," won nationwide.

Violence against Blacks increased, and in reaction more people were endorsing the April 24 march. However, redbaiting was also rearing its ugly head. Mac Warren, newly announced SWP candidate for Congress for Roxbury, attended one meeting of Black opponents of April 24, where he was denounced by the All African People's Revolutionary Party (AAPRP) as a member of the SWP and kicked out. The AAPRP was a small group, led by Stokely Carmichael, which was against busing, opposed any political collaboration between Blacks and whites, and had physically threatened NSCAR staff. For Carmichael, this represented a sad political degeneration from his days as chairman of the Student Nonviolent Coordinating Committee in the 1960s. However, others picked up on the redbaiting of NSCAR, attacks which were aimed at scuttling the April 24 action.

Meanwhile, the police began to circulate the falsehood that Progressive Labor and CAR were behind April 24. This was further confused by the similarity of the names CAR and NSCAR. It was known that CAR had provoked violence. Was a police trap being set up for April 24?

Tensions in the city were high. Racist gangs had driven into Roxbury, shooting at a Black housing project. In retaliation, a group of Black youth attacked a white motorist and severely beat him. The racists seized on the incident, as did the press, and clamored for the city administration to contain "Black violence." Immense pressure was brought to bear on leaders in the Black community by the Democratic city administration.

While the building for April 24 had been going very well, with a broad list of speakers and endorsements, the situation was appearing more and more dangerous. NSCAR had trained over 1,000 well-disciplined marshals, but would this be enough? The police could not be relied on, and might repeat what they did at Carson Beach and attack the march under cover of their smear that it was a CAR affair.

The party and YSA had a well-organized fraction of comrades who worked with NSCAR and met daily to discuss tactics in the struggle. Malik Miah, who coordinated with our national office, Maceo Dixon and Mac Warren worked as a team to lead the work. The fraction discussed the situation and came to the conclusion that it was becoming more and more doubtful that the march could be successfully brought off. It was decided that Dixon and Warren should meet with the other leaders of the march to take stock of the situation.

According to Hillson, "Conversations of Dixon, Warren and the key community and coalition leaders working on April 24 painted a gloomy picture. Political pressure, intertwined with the awesome security problem, made it inadvisable, they agreed, to carry through the demonstration. The police had virtually stopped talking to the coalition leaders. And unremitting red-baiting of the action, coupled with death threats [against the march organizers], stirred further apprehension."[13]

Several days before April 24, Dixon, Warren and the Black community leaders behind the march made the hard decision to call it off, given these circumstances.

Meanwhile, there were three appeals of Garrity's order before the U.S. Supreme Court, filed by Mayor White, the Home and School Association (a front for the racist mobs), and the Boston School Committee. Also before the Court was an appeal by the Boston Teachers Union of one part of Garrity's order mandating the hiring of Black Teachers until their numbers reflected the proportion of the city's population who were Black. The BTU was 96 percent white in a city where the Black population was 20 percent.

President Ford flirted with also appealing Garrity's order, pulling back only when there was a major outcry, including in such ruling-class mouthpieces as the New York Times. The more far-sighted among the capitalist politicians realized that if the Justice Department joined in this attempt to roll back the 1954 court decision, it would create great turmoil among the nation's Black population, perhaps leading to new explosions of protest. They were also afraid that America's image would be tarnished throughout the world.

On June 14, the Supreme Court summarily refused to consider the appeals, and Garrity's order was thereby upheld. The Court had no choice unless it itself was ready to reverse its own 1954 decision. The racists were forced to back down, and became demoralized. Racist whites moved to the suburbs or enrolled their children in private schools.

Notably, on the same day as this decision, the Court also upheld an appeal by the Pasadena, California School Committee of a Federal District judge's order in a related busing case. In the process of desegregation of the city's schools, originally ordered by the same judge, there were demographic shifts among the white population that re-segregated the schools. Consequently, the judge had instituted yearly adjustments in the busing order to keep no school in the district more than 50 percent Black. The school board had appealed this decision. Thus, while the Court had upheld Garrity's decisions to enforce the 1954 ruling where the Boston authorities had in fact imposed legal segregation, in the Pasadena case it upheld re-segregation due to "population shifts."

While the overturn of *de jure* segregation in the Boston schools was a victory for Black rights, the ruling class adapted to the new legal changes. The Pasadena case gave the green light to stifle new busing plans based on *de facto* housing segregation, with the result that schools either remained segregated or were re-segregated by white flight.

Today, Blacks who have the money can freely move around the country to work and live where they want, unlike in the days of Jim Crow. And as a result of the overthrow of Jim Crow substantial numbers of Blacks have been able to move into the middle class, and a few into the capitalist class. Affirmative action, another victory of the Black struggle of the 1960s, has enabled many Black workers to move into better-paying jobs. But institutional racism still exists, with most Blacks not having enough wealth to move out of the Black communities. The resulting *de facto* segregation in housing continues to be by and large prevalent to this day, and as a result school segregation remains a fact of American life, with schools today more segregated than in 1970.

The Boston busing war proved not to be the opening of a new upsurge of the Black struggle, but rather the final flaring up of the great civil rights battles of the 1950s and 1960s.

There were many heroes and heroines in the Boston fight, including the Black community leaders who stepped forward. The real heroes were the Black students, male and female, who faced the racist violence daily and who would not give up.

The part played by the Socialist Workers Party and the Young Socialist Alliance in this war was a proud achievement, one which had an impact far greater than our numbers.

---

1 See the famous book by Jonathan Kozol, *Death at an Early Age* (Penguin Books, 1967).

2 Jon Hillson, *The Battle of Boston* (Pathfinder Press, 1977), p. 26. This book is the best overall treatment of the struggle.

3 Ibid., p. 1.

4 Ibid., p.70.

5 Ibid., p 72.

6 Ibid., p. 79.

7 Ibid., pp. 96-97.

8 Ibid., pp 120,121.

9 See Max Elbaum, *Revolution in the Air* (Verso, 2002) for a detailed description of the Maoists' intervention in the Boston busing war.

10 Hillson, op. cit. pp. 138-139.

11 Ibid., p. 140.

12 Ibid., p. 169.

13 Hillson, op. cit. p. 241.

CHAPTER NINE: REVOLUTION IN PORTUGAL

In the early 1970s the two countries of the Iberian Peninsula were still under brutal military dictatorships that had their roots in fascism. Spain was ruled by Francisco Franco, whose fascist Falange movement came to power in the 1930s, defeating the Republic in the Civil War with the support of Nazi Germany and Fascist Italy. Marcelo Caetano, protégé of the fascist Antonio de Salazar who came to power in 1928, headed the regime in Portugal.

Caetano was overthrown by a military coup in April 1974, which unleashed a massive upsurge of workers, peasants, shopkeepers and other small business owners—an upsurge that swiftly became a pre-revolutionary situation.

The background of the coup was a rebellion in the army ranks and lower officers as a result of the failure of a 13-year war to suppress liberation movements in the Portuguese African colonies of Angola, Mozambique, and Guinea-Bissau. These wars were eating up 40 percent of the government's budget causing inflation to soar, and had become so unpopular that 50 percent of young men drafted refused to show up.

"The overturn of the dictatorship of Marcello Caetano has brought forth a storm of political activity, discussion and jubilation from the Portuguese people," Caroline Lund wrote in *The Militant*. 'The military coup, headed by General Antonio de Spinoza, set up a junta that promised the restitution of civil liberties and 'general elections for a constitutional national assembly,' which would 'permit the nation to choose freely its own form of social and political life.' Another promise of the junta was an end to the colonial wars in Africa, which had eroded the grip of the old regime."[1]

The new military leadership formed a provisional government. The SWP immediately sent Gerry Foley to Lisbon to report first hand for *The Militant* and *Intercontinental Press*. He was at the huge May Day demonstrations that took place shortly after the coup. "'The explosion of joy that swept the entire country has no parallel since the demonstrations at the end of the war marking the liberations of nations occupied by fascism-Nazism.' That was the way *Diario de Lisboa*, the first paper to come off the press following the May 1 demonstrations, described the massive outpouring in celebration of the fall of the fascist government of Marcello Caetano," Foley wrote.

General Spinola had been a fascist from his youth. But he had begun to recognize that the colonial wars in Africa were being lost, and he wrote a book to that effect that was widely read in the armed forces. This caused him to fall from favor with the Caetano government, and he countered with the coup before it could act against him.

The objective of the military junta went beyond abandoning direct control of the colonies in favor of a policy of neo-colonialism that maintained Portugal's economic domination. It also sought to modernize the economy stifled under the fascist regime, joining the rest of Europe by moving toward bourgeois democracy. But the social explosion from below threatened to go much further.

Both the Communist Party (CP) and the Socialist Party (SP) grew as workers poured into their ranks. A broader layer of workers joined the formerly illegal trade unions. Peasants in the south of the country began to seize land from the landlords' estates. This reflected the growing radicalization of workers and other producers, who were moving toward socialism as their goal and these parties seemed to embody that desire. However, the leaderships of both the SP and CP sought to keep the struggle limited to winning democracy within capitalism, while using militant and leftist rhetoric in appealing to the workers. The Armed Forces Movement (MFA), as the military elements now in charge called themselves, sought the help of these parties in keeping things under control.

The MFA, seeking support among the masses, soon formed a second provisional government with CP participation. In spite of opposition from the CP and SP, however, in July 1974 it passed a law clamping down on strikes and worker occupations of factories, which were mushrooming. It also freed many fascists initially arrested after the coup. This law turned out to be a paper tiger that was ineffective in containing the workers' upsurge.

The rightists, including fascists, sections of the clergy (the Catholic Church was the state religion under the fascist government) and bourgeois parties, began organizing. In September, Spinola sought to reverse the situation by calling for a mass demonstration in the capital, Lisbon, to "support President's Spinola's speeches and the program of the MFA." Air force planes dropped posters backing the demonstration. The mass rightist mobilization was designed to create the conditions for another coup to crush the upsurge militarily.

The CP and SP finally woke up to the danger when it became clear they would be smashed. Spinola's plan was thwarted by a mass counter-demonstration by the workers, who barricaded the streets around the site of the proposed demonstration and formed defense pickets. The rightist demonstration never materialized. Spinola was forced to resign from the government. The net result was to strengthen the confidence of the workers.

Spinola would try again early in 1975. This time he relied on paratroopers, whose planes on March 11 flew low over the city in an attempt to frighten the residents. They strafed an artillery base opposed to Spinola. Once again, the workers defeated the coup attempt, leading a huge mobilization that was even greater than the September mobilization. Spinola and 27 other officers were placed on a list to be arrested. Spinola fled the country and conservative officers were purged. A new MFA government pledged, "to lead the revolution."

The working class and its allies had felt their power, and in the months ahead strikes and factory occupations multiplied. The CP moved to take control of much of the now nationalized press.

Throughout the nineteen-month long pre-revolutionary situation, the CP and SP waged a factional struggle against each other in vying for MFA approval. Whichever party was on the outs would point to the shortcomings of the government, often using leftist language and mobilizing its membership in demonstrations. However, both pledged their continued allegiance to the MFA, which retained ultimate control throughout. The different MFA coalition governments remained capitalist governments, in reality military dictatorships, which sought to maintain capitalist rule in the turbulent situation, even as they had to increasingly rely on leftist rhetoric to maintain popular credibility.

Smaller groups to the left of the CP and SP (the "far left") also emerged and grew. These included Maoists, anarchists, "sovietists" (who hoped that broad workers councils could seize power directly) and others. Among these were two formations that considered themselves Trotskyist and supporters of the Fourth International, the International Communist League and the Revolutionary Workers Party (LCI and PRT in their Portuguese initials). In the International debates the LCI leaned toward the IMT and the PRT toward the LTF.

The orientation of the IMT and LCI was to try to form a united front of the far left, which they called "the new mass vanguard." As previously explained, the idea was that this united front could take audacious actions that would in turn draw the masses into a revolutionary struggle for power.

Both the LTF and IMT recognized that a pre-revolutionary situation had emerged after the April 1974 coup overthrowing the Caetano regime. But as the upsurge deepened, important differences arose between the two factions. One of these concerned how to respond to the April 1975 elections to the Constituent Assembly.

Held one year after the Caetano regime was overthrown, the elections reflected the deepening upsurge. The combined vote for the CP and SP candidates was slightly over 50 percent. If some smaller groups that claimed to be workers' parties were included, the left vote was about 60 percent. The SP had received the largest vote among the left parties.

The election results alarmed the MFA, as well as the CP, which backed a law that would bring the unions under its control and squeeze out the SP. Those in the MFA who presented the most demagogically leftist line, especially General Otello de Carvalho, came to the fore. They issued a call for the dissolution of the Constituent Assembly by promising that the MFA would support a government of peoples or workers councils. The CP supported the MFA in this maneuver, and the gullible "far left" fell into line behind the CP. The SP defended the Constituent Assembly against this onslaught aimed at itself.

The IMT international leadership, including Ernest Mandel, Pierre Frank and Livio Maitan, were drawn into this trap by their orientation toward the "far left." The LCI in Portugal followed suit.

An article in *Rouge*, the paper of the French Revolutionary Communist League (LCR), illustrated the differences over the objective situation. The article was by Charles Michaloux, who together with Charles-André Udry, were the younger leaders of the IMT international leadership most responsible for its intervention in Portugal.

Michaloux analyzed the stage of the class struggle the following way:

"For the first time, the barracks are concretely proceeding to organize meetings to elect assemblies of rank-and-file delegates, based on democratic guidelines that go beyond the tortuous recommendations of the MFA. Last Sunday, general assemblies in two Lisbon barracks passed motions and initiated election procedures, in many instances with the active encouragement of MFA officers. On Saturday and Sunday People's Assemblies were held in almost all the neighborhoods, districts and urban centers.

"The coordinating committee of all the Lisbon committees issued a call for a demonstration tonight [July 16, 1975] with the open support of the assembly of [the more radical] soldiers....

"In Portugal, the governmental power is vacillating, while the power of the rank and file is taking shape. It already has a name: the People's Assemblies, which will elect a National Assembly of the workers and soldiers. This National Assembly will create a Workers and Peasants Government, which the international solidarity movement must help to defend against the blows that the reaction is already preparing against it."[2]

This assessment was wildly inaccurate and overblown. It should be noted that Michaloux did not suck this out of his thumb. This was the view of all the organizations of the far left. The demonstration Michaloux referred to turned out to be no more than 7,000 strong. No such National Assembly was ever elected, and obviously no Workers and Peasants government was formed. This view that People's Assemblies or other forms that could become soviets were soon to challenge the government for power, led the IMT leaders to make some big errors.

It was true that factory and neighborhood committees had formed, but they were embryonic and never developed into mass organs capable of taking power and establishing a workers' democracy that could replace the bourgeois democratic forms that had arisen as exemplified by the newly elected Constituent Assembly. Further, many of these committees were small front groups of the various ultraleft organizations.

We in the SWP firmly opposed the call for the dissolution of the Constituent Assembly. The elections to the Constituent Assembly were key for they showed that a majority of workers had voted for socialism. They did this by voting for the CP or SP, which they (mistakenly) thought were sincere in advocating socialism. We proposed instead that our groups in Portugal call on the CP and SP to form a "Communist-Socialist" government to replace the MFA-dominated governments, and begin the transition to socialism.

This proposal did not mean that we had any illusions in the CP or SP. But we recognized that the great mass of workers did have such illusions. The call for an SP-CP government would expose the real intentions of both parties to continue to support the bourgeois government. Their likely refusal to accept the mandate the working people had bestowed upon them would go a long way toward dispelling workers' illusions in the CP and SP as revolutionary parties. Such a proposal would also popularize the idea that there should be a workers' and peasants' government that would break with the capitalists. At the same time, if by some unlikely development the SP and CP actually formed such a government, it would open the field for the working people to organize to demand that such a government carry out their aspirations for socialism.

Such a call could greatly help small groups such as ours to reach the masses, begin to recruit the vanguard of the workers and their allies, and to step forward as leaders.

To call for the dissolution of the Constituent Assembly in the name of replacing it with as yet purely embryonic and minority forms of workers' democracy was not only utopian, it was also undemocratic. The great mass of working people had voted for the Constituent Assembly and to call for its dissolution went directly against the wishes of the masses as expressed in their democratic vote.

This difference between the IMT leaders and the majority of the LTF led by the SWP raised the related debate of our attitude toward bourgeois democracy and workers' democracy. The IMT correctly said workers' democracy was superior to bourgeois democracy. But they drew the conclusion that in the concrete situation in Portugal we should oppose bourgeois democracy in the form of the Constituent Assembly, in favor of a non-existent power of mass People's Assemblies.

We said that until and unless the working people are organized to actually have the power to replace bourgeois democracy, we must defend bourgeois democracy against attempts to overthrow it in favor of a bourgeois government under the control of the military, as the MFA and the CP, with the ultraleft in tow, were calling for. After many decades of fascist rule, the masses were enjoying their newly found democratic rights, and rejected the call for the dissolution of the Constituent Assembly. For our small groups to tag along with the ultraleft opposition to the Constituent Assembly put us in opposition to the masses.

There was another instance where our differences over democracy exploded in the Fourth International. This involved the takeover of a newspaper on June 18 by workers in the print shop that published it. The name of the newspaper was *Republica*, and it was a paper that was identified with the SP, although it was not an official organ. The IMT supported the takeover by the print shop workers, as did the CP and "far left." We opposed it.

In our opinion, the issue was the democratic rights of the SP. The IMT saw the action by the print shop workers as an assertion of workers' control, like the occupations of factories and other capitalist enterprises that had become widespread.

The IMT view conflated two separate issues, workers' occupations carried out to further their demands against the bosses, and the suppression of a newspaper of a workers party. The takeover of *Republica* by a hundred workers or so violated the rights of millions of workers who supported the SP. Moreover, it turned out that Maoist groups had a base in the print shop, and carried out the takeover because they were politically opposed to the SP, not because they were furthering workers' control. In our view, the wrong policies of the SP had to be fought politically, not by suppressing its democratic rights.

I made a speaking tour around the United States, explaining our position on the Constituent Assembly and the *Republica* takeover. In each city people from other tendencies spoke challenging us, frequently along the lines of defending the Portuguese far left and the MFA. These discussions were lively.

We held an SWP convention in August 1975, which discussed the international situation and the debate inside the Fourth International. Portugal was at the center of both discussions. I gave the report about the development of the struggle in Portugal. Jack Barnes made the report on the differences concerning Portugal in the International. Under both reports a leader of the IMT was given equal time to present their views. Alan Jones, a leader of the British International Marxist Group (IMG) spoke for the IMT. Time was also granted to representatives of the many sections and sympathizing groups of the International to speak. Included in the latter were the LCI and PRT from Portugal, whose speakers were given standing ovations, as was Jones, reflecting the spirit of internationalism that pervaded the convention.

In the International discussions, we emphasized that the *Republica* affair was part of the MFA offensive against the democratic vote of the masses in the Constituent Assembly elections. For its own sectarian reasons in its struggle with the SP, the CP supported the MFA campaign. But by backing the *Republica* takeover the MFA, utilizing leftist demagogy, had struck a blow not only against the democratic rights of the SP, but of the working class as a whole.

As a result, the SP left the government on July 11 and called for mass demonstrations in its defense. Hundreds of thousands of workers poured into these rallies on July 18 and 19. The CP, joined by some of the far left groups, tried to set up barricades to prevent these rallies from taking place, but the workers smashed right through them. Even most CP members did not join these miserable barricades, which crumbled at the first encounter with the workers.[3]

The MFA began to turn then on the CP, and the Stalinists themselves began to fear their democratic rights were in jeopardy, as there began a wave of attacks on CP headquarters after the SP left the government. Although it did fail to vigorously defend the CP, the SP denounced the anti-Communist attacks. This did not stop some IMT groups from charging that the SP, in alliance with the Catholic Church, was behind the attacks, and therefore the SP should be suppressed. In fact, what was actually needed was a united front defending the democratic rights of both the SP and CP as well as the smaller organizations.

The radicalization of the masses did penetrate into the ranks of the armed forces. In some units, left leaning soldiers were in the majority. A wing of the MFA sought to become the spokesmen of this radicalization. General Otello de Carvalho became the best known. But he and other "leftist" officers remained loyal to the MFA, which tolerated them to exert control over the radicalization in the ranks.

The MFA organized a new government, the sixth provisional government, in September 1975, with the participation of the SP and CP. The SP was the dominant party in the new government. The economic situation was worsening, while the government called for austerity. Consequently, unrest in the working class was deepening. The atmosphere was one of defiance of the new government in the military and the labor movement. The CP encouraged this climate through its control over most of the press. The CP did so only to exert pressure to regain a larger share of posts in the government.

This unrest climaxed in a huge demonstration of striking construction workers on November 12, with thousands of workers surrounding the parliament. The CP had led the construction workers' strike, although its leaders did not want a strike of this character. But they were unable to control the movement they had unleashed.

"The construction workers' demonstration," wrote Gerry Foley in *The Militant,* "was the first really massive, concentrated, and determined struggle by a section of the Portuguese working class. It was all the more powerful because it was waged by the most disadvantaged layer of the working class, including a large percentage of Africans."[4]

The organizations of the "far left" had formed an umbrella group called the United Revolutionary Front (FUR in its Portuguese initials). One of the organizations of the Fourth International, the LCI, joined the FUR. The most important organization in the FUR was the Revolutionary Party of the Proletariat (PRP). In the atmosphere of rebellion in the armed forces and labor movement the PRP issued a manifesto calling for an armed insurrection. The PRP and the FUR in general had greatly misunderstood the real situation, becoming heady with the view that organs of workers power were already in existence, and that the capitalist state was virtually non-existent.

"But despite their intentions, the Social Democrats and the right in general have no army in Portugal. If they want to stage a confrontation with the proletariat, they will have to resort to mercenaries hired in Spain or simply invaders from NATO and the USA," the PRP manifesto stated.[5]

Events soon punctured these illusions. The MFA majority removed Carvalho, who had gone into opposition to the government three weeks before, from his command in Lisbon. A military dictatorship, even one with a democratic and socialist veneer cannot long tolerate divisions in its officer caste or unrest in the ranks. The November 12 construction workers' demonstration threatened a renewed and determined upsurge of the working class as a whole, a danger that the MFA as well as its SP partners decided to nip in the bud. Leaders of the paratroops corps fell into the trap, believing the overblown rhetoric coming from the CP and its FUR allies.

On November 25, left-wing paratroop units in the Lisbon area seized the radio and television stations and broadcast appeals to support their military coup against the sixth provisional government. They suddenly found themselves in a void. Their appeals failed to win mass support, and even the CP beat a hasty retreat. The bourgeois state, supposedly dead, sprang into life. The armed forces quickly smashed the ultraleft coup. Carvalho was rehabilitated and he came out in support of the government. The groups in the FUR were summoned to the seat of government, along with all legally recognized parties. There they were all instructed to turn in their arms and radio transmitters, if they had any, to prevent any demonstrations, and to "stimulate productivity" (pledge their political support for austerity).

This proved to be the turning point. The SP-backed government launched a wave of repression, although brief, which led to the retreat of the masses over the next months. The pre-revolutionary situation had come to a close, and gradually a "normal" bourgeois-democratic regime was established.

The orientation of the IMT toward the far left, hoping to weld it into a force capable of leading a revolution, had been shown to be bankrupt, although they didn't recognize it immediately. The FUR disintegrated. The grave mistake of the FUR in turning its back on democratic rights and the Constituent Assembly, chasing instead the will o' the wisp in the imminent seizure of power by still-embryonic grass roots organizations of the workers, contributed to this disaster. Of course, the main culprits on the left were the SP and CP, with their class-collaborationist support of the MFA and the bourgeois governments it controlled.

On December 14, there was symposium on Portugal of various tendencies on the U.S. socialist left organized at Boston University. I represented the SWP. Other speakers included Arthur Simson of the CP, Joan McBride of the International Socialists, Patrick Smith, a writer for the pro-Maoist *Guardian* newspaper, and Dan Burstein of the Maoist October League. The differences were sharp.

I characterized the nature of the revolution as socialist. The CP and *Guardian* speakers said the goal was a democratic capitalist regime, and that socialism was a long-term objective. Both supported the fifth provisional government, which was replaced in late August. Both supported dissolution of the Socialist Party as rightist, and both claimed that the greatest danger was the possible dissolution of the MFA. Both denied that there had been any ultraleft coup attempt.

McBride championed the positions of the Portuguese PRP, which itself was soft on the fifth government. I pointed out that most of the far left groups tended to look to the most radical-sounding officers including General Carvalho, whom the PRP characterized as part of the "revolutionary left." Tellingly, the International Socialists newspaper *Workers Power* in their November 28 issue, echoing the PRP call for insurrection, featured the headline: "Portugal–All Power to the Workers!" Under this the lead story began, "The first shots in the Portuguese civil war have been fired. The lines have been drawn and there can be no turning back."

On January 1-4, 1976, there was a meeting of the SWP National Committee at which I reported on the Portuguese events. The meaning of the November 25 ultraleft coup attempt and its aftermath was becoming clearer. "The government was interested in provoking the kind of thing that happened on November 25, not a confrontation with the working class itself," I said. It utilized the ultraleft action to begin the process of demobilization of the workers.

Early in 1976, the current in the LTF led by Hugo Moreno, broke with both the SWP and the LTF. This current had sent cadres to Portugal who became the leaders of the PRT. Although the PRT had not supported the FUR, it shared some of the positions of the IMT. Among these was the misestimation that the embryonic organizations of workers' councils and commissions were in fact rapidly becoming mass soviets that could overthrow the bourgeois state and take power. As a consequence, it rejected the call for an SP-CP government. It was ironic that they took this position *after* the smashing of the ultraleft coup, when even these organizational embryos had disintegrated.

A difference Moreno had with the IMT was that he did not look to the FUR to be the instrument to lead this development, but to the rapid growth of the PRT. Early in 1977 I went to Portugal to meet with leaders of one wing of the split engineered by Moreno in the PRT, the wing that rejected Moreno's course. I found that the PRT had indeed recruited many young people, who were subjected to a crazy forced march to rapidly build a party that could lead the working class to power. These enthusiastic young people, and many were in their teens, were told, among other things, to steal money and jewelry from their parents, to finance the effort. They were driven to sell their paper and be active all the time, with very little sleep. Over months of this insanity, most became burnt-out. I met with many of them, and they told me their horror stories. I wrote a report on this fiasco.[6]

In the summer of 1976, the party held another national convention. Portugal was again on the agenda, and again there was a large participation of international observers. I gave the report for the outgoing National Committee. There were still differences within the Fourth International, now about the recently held presidential elections in Portugal.

The two Fourth International groups in Portugal had called for a vote for the candidate of the CP, while opposing its class-collaborationist program. We agreed with this position. But a few other groups in the International came out in support for Carvalho, who was one of three MFA-supported candidates. Their support appeared in my opinion to be a kind of nostalgia for Carvalho's and their own ultraleftism in 1975. Unlike the CP, Carvalho did not represent a party in the working class, but the bourgeois MFA.

•••

On a related point, we in the SWP made an important error, while the leaders of the IMT got it right. That concerned the situation in the former Portuguese colony of Angola in Africa. As the hold of Portuguese imperialism weakened, a war broke out between the three national liberation movements that had opposed Portuguese rule. These were the FLNA (National Liberation Front of Angola), the MPLA (People's Movement for the Liberation of Angola), and UNITA (National Union for the Total Independence of Angola). All three had played important roles in fighting the Portuguese colonists.

The three movements were based in three different ethnic groups in different parts of the country. In light of this fact we initially took no side in the struggle between them. Of course, we were opposed to any intervention by the United States, Portugal, or South Africa. But what we failed to understand was that on the ground imperialism had taken sides, and was actively intervening through political and military support to the FLNA and UNITA. Washington supported the FLNA, based in northern Angola. Both the United States and South Africa were supporting UNITA, which was operating in southern Angola, on the South African-controlled border with South West Africa (later called Namibia after its liberation in the 1980s).

We also failed to understand the intervention of Cuban troops into Angola, which fought against South African military advisors to UNITA. These troops were decisive in pushing back South Africa and its UNITA cats paw. (In the 1980s, Cuban troops would again fight the South African army in Angola, inflicting a decisive defeat on the apartheid regime, which was an important factor in its disintegration.)

The IMT comrades understood the situation. In part because of their arguments we switched our position to theirs. The situation was also becoming clearer from pronouncements by Washington itself what the score was.

The MPLA emerged as the government of Angola after the Portuguese MFA governments reluctantly recognized Angolan independence, along with independence for Mozambique and Guinea-Bissau. The whole Fourth International understood that the MPLA was not socialist, despite its assertions to the contrary. The MPLA's record in power in the coming years demonstrated in fact that it was not socialist.

---

1 *The Militant,* May 10, 1974. The SWP put out a pamphlet on Portugal with the first three articles Caroline Lund wrote about the upsurge.

2 See the Oct. 15, 1975 issue of *Intercontinental Press* for a full description of these events and the debate between the IMT and LTF.

3 *Intercontinental Press,* Aug. 4, 1975.

4 Ibid., Dec. 8, 1975.

5 *Jornal Novo*, Nov. 14, 1975.

6 Gus Horowitz, "The Differences Over Portugal," SWP Internal Information Bulletin, March 1977.

CHAPTER TEN: NEW CAMPAIGNS

The convention of the YSA held at the end of 1974 met in the context of the Boston busing battle and a deepening worldwide recession that lasted into most of the next year. This was also the convention the FBI was ordered not to infiltrate by the judge presiding over our lawsuit against government spying and disruption.

Held in St. Louis, the convention decided to intensify the YSA's campaign in support of the Boston Black community. The YSA also decided to utilize the SWP Presidential campaign launched at the party's last convention to spread socialist ideas, help mobilize support for the struggles we were involved in, and build the party and YSA. We decided to launch our 1976 election campaign this early so we would have almost two years to take advantage of the special opportunity to present our ideas to a wider audience that an election campaign provides.

The SWP nominated Peter Camejo for President and Willie Mae Reid for Vice-President. Our campaign platform in an election year celebrating the 200th anniversary of the Declaration of Independence was "A Bill of Rights for Working People." The recession was in full swing. At the press conference announcing the campaign, Camejo declared, "Nearly 200 years after winning independence, America faces a growing crisis. There is mass unemployment and soaring prices. Pollution is destroying our environment. Lynch mobs roam the streets of Boston. We continue to be threatened by the outbreak of new wars. The FBI and CIA are fighting each other over how to best violate our constitution. Working people must have a decent life. They want programs to get out of the growing crisis. Our proposed Bill of Rights for Working People has as its purpose expanding the Bill of Rights in the Constitution to include proposals to address new problems created by present day capitalist society."[1]

This turned out to be the most important Presidential campaign the SWP held before or since. Indeed, it was the largest socialist campaign since those of Eugene Debs for the Socialist Party in the early 1900s, although nowhere near the size of those campaigns.

Camejo was the first Latino to run for President. He had been a central leader of the YSA in the early 1960s, and then of the SWP in the San Francisco Bay Area in the mid-to-late 1960s. He became a central leader of the student and antiwar movements at the University of California at Berkeley. Ronald Reagan, then Governor of California and later President, denounced him as "involved in every large-scale demonstration" and as the "most dangerous man in California." Peter then moved to Boston, where again he became a central leader of the antiwar movement. In 1970, he ran as SWP candidate for U.S. Senate against the liberal Ted Kennedy. The pro-Kennedy *Boston Globe* admitted, "The young man Camejo draws a big response from students in greater Boston who hear him, more than Senator Edward Kennedy on the same campus forum." (See Volume One of this work.) Camejo then began to do more traveling in Latin America for the SWP, and was on leadership bodies of the Fourth International. He continued to speak around the United States. He was the best public speaker by far of anyone in the party of my generation, and was the most loved by the membership.

While we were thinking about whom to run, Jack Barnes brought up that perhaps he should be the candidate. But the demand from the party ranks for Camejo to be the candidate was overwhelming. I believe Jack was jealous of Peter's standing in the ranks of the party, as well as of his public speaking ability.

Willie Mae Reid, like Camejo 35 years old, had spent her entire youth as a Black woman in the officially segregated Jim Crow South. When the civil rights movement came to her hometown of Memphis, Tennessee in 1958, she joined the "ride-ins" and bus boycott that ended segregated seating on city buses. She had a job as a kitchen worker. Reid moved to Chicago where she worked in the garment industry, as an office worker, and computer programmer. She became active in organizing in the Black community, and as a student at a junior college. She began to be influenced by Malcolm X, whose speeches she heard over the radio. She also became a supporter of the women's liberation movement. Reid joined the Party in 1971, and ran against the notorious racist Mayor Daley in the spring of 1975 while she simultaneously launched her campaign for Vice-President. She was one of the nicest people I've known.

•••

In 1974 there was an ominous development in a group whose origins went back a decade earlier in a split from the SWP. The Workers League was affiliated with an international group, the International Committee of the Fourth International (IC), led by Gerry Healy of the British Workers Revolutionary Party. In spite of its name, the IC was not affiliated with the Fourth International. In 1963, Healy had refused to join with the majority of other sections in the IC in reunification with the Fourth International. The Healyites' rump version of the IC instead became vociferous in their denunciations of the Fourth International and the SWP, and the Workers League followed suit.*

The central leader of the Workers League was Tim Wohlforth. At a summer camp held by the Workers League in 1974, Gerry Healy came over from Britain. His mission was to denounce Nancy Wohlforth, Tim's wife, as a CIA agent, and to use this preposterous charge to remove Tim as the Workers League national secretary. The Workers Revolutionary Party, as Healy's group in Britain was called, and the International Committee had long since degenerated into a cult around Healy, who had become profoundly paranoid, seeing spies and potential assassins everywhere.

Tim and Nancy wrote a long document detailing their horrible ordeal and break from Healy and Healyism. They sent it out to many organizations on the left. Only one, the SWP, took notice. In February 1975, *Intercontinental Press*, edited by SWP leader Joe Hansen, began to publish their document serially. This resulted in Tim and Nancy having discussions with the SWP, which led to Tim rejoining and Nancy joining the party.

Healy's response was to open a campaign denouncing Hansen as an agent of both(!) the FBI and of the Soviet GPU (forerunner of the KGB). He charged that Joe, as one of Trotsky's secretaries, was responsible for the murder of the great revolutionary leader. When George Novack came to Hansen's defense, Healy included him as an agent, too. Eventually, the campaign became ever more vituperous and widened to include many of the younger SWP leaders. Healy produced voluminous material in 1975 and 1976 trying to substantiate his ridiculous Big Lie.[2]

We decided to hold a big meeting to bring together all in the wider movement who were appalled at Healy's campaign, to be held in London to make it easier for European comrades to attend. The British International Marxist Group (IMG) organized the meeting in a large hall in January 1977. The hall was packed with over 1,000 in attendance.

We sent Tim Wohlforth and George Novack to be our representatives. (Joe Hansen's health precluded him from attending.) In addition, the dais included representatives of different Trotskyist tendencies. Tariq Ali, of the IMG, chaired the meeting. Ernest Mandel spoke for the United Secretariat; Pierre Lambert for the French Internationalist Communist Organization (OCI); Betty Hamilton, who had been with Healy's group since the Second World War but broke with him as he degenerated; and Tamara Deutscher, the wife of Trotsky biographer Isaac Deutscher. Michel Raptis (Pablo), who had been the International Secretary of the Fourth International since after the war, but who broke away after the 1963 reunification, sent a message—he couldn't attend because his wife was ill.

Others who rallied to the victims of the Big Lie were six former guards and secretaries to Trotsky; Trotsky's grandson Esteban Volkov; Marguerite Bonnet, the European executor of Trotsky's literary estate; French writer Daniel Guerin; and C.L.R. James, a West Indian writer of some note who had been for a time in the SWP.

Healy's cult later exploded when revelations came out publicly that he had made virtual sex slaves of 26 women members of his group for at least two decades. These victims had maintained their silence in deference to the cult leader.

•••

Bombings and fire-bombings of our headquarters, as well as of other socialist groups, had occurred in the 1960s and 1970s. The most serious attack against us was in Los Angeles on February 4, 1975. Lew Jones was city organizer at the time with an office in the same headquarters as that of one of the branches, on the second floor of a building. Jones was about to leave, and as he came to the head of the stairs, he saw a "person halfway up the stairs lighting a fuse," Harry Ring wrote in *The Militant*. "He shouted at the person and began running down the stairs toward him. The man hurled a pipe bomb at Jones, and it went past him, falling on the top landing. Jones pursued the man out of the building, but he escaped.

"Meanwhile, Jones' shout was heard by Tim Mallory, Socialist Workers candidate for the Pasadena, California school board. Mallory rushed to the landing and saw the bomb with its burning fuse. He slammed the door shut and quickly warned those inside to leave by the rear exit. Within less than two minutes, as they were halfway down the rear stairs the bomb exploded with tremendous force. The entrance door was completely demolished, and part of the downstairs street door was ripped off by the blast. A half-dozen windows were blown out, and fragments of the bomb penetrated a wall 30 feet down the corridor. Residents of a neighboring apartment building reported some 30 broken windows."[3]

The bomb was packed with nails and ball bearings, which blew through the walls. There were some 25 people working in the headquarters at the time. Many would have been hurt or killed had not Jones seen the attacker, and had not Mallory swiftly acted.

I flew out to Los Angeles to help in mapping out a public response, and also to show the solidarity of the national party with our local comrades, who were understandably shaken up. I found Lew Jones upset that he didn't do more. He thought maybe he should have run back up the stairs to warn the people in the headquarters. I reasoned with him that it would have been crazy to run back up toward a bomb with a burning fuse. I understood that he felt responsible as the city organizer for the comrades, but he had done well in shouting and trying to stop the guy from lighting the bomb and throwing it. He could have been killed had he stayed in the stairwell. Lew saw that I was right and calmed down.

In such situations it is important that comrades be mobilized to take action, and not stew over the events, to turn the attack into a political counter-attack. The party went on a public campaign nationally and locally to demand that the mayor see to it that the police made a serious attempt to find the terrorist. They did catch him later through tips from acquaintances of his Nazi Party friends.

•••

In the face of mounting unemployment the AFL-CIO called for a national demonstration in Washington, D.C. on April 26, 1975. As *Militant* reporter Andy Rose wrote, the event was "officially sponsored as a 'Rally for Jobs Now' by the Industrial Union Department of the AFL-CIO. It was an action without precedent for decades in this country: a national protest demonstration called by major trade unions to advance political demands." While we didn't know it at the time, it was also the last such national labor action, although individual unions, especially the United Mine Workers, did organize demonstrations in the following years.

Some 60,000 union members and their supporters joined the action. While the AFL-CIO tops wanted a carefully controlled rally only, a march to the rally was also organized. According to *The Militant*, "The march—the most militant and inspiring part of the day's events—was sponsored by the coalition of New York-area unions, not by the AFL-CIO. According to an article in the April 21 *New York Times*, conservative AFL-CIO officials were worried about 'participation in the march of radicals' and about 'possible injection of the Vietnam issue into the demonstration.'"

But that's just what they got. The New York march organizers welcomed antiwar banners and literature. The rally actually turned into an antiwar event, as well as a demand for jobs. The National Peace Action Coalition, the major antiwar group, distributed many thousands of leaflets. As *The Militant* reported, "The unionists gave a warm response to activists from the National Student Coalition Against Racism (NSCAR), who joined the march under their own banner and distributed more than 20,000 leaflets about the May 17 march against racism in Boston, sponsored by the NAACP. A thousand marchers bought NSCAR buttons."[4]

The SWP Presidential campaign was well received, too. Peter Camejo rode down from New York on the train organized by the American Federation of State, County and Municipal Employees. He walked up and down the entire train, introducing himself as the SWP nominee. "You can bet I'm the only Presidential candidate who will be marching with you today," Camejo told many of those he met on the train. Some unionists already knew about him from an article on the socialist campaign in the *New York Times*. Some 23,600 copies of the Bill of Rights for Working People were distributed at the day's events, and 1,500 copies of *The Militant* were sold.

•••

On April 30, 1975, the puppet regime in Saigon fell to the advancing North Vietnamese and National Liberation Front forces. This great victory dealt a major blow to U.S. imperialism. (See Volume One of this work as well as the book *Out Now!* by Fred Halstead.)

Earlier in April there appeared to be another anti-imperialist victory, when the Khmer Rouge guerrilla movement overthrew the pro-U.S. regime in Cambodia. But then the truth began to trickle out. People in Phnom Phen, the capital, initially poured into the streets to greet the Khmer Rouge fighters. This was understandable, since the whole country had suffered intense U.S. bombing and the puppet government installed by a U.S.-orchestrated coup was hated. Unexpectedly, the Khmer Rouge attacked the population of Phnom Phen and forced them to leave the city. Similar forced mass evacuations of the other cities and towns occurred.

It still wasn't known how far the Khmer Rouge would go with this policy. But we were concerned. Joseph Hansen wrote that we should be on guard against any attempt by imperialism to once again intervene in Cambodia. "Nonetheless," he argued, "revolutionary Marxists are duty bound to voice their concern over the program being followed by the national liberation forces in Cambodia. It is not a communist program.

"Consider the class composition of the cities and towns. The very thin layer of capitalists, or would-be capitalists, left Cambodia before the collapse of [US installed dictator] Lon Nol.... The fact is the bulk of the city population in Cambodia consists of workers and artisans. To view them as potential, if not actual, class enemies is not Marxist. And to drive them into the countryside for 'reeducation' does grave injury to the Cambodian revolution. The same layers, in alliance with the peasants, constitute the key force required to move toward a socialist society."[5]

The extent of the insane course of the Khmer Rouge would gradually become known, as it killed millions. Some "reeducation!"

During the war the Khmer Rouge had grown in the countryside as peasants found the U.S bombing and the pro-landlordism of the Lon Nol regime increasingly intolerable. There are similarities to the situation in China in 1949, after the peasant army under Mao Zedong overthrew the pro-US regime of Chiang Kai-Shek. Workers in the cities welcomed the Maoist armies, but their demonstrations were suppressed. However, the similarities stop there. The workers and artisans in the cities in China were not expelled. In the context of the Korean War, when the United States threatened China, the regime mobilized the city people in a controlled way to overthrow capitalism. A Stalinized bureaucratically deformed workers state was established by 1952. The Chinese revolution was one of the most important events of the twentieth century, dealing a major blow to imperialism and giving a mighty impulse to the colonial revolution worldwide.

The Khmer Rouge thought of itself as Maoist, but acted like Maoism on meth. Its peasant army was inculcated with the idea that the problem was the "cities," identifying all the people in the cities with the hated regime. There was no differentiating between classes in the cities. Obviously, the depopulation of Cambodia's cities was a severe blow to economic production and culture. Such an anti-working class regime was clearly opposed to Marxism. The Khmer Rouge experiment to establish a peasant regime led by elite intellectuals was a utopian pipe dream. It led instead not to utopia but to the ruination of Cambodia and mass murder on a scale that it should be called a holocaust.

The Khmer Rouge regime and state was not like the Stalinized countries. It was an extreme *right-wing* state.

Many on the left were slow to realize that something evil was happening in Cambodia, falling for the claptrap about the peasantry under an idealistic and benevolent leadership creating a "pure" and "simple" society. The peasantry can be a great revolutionary force in alliance with and under the leadership of the working class. The Russian and Cuban revolutions have been the greatest examples of the revolutionary potential of the peasantry. The Chinese revolution was also, in spite of its Stalinist distortions. But in Cambodia the peasantry was not led by a workers' party, but by a (petty) bourgeois force.

In the United States, Maoists groups continued to defend the forced depopulation of the cities for years to come.

•••

In the summer of 1975, two long-time leaders of the SWP died. One was Larry Trainor, who had recruited me and Peter Camejo in November 1959 and helped recruit many others in the Boston area in the 1960s, including my brothers Roger and Roland. Larry had joined the Trotskyists in the 1930s. He was a founding member of the SWP in 1938, and was elected and re-elected to the party's National Committee from 1938 until 1973. He died of Lou Gehrig's disease (ALS), the same relatively rare fatal disease that claimed my companion and comrade Caroline Lund many years later, in 2006.

In his more than 40 years in the revolutionary socialist movement, Larry was an agitator for socialism, an organizer of the revolutionary party, and an educator of Trotskyist cadres. I was one of the speakers at his memorial meeting, and I stressed some of the lessons he taught us. "He taught us class hatred—hatred of capitalism and the capitalist class. He taught us party professionalism. He taught us party patriotism, not as a religious concept but from consciousness. From consciousness that to build the kind of party we are building its members must be dedicated. They must be loyal. They must want to build this party, and have a readiness to make sacrifices for it."

As I write this in the first part of the 21st century, I still believe in these concepts. Some people have come to the conclusion that party loyalty led to the degeneration of the SWP. That is false and anyone who rejects loyalty to a revolutionary socialist party will not be able to build it. By "loyalty," I mean the conviction that the revolutionary party is your party and you want to defend it and build it, however much you disagree with its majority decisions and even if you think that the leadership must be changed. To put the same point in a negative way, I clearly am not today loyal to what still goes by the name "Socialist Workers Party."

Likewise, anyone who rejects party professionalism will not be able to help build the kind of party needed to overthrow capitalism and lead the transition to socialism. The SWP and YSA were effective way beyond our numbers would indicate because of our professionalism in thinking through our politics in the situations we faced and our professionalism in carrying out what we decided to do. We often referred to the slogan of the members and organizers of the great 1934 Teamster strikes in Minneapolis: "Whether a picnic or a strike, we do it right!"

•••

James P. Cannon, the founding leader of the Trotskyist movement, died in Los Angeles during the SWP convention in August 1975. We were holding a meeting of the steering committee of the convention when we were told there was an urgent telephone call. I went to answer it. Dave Prince, who was Cannon's secretary and live-in helper at the time, told me of his death. I went back to the meeting, and said, choking, "James P. Cannon is dead." Immediately, we changed the convention program, and scheduled a meeting to honor him. Joseph Hansen spoke to a packed audience of 1,250 on his life and character.

Cannon became a revolutionist as a teenager, and joined the Industrial Workers of the World (IWW), and then the Socialist Party (SP). His leadership qualities were soon recognized in both organizations. After the 1917 Russian Revolution, he was one of the leaders of the left wing of the SP and IWW that led a split, which in a few years, led to the formation of the Communist Party (CP). He was not only a leader of the new CP, but was elected to the International Executive Committee of the Communist International. Later, he opposed the Stalinist degeneration of the CP and the International and became a supporter of Leon Trotsky.

Cannon was the central leader of the Trotskyist movement in the United States from the time the supporters of Trotsky were expelled from the CP and Communist International in 1928, through the 1930s and the founding of the SWP in 1938. He was one of the leaders of the SWP convicted under the thought-control Smith Act in 1941, and imprisoned. He remained the central executive leader of the SWP up until Farrell Dobbs took on that responsibility in 1953 and Cannon moved to Los Angeles into semi-retirement. He remained on the National Committee until he left that post in the transition of leadership to a new generation in the early 1970s, when he became Chairman Emeritus.

I met Cannon at my first SWP convention in 1961, when he approached me with the proposal that I move to New York to become part of the YSA leadership. I heard him speak at the 1965 convention, the last one he attended because of increasing health problems. After his life's comrade and companion Rose Karsner died in 1968, we arranged for younger comrades to do a stint as his secretary and live-in helper.

I would meet with Cannon whenever I was in Los Angeles, and from time to time when I lived there. (For more on my relations with Trainor and Cannon, see the first volume of this work.)

•••

The August 1975 SWP convention was held in Oberlin, Ohio, as had our yearly national gatherings, alternating between conventions and educational conferences, since 1970. There were more than 1,600 delegates and observers present, making this the largest party convention to date. The attendance reflected continued growth, both in terms of new branches and recruitment. Our involvement in the fight for community control of the schools on New York's Lower East Side and in the Boston busing struggle were highlights.

The Presidential election campaign was in full swing. Camejo and Reid had been speaking all over the country, to substantial audiences, and recruiting new people who heard them. We were getting more media coverage than in previous campaigns. The Political Rights Defense Fund (PRDF) endorsed suit was winning more support in the post-Watergate era. By the time of the convention, we had established branches in five new cities: Newark, N.J.; Baltimore; New Orleans; San Antonio, Texas; and San Jose, California. A big election rally with the candidates brought down the house.

Our conventions usually began with a discussion of the world political situation, so that our consideration of domestic questions would be placed in the international framework. This year our focus was on the revolutionary upsurge in Portugal, and the situation in the Fourth International in that light. A big banner that hung above the speakers' platform declared: "Solidarity with Portuguese Workers! Portugal Out of Angola!" Two reports were given on Portugal, one by Jack Barnes and one by me.

We projected that the period ahead would be one of increased class polarization and working class struggles in the communities of the oppressed nationalities and on the job. We expected such developments and posited a turn to the working class as they developed. What this meant in practice was the beginning of a process of dividing the branches into smaller units. The projection was that such smaller units could more effectively relate to working class communities.

Our projections proved false. Struggles in working class communities like the ones in Boston and New York's Lower East Side had not become generalized. We soon saw that we had over-divided the branches, which were not immersed in community struggles, and we moved back to larger branches more suited to the actual opportunities before us.

---

* For a full discussion of the political and organizational issues in this split, see Volume One of this work.

1 *The Militant,* Jan. 17, 1975.
2 See Tim Wohlforth, *The Prophet's Children* (Humanities Press International, 1994).

3 *The Militant,* Feb. 14, 1975.
4 Ibid., May 9, 1975.
5 Ibid.

CHAPTER ELEVEN: CONTINUED GROWTH

The SWP and YSA were becoming better known and more central on the left in 1976. The Presidential campaign of Camejo and Reid and increasing support for our civil liberties lawsuit against the government were major reasons for this positive trend. Also important were our involvement in a powerful rank-and-file movement in the United Steelworkers, called Steelworkers Fight Back; the struggle to win the Equal Rights Amendment (ERA) for women; and the Raza Unida Party, an independent Chicano political formation. As we entered the Presidential election year our role in the Boston busing battle had also raised the party's prestige

Consequently, we drew renewed attention from the far-right "U.S. Labor Party," an electoral front for the National Caucus of Labor Committees (NCLC), a cult around Lyndon LaRouche with a history of violent attacks on the SWP, Communist Party (CP) and other socialist organizations, as well as anti-labor and anti-Black activities. Like historical fascist organizations, it claimed to be anti-capitalist and even socialist (Hitler's National German Socialist Workers Party, better known by the acronym Nazi, comes to mind).

The growing public impact of the Camejo-Reid campaign stuck in LaRouche's craw. In January 1976, the NCLC stepped up its harassment against the SWP. Its members would telephone SWP headquarters and members at odd hours to create a general atmosphere of intimidation. The NCLC demanded that radical groups be barred from some campuses and disrupted our public meetings.

The NCLC advertised for their public meetings with such headlines as "How the Socialist Workers Party and the Communist Party (USA) participated in the murder of John F. Kennedy." One leaflet reproduced a photo of Kennedy's alleged assassin, Lee Harvey Oswald, distributing handbills of the Fair Play for Cuba Committee, with the caption "Oswald passing out leaflets for an SWP front group in New Orleans prior to J.F.K.'s assassination." Such charges dovetailed with the government's own charges that the SWP is made up of conspirators plotting violence, used to try to justify the government's actual dirty deeds against us that we were fighting with our lawsuit.[1]

The *New York Times* featured a front-page story on our suit on March 14, 1976, under the three-column headline "F.B.I. Burglarized

Leftist Offices Here [New York City] 92 Times in 1960-66, Official Files Show." Below the headline was a picture of Camejo, who was quoted in the article. This was but one story about our suit and the Camejo-Reid campaign that broke into the daily press. In previous campaigns it had been hard to get any coverage of our election efforts in the capitalist press.

The Political Rights Defense Fund (PRDF) released voluminous government documents concerning FBI break-ins of our headquarters across the country. The story generated headlines in major dailies across the United States, not only in New York. As it was set up, the PRDF represented a broad coalition to publicize the lawsuit, raise money for the legal fees involved, and garner support. As in other defense efforts (while our suit took the form of an offensive against the government, it was in fact a defense of democratic rights), we were scrupulous in insisting that endorsers of the suit were not in any way expressing support for the program or policies of the SWP and YSA.

Another example of coverage of the election campaign was a front-page interview with Camejo in the *San Francisco Chronicle* that detailed our socialist positions on the issues.*

Besides speaking throughout the United States, Camejo and Reid spoke in many countries in the world, in engagements set up by our cothinkers. Peter, who was fluent in both English and Spanish, toured Latin America. He also went to Spain, which was in massive ferment following the death of the fascist dictator Franco in late 1975. In January 1976 a massive strike wave of 250,000 workers broke out, demanding political rights as well as long-overdue increases in wages and benefits. Workers Commissions, which had been formed underground by the Spanish Communist Party and supported by groups to the left of it, helped lead the strikes. Often these strikes broke out spontaneously, with the Workers Commissions joining in after the fact.

The Spanish dictatorship, while crumbling, was still in place. The capitalist class opted for a return to the monarchy, installing Juan Carlos I as king, and promising a gradual democratization of the nation. Workers, farmers, and national minorities suppressed under the fascists began to take matters into their own hands. The Communist and Socialist parties emerged into the open, together with the Workers Commissions and unions orienting toward the Socialist Party. The Communist Party and Socialist Party both grew, as did the organizations to the left of them, including Trotskyists, all of whom were still technically illegal.

Camejo traveled to Spain in May 1976 where he spoke to some 4,000 workers and students in a nine-day tour of three cities—

Barcelona, Valencia and Madrid. The fascist Civil Guard broke up one meeting in Madrid, but others were held after protests. His tour was extensively covered in the Spanish press. He met with the organization secretary of the General Workers Union, which was aligned with the Socialist Party, as well as the most well-known leader of the Workers Commissions, and other trade union leaders.

As Joanna Rossi reported in *The Militant:*

"A public meeting, held May 27 in the Barrio Pilar, a large working class neighborhood in Madrid, was a high point of the tour. Camejo had been invited to speak ... by the Santa Maria del Val Club, an organization of young workers. The meeting was packed with more than 500 young workers, some students, and a number of older persons. It was an enthusiastic crowd, hungry for revolutionary ideas. They applauded and laughed as Camejo spoke in Spanish, punctuating his talk with jokes at the expense of bourgeois politicians, the FBI and CIA....

"One of the points he stressed—and this touched on a topic under sharp debate within the Spanish left—is the need for the working class and its parties to remain independent from bourgeois parties and programs. Camejo explained that in the United States, as in the rest of the world, the Communist Party and Social Democracy do not hold this view, traditionally seeking blocs with the 'liberal' bourgeoisie.... The audience rocked with laughter at his reference ... to the deals the Spanish reformist parties are trying to establish through a 'junta' with their bourgeoisie. The applause was loud and prolonged. The audience included a number of Spain's large, underground Communist Party. Their faces grew serious as Camejo denounced international Stalinist politics, past and present. 'But,' Camejo went on, 'we must not confuse the rank and file of the Communist or Socialist parties with the disastrous lines of their leaders. We must be able to work together, to unite, around many important issues we all support....' This touched a responsive chord throughout the audience, which burst into a new round of applause."[2]

In August 1976, the SWP's 28th national convention was held at Oberlin College in Ohio. Since its previous convention the year before, the SWP had expanded into 15 new cities. In attendance were representatives from two U.S. organizations interested in common work with us: the Revolutionary Marxist Committee, which emerged from a split in the International Socialists, and Spark, a small group with ties to the French Lutte Ouvriere (Workers Struggle) organization. There were 200 observers from countries around the world, most from groups in the Fourth International. Two international Trotskyist currents not in the International also sent greetings. These were Lutte Ouvriere and several national groups affiliated with the Organizing Committee for the Reconstruction of the Fourth International (OCRFI).

The convention discussed our work in the unions, Black and Chicano organizations, the National Organization for Women, our lawsuit against the government, our election campaigns, and other areas of work. The convention projected we would recruit 300 new members in the next six months, and win 20,000 new readers to *The Militant*.

A rally at the end of the convention attended by 1,650 featured speeches by Peter Camejo and Willie Mae Reid. The party and YSA made a major effort to put the Camejo-Reid ticket on the ballot in as many states as we could. This was very difficult, as most states have undemocratic election laws that make the task for third parties to win ballot status quite onerous. Huge numbers of signatures of registered voters had to be gathered on petitions. On the positive side, the petitioning effort did help spread the news of the campaign more widely. We finally won ballot status in 28 states, significantly more than the other socialist parties. The greatest effort was in California, where almost 100,000 signatures had to be gathered and approved by the Secretary of State. About 289,000 signatures were turned in for Camejo and Reid, as well as for our candidate for Senator, Omari Musa. About 110,000 were approved.

We fielded many other candidates for federal, state and local offices across the country. One of these was Sylvia Weinstein, who ran for San Francisco Board of Education. Sylvia was one of the coordinators of Child and Parent Action, which was backing a ballot proposition to provide for low-cost quality childcare for all parents in San Francisco. Sylvia was also a leader in the broader women's movement in the city. The proposition was defeated by a scare campaign orchestrated by the city's Board of Supervisors that there wasn't enough money. Sylvia countered that the funds should come from "the banks and other big business concerns, not the already overtaxed working population."

The SWP Presidential campaign received wide support on the left (with the exception of the pro-Moscow and pro-Beijing Stalinists), among civil libertarians, artists and other intellectuals, fighters for Black and Chicano rights, leaders of the former antiwar movement, and people in the women's movement. Camejo and Reid were also endorsed by a number of local labor leaders. The *New York Post* ran a spread in its October 23 issue on third parties in the election. It said, "The most successful of the left-wing parties on the ballot in terms of recent elections is the Socialist Workers Party."

Under the pressure of the SWP campaign the CP did not call for a vote for the Democratic Party candidate, Jimmy Carter, who was running against Republican Gerald Ford. This represented a tactical shift for the CP, which ran Gus Hall for President. Since the middle of the 1930s, the CP had mainly supported Democrats (and once again reverted to style after 1976). While calling for a vote for Hall, the CP also supported Democrats for other offices, making clear it was not changing its basic electoral orientation.

The main Maoist groups and the Maoist *Guardian* newspaper called for a boycott of the elections, as did the International Socialists. The Social Democrats USA, the right wing of the social democratic movement in the United States, had campaigned in the Democratic primaries for Henry Jackson, the U.S. senator and the most vociferous of the anticommunist "cold war" Democrats. When it turned out that Georgia Governor Jimmy Carter beat their candidate for the nomination, they switched to Carter. The moderate wing of social democracy, the Democratic Socialist Organizing Committee, also backed Carter. The Revolutionary Marxist Committee (RMC) called for a vote for the SWP, although they called us "opportunist and tailist." The RMC would soon move closer to the SWP politically and would merge with us. Spark called for a vote, with criticisms, for the SWP. The sclerotic Socialist Labor Party and the small Socialist Party ran their own candidates.

The SWP supported the candidates of the Chicano Raza Unida Party in Texas, California, New Mexico and Colorado. In Texas, Raza Unida had won some local elections and individual Raza party leaders and leaders of other Chicano organizations called for support to Camejo-Reid. The SWP also called for a vote for General Baker, a candidate of one of the smaller Maoist groups, the Communist Labor Party. Baker had come out of the Dodge Revolutionary Union Movement, a Black-led militant caucus of the United Auto Workers in the late 1960s.

One result of the PRDF and our election campaigns was a long feature article in the left-liberal magazine *The Nation* on the SWP by Walter and Miriam Schneir. The couple had written a study of the case of the Rosenbergs, who were executed as spies at the height of the witchhunt in 1953. Miriam Schneir was also the editor of a popular book, *Feminism: The Essential Historical Writings*.

The title of their article, "Square Target of the FBI," referred to things such as our prohibition of members' use of illegal drugs, which differentiated us from much of the "New Left," as well as to our organizational seriousness.

They wrote:

"Assessing the strength of the SWP by the number of its members—nearly 1,500 in the party itself and about 1,000 in the closely related Young Socialist Alliance—can be misleading. Membership in this cadre-type party is not at all a casual matter; it represents a deep personal commitment. The constitution of the SWP mandates democratic control of its governing bodies and party democracy is a fundamental principle. But once a decision is reached, it is 'binding upon members.' Socialist Workers agree to submit to party discipline....

"The party's national headquarters in New York City, located on the downtown waterfront at 410 West Street, is a solid 5-story former marine repair shop that has been completely refurbished by volunteer SWP labor. Seventy-year-old SWP theoretician George Novack, who remembers when it could barely afford one telephone, notes with pride: 'We have an infrastructure for a party of about 100,000.' A visit to the headquarters reveals that Novack is not exaggerating. It is a hive of activity staffed by about 120 persons.... By comparison, at the height of its strength in the late 1960s, Students for a Democratic Society, the organizational heart of the New Left, had a debt-ridden national headquarters consisting of a single floor of dilapidated offices run by ten-to-fifteen overworked and overwhelmed individuals. The atmosphere at Socialist Workers headquarters is cheerful but businesslike....

"Born out of the bitter clashes between Stalinists and Trotskyists that rent world communism in the 1920s and 1930s, wounded almost mortally by the Smith Act convictions of its entire leadership in the 1940s and the McCarthyism of the 1950s, the Socialist Workers Party re-emerged during the turbulent 1960s with a new, young, vigorous and confident membership."[3]

The Schneirs concluded by calling for a vote for Camejo-Reid.

Another indication of new respect for the SWP was that the bourgeois right felt the need to confront the party. One example was a debate before a large audience between Phyllis Schlafly, the most well known of the opponents of the ERA and abortion rights, and the SWP's Dianne Feeley at Georgia State University. Feeley was also the head of the ERA Committee of the New York National Organization for Women. There was a "Debate on the CIA" before 1,000 at Southern Illinois University (SIU) at Carbondale between former CIA director William Colby and Syd Stapleton, an SWP National Committee member and the National Secretary of the Political Rights Defense Fund. The debate was organized by SIU student and YSA member Mark Harris and was also broadcast live on the campus radio station. The two also debated at Cornell University.

Camejo began in his speeches to single out another election campaign that occurred in 1976, in the United Steelworkers (USWA) union. "A major challenge to the entrenched bureaucracy of the United Steelworkers of America is shaping up behind Ed Sadlowski, the insurgent director of USWA District 31," wrote Andy Rose in *The Militant.* Sadlowski was running for union president against Lloyd McBride, the candidate of the bureaucracy to succeed I.W. Abel, who was retiring. Abel preached that the interests of the workers and the capitalists were basically the same, and had signed a no-strike pledge with the big steel companies.

As Rose noted, "Sadlowski won national prominence in 1974 when he wrested the directorship of the Chicago-Gary district, the largest in the USWA, from the bureaucracy's handpicked candidate. Now Sadlowski has launched a nationwide movement called Steelworkers Fight Back. Its avowed purpose is to restore democratic, rank-and-file control over the steelworkers union so it can fight effectively for the needs of working people [and create] 'a tough, democratic labor movement.' In a widely circulated letter appealing for support to Steelworkers Fight Back, Sadlowski describes the purpose of the new movement: 'We are determined to eliminate the kind of tuxedo unionism some of our leaders have practiced in the past....'

"An immense economic and social gulf separates the top officials from the ranks, Sadlowski charges. '[I.W.] Abel makes $75,000 a year as President of the United Steelworkers where the average member makes about $5 an hour.' Sadlowski hits the AFL-CIO leadership's flag-waving support to the Vietnam War as prime example of a stand directly contrary to the interests of the workers. 'Who's the guy that was going? It was my son that works in the steel mill. It's not the banker's boy. The kid in the damn trenches in Vietnam, that was the working-class kid.'"[4] He also spoke out against racism in the plants and union.

The SWP had some members in the USWA for some time. Younger comrades got jobs in steel as a result of the Sadlowski campaign. These members jumped into support of the Fight Back movement. Branches in cities with steel mills helped the movement in other ways, including with leafleting and getting the word out to other workers

The McBride forces red-baited the insurgents. A McBride rally in Pittsburgh turned into an anticommunist rant, with Joe Odorcich, director of District 15, using the platform to denounce prominent Sadlowski supporter Jim Balanoff as a "communist." Balinoff was the President of the 18,000-member Local 1010 in East Chicago. The McBride rally had about 200 people present, compared with an earlier Sadlowski rally of 500 in Pittsburgh. The McBride event included union staffers, lawyers, etc. while the Sadlowski rally was mostly rank-and-filers. At a rally in Cleveland, Sadlowski responded, declaring that racism and red-baiting are incompatible with trade unionism. "That's the bosses game," he said. "That's the divide-and-conquer game." The union's anticommunist clause "doesn't belong in a labor union constitution." During the witchhunt most unions adopted positions barring "communists" from membership, and these were often still on the books.

Violence was another tactic. Ben Corum, one of a team of Sadlowski supporters from the Chicago-Gary district was in Houston leafleting at the Hughes Tool Company when he was shot from behind by three thugs in a car that sped away. The bullet hit Corum in the neck, and narrowly missed his spinal cord. The team was touring steel plants across the South. Camejo and Reid sent a telegram to I.W. Abel and Sadlowski, stating: "The attempted murder of Ben Corum, a member of the United Steelworkers of America...is an attack on the steelworkers union and the entire labor movement. It is typical of the violence promoted by the open-shop movement, the Ku Klux Klan, professional strikebreakers, and others used by corporate management to weaken and destroy unions. We support wholeheartedly actions by the Houston labor movement and by all leaders and locals of the United Steelworkers to see that those responsible for this crime are apprehended and prosecuted." But the Houston police swept the crime under the rug and no one was ever apprehended.

On the first day of the USWA convention in August a Sadlowski delegate, Cliff Mezo from Local 1010, was severely beaten by Abel's henchmen and his camera smashed. Mezo had taken a photo of people forging a delegate's credentials. Balanoff took the floor to demand an investigation, and Abel, tongue-in-check, said Mezo shouldn't have been attacked, but also insinuated that Sadlowski's ideas were so outrageous that some steelworkers would just naturally start swinging. "I sometimes have to restrain myself," Abel said. "We steelworkers are made that way." He also said that Mezo had "provoked" the attack by taking the photo.

As a result of our support to the Sadlowski campaign, we expanded our fraction in the United Steelworkers, urging members where possible to get jobs in steel. Our steelworker members functioned as active unionists, taking responsibilities in Steelworkers Fight Back. One of our disabled members, Robin Maisel, helped staff Sadlowski's campaign headquarters. In December SWP and YSA activists in the union from California, Illinois, Michigan, Ohio, Pennsylvania, Texas and Wisconsin met to discuss their experiences in Steelworkers Fight Back and to decide their ongoing work. Frank Lovell, our national trade union director, opened the meeting.

The United Steelworkers election was held in February 1977. McBride won in the union as a whole, but Sadlowski won in the basic steel plants. The difference in the vote had to do with the smaller shops organized by the USWA that were not related to the steel industry. The steelworkers' Fight Back campaign was a high point, along with the United Mine Workers' strike in 1978, of labor militancy in the second half of the 1970s.

By early 1977, SWP fractions in rail, auto, steel and coal were firmly established. Many women comrades were in these fractions, taking advantage of rulings and laws passed in the early 1970s that opened the way for women to be hired in "male" industries. These opportunities for women came as a result in part of earlier victories by the Black struggle in opening more industries for African-Americans, combined with the struggles of the new women's liberation movement.

At our August 1976 convention, we had projected recruiting 300 members in the next six months. We actually recruited 326 new members by early 1977. These were "provisional members," who participated in party meetings and work for three months, during which time they could familiarize themselves with the party and make a final decision to join. Previously, most party recruits had come through the YSA, and got to know our movement through that experience before they decided to join the SWP. Now we were recruiting more people who were a little older and weren't joining the youth group.

I still had duties related to organizational questions. In 1977, I did a survey based on branch reports, and concluded that the SWP had 1,760 members, with another 2,000 in the YSA. There was an overlap of membership, so there were about 3,000 organized members of our movement. This was our high point.

In early 1977, I worked on *Intercontinental Press* (IP) to help relieve the workload on the publication's editor Joseph Hansen, who had health problems. While I was there, the IP staff helped build another staff of Spanish speakers to launch a new magazine in Spanish called *Perspectiva Mundial*, which was largely composed of translations from IP. More and more in 1977, my work centered on the Fourth International. Through 1979, of course, the party continued to be active in many areas, although I was not directly involved and was mostly out of the country.

---

* I learned years later about an incident surrounding Camejo's *San Francisco Chronicle* interview. Jack Barnes had called Camejo into a private meeting and violently berated him because the interview quoted Peter on our anti-Stalinist stance, but left out our defense of the Soviet Union against war threats by the United States. In the first place, this was insignificant compared to the fact that our campaign was on the front page of a major newspaper in the country read by hundreds of thousands. Also, Peter was not responsible for what the *Chronicle* interviewer wrote. The real import of Barnes' tongue-lashing was that it demonstrated a negative tendency of arrogance toward others in the leadership, a trait that would become dominant later.

1 *The Militant,* Jan. 16, 1976.
2 Ibid., June 11, 1976.
3 *The Nation,* Sept. 25, 1976.
4 *The Militant,* Feb. 20, 1976.

CHAPTER TWELVE: A NEW SITUATION IN THE FOURTH INTERNATIONAL

Late in 1976, the Steering Committee of the International Majority Tendency (IMT) adopted a "Self-Criticism on Latin America." I received a copy of the English translation as a member of the Political Committee (we soon published it in the English version of the International Internal Discussion Bulletin).

I brought my copy home to our apartment in Hoboken, New Jersey. I started to read it, but put it down, irritated by an introduction that was a tirade against the Leninist Trotskyist Faction (LTF). While I was preparing supper, Caroline read it through. When she was done, she exclaimed, "We won!"

Caroline was right. The long faction fight in the Fourth International was over. While other differences became involved, the origin of the struggle was the adoption at the 1969 World Congress of a sharp turn toward advocating that our sections in Latin America initiate or prepare to initiate rural guerrilla war throughout the continent. We were among the minority that voted against this new orientation.

The guerrilla orientation initiated a wider turn toward ulraleftism by the majority. The "Self-Criticism" was a full reversal of the 1969 position on Latin America. As such, it pulled the rug from under subsequent positions taken by the majority on Europe and other questions, which we characterized as ultraleft.

During the long fight the two factions had hardened. We saw the "Self-Criticism" as the opportunity to break through this situation. At a meeting of the National Committee of the SWP on January 7, 1977, a report given by National Secretary Jack Barnes was unanimously adopted, titled "The Meaning of the IMT Self-Criticism on Latin America."

Jack's report summarized the content of the new IMT position, as well as the history of the faction struggle. He concluded:

"I was thinking about how long this debate has been frozen. Rather than a collective give and take, we have had a confrontation of resolutions and editorials. That has to end. Finally, I think it is now obligatory to dissolve the structures of the two main factions in the Fourth International. This would greatly facilitate forging a new majority of perhaps eighty or ninety percent of the International on a whole number of key questions as we proceed to settle the old questions.

"We have a powerful new reason for ending factional operations. The factions originated precisely in the struggle that broke out at the Ninth World Congress over two counterposed lines on a key question for the International. Something new has developed: a recognition by comrades who carried the line that whole elements of it were wrong and must be discarded. It was the refusal to recognize this that in our opinion led—regardless of the intentions of the comrades involved—to the organizational practices that necessitated forming a faction [the LTF]. Now the situation has changed.

"We can go back to the norm in a Bolshevik organization of temporary alignments, give and take in leadership relations, the possibility of different lineups on different questions. We can agree today, disagree tomorrow, agree the next day after events show who was right and who was wrong. We can seek a homogenous leadership.

"There is not only cause for optimism but reason for determination in pressing forward. The next world congress, which will probably be held sometime in 1979, will take place soon after the fortieth anniversary of the founding of the Fourth International, where the Transitional Program was adopted and the validity of the Leninist strategy of party building was reaffirmed, laying the foundations for the Fourth International today. If we can collectively take advantage of the new situation in the International and move forward together, there will be an extremely large majority of comrades who will again reaffirm this course at the next world congress. That should be our goal."

There were a large number of international guests at the National Committee meeting, including a representative of the IMT, Alan Jones, and representatives of the LTF from around the world. The LTF steering committee had called for a meeting of the faction to follow the National Committee meeting. We were convinced we would have to take the bull by the horns and immediately dissolve the LTF, which would pressure the IMT to do likewise. We knew there were recalcitrant leaders of the IMT who would oppose its dissolution, and a few on our side, too.

At the meeting of LTF leaders, I gave the report proposing that we immediately dissolve the faction. Some in the LTF who were members of the French LCR were opposed. After a thorough discussion, the faction voted in a large majority to dissolve.

In the aftermath of this decision, the French Internationalist Communist Organization (OCI) soon withdrew from seeking an accommodation with the Fourth International. This was an unfortunate development. It had been clear that the OCI leaders were supporters (critically) of the positions of the LTF. But their sectarianism toward the LCR blinded them to the fact of the new situation in the International (including the LCR), which objectively had come closer to their positions.

In the coming months international work was my primary task. To actually dissolve the factions and lay the foundations for a new leadership structure in the International required a lot of work and negotiations. I made many trips to Europe, attending meetings of the United Secretariat, visiting sections, and participating in negotiations with leaders of the IMT. Jack Barnes accompanied me to the most important meetings. One issue we discussed concerned the principle that all former members of the LTF and IMT be accepted in the Fourth International. There was one small group that had joined the LTF in Costa Rica, led by Fausto Amador, the brother of Carlos Fonseca Amador, a founder of the Sandinista National Liberation Front in Nicaragua (FSLN). The IMT leaders objected to accepting this group in the Fourth International.

It turned out that Fausto had earlier joined the Belgian section, but ran into a problem. Belgian comrades learned that he had gone on Nicaraguan TV during the Somoza dictatorship, while the FSLN was waging a guerrilla war against the regime, to urge his brother and the FSLN to turn themselves in. He said they would not be arrested, but could function as a legitimate political group, a highly dubious assertion.

The FSLN considered Fausto a traitor. Apparently, after news of this betrayal surfaced in Belgium, Fausto quickly left the country and went to Spain, where he organized a small group, and then took the group to Costa Rica. That's when he asked to join the LTF. We had thought he and his group were a legitimate part of the Fourth International, as Jack and I insisted at a meeting in Brussels that went into early morning (when we were more awake than the European comrades because of our jet lag). Finally, the IMT leaders gave up and agreed.

This was a mistake on our part. We had serious doubts about the validity of the charges against Fausto. We were leery of assertions by guerrilla groups that someone is a traitor, as there have been executions of leaders of such groups who later turned out were innocent. But we should have more carefully looked into the case. In hindsight, it would have been better to refer the issue to the International Control Commission for investigation. Such a commission could have interrogated the Belgium comrades, Fausto himself, and others to get at the truth. A commission would have found that the charges against him were true, his appearance on TV and what he said were public facts. When the FSLN triumphed a few years later, the affair would come back to bite us.

•••

In 1977, I had been visiting many countries around the world to meet and discuss with groups that were in the LTF, mainly in Mexico and Europe, but also with supporters of the IMT. Caroline was on a tour of Spain writing articles for *The Militant*. She also met with supporters of the Fourth International as well as other revolutionists. SWP leader Jose Perez also toured Spain, traveling to different cities. Caroline was especially impressed with fighters in the Basque country, supporters of the Revolutionary Communist League (LCR) who were struggling for independence as well as for socialism. One of them gave her a nice woolen vest with Basque symbols. She wore this vest for many years.

Another important oppressed nationality, in addition to the Basques, were the Catalonians. Their language was also suppressed by the dictator Franco, as Basque was. The largest city in Catalonia is Barcelona. I had visited Barcelona many times since the 1974 World Congress to meet with leaders of the Communist League (LC), the Fourth International group associated with the LTF. Caroline and I met up in Barcelona, and attended a big mass meeting of thousands, organized by the LCR, which was held in a huge tent. The LCR was associated with the IMT.

This very spirited meeting's themes included the call for a republic and socialism, as well as immediate demands of the workers, peasants and oppressed nationalities. The majority of workers' parties supported the demand for a republic, as part of the fight for democracy against the remnants of the fascist regime. The slogan also embodied the fight against the monarchy. Franco had launched the Spanish Civil War in the 1930s against the formation of a republic. This was also deep in the historical memory of the working class.*

Caroline and I found time to visit many sights in the beautiful city, including many striking buildings built by the famous architect Gaudi. One of these is the unfinished "Holy Family" cathedral. Another site we visited was the old fort overlooking the city and the Mediterranean, accessible by cable car. Comrades took us out to eat at one of the city's famous seafood restaurants.

Both sides in the International came to agreement that a team of younger leaders of the LTF would move to Paris to work on a daily basis with a team of younger leaders of the IMT. The SWP proposed that Caroline and I be part of the new day-to-day leadership.

Jim Percy, the National Secretary of the Australian Socialist Workers Party and one of the younger leaders of the LTF, had joined me on one of my trips that summer. While we were on the ferry crossing the English Channel going back to Paris from London, I raised with him over lunch the suggestion that he and his companion, Nita Keig, join Caroline and I in Paris as part of the day-to-day leadership group. (Actually, not only Jim, but also Caroline and Nita were younger than I by many years.)

This proposal was formalized by the appointment of Nita to the International Executive Committee (Caroline, Jim and I were already members) and the four of us to the United Secretariat. Subsequently, the United Secretariat elected us to the Bureau, a subordinate body of the United Secretariat responsible for day-to-day work. From the IMT side the Bureau also included Charles-André Udry from Switzerland, Charles Michaloux from France, Lahire (a pseudonym) from France and Jacqueline from Switzerland.

I later learned from Michaloux that it was the younger leaders of the IMT, especially himself and Udry, who led the fight within the IMT to adopt the "Self-Criticism." Livio Maitan was opposed, while Ernest Mandel sat on the sidelines. Hugo Moscoso of the Bolivian Revolutionary Workers Party (POR) played an important positive role. Moscoso had been one of the leaders at the 1969 World Congress who proposed the turn toward the guerrilla war strategy for Latin America, and his POR suffered greatly as a result of trying to put it into practice. Thus, his new position calling for a reversal of the policy carried great weight within the IMT leadership. It also demonstrated his revolutionary and moral character.

* It was in the context of this particular historical struggle for a republic in Spain that Jack Barnes made a political error. Back in New York, he decided that the call for a republic was reformist and we should call for a workers and peasants government instead. The call for a republic of course was not counterposed to that for a workers and peasants government. This was a minor error, but foretold similar errors later, where positions were taken by Jack that were in part motivated by seeking to "differentiate" from the broader left.

CHAPTER THIRTEEN: REBUILDING THE INTERNATIONAL

In the fall of 1977 Caroline and I replaced Gus Horowitz and Becky Finch as the party's full-time representatives in Paris. We would move into the party apartment Gus and Becky had occupied. Caroline went to Paris at the end of September 1977, and I arrived a week or so later. After the flight of six or seven hours, I was waiting for my luggage when my name was called over a loudspeaker, and I was directed to go to passport control. From there I was whisked into an interrogation room. Two policemen went through my luggage in the room, and found a bundle of English language International Internal Bulletins. One of the cops said to the other "truc Trotskiste"—Trotskyist stuff.

I wasn't answering them beyond my name, my address in the United States and such. But they told me who I was, a leader of the SWP and a member of the United Secretariat, and so forth. It was hardly a secret. My name was on the bulletin as the author of one of the articles, my report on what I had found out about the Morenistas' disastrous intervention in Portugal. The cops didn't get very far with me. One of the cops said that I was unnaturally calm and cool, and that meant I was not an ordinary traveler.

Caroline, who had been waiting for me at the airport, became alarmed. She got in touch with the Revolutionary Communist League (LCR), which began to make inquiries with the government. Probably under this pressure, after some hours the cops told me I was barred from France and would be sent back to the United States. I tried to get them to send me to Belgium, where the SWP had another apartment, but they insisted on sending me back to New York.

Then they left, and a young, good-looking woman came in and asked me in very good English, all friendly, if I would agree to pay for my ticket back, since they had found a few thousand dollars in travelers checks on me. I was amused that they thought this might work. They put me on an Air France plane, in the front row with some kind of officer beside me. When I got back to New York, I had been up for about 40 hours. I got some sleep, and the next night flew to Brussels. Caroline took a train up from Paris to Brussels to meet me. It was my fortieth birthday, and we celebrated by eating at a good restaurant. The next day we went to Paris by train with no problems.

After talking with comrades in Paris, I learned that the French authorities had decided that the United Secretariat was a "terrorist organization," probably based on what I referred to in an earlier chapter about the assassination of Carrero Blanco in Spain. Apparently, at the airport I had been picked at random from the passenger list for screening, and then my name popped up as associated with the United Secretariat. The French government knew this designation of the United Secretariat as terrorist was bogus, and didn't try to enforce the ban very vigorously. I had no trouble after this incident.

When Caroline and I were in Brussels in 1968-70, I was the SWP representative to the United Secretariat. At the time there was no office for the Bureau of the United Secretariat, which comprised exactly three people—Ernest Mandel, Pierre Frank, and myself. We met in Ernest's home, and the larger United Secretariat met in the headquarters of the Belgian section. Now in Paris there was a large office, with a paid staff kept busy with correspondence with the sections, preparing the international bulletins, publishing the Fourth International magazine, *Inprecor*, typing minutes and so forth.*

Caroline, in addition to functioning on the Bureau, worked in the office. She was a crack typist. One of the office workers was a woman from Brazil, which was still under a brutal military dictatorship, one of the many in Latin America established by Washington. She and her husband were members of the underground Brazilian section. The political police captured her husband, but she managed to escape. She had kept some of his clothes for the day when he would be released. But as years went by, she faced up to the fact that in all probability he had been murdered. She and Caroline had become good friends, and she gave a pair of her husband's pants to me as she thought we were about the same size. I wore them for many years.

In Spain, Portugal, Mexico, the United States and Canada there had been splits during the long faction fight, with different groups identifying with one side or the other. One of our jobs in the Bureau and United Secretariat was to work toward reunification of these groups. Accordingly, I went to Spain to meet with the leaders of the Communist League (LC), the group identified with the LTF, urging them to begin negotiations with leaders of the IMT-identified Revolutionary Communist League (LCR).

In Britain, the International Marxist Group (IMG) had not split, but there was a very tense situation between the IMT majority and the LTF minority. Two of the older LTF comrades were Connie and Alan Harris, who had become good friends with Caroline and I since our days in Brussels in 1968. In the intervening years, I and other SWP comrades arriving from New York would often stay at their apartment before going on to "the continent" by train and boat. I had the British beat in the new situation, and became friends also with former IMT leaders in the IMG including Alan Jones, Brian Grogan and Dodie Weppler.

Since Caroline and I went back to the United States every so often, I would also travel to Mexico for discussions with the Socialist League (LS), urging reunification with the Revolutionary Workers Party (PRT). I knew comrades from both sides fairly well as I had made many trips to Mexico in the preceding years. In regard to Portugal, as I explained in a previous chapter, the Portuguese pro-LTF group had been destroyed by the intervention of the Morenistas. In Canada, the IMT leaders had been in close touch with the Revolutionary Marxist Group (RMG), while the SWP was close to the League for Socialist Action/Ligue Socialiste Ouvriere (LSA/LSO, the LSO being the Quebec wing of the section).

In Australia, a small pro-IMT group developed during the fight outside the Australian SWP. There were steps taken by both groups to unify before the splits were healed in other countries.

In the United States, the Internationalist Tendency (IT) had split from the party in 1974, as explained in an earlier chapter. The International by majority vote considered them to still be a sympathizing group of the Fourth International, which was the same formal legal status of the SWP. (We didn't object to this decision.) They never did set up a public group of their own, but maintained that they were unjustly expelled. I'm convinced they took this stance under pressure from the IMT leaders, who correctly thought a small group could not challenge the SWP for political space on the left while maintaining ties to the Fourth International. In addition, the IMT wanted to fan the organizational flames against the SWP with the charge that the party was undemocratic. Some IT members then drifted away, discouraged because they had been looking forward to launching their own party as a sympathizing section, after what they believed would be a split in the Fourth International. The IMT "Self Criticism" and the subsequent dissolution of the factions dashed that hope.

There were former IT members who did want to reintegrate into the SWP after the factions dissolved. Formally, we welcomed these comrades to rejoin. But we insisted that each of them apply to rejoin as individuals, and not as a group. We made no provision to integrate their leaders into the Political Committee and National Committee. Admittedly, this procedure ran counter to what we were furthering in other countries. I believe how we handled the reintegration of the IT was a mistake. We should have approached the situation as we did the dissolution of the factions internationally, taking the lead in welcoming these comrades back into the SWP, with no preconditions. Looking back, this experience was evidence of a factional attitude creeping into the leadership of the party. I include myself, since I merely accepted this procedure without much thought.

Another thing we did in the Bureau was to attend the important meetings, including conventions and national committee gatherings of the sections. We decided that to emphasize the new situation in the Fourth International, we would be sure to send delegations that included representatives from both the ex-LTF and ex-IMT. From our side, this meant Caroline, Nita, Jim, or myself.

Another job of the Bureau was to prepare the meetings of the United Secretariat. We would put together the proposed agenda, prepare materials for the various points under discussion, propose reporters, and make practical arrangements. At this time these meetings would take place in Belgium, because of the possibility of members from outside France being denied entry into Paris.

The SWP apartment in Brussels was large with a number of fold-out beds. We were thus able to put up a dozen or so United Secretariat members. Jim, Nita, Caroline and I would arrive a day or so early to clean up the apartment. Jim was a good cook, and he and I would do a giant shopping to prepare big stews, salad fixings, potatoes and vegetables, desserts, wines, breakfast stuff, lunch meats and bread. Everyone was able if they wished to take sandwiches and fruit to the meetings. Some would instead go to restaurants for lunch. We cooked breakfast and the evening meals. Others would pitch in to do the dishes.

The real bottleneck was showers in the morning. The four of us would get up early to get our showers out of the way, and then wake the others for their showers while we set up the breakfast table and cooked. We always got everyone to the meetings on time.

The Italian section had always been weak, in spite of a favorable objective situation following the 1969 wave of strikes, factory occupations and demonstrations. It was true that the large Communist Party was an obstacle, but this was true in France, too, and the French LCR grew to be the strongest section in Europe. Many of the younger European comrades we were working with blamed the main leader of the Italian group, Livio Maitan, for this situation. In fact, Livio had ceased to be active in Italy and had joined the French LCR. He also came to United Secretariat meetings.

We learned that the Italian section was indeed a bit weird. For example, each branch had its own Control Commission with the power to expel. Sometime in the autumn of 1977, the Italian section had voted to dissolve itself. We discussed this in the Bureau. With the exception of Jim Percy, we decided to try to dissuade the section from carrying out this decision. Jim thought we should just let the section die, because it was in such bad shape. We informed the Italian leaders of our decision and asked them to hold off until we could send a delegation to talk to them. They agreed. We sent Caroline and Charles-André Udry. They began to go to Italy on a regular basis. Sometimes Nita or others would join them. One result of these trips was that Caroline would come back with new recipes for me to cook of Italian dishes she had tried on her visits. She also began to learn Italian.

---

* During the faction fight, the comrades in the majority began to publish *Inprecor*, as an alternative to *Intercontinental Press*. With the dissolution of the factions, both publications continued, but now as complimentary not competitive resources.

CHAPTER FOURTEEN: DISTURBING DEVELOPMENTS

At the end of 1977 Jack Barnes and Mary-Alice Waters came over to Europe for an expanded United Secretariat meeting. They stayed in our small apartment. They also visited Jim and Nita. Around this time Jim had raised with me that he thought he, Nita, Caroline and myself should meet together before Bureau meetings to work out a common position. I rejected this as completely contrary to the job we had to do in breaking down the old factional lines.

Jack and Mary-Alice came back from their meeting with Jim and Nita, and implied that Caroline and I were doing something wrong, without directly saying what. From hints, I gathered they agreed with Jim on two points, that we should have what amounted to faction meetings, and that it was a mistake to try to save the Italian section. I asked to have a meeting between Jack, Mary-Alice, Caroline and myself to get out in the open what they were only hinting at. They kept putting this meeting off, and finally left for New York without discussing with us.

This disturbed me for two reasons. First, Jack was hinting at reversing the position he argued previously, and which the SWP leadership and the LTF had adopted both on the issue of holding faction meetings and by taking what was a factional stance on the Italian section. Caroline and I rejected both positions. In fact, Caroline continued to make the trips to Italy, which were productive and gave the section a new lease on life with renewed vigor.

The second thing that disturbed me was the high-handed way Jack had treated us in avoiding a discussion on a major point. It made me think back about meetings of the Political Committee I had attended in the mid-1970s (when I was not away on international trips). I recalled that on a number of occasions a newer member of the Political Committee would be asked to make a report, but after the discussion proceeded awhile, Jack would take issue with the report. Actually, it was Jack's responsibility as National Secretary when asking a comrade to make a report, to go over it with him or her beforehand, not to sandbag them in the meeting itself. If something had to be corrected, he should take it up privately with the individual after the meeting. As can be imagined, the comrade involved was often embarrassed, flustered and as a result lost confidence.

Our tradition had always been to help newer members at any level of the organization to gain confidence as leaders. Jack's behavior cut across the grain of our leadership traditions as I had experienced them since first joining the SWP, as a new member of the Boston branch, as a YSA leader who consulted with the experienced party leaders, and as a new member of the Political Committee and National Committee. I had always been treated by the older comrades with respect and encouragement, and had tried to do the same in my role as a YSA and then party leader.

Early in 1978, Mary-Alice came over to a Bureau meeting alone. Caroline was away on a trip to Italy, and as we were riding the Metro on our way to the office, Mary-Alice told me over the noise of the train that she and Jack had broken up. She was shaken, and I suppose found it easier to give me the news this way rather than in private.

Later that evening as we were eating a dinner I had made of rabbit in wine, I raised how she and Jack had treated Caroline and I on their previous trip. She agreed it was untoward. I felt I could raise my more general concerns about how Jack had begun to act in the Political Committee. My thinking at that point was that Jack was functioning in a way I had never seen before, since I first met him in the early 1960s. In fact, his behavior was contrary to the way he had previously acted. He was "turning the PC into a one-man band" was how I put it to Mary-Alice. I didn't use the word "cult" because I thought Jack was making mistakes, not consciously furthering a cult of himself, and that it could be corrected. We talked late into the evening, and came to complete agreement.

I resolved to talk to Jack about the matter the next time I was in New York, which turned out to be at the February 1978 National Committee meeting. Charles-André Udry and John Ross were with me, and afterward we went up to Canada to further the reunification. While in New York, I asked Jack to have a private meeting, where I raised the discussion Mary-Alice and I had. I fully expected him to react by being somewhat shocked, but also to want to discuss how the situation could be corrected.

But after I had finished my somewhat lengthy remarks, Jack's only response was to say, "I can't imagine the SWP without you or Mary-Alice." That was all. The meeting was over. I was stunned by this threat to expel us if we took our criticisms any further. From that point on, I knew I would be pushed out one way or another, and although I tried to suppress the knowledge back into my unconscious it bubbled to the surface in the next years.

As far as Jim and Nita were concerned, the issues about Italy and meeting separately were forgotten, and we remained good friends and collaborators. We kept working as before together with the European comrades, especially the "two Charleses." We were successful in breaking down the old divisions in the Bureau and were discussing politics and organizational problems in a free and open manner, and most often came to agreement. We were also able to informally discuss the factional excesses that had occurred on each side in the past, and could now laugh at them. In late 1978 Nita went back to Australia to help out in the fusion of the two groups there.

Gus Horowitz and I crossed paths once in Mexico around this time. He was there for his work on the Latin America resolution for the Fourth International, and I to collaborate with the Socialist League (LS) and the Revolutionary Workers Party (PRT) concerning fusion. During a break, Gus and I went out to a wine bar for a snack. We began warily feeling each other out about the situation in the SWP. I knew he supported George Breitman's position on Cuba (see Part Two, Chapter Ten). Gus had the suspicion that perhaps this tendency wasn't being treated fairly. We found we agreed there were problems in the Political Committee along the lines that Mary-Alice and I had discussed. While we still thought the chances were remote for a full-fledged cult to develop in the party, the very fact that the subject was broached, and the word "cult" was used, is worth noting.

In December 1977, there had been a shake-up in the functioning of the Political Committee related to the separation of Jack Barnes from his companion Mary-Alice Waters. Jack had established a relationship with another woman. Soon after the February 1978 National Committee meeting, Barnes and his new companion decided to leave New York, and drove to California. They were on the road for a few months, and arrived finally in the San Francisco Bay Area, where comrades had helped set up an apartment for them in the house of an older comrade, Ray Sparrow. It seemed that Jack had decided to leave the center and his post as National Secretary. What he was going to do in California was not clear. He had avoided visiting SWP branches on the cities they drove through. They had been setting up their library in their new apartment when Mary-Alice flew out and had a private meeting with Jack. Subsequently, Jack decided to come back to New York, and he and his new companion made the trip back in July 1978.

Gus Horowitz and Becky Finch had been in Paris in 1976 and 1977, as SWP representatives to the United Secretariat of the Fourth International. When Gus returned to New York in September 1977, and resumed his elected position as a member of the Political Committee, he noticed a change in the atmosphere of the meetings. Jack had assumed a more domineering attitude, Gus later told me, and there was tension in the meetings. In the weeks when Jack had left for California, Gus noted, the PC meetings became more relaxed and comradely. Mary-Alice and Larry Seigle were functioning as a team to prepare the meetings, a duty of the National Secretary, and they encouraged full discussion and participation, a change from what Gus had discovered upon his return from Paris.

When Jack did return, Gus told me, he seemed "like a man on a mission." During his sojourn to and from California he apparently had some kind of epiphany, like Saul on the road to Damascus, and had seen the light illuminating the road forward for the SWP. Gus thought that some of the important policy changes that Jack was to introduce emanated from this whole period.

CHAPTER FIFTEEN: THE TURN TO INDUSTRY

Early in 1978, the party leadership proposed a major political "turn" or reorientation. This reorientation involved getting a "large majority" of the membership into industrial unions. A report by Jack Barnes to that effect was adopted enthusiastically by the National Committee on February 24, 1978.

The selected quotations below are from the printed (edited) version of the report. They highlight the political basis of the turn to industry.

"What we propose is a *political* move, not a hygienic or therapeutic move for the party. We are not doing this to cleanse the party of petty-bourgeois elements or any such nonsense. Our judgment that this political move is necessary and timely flows from the big changes in the situation facing the capitalist class on a world scale, the need of the American ruling class to drive forward their offensive, to more and more make the industrial workers and their unions the target. Our judgment flows from the changes in the attitudes of the working class in response to this offensive."

"We are still in a preparatory period—not a period when we are leading mass class-struggle actions. We must make no mistake about that. But it is a preparatory period in which the *center of American politics has shifted to the industrial working class*. That's the central political judgment we put before the [National Committee]."

"But one can't end there. Although we are not proposing this move for therapeutic or hygienic reasons, the question of the composition of the party poses a challenge. We will not become a party whose big majority are industrial workers automatically. It must be consciously *led* and it must be organized."

The report included the prediction that a political radicalization—not only a radicalization on economic issues—of the working class was in the immediate offing.

We were all aware that the composition of the party was a problem. The majority of the young people we had recruited in the radicalization of "The Sixties" and its aftermath in the 1970s had a student background, even if they mostly came from working class families. This was natural, since the center of the youth radicalization had been among students. When these members graduated or otherwise left campus, their training led them into "white collar" jobs such as teaching, social work and other government jobs, skilled technical work, and so forth. Our composition was disproportionably tilted toward this section of the working class. Of course, we had recruited some young industrial workers as the youth radicalization spread. Some students we recruited had also gotten industrial jobs.

The largest union fraction we had built was in the teachers' unions, comprising some 110 comrades. This fraction was led by Jeff Mackler and had done important work for over a decade in the left wing of the American Federation of Teachers (AFT) and the National Educational Association (NEA). In New York City one of our members, Ray Markey, had been elected president of the library workers in the American Federation of State, County and Municipal Employees (AFSCME). He was elected because he was a class struggle fighter. Both Mackler and Markey were members of the National Committee, in part because of their union work.

As Jack indicated in his report, "Saying we are going into industry doesn't mean we are demeaning our AFSCME or our teachers work. To the contrary, by building a more powerful proletarian party, better equipped, we will be strengthening this work, making it better, and increasing the rate of recruitment in it. We will build bigger and better fractions. If out of all this, five years from now, three years from now, two years from now, we don't have a bigger and more powerful teachers fraction, or an AFSCME fraction, due to recruitment and increasing influence, then we've messed up."

To make the point explicit, he added: "We are *not* deciding, by the way, to pull our national leaders out of AFSCME or the teachers. We would be out of our minds to pull Jeff out of the teachers....Ray is *the* spokesperson for a class–struggle, pro-independent political action opposition to the [bureaucracy] in AFSCME."[1]

In the discussion that followed, National Committee members fleshed out the report. Our comrades in industry would be wearing "three hats," as one member put it. First, they would be workers, becoming integrated into their workplaces and among their workmates. Second, they would be trade unionists, active in their unions. Three, they would be socialists on the job. They could do this because coming out of the radicalization of the 1960s-1970s, red-baiting had diminished effectiveness in most workplaces.

For some time we already had an established fraction in the railroad unions. Our steel fraction was also built up as a result of our work in the Fight Back campaign in the United Steelworkers (USWA). Soon we would also have a fraction in the United Mine Workers (UMWA).

In fact, this National Committee meeting was held during the historic UMWA strike of 1978. The victory of the Miners for Democracy group in democratizing the UMWA demonstrated the importance of union democracy in mobilizing the power of the rank-and-file. President Carter tried to force the coal miners back to work by invoking the "slave labor" Taft-Hartley act passed in 1947. The coal miners simply ignored Carter and Taft-Hartley. Technically, the miners were now criminals. But their collective power smashed this union-busting attempt, and they reached a contract with the coal bosses.

As a result of the turn, we rapidly built fractions in the International Association of Machinists (IAM), mainly in maintenance at the airlines, and the United Auto Workers (UAW). In December 1976, our steelworker comrades had held their first national fraction meeting. By the summer of 1979, over 100 SWP steelworkers were in the fraction.

We took some casualties in the coal mines in the South. A number of comrades in the UMWA were attacked by right-wing groups in the mines. It was clear they did this with the support of the mine owners. In one mine, two women SWP members and a Black woman miner had their cars and other property fire-bombed and otherwise vandalized. These three were singled out because they had fought the company to hire women. Company security and the local police looked the other way.

We learned that our miner comrades in the rural south had to be more cautious in "coming out" as socialists. There were white racists in the mines and hostility to hiring women. These types could be instigated and used by the bosses to create divisions in the workforce.

Our goal was to build fractions in select unions. We envisioned these fractions not just as a collection of SWP members in a given union or workplace, but organized along democratic lines. That is, the fractions would elect their own leaders, and would soon elect national fraction steering committees and organizers at national meetings. They would be subordinated to the elected political leaderships at the local and national level, but would have leeway in deciding their own activities and policies in their union work. In one report, Jack emphasized that the fractions would become parallel institutions to the branches and leading committees of the party. It was hoped that they would be training grounds for new party leaders rooted in their experiences as activists in industry and that this experience would be transferred to the party as a whole, enriching our overall work and campaigns. This could only develop if the fractions had enough freedom to talk through and decide their work, make mistakes, and go through a process of selecting their own leaders, without much outside interference from the other party institutions.

1 SWP Party Organizer, Vol. 2, No. 2, April 1978.

CHAPTER SIXTEEN: THE IRANIAN REVOLUTION

In 1978, demonstrations against the Shah of Iran swept the country in ever more powerful waves. Shah Reza Pahlavi had been installed in a CIA-backed coup in 1953 that overthrew the democratically elected nationalist regime of Mohammed Mossadeqh two years after it had nationalized the oil industry. The Shah's dictatorship was characterized by unbridled brutality, murder and torture. The hated political police, SAVAK, had been organized by the CIA and Israeli intelligence. There were tens of thousands of U.S. military personnel in Iran training the army and the Shah's elite Royal Guard. The jackboots of the United States were everywhere. The U.S. embassy, the final seat of authority, was huge, occupying a square city block. Iran was a bastion for Washington in the Middle East along with the garrison state of Israel. The Shah maintained close relations with the Zionist regime, in an alliance against the Arab countries and the Palestinian people. Bordering the USSR, Iran was also a high-tech U.S. listening post monitoring the Soviet Union.

Millions of migrants from the countryside, forced off the land, lived in the slums in southern Tehran. They had demanded the government provide services such as electricity, running water, sewer systems, health centers and transportation, but their pleas fell on deaf ears. The inhabitants resorted to tapping into electric and water lines. The regime had tried for some time to evict the settlers, and in the summer and fall of 1977 the shantytowns had become a violent battleground. The regime sent in demolition squads escorted by hundreds of paramilitary soldiers with dozens of bulldozers, trucks and military jeeps.

The people fought back with shovels, clubs, stones and anything else at hand. Government cars were set on fire and offices ransacked. Some demolition squad agents were killed. The authorities agreed to negotiations, and the Shah retreated and halted the demolitions in October. These millions of super-exploited people, most of whom were employed on and off again in industries such as construction, had struck the first blow in what would become an upsurge so powerful it would overthrow the Shah in less than two years.

Demonstrations against the US-backed despotism became larger and larger during 1978. In September, some 3-4 million took to the streets. The Shah responded by declaring martial law on September 8, unleashing murderous repression. Hundreds of unarmed demonstrators were gunned down in Tehran alone. Massacres occurred in other cities throughout the country. However, not only did the repression not crush the movement, it spurred millions more to take action.

During the year, weekly demonstrations following Friday prayers, and especially the commemorations after police and army massacres, became the calendar of ever more massive peaceful demonstrations. In Islamic tradition, there is a forty-day mourning period after a death. In the absence of any national organization, these dates provided the broad masses with a schedule for the next actions. In some instances, demonstrators would wrap themselves in white clothes, the Islamic burial dress, before going out, signifying their willingness to die.

On October 3, employees of the National Bank walked out and in a matter of hours all bank workers were on strike. They were followed by teachers, journalists, telegraph and postal workers, radio and television personnel, and then virtually all sectors including the industrial workforce. The oil workers were key, given the central role oil played in the Iranian economy. Thus began one of the most powerful general strikes in history, with both economic and political demands aimed at the regime. The oil workers, while shutting down production for export, kept up enough production for domestic use including gasoline and heating oil—vital in Iran's cold winters.

Mass demonstrations continued daily. Battles between the determined but unarmed populace and the police and army resulted in many casualties.

The Shah's renewed bloody repression was combined with concessions. Big wage increases were granted. Some of the thousands of political prisoners were released. But their stories of torture only fueled the rebellion. The despot also promised elections, but the general strike and the mass mobilizations continued.

As the regime crumbled, Washington reiterated its support. President Carter praised the Shah as a force for democracy. On November 5, the demonstrations exceeded even those in early September. The next day, the Shah appointed a military government. The State Department endorsed it and Carter, who had become a master of Orwellian doublespeak, said it was a step toward "liberalization."

However, behind the scenes, Washington was demoralized. "The military government is about the last card the shah has to play," one U.S. official told the *Washington Post*. "He doesn't know what to do next, and neither do we. It will be a miracle if he is still around to hold the elections he has promised."[2]

The Militant and *Intercontinental Press* covered the events weekly and extensively. We were aided greatly in this by Iranian militants in the United States who were drawn around the SWP in the 1960s and 1970s. The Iranian comrades were able to get through to people in the country, making our coverage lively. No other tendency on the left came near to matching our coverage.

•••

Iranian students in Europe and the United States formed the backbone of a worldwide Confederation of Iranian Students opposed to the Shah's dictatorship. It was led by Mossadeqh's National Front, a bourgeois nationalist movement, and Maoists. The latter, under the influence of Beijing's position in the Sino-Soviet conflict, had come to see the Soviet bloc and Cuba as the "main enemy" and to support Washington in the Cold War. The pro-Moscow Tudeh (Masses) Party was sidelined in terms of numbers and influence.

During the last decade of the Shah's rule, a current had developed among Iranian students in the United States that sought political independence from the National Front and the Stalinists of both the pro-Moscow and pro-Beijing varieties. This tendency published its own paper, *Payam Daneshjoo* (Student Correspondence). We in the SWP found opportunities to collaborate with the new current in the areas of civil liberties and anti-deportation campaigns in the face of U.S. government hostility. In this process, the Sattar League, a revolutionary socialist group, was formed. It developed a program for national liberation and socialism in Iran. While working closely with the SWP and the YSA, the Sattar League had its own democratic structure and elected leadership, and decided its positions autonomously.

Many ad-hoc activities in defense of Iranian political prisoners enabled the League and the SWP, together with Iranian intellectuals in exile, to form the Committee for Artistic and Intellectual Freedom in Iran (CAIFI). During the 1978 upsurge, CAIFI held meetings and demonstrations around the country to draw attention to the situation and to call for the United States to stop supporting the Shah.

Unfortunately, these activities were hampered by sectarian opposition from Maoist elements within the Confederation of Iranian Students. Fervent anti-Trotskyists, they physically attacked CAIFI meetings. The attacks were successfully repelled by defense guards organized in the main by the Sattar League along with the

SWP and YSA. Ultimately, however, the Maoists were successful in expelling *Payam Daneshjoo* supporters from the Confederation.

Both Moscow and Beijing fell over themselves to indicate their support to the Shah during the general strike. Soviet Premier Leonid Brezhnev sent the Shah birthday greetings on October 26, 1978, addressed to "Your majesty Mohammed Reza Pahlavi, the light of the Aryans, king of kings of Iran"! (The Shah liked to refer to himself as the "Shah an Shah"—"king of kings.") In a fall visit to Tehran, Chinese Premier Hua Kuo-feng hailed the Shah, shaking the despot's hand in a photo-op. Both Stalinist regimes were seeking favor with Washington. One result was the paltry coverage of the anti-Shah upsurge in the pro-Moscow and pro-Beijing newspapers.

In addition to the Sattar League in the United States, there developed a group of Iranian supporters of the Fourth International in Europe. The two groups were in touch, and projected a course toward unity. The Sattar League had helped publish *Payam Daneshjoo* for five years as a monthly. Babak Zahraie, the central leader of the Sattar League, told *The Militant* that it would begin publishing weekly. The paper "is the most widely circulated Iranian publication abroad," he said. "Before the military government, there were five articles in a row in the uncensored daily press in Iran about Iranian papers abroad. Every one of them mentioned *Payam Daneshjoo.*"[3] The European comrades had been publishing *Kandokav* (Search). Unity would mean the merger of the two publications.

Carter began to hint of direct U.S. military intervention if the Shah fell. This alarmed the Kremlin. Even though he supported the Shah, Brezhnev issued a sharp warning on November 19: "It should be clear that any intervention, and still more any military intervention in the affairs of Iran—a country that borders directly on the USSR—would be regarded as affecting the interests of the security of the USSR."[4]

The Iranian masses knew that their struggle was against not only the Shah, but also U.S. imperialism. The Shah was a U.S. puppet who administered pro-imperialist policies to the detriment of the Iranian people. The draining of Iran's oil wealth was one aspect of this policy. Another was the Shah's agricultural policy (dubbed the "White Revolution") favoring big farms growing crops for the imperialist-dominated world market. Peasants were driven off the land, crowding into the cities to become impoverished workers going from one low paying job to another, and sometimes going back to the land for a time. These workers, tens of millions, retained family and other ties to the peasants in the countryside. It was no wonder that the peasants began to join the struggle with their own demands for land, better prices for their produce and so forth.

Within Iran the majority were Persian, their language Farsi. In addition, there were many oppressed nationalities. One of the largest was the Turkish-speaking peoples of the province of Azerbaijan. Another was the Kurds. The Arab southwest was a center of the oil workers. Turkmens had ties to people in Soviet Turkmenistan. Baluch nationalities in the east extended into Pakistan and Afghanistan. The Shah had severely repressed these peoples, who totaled in the millions. The anti-Shah rebellion in these areas also became struggles for their liberation from Persian oppression. Often, they were in the vanguard of the movement. For example, in one of the initial anti-Shah actions, in February 1978, demonstrators had temporarily seized control of Tabriz in Azerbaijan.

•••

The Iranian revolution combined the fight for *Azadi* (freedom or political democracy), a key slogan of the demonstrations, for the rights and living standards of the workers, for the interests of the peasantry, and for the freedom of the oppressed nationalities, with a fight against U.S. imperialism expressed in the historic demand for *Esteghlal* (independence). *Azadi* and *Esteghlal* are revolutionary demands that go back to the onset of the revolutionary national awakening of Iran at the beginning of the 20th century.

While the working people were the base of the rebellion, they lacked a mass political party to fight for their interests. The oldest left party, the pro-Moscow Tudeh party, had been discredited by its failure in 1953 to fight the imperialist-backed coup. It had also supported the Shah's White Revolution and his governments in the early 1960s. At the time, the Soviet bureaucracy had reached an accord with the Shah. Pro-Moscow parties around the world and in the United States hailed the Shah's regime as "progressive."

The Maoist groups were small reflections of organizations that had grown in the United States and Europe. The Fedayeen and Mujahadeen were groups formed in Iran with sizable followings. They looked to the Palestinian resistance as a model and had waged guerrilla armed struggle against the regime. The Fedayeen was built by youth supporters of the Tudeh Party in the decade after the 1953 coup. They had concluded that armed struggle was the missing strategy that allowed the victory of the coup without a battle. The central leaders of this tendency were either killed during armed actions or were condemned to execution by military tribunals. Their founder, Bijan Jazani, was among ten members murdered by the SAVAK while serving long prison terms.

The Mujahadeen, known as a left Islamist group, had their roots in the National Front and a religious splinter of the Front called Nehzat Azadi. They were for an Islamic government without the clergy. Armed struggle gave them a more militant stance than more traditional Islamic groups. Their central leaders, like those of the Fedayeen, had been eliminated by the regime. They also suffered internal purges leading to the physical annihilation of some of their leaders by others who had become Maoists. These murders were lauded by many Maoists abroad.

The Fedayeen and Mujahadeen each had at most a few thousand supporters by the time of the 1978 upsurge.

•••

It was the Islamic clergy, however, that stepped into the leadership vacuum. Notably, the Shah had allowed the mosques to function during his rule even as he shut down all other institutions and organizations that could become potential centers of opposition. He was forced to do this because to take on the religious establishment directly would have made it impossible for him to consolidate his rule after the 1953 coup. The coalition that was built to carry out the coup focused instead on destroying the communists, terrorizing the working people, and co-opting former oppositionists. This was in line with Washington's line internationally in the Cold War. Thus it was natural that the mosques would become centers of organization of the rebellion.

The more secular bourgeois nationalists, while opposing the Shah, sought an accommodation. They had formulated a policy to safeguard what they defined as the three pillars of Iran—the Shah, the army, and the support of the United States. However, they sought to replace the Shah's absolute monarchy with a constitutional monarchy, much like Britain's parliamentary system under its monarch.

The most popular opponent of the Shah was the Ayatollah Ruholla Khomeini. He had supported an unsuccessful uprising against the Shah in 1963, leading to his forced exile, first in Baghdad and then in Paris. In exile, Khomeini maintained contact with the young clergy in the mosques, largely by smuggling in tapes of his speeches. His prestige grew during the rebellion because of his consistent opposition to the regime, in contrast to most of the clergy higher-ups who sought a compromise with the Shah. While many of the best-known leaders of the clergy were in prison, the lesser-known younger members of the clergy in the mosques were pro-Khomeini and stood for abolishing the monarchy.

Khomeini had formulated his ideas about an Islamic Republic in writings after the 1953 coup. In these he polemicized against Marxism and the Tudeh Party, which had been strong before the coup. Thus it was no surprise that while he uncompromisingly opposed the Shah and the monarchy, he would not further the other aspirations of the workers, peasants and oppressed nationalities that came to the fore in the uprising.

However, during the 1978 uprising, Khomeini's weekly addresses played in the mosques supporting the general strike and urging the demonstrators to continue their protests and to attempt to win the soldiers to their side. Because of his uncompromising stance, Khomeini became the symbol of the anti-Shah fight.

Demonstrations on December 10 and 11 were the largest to date. David Frankel reported in *The Militant*:

"Opposition leaders asserted that 7 million protesters—*one fifth of the country's population*—marched in opposition to the regime on December 10.... CBS News estimated that 1.5 million marched in Tehran alone. 'The sheer weight of numbers of the procession took even seasoned observers by surprise,' Tony Allaway reported in the December 11 *[Christian Science] Monitor*. 'More than a quarter of Tehran's population had turned out to register their protest.'

"Although the shah had threatened to ruthlessly suppress the December 10 and 11 protests, the determination of the masses forced him to back down. Clearly, he was afraid that the army would crack if ordered to fire on such throngs....

"According to wire service reports, numerous placards demanded: 'US imperialists pull out of Iran.' Students insisted that reporters 'tell Jimmy Carter we want democracy and not a royal tyrant.'

"One demonstrator told Allaway: 'It is wrong that we hate foreigners. That is the government telling lies so that the foreigners will hate us.... All we want is to tell the Americans that we don't want their Shah anymore and we want the Americans and British to stop stealing our oil.'"5

On January 16, 1979, the Shah fled, following other members of his family into exile. The country erupted in celebration. Just before his precipitous exit, the Shah appointed Shahpur Bakhtiar as the new prime minister.

Reporting from Tehran in *The New York Times*, Nicholas Gage wrote: "The streets, nearly empty during recent days of strike and gasoline shortages, were quickly clogged with automobiles that added the sound of horns to the din, as people threw flowers at soldiers, who seemed to share their high spirits. The cacophony of celebration continued all afternoon and well into the evening."

The next day, members of the Sattar League and supporters of *Payam Daneshjoo* began to return to Iran, as did the European comrades. The Bureau of the United Secretariat of the Fourth International decided to send me and Brian Grogan to Iran. Brian was a leader of the International Marxist Group in Britain, and had been a supporter of the IMT. This was in keeping with our practice of teaming former members of the LTF and IMT on international assignments. One of our objectives was to facilitate the unification of the two Iranian groups. Before we could get there, a strike by Iran Air employees blocked commercial flights. However, the SWP was able to send Cindy Jaquith in under the wire to begin reporting firsthand for *The Militant*.

Cindy Jaquith reported that Bakhtiar had launched a "bloody crackdown against the movement" following an announcement by Khomeini on January 25 that he was flying in from Paris the next day. Iran Air employees announced they would end their strike for one day to allow Khomeini to arrive.

As Jaquith noted:

"The army then surrounded the airport with tanks and closed it down. Angry students demonstrated the next day at Tehran University. They were met with army machine guns that killed more than 100.... The blood of slain students was still on the streets when 1 million people poured out here today [January 27] to vent their anger at the Bakhtiar regime.

"As I join the march, demonstrators are chanting, 'my brother, you are gone, but we will continue.' Along with other journalists I am swept along in a sea of humanity down the street where the students died.

"To our left is a contingent of 1,000 women, all in black veils, with raised fists. Women are nearly half the demonstration. These sisters chant: 'It is good the students and workers are getting together.'

"Behind them are signs denouncing Jimmy Carter and Shahpur Bakhtiar. 'Death to Carter, the shah, and Shahpur' is a popular slogan. 'If Khomeini comes late, we will kill you Bakhtiar,' is another.

"Word passes quickly through the crowd that 160 airmen were executed this morning for mutiny. 'Oh you airmen, you are the light of our eyes,' the demonstrators shout.

"This demonstration has been organized overnight by supporters of Khomeini. It coincides with the traditionally observed anniversary of the death of the prophet Mohammad. Many of the slogans combine religious and political messages. The focus is on the massacre of the students, the call for an Islamic republic, and the demand that Khomeini be allowed to return."[6]

On January 22, the comrades of the Sattar League held a news conference attended by all the daily press and most foreign journalists to announce the formation of a new party in Iran, the Hezb-e Kargaran-e Sosialist [HKS–Socialist Workers Party]. Babak Zahraie gave an overview of the party's program, which supported the demands of the workers and peasants and called for a workers and peasants government to replace the government beholden to the capitalists and imperialists. The program included among its demands for freedom and democracy full rights for women and the oppressed nationalities. The central immediate demand was for an elected constituent assembly to draft a new constitution. The full program, called the "Bill of Rights of Iranian Working People," was printed and distributed by the thousands. It became a reference point for leaders of all tendencies released from prison.

Comrades from the HKS accompanied Jaquith and translated for her. When Grogan and I arrived, we were similarly escorted by our cothinkers.

Subsequently, Bakhtiar was forced to retreat and allow Khomeini's return on February 1. The day before, a flight of journalists was allowed in. Brian Grogan and I were on that flight. As we approached the airport, I saw a fighter jet come alongside us, very close, but it apparently had orders not to interfere. After we landed I was surprised that there were no customs or border officials—they were on strike. HKS members were joking with baggage handlers and we were whisked away and taken to the Intercontinental Hotel.

•••

The next morning we watched a live broadcast on the TV in our room of the arrival of Khomeini's plane and the beginning of his drive into the city. There were throngs along the route. Suddenly, the newscast was cut off, and the Iranian flag filled the screen accompanied by military music. If this was designed to prevent people from observing Khomeini's return, it backfired when the disappointed viewers rushed out to swell the throng. HKS comrades came for us and we joined the massive demonstration, crushed into a side street. We were looked at somewhat askance as the Yankee and Brit we were. Our comrades explained in Farsi that we were against Carter, and the mood changed instantly. Scowls became broad smiles. One family brought us into their house and up onto the roof where we got a good view of the massive crowd. Girls of the family, smiling shyly, brought us tea and sweets.

When the cars carrying Khomeini and his entourage passed, the crowd broke up. We went out into the street with our HKS friends, into a crush of people. An old man shook his fist in my face, and said in halting English, "Shah finished!" before it could be explained that we were on his side. The swirl of the crowd whisked him away.

The next days were spent by Brian and I with leaders of the HKS and some European supporters of the Fourth International, negotiating a fusion of the groups. We met mostly in homes and apartments vacated by parents of members. These were in better off sections of the city—not the most rich, but reflecting the middle class of professionals who generally feared the revolution even though their children had become revolutionists as students abroad. Cindy was often in these meetings, although she actually spent much of her time out in the streets observing the demonstrations and the continuing battles between the people and the armed forces.

One such confrontation she told us about was an attempt by Bakhtiar to crush an action of tens of thousands of demonstrators. The prime minister had sent tanks into the streets. These were huge British Chieftain tanks that roared along at high speeds, smashing and riding over parked cars, firing at demonstrators with artillery and high-powered machine guns. Many of the white-dressed protesters were killed or wounded, but the crowd continued to fight back. One tactic was for a group to hold up steel I-beams gathered from construction sites, and charge the tanks. While many were killed in the charges, they were replaced by others. Those who got through used the I-beams to smash the tanks' treads. The immobilized tanks could still fire on the people, but many demonstrators could get close enough to set the tanks on fire with Molotov cocktails. The soldiers inside would either be baked to death or forced to flee into the crowd and be killed.

I went on a demonstration at a plaza featuring a large monument called Shahyad (Shah's Remembrance—later changed to Azadi) on the road from the airport to the city. There were hundreds of thousands of people—there was no way I could get an accurate number. There were big contingents of women dressed in the *chador* (veil), a black garment from head to toe with only the face showing. Suddenly an American-made fighter jet roared low overhead. The noise was terrific, and I flinched. The crowd just shook their fists at the plane in defiance. I was impressed by the women dressed in black shouting their anger with raised fists.

Brian and I were put in an empty apartment by our comrades. While we were there and discussing with HKS members one night, they overheard the concierge of the building calling SAVAK about us, saying we were suspicious. That a concierge would do this was not uncommon in the police state. They often were employed as eyes and ears for the hated institution. It was after 9 p.m., there was a 10 o'clock curfew, and the army would open fire on anyone in the streets after that. It was necessary for us to get out of there and to a safe place quickly. There were no safe homes close by. Babak's brother Siamak was one of those in the apartment with us, and he had a jeep. We got in and Siamak drove across town at high speed. Tehran is a sprawling city, like Los Angeles and we made it in the nick of time to the home of the parents of Kateh Vafadari, Babak's companion and a leader of the HKS.

At night, masses of people went to their rooftops, chanting "Allah Akbar"—God is Great—effectively breaking the curfew. The monarchy and army top brass were becoming more and more isolated in face of the strike and demonstrations, which were producing deep fissures in the ruling circles.

During the day, Brian and I continued to meet with leaders of the two groups. A formula for unification was agreed upon. A person we knew as Hormuz became the national chairman of the unified group and Babak became the editor of the new newspaper. It was agreed to keep the name HKS. At my suggestion, the unified newspaper was called *Kagar—The Worker*. This name, while a good one to project the HKS' politics, did not have the connotation it did in the United States, where for decades it was the name of the Communist Party (CP) paper.

•••

Upon his return Khomeini appointed his own cabinet with Mehdi Bazargan as prime minister, in opposition to the Bakhtiar-led military regime. Bazargan had served as the head of the oil industry after its nationalization by the National Front government of Mossadegh. Although the National Front no longer played much of a role, Bazargan represented a religious wing of the Front called Nehzat Azadi. On February 8, there were demonstrations in support of the Bazargan cabinet against the Bakhtiar regime. In Tehran, one million marched.

Joining the action was a contingent of 1,000 airmen from the Doshan Tappeh airbase. During 1978, homofars (mechanics) at air bases around the country had begun to organize and hold demonstrations of their own. At the Doshan Tappeh base the next day, February 9, homofar trainees staged a demonstration. It was attacked by the Royal Guards, who inflicted many casualties. On February 10 the homofars themselves, who did not live on the base, returned to work and saw the carnage. They refused to work and started demonstrating. The Royal Guard attacked with tanks, machine-gunning everyone they could.

The civilian population around the base came to the homofars' aid. The airmen raided the base armory to get guns, arming themselves and distributing guns to civilians outside. Everyone on the base, knowing that the Royal Guard intended to kill everybody, joined the action—even the elite Green Berets. Women and children attacked the tanks with Molotov cocktails, setting some on fire. The homofars inside the base were joined by civilians firing on the Guards outside. The Guards were driven back block by block, the homofars and civilians building barricades as they advanced.

As we were being driven to and from our meetings, we noticed cars with white flags, some bloody, that had handmade scrawls on their doors indicating they were ambulances. We didn't know it at the time, but these were taking the wounded from the battle to hospitals. The army was no longer in control of the streets. The insurrection had begun although no one knew it, and attacks on army, police, Royal Guard and SAVAK headquarters spread.

We were eating with comrades in a restaurant when about 2 p.m. a waiter came over and told us that the army had moved the curfew up from 10 p.m. to 4 p.m. We hurriedly drove back to the apartment we were meeting in. At four o'clock we all went up to the roof. We could hear from everywhere shouts of "Allah Akbar." A military helicopter flew overhead, firing. We ducked for cover in the stairwell. When it was gone, we went back out. We could see fires and burning tires to the south, in the huge slums of the poorest section of town. Later we would learn that the masses in the south had openly defied the curfew and come out into the streets.

In the face of this show of force by millions, the army cracked. The high command issued a notice that the army would no longer attack the people. The army disintegrated, and the soldiers joined the people. The Bakhtiar government was overthrown.

The next day we awoke to the sound of car horns blaring. We drove out into the street, joining cars honking with their lights on, in celebration of the victory. We were swept along with cars converging on an armory. When we got there we saw people taking automatic rifles, machine guns, bazookas and other arms.

Battles continued two more days against holdout SAVAK and police headquarters. People from the guerrilla groups Fedayeen and Muhajadeen were joined by many other armed civilians. Over 1,000 revolutionists were killed in these final operations.

During these last battles, I went with comrades to a square near an army hospital. Wounded and bandaged soldiers were milling with the crowd. When told who I was, they crowded around, wanting to tell their stories. One joyfully said "I'm so happy we are finally with the people!" Just then a rumor swept the crowd that a SAVAK force was descending on the square. The rumor was false, but the crowd ran in all directions. I got separated from my Iranian friends. I did not have any addresses, and could not speak the language. I spent some anxious moments before I was found.

•••

The Tehran insurrection rapidly spread throughout the country following the stand-down by the army.

During the insurrection the state television station had been taken over by anti-Shah journalists. The station became an organizing center of the struggle, directing fighters to pockets of resistance, based on reports the station received from the field. Following the victory, it broadcast reports of further actions by armed groups of citizens taking control of the city.

Driving with comrades at night, we came across roadblocks at every major intersection; militants stopped cars and questioned their occupants in the search for supporters of the overthrown regime who might be trying to regroup. After explaining who we were and that we had no weapons, we were waved through. Neighborhood committees formed during the revolution manned these roadblocks. In the general strike they distributed scarce supplies, dealt with health problems, and carried out some self-defense activities. They armed themselves during the insurrection.

Air traffic was halted to try to prevent top figures in the old regime from escaping. This had the effect of keeping us. in the country, too.

We had been telephoning the United States to transmit our stories. Jaquith wrote the articles with help from the Iranian comrades, who had their own first-hand sources and translated from the daily press. I would go over the articles. Also present were journalists from *International Viewpoint, Rouge* (the paper of the French Revolutionary Communist League (LCR)), and from *Informations Ouvrières* (Workers' News), published by another French Trotskyist organization. We all collaborated.

Shortly after the insurrection, we were in the apartment of a friend of the LCR who was living in Tehran. We planned to telephone in a joint article to be shared by all these newspapers in addition to *Intercontinental Press* and *The Militant*. But the phones were not working. We didn't know it then, but international telephone service had been cut to block communications by Shah supporters with their international backers. This apartment was located on a street where many of the foreign embassies were. Suddenly, the street was raked by sustained heavy machine gun fire. We had become used to the sound of automatic rifles, but these guns were using high caliber ammunition, and it was loud. Some bullets hit bars on a window where we were. We were pinned down, and couldn't get out. This was the most frightening time of my stay.

When the firing stopped, comrades were able to get through and get us out of there. We soon saw on TV that the real target of the counter-revolutionaries was not anything in our location—those shots had been a diversion—but the TV station itself, which was coming under heavy fire from three surrounding hilltops. We could hear the gunfire over the TV. The announcer appealed to "armed people" to come down to the TV station. Immediately, we heard a commotion on the street below and saw cars heading for the station. Confronted by large numbers of armed civilians, the attackers fled.

We also witnessed on TV the SAVAK torture chambers that the people were uncovering. These were truly horrifying. One was a room with electrical equipment where people were given electric shocks. In a blood-stained room were a woman's bra and panties on the floor—the CIA-trained goons hadn't had time to clean up as they fled before people found the site. Another was of a small closet-like room, where the walls could be heated to scorching temperatures. Human skin was still stuck to the walls.

One complex was found almost by accident, when people noticed air vents coming up from the ground next to a steel mill. A tunnel was found leading to a prison complex, with people still inside, where "suspect" steel workers had been sent for interrogation and confinement.

The Khomeini-Bazargan government found itself in power through an insurrection it had neither called nor wanted. "The Iman [Khomeini] himself couldn't have predicted this," one person on the street told the press.

The new government was under immense pressure to meet the demands of the people. To divert mass anger, it put on trial some of the hated officials of SAVAK, the Royal Guard and the army who had been captured. They were quickly shot. The trials were held in secret at Khomeini's compound behind closed doors. Thus the facts of their connections with the United States as well as the full extent of their knowledge of the crimes of the Shah's regime and its connections to the state bureaucrats now under the new government were kept secret.

I went down to Khomeini's compound during one of these trials. People who sought justice were also there. I met a young person who spoke English. He had been a law student when arrested by SAVAK.

He showed me his crooked arm, which had been broken in multiple places. The bones healed at unnatural angles while he was imprisoned. He wanted to testify, as did others there and many more, but they were not allowed into the trials.

I learned from him and others that the Shah's regime had begun arresting anyone wearing hiking boots. Anti-Shah students had formed groups to climb the mountains overlooking Tehran where they could meet and discuss, away from the listening devices of the totalitarian regime.

•••

The new government wanted to keep intact as much of the old state apparatus as it could.

Once phones were working again, Cindy Jaquith sent in a report. "...[S]ince taking office, the new government has carried out no social or democratic reforms," she wrote. "In line with the bankers, businessmen and landlords this government is responsible to, Bazargan has been preoccupied with trying to restore capitalist law and order.

"The workers, on the other hand, returned to the job with the opposite goal in mind. Their attitude is: 'We've gotten rid of the shah and his U.S. advisors. So now the factories belong to us. *We* will run them from now on, through our own democratically elected bodies.'..."

Workers did begin to elect their own committees. Bazargan went on TV to counter this trend.

As Jaquith went on to report:

"It's all right if workers form committees that play a 'consultative role' in decision making, Bazargan said. But there is a 'dangerous logic' if the workers begin thinking they should elect their own leadership—either at the factory level or higher.

"After all, he explained, if workers elect representatives to run the factories, why not elect representatives to run the cities? And if workers are to decide who runs the cities, why not elect the representatives that run the provinces and the central government as well. For that matter, why not elect the leader of the revolution itself?

"'Ah, but this cannot be,' Bazargan insisted, 'for we have our national leader—Imam Khomeini....' The next night another glum-faced representative of the government appeared on television to lecture viewers on workers' control of industry. 'The workers want to control the factories, what is produced and how,' he complained. 'But this is against all laws of commerce and capitalism. In fact, it is the exact opposite of our system.'"7

The Bazargan government was weak. He was not a popular figure. He was seen by the masses as tilting toward the West. He made repeated appeals for the revolution to stop, to allow the new government to consolidate. The real decision maker was Khomeini—either in his own name or in the name of the Islamic Revolutionary Committee, a ruling council set up by Khomeini and Bazargan. Khomeini had gone to the holy city of Qum, saying he trusted his representative on the Committee, Ayatollah Morteza Motahari, the youngest and most erudite among the clergy, in disputes on the Committee. Bazargan soon asked Khomeini to come back, however. Thus, Khomeini became the arbiter among the contending factions.

Jaquith's report analyzed Khomeini's unique leadership role:

"Because of his uncompromising stand against the shah throughout his exile and upon his return to Iran—while members of his newly-appointed cabinet wavered on the monarchy—Khomeini earned the respect of the Iranian masses. The new regime is now banking on his past record to bring those same masses into line.

"Thus it was Khomeini, not Bazargan, who called on civilians to turn in their arms after the insurrection, telling the masses it was a 'sin' to hold onto their guns. It was Khomeini who ordered the banning of all demonstrations. And it is Khomeini who has launched the sharpest attacks on those advocating democratic rights, labeling them 'antirevolutionary'....

"Wherever possible, Khomeini has sought to use the Islamic Revolutionary Committee to absorb the independent committees that have sprung up, or to take over the leadership of these committees where necessary.

"No one knows who is on the Islamic Revolutionary Committee, which has been centered in Tehran. Its meetings are secret. Similar committees have been set up in other major cities, where they appear to play the same role of directing local government."8

It should be noted that while Khomeini was the figure publicly issuing these attacks on democracy and the masses, the Bazargan wing of the government fully supported them.

The community committees retained their arms. The regime sought to confront this danger to restoring "law and order" by incorporating these armed contingents into a new National Guard.

But as one "Western expert" quoted in the March 5 *U.S. News and World Report* put it, "This country has tasted revolution. The

Ayatollah may find that stopping one is much harder than starting it."

We went on a demonstration in support of democratic rights. It was attacked by Khomeini supporters who had been told it was a counter-revolutionary action fomented by the BBC. Suddenly some armed youths in the keffiyeh scarf made popular by the Palestinian fighters and adopted by the Fedayeen appeared on the rooftops, scaring off the attackers. At the same time, workers drinking tea in a nearby tea bar, pulled the foreigners inside to protect us. Through our interpreters, they expressed support for the demonstration, and we had a congenial discussion until they decided the coast was clear and we could go out.

In a week or so air travel was restored. Cindy Jaquith and I flew out with the French comrades to Paris. After staying over one night, we went back to New York, where I was reunited with Caroline. On March 4, Cindy and I addressed a large meeting on the revolution in New York.

•••

The HKS continued organizing in Iran. Its newspaper *Kargar* called for the "development, extension and coordination of the democratic committees of the toiling masses in the factories and offices, in the armed forces and in the neighborhoods." The HKS also raised the issues of equal rights for women and freedom for the oppressed nationalities.

The HKS began a campaign for its right to function openly and for the democratic rights of all political parties. On March 2 the campaign was launched at a rally of 2,000 at the Polytechnic University. In addition to students, those attending included a busload of workers from a cement factory as well as autoworkers from a General Motors plant and the Iran National auto factory.

A Maoist sect had put up posters a day earlier denouncing Babak Zahraie and revolutionary poet Reza Baraheni as CIA agents. Baraheni had been a leading figure in CAIFI. The Maoists chained the gates of the University. The crowd began to chant "The chains belong to SAVAK!"

Ten armed representatives of the Islamic Revolutionary Committee arrived. They said the socialists had a right to hold their meeting, and that the gates should be opened. But they refused to defend the meeting and they left. Maoist goons attempted to start a fight with the rally defense guards. To prevent a confrontation, the monitors allowed one of the thugs to speak. He launched into a diatribe again accusing Zahraie and Baraheni of being CIA agents.

He demanded the crowd leave. When no one did, he left the podium hailing "the great Stalin."

The disrupters, who were from various Maoist groups, brandished switchblades. The rally organizers decided to discontinue the meeting in order to protect the crowd. The disruption was reported the next morning on the front page of the daily *Ayandegan*, and became part of a broader discussion of democratic rights. Still calling themselves communists, the Maoists had become part of the government's attack on democratic rights, another expression of the degeneration of this current.[9]

•••

The HKS also initiated an Ad Hoc International Women's Day Committee to hold a celebration on March 8 of the international holiday. Kateh Vafadari was the head of the committee. Women handing out leaflets for the meeting were harassed and threatened with violence. In response to the women's demand that the Islamic Revolutionary Committee defend their right to hold a planning meeting on March 3, two armed guards were sent. When about 70 thugs armed with knives broke into the meeting, one of the guards lowered his automatic rifle at the thugs and said, "you take one step closer and I'll shoot you." The attackers retreated, but the women decided they couldn't continue their meeting. As they marched outside, the angriest were the women workers. Many wore the *chador*. Raising their fists at the goons, they shouted, "We went in front of tanks! Do you think we are afraid of you?"

There were several rallies on March 8 and thousands attended them. "What sparked the outpouring in Iran," *The Militant* reported, "was a March 7 statement by Ayatollah Ruholla Khomeini that female government workers could not go 'naked' to work" but must wear the chador. "The government had also made statements against equal rights for women in divorce, against coeducation, abortion, and laws outlawing polygamy." The Ad Hoc Committee changed its name to the Committee to Defend Women's Rights.

As *The Militant* report noted:

"High school women took the lead in the big demonstration that followed these rallies. Thousands of these students had gone on strike that day for women's equality. Some 20,000 women marched from Tehran University to the offices of Prime Minister Mehdi Bazargan, denouncing government attacks on women's rights....

"Rightist goons attacked the marchers [but were unable to disperse the march]. But on March 10, 7,000 women returned to protest, holding a sit-in at the Justice Department. They were joined by a march of 10,000 women....

"Public employees struck to protest government attacks on equal rights. Nurses, high school teachers, and women in the ministries of agriculture and foreign affairs walked out. Women workers at Iran Air issued a statement that the only veil women need is 'a veil of purity in their hearts.'"[10]

Mark Harris remembers *NBC News* covered the march, and he recognized one of the women speakers from when she was a member of the Sattar League.

Rightist thugs continued their attacks. As *The Militant* reported, "On March 11, women activists held a news conference to declare they would not be intimidated by violence. Speaking for the Committee to Defend Women's Rights, Kateh Vafadari announced there would be another rally the next day. She demanded that the Bazargan government halt the attacks on women protesters."

Present at these meetings and demonstrations was Kate Millett, an American feminist scholar and author of *Sexual Politics*, one of the most influential feminist books to emerge from "The Sixties." She had also worked with the SWP and the Sattar League in CAIFI. She came to Iran at the invitation of CAIFI and the Ad Hoc Committee. Millett chronicled her experiences in a book, *Going to Iran.*

Millett described Kateh Vafadari's presentation at the news conference as she faced pro-Shah Western "reporters" and other hecklers.

"Her hands tremble, she goes on with bravery and with polish; one sees only the courage and beauty, the ardor, the youth. 'We are calling on all women, all Iranian women, and on our brothers who are in support of our democratic rights, to come out tomorrow in the streets of Tehran.' I remember her forbearance when she told me late last night by the hotel desk that the Fedayeen did not see their way to protect our demonstrations. Nor the Muhajadeen. 'But we need this coalition of leftists and women.'

"'Of course, but we will also go it alone when we have to....' Kateh determined. Kateh intoning now the translation, the official statement. 'We all want to unite, with veil or without veil. They are trying to separate us; they are trying to put us against each other. We all fought together, all the men and the women with all different ideas, all different beliefs--against the tyranny. *We* threw out the

Shah. Today we don't want anybody to separate us. There is freedom if all the Iranians are free, both men and women. '"[11]

The Militant reported:

"Fifteen thousand turned out for the March 12 rally at Tehran University. A few speakers urged the crowd to refrain from more demonstrations, as right-wing hecklers shouted that women were 'creating havoc and anarchy and trying to create divisions within the revolution.'

"But speakers from the Committee to Defend Women's Rights argued that women must stay in the streets until their demands are won. The crowd voted with its feet, marching out onto Shah Reza Avenue.

"Bank workers, hospital workers, students and teachers participated. There was a contingent of radio and television workers there to protest the firing of women in the media and government censorship.

"Women students and nurses waved from their buildings as the march passed by. The demonstrators chanted: 'To deny women freedom is to deny freedom to the rest of society.'

"In the face of these unprecedented mobilizations, the government has been badly shaken. Khomeini retreated on his statement about the *chador*, saying that wearing it is a 'duty' not an 'order.'

"United Press International also reported that Khomeini disavowed those attacking the demonstrators *and warned them of 'harsh punishment' unless they stopped their assaults."*[12]

The government would impose the chador little by little. By June of the following year, it became compulsory for all women working in the public sector.

•••

The government decided to call a referendum for or against an Islamic Republic, as one prong of its attempt to put a lid on the masses. It also began to use remnants of the army that had survived the insurrection in some cities outside Tehran. These were now under the control of the Khomeini-Bazargan government.

Gerry Foley was sent to Iran as a reporter for *Intercontinental Press* and *The Militant*. His articles were picked up by Fourth International publications around the world.

Foley wrote:

"By the third week of March, the reactionary offensive of the authorities had gone as far as a military attack on the Kurdish people, resulting in hundreds of deaths.

"The central government was not able to extend its authority to Kurdistan after the insurrection.... The people have kept their weapons and give their allegiance to Kurdish-controlled committees. As an oppressed nationality, they are demanding the right to set up their own local government.

"Fearful of solidarity with the Kurds, the government has carried out its operation in Kurdistan as secretly as possible. Nevertheless, reports reaching Tehran tell of helicopter gunships and heavy weapons being used against the crowds in [the Kurdish city of] Sanandj.

"In the Azerbaijani towns bordering Kurdistan, tens of thousands have reportedly demonstrated against the massacre of their sisters and brothers."

Foley gave a thumb-nail sketch of the struggle on the ground.

"The process of organization among the masses that began in the fight against the shah has not been broken off. It continues to give political life to the organizations that remain from the period of the insurrection, such as the neighborhood defense committees, although these have been brought under the tutelage of the religious hierarchy.

"In most of these organizations, there was little consciousness of the need for class independence. As a result the religious leaders were able to assert their control over the local groups through coordinating committees—the so-called Imam's committees.... The committees are not elected, but are chosen through a combination of appointment and co-option. The local and factory committees have been subjected to a process of purging and to introduction of right-wing elements, including former SAVAK agents.

"The features and contradictions of this process are well-illustrated in Ahwaz. Harassment and intimidation of left activists by the Imam's committees have been widespread in the last few weeks. But this has been particularly intense in this hub of the oil industry and has focused on the Iranian Socialist Workers Party (HKS) branch in that city. Its members report that they are continually arrested by the local committees, often several times a day. They are taken to committee headquarters and threatened. They are followed by members of the central Imam's committee and committee cars are stationed in front of their homes. They are subjected to physical attacks.

"But when they are taken in front of the committees and subjected to anticommunist inquisitions, they are able to argue with the groups and sometimes make such an impression on the members that the red-hunters have to back off. On some occasions they have been able to win over members of the committee to their political views."[13]

The referendum for or against an Islamic Republic was held March 30-31. The "yes" won, but the referendum did not create general enthusiasm. Foley reported that the Kurds and Turkmenis (another oppressed nationality) did not vote nor did a large percentage of the Arabs in Khuzestan. The government claimed an overwhelming turnout, but Foley, observing the polling stations in Tehran, thought the official figures were inflated. However, a large section of the population in the Persian areas did vote "yes," he reported.

The pro-Moscow Tudeh Party urged a "yes" vote, a position echoed by the CP in the United States. Writing in the March 21 *Daily World,* Tom Foley said, "The Tudeh Party in its statement declared its support for the Ayatollah Ruhollah Khomeini and for the creation of an Islamic Republic." In the same issue it smeared the big women's demonstrations: "...the question of the behind the scenes hand of the CIA cannot help but be raised. It [the demonstrations] has the stamp of their typical handiwork: utilize a legitimate demand in order to disrupt the revolutionary process." The HKS, too small to mount a boycott campaign, said the vote was undemocratic and explained that the content of an "Islamic Republic" was unknown and left up in the air.

Shortly after the vote, Bazargan attacked those opposed to the vote, singling out the Trotskyists. Following his address there was stepped up harassment from the Imam's committees of activists selling *Kagar.* One woman comrade was badly beaten in Ahwaz.

Abolhassan Bani-Sadr, a theoretician and finance minister of the regime, challenged the Marxist groups to debate him. Only the HKS accepted the challenge, as the others shied away from talking publicly about socialism. The debate was held on national television on April 11, with Babak Zahraie speaking for the HKS. An estimated 22 million watched.

Bani-Sadr "could come up with little more than vague formulas" Foley reported, "and he was obviously floundering about."

By contrast, Zahraie offered concrete immediate solutions to the burning questions of unemployment, inflation, food shortages and so on, linking these to steps to attack the backwardness of Iranian agriculture.

As Foley noted:

"The favorite formula of the Muslim politicians is that the Islamic Republic means national independence. Zahraie demolished that point by showing how the Bazargan government is doing nothing to combat the wrecking of the economy by the big imperialist corporations. He contrasted this passivity with the bold moves the Castro leadership took in Cuba to break the power of the imperialists and rebuild the economy....

"The two major Iranian dailies, *Kayan* and *Ettela'at* ran the full text of the debate along with editorials about the importance of public discussion of these problems.

"There has been a wave of sympathy with the HKS. This has, for example, forced the Imam's committee in Ahwaz to back away from its persecution of Trotskyist activists.

"There are many reports of workers in the plants saying that Zahraie said exactly what was on their minds.

"Even many Tudeh (Communist) Party members have called Zahraie to congratulate him for raising the voice of socialism in the country as it never has been raised before. And rank and file members of some of the sectarian Maoist groups, which in the past have disrupted HKS meetings and called the Trotskyists CIA agents and traitors, are now coming to the HKS to apologize for their actions."[14]

The Tudeh Party published an article after the debate entitled "Trotskyism, Handmaiden of Imperialism." In it the Stalinists denounced not only the HKS but the national radio-TV network for airing the debate. It accused the network of "helping to mislead the people," "besmirching socialism," "dimming the luster and weakening the attractive power of scientific socialism," and promoting "division, confusion and deviation among the revolutionary forces."

No further televised debates were held.

There were big demonstrations on May 1, May Day. The *New York Times* reported May 2 that "the call for marches and rallies to mark the traditional workers' holiday was first issued by leftist groups. However, in recent days, the call was taken up by the religious revolutionary leadership in an apparent attempt to reduce its leftist content."

Foley described the mass demonstrations for our press:

"Unfortunately, the mobilization of working people in Tehran was not united or on a clear class basis. There were several demonstrations. The two largest were called by the Islamic Republican Party led by Khomeini's ideologist Bani-Sadr and by the

Coordinating Committee.... One to two hundred thousand persons participated in each. The Coordinating Committee, an attempt to set up embryonic unions, was dominated by the Fedayeen.

"In addition, tens of thousands of persons attended a rally called by the Mujahadeen-e Khalq.... And the Stalinist Tudeh Party held its own much smaller rally.

"The Islamic Republican Party leaders tried to tried to turn the demonstration they called in a rightist direction. Groups of rightists within it raised anticommunist slogans. But large numbers of working people also shouted demands for the nationalization of industry. The Iranian Trotskyists sold their paper on this demonstration, getting a generally friendly reception."[15]

On May 30, there was another debate between Bani-Sadr and Zahraie at the Teachers Institute in Tehran, on the topic, "Property, National Independence, and the State." Some 70,000 attended the outdoor meeting. On June 1, Zahraie was scheduled to speak at the University of Tabriz in Azerbaijan Province. Seven thousand gathered for the meeting, but the organizers decided to postpone it when a gang of about 100 hoodlums showed up, armed with knives, swords and revolvers. Comrades reported that the disruption became a topic of discussion in the streets. Residents expressed their outrage at the attack on freedom of speech. When one of the thugs returned to his house, a crowd of neighbors surrounded him and demanded he get out of the city because he had "besmirched the good name of Tabriz." However, a month later Zahraie spoke to 6,000 at a rally organized by the HKS in the port city of Anzali on the Caspian Sea, the hub of the Gilak nationality and language.

Gerry Foley visited Turkmenistan and Kurdistan. (His impressive facility with languages helped him communicate with many Iranian peoples.) The army had pulled back from its initial assault on Kurdistan, and there was an uneasy truce there and in Turkmenistan. In both places, the general leadership view, he reported, was that "revolutionary fortresses can be built among the oppressed nationalities, and after that revolutionists can sit back in those areas and wait for the revolution to advance in the rest of the country." This proved to be a dangerous illusion.

The Khomeini regime played on the racist fears of the Persian majority to oppose the demands of the oppressed minorities.

These included the Arabs in Khuzestan. Fred Murphy wrote in *The Militant*:

"Strikes and mass demonstrations by thousands of Arabs in Khuzestan province, which contains Iran's main port and oil-producing centers, have sparked a crackdown by the capitalist Khomeini-Bazargan government. The aim is to disarm revolutionary-minded workers there and crush their protests for national and trade union rights....

"Customs workers in Khorramshahr—the majority of whom are Arabs—began a strike in mid-May for higher wages and recognition of their union. On May 29 a right-wing gang fired on the striking workers, wounding two.

"At around the same time some twenty steelworkers leaders were arrested in Ahwaz, and a central Arab leader of the oil workers council there was seized and taken to Tehran.

"On May 30, elite units of the Iranian navy launched predawn assaults on two Arab cultural centers in Khorramshahr, where Arab activists had been conducting sit-ins in support for their demands for national autonomy and cultural rights.

"An Arab cultural center in Ahwaz was also attacked and occupied by military forces of the central government on May 30, and a wave of arrests was launched against Trotskyist supporters of the Arab struggle...."

There were more attacks, and the "Arabs resisted, and fighting spread to other parts of Khorramshahr and to the neighboring oil-refining center of Abadan.... The central police station in Khorramshahr, the post office, a government tobacco factory, and various stores and shops were set afire."[16]

In another report, Cindy Jaquith wrote:

"As 200 oil workers began a strike and sit-in demanding the release of their leaders in jail in Ahwaz, Iran, pressure intensified on the Khomeini-Bazargan government to free the hundreds of worker militants imprisoned in Khuzestan Province since late May.

"The mass arrests occurred during the wave of protests by Arabs for their national and cultural rights in the province....

"Among those jailed were three members of the oil workers council, some twenty steelworkers, and nine members of the Hezb-e Karagan-e Sosialist, the Iranian section of the Fourth International.

"Two of the HKS members, Omid Mirbaha and Mohammed Poorkahvaz, are being held in Karoun prison along with the three oil workers leaders—Javad Khatemi, Nasar Hayati, and Shobeyr Moiyo—and others. The oil workers and HKS members are on a hunger strike...."

"Prominent writers and intellectuals in Iran, with long records as anti-shah fighters, have joined the campaign to free the HKS members and the oil worker leaders."[17]

•••

Members of the Fourth International began an international campaign to free the HKS members and oil workers, enlisting protests from prominent people. In France, these included the feminist writer Simone de Beauvoir and the head of the Socialist Party. The president of the New Zealand Labour Party, the chair of the Danish Federation of Transport and General Workers, the Danish Metalworkers Federation and Office Workers were among the many joining the campaign from around the world. In Paris, 1,000 demonstrated at the Iranian embassy, and a delegation from the LCR, the OCI, the League for Human Rights and trade unions entered the embassy to meet with officials. In Sri Lanka, Bala Tampoe, a leader of the FI and general secretary of the Ceylon Mercantile Union, sent a letter to Barzagan. Protests were pouring in from around the world.

In the United States we went on a similar campaign, enlisting unionists, Palestinian fighters, clergy, civil libertarians and many more. In New York, we organized a picket of the Iranian embassy.

On June 29 more than 50,000 people attended a rally in Tehran, called by the Fedayeen to honor guerrillas killed in the struggle against the Shah. The gathering also called for the release of the more than 40 members of the Fedayeen imprisoned by the Khomeini-Barzagan regime. Although the Fedayeen were sectarian opponents of the Trotskyists, one speaker called for the release of the HKS members.

At the request of the International Federation for the Rights of Man in France, two lawyers, Mourad Oussedik and Michel Zavrian, went to Iran to make inquiries about the HKS prisoners. The international and domestic campaign clearly was having a big impact. After much bureaucratic evasion, the Ministry of Justice authorized the lawyers to visit the prisoners.

Their report, published in *Informations Ouvrières* and translated in *The Militant* and *Intercontinental Press*, detailed the horrible conditions and brutality meted out in the prison where the 14 were held. From what they saw and heard, the lawyers concluded that there were three categories of prisoners. One was "those who can be called the 'indeterminates,' arrested without the slightest reason" and without charges. The second were the Arab prisoners. "The only charge against them is being Arabs." They were brutally tortured."

As the lawyers' report documented:

"For them the exactions of the old regime, based on the local feudal rulers continue, oppressing them both economically and socially. The same feudal rulers are today allied with the officials of the new regime.

"The third category is the militants of the Socialist Workers Party [HKS]. We were able to talk with them. All have suffered brutal treatment.... The sole proposal that has been made to them is that they would be released if they would sign a written statement recanting their views—an offer they have rejected for obvious reasons. Their political maturity, their refusal to compromise, and the influence they have won over their fellow prisoners through their dignified comportment and their solidarity have won them the hatred of the Islamic Committee...."[18]

Repeated demonstrations and sit-ins, including a mass demonstration of 30,000 on July 10 in Ahwaz, demanded the release of Arab prisoners and the withdrawal of government troops enforcing martial law in Khuzestan. These troops were drawn from Persian-dominated cities in the north of the province, stirred up by government lies about "Arab terrorists" that played to the racism and fears of the Persian majority.

Repression against the Arabs in Khuzestan took a sharp escalation when the Khomeini-Bazargan government shot five Arab prisoners on July 27. This was the first time since the overthrow of the Shah that anti-Shah fighters were executed.

Two weeks earlier there were the first reported clashes between government troops and Azerbaijani armed committees in the town of Meshkinshahr.

The oppressed minorities had been in the forefront of the anti-Shah movement. The government crackdown on them reflected a fear that the movements for national rights by these oppressed peoples could link up with increasing workers' struggles throughout Iran, including among the Persian majority.

One Iranian banker told a *Washington Post* reporter that the labor force "was in a state of rebellion" and that industrialists "spend all their time trying to placate rebellious workers who have unrealistic expectations under the new regime." He said that "workers want housing, more meal allowances, longer vacations, profit sharing and say they want to run the company." Armed revolutionary committees have prevented many companies from laying workers off, and in some cases have forced the rehiring of fired workers, the reporter said.[19]

Under this pressure, Bazargan announced the nationalization of some major industries on July 5—a victory for the workers.

But at the same time, the repression became more generalized. "Confronted with rapidly mounting struggles by the Iranian masses to defend and extend the gains of their revolution," Gerry Foley wrote, "the Khomeini-Bazargan government has launched a major crackdown aimed at smashing all opposition. The crackdown occurs in the context of a sharpening of class battles and a polarization on all fronts in the country—from national and peasant struggles, to protests in factories and the armed forces, to deepening opposition to press censorship and curtailment of democratic rights."[20]

On August 18, Khomeini announced his intention to turn Iran into a one-party state. He launched a furious campaign to whip up chauvinism against the Kurds, calling for a "holy war" against them. Leftist newspapers were banned, including *Kargar*. Twenty-six papers in all were shut down, including some pro-capitalist publications. Public meetings and demonstrations were banned. The central leaders of left groups all went underground.

On August 26, twelve of the imprisoned HKS members were sentenced to death after a secret trial, and two others, women, to life imprisonment. The accused were denied any legal representation and the right to call witnesses or even to speak in their own defense.

The HKS went on a campaign to stop the executions. In the United States we mobilized the party and YSA, based on our pre-existing campaign, to reach out to wider forces. Our co-thinkers around the world did likewise. Telegrams poured into the government, there were demonstrations at Iranian embassies, and other forms of protest from Britain to Japan, from Canada to Argentina, and countries in between. Many were reported in the major Tehran dailies.

The powerful campaign blocked the government from immediately carrying out the executions. The Iranian embassy in Washington, where we had helped organize demonstrations, even denied that any verdict had been reached against the 14, reflecting the impact of the worldwide protests. The embassy's press release included absurd charges against the HKS prisoners such as "carrying out anti-people activities; the blowing up of an oil pipeline; creating chaos and disorder; instigating and encouraging people to participate in armed warfare against the central government, and so on." A pipeline *had* been blown up—when the 14 were in prison. The HKS was well known for its opposition to acts of terrorism. The charges, when not ridiculously vague, were transparent lies.

The U.S. SWP launched a "Committee to Save the Iranian 14," which immediately garnered broad support among trade union officials, figures in the Black and Chicano movements, prominent writers such as Noam Chomsky, human rights fighters, and many more.

•••

Despite the repression, the Iranian revolution continued to deepen, as workers, peasants and oppressed nationalities mounted increased struggles in the latter part of 1979. Khomeini's "holy war" against the Kurds was met with increasing resistance.

A report by Fred Feldman in *The Militant* described the deepening struggle:

"A new popular uprising is taking place in the cities and villages of Kurdistan, which were occupied by government troops and Pasdaran (Islamic Revolutionary Guards). As of October 21, fighters were reported to be in control of most of Mehabad [the capital of Kurdistan] including the army barracks.

"The regime failed to maintain the chauvinist fervor it tried to whip up against the Kurds. Slogans have appeared and meetings in solidarity with the Kurds' just demands have taken place at some universities.

"A representative of the 'Imam's office' in Qum, who was sent to Kurdistan to investigate the situation, has publicly denounced the massacres perpetrated against the Kurdish people.... He pointed to the slaughter of the entire population of the village of Gharna—more than eighty people—as an example.

"Land seizures in southern Kurdistan—which Khomeini sought to crush with his anti-Kurdish drive—have continued and spread to the southern districts of neighboring Azerbaijan."[21]

Popular resistance to repressive measures was reflected in a conference of Islamic judges held in Qum in October. Many of them expressed opposition to arrests without charges, executions for violations of "morality," and right-wing hooliganism.

The government backed down on some of its repressive measures. On October 10, Khomeini declared a moratorium on executions. The outlawing of newspapers was lifted, and publications of the left wing organizations began to reappear, including *Kargar*.

On October 20, the Committee to Defend Political Prisoners, which the HKS had helped to establish, held a news conference to demand the freeing of 1,500 political prisoners, most of them in Kurdistan and Khuzestan.

At a news conference called by the HKS on October 21, Babak Zahraie revealed that the HKS prisoners, twelve of them still under threat of execution, were being brutalized and denied access to radio, newspapers and visitors. Three of them were being denied needed medical treatment. Zahraie demanded an end to this mistreatment and the transfer of the prisoners to Tehran. The HKS also called for a review of the cases in an open letter to the head of the Islamic Revolutionary courts. Two major dailies reported the conference on their front pages, one under the headline "Socialists Imprisoned for Beliefs."

There was no attempt by rightist thugs to disrupt either news conference, in contrast to the free rein given to these gangs in the summer. A rally of 10,000 called by the Tudeh Party also took place without any attacks.

In the Caspian seaport of Bandar-e-Enzeli, *The Militant*'s Fred Feldman reported, thousands of fishermen protested a government ban on plying their trade, an attempt by the government to guarantee a monopoly of state-owned fisheries.

Feldman wrote:

"Ten people were killed October 16 when the Pasdaran fired on a protest of 5,000 to 10,000 people. Fighting spread throughout the city and demonstrations grew, demanding the punishment of the Pasdaran. The police headquarters was burned to the ground. A demonstration of 10,000 took place in the neighboring city of Rasht."

In response, the government lifted the ban.

"Two members of the HKS were arrested during the demonstrations in Bandar-e-Enzeli and questioned by the Pasdaran. One of the socialists had run an election campaign for the local city council, in which the HKS also backed independent fishermen candidates.

"After talking to the guards about their politics, the HKS members were able to win over some of the Pasdaran. The government not only had to release the socialists, but had to order them expelled from the barracks where they were continuing to hold discussions with the Pasdaran.

The nationalization of many industries in July led workers to believe that "if the factories belong to us, then we should be the ones to decide how they are run," the HKS reported to *The Militant*.

Shoras, or factory committees, began to be set up. The late Ayatollah Taleghani, the highest-ranking clergyman in Tehran, was said to have called for such *shoras* shortly before his death. The *shoras* varied from plant to plant. In some, pro-government employees and more conservative technicians had the upper hand, while in others production workers were increasingly playing a dominant role. The *shoras* spread to cities outside Tehran and to privately owned companies.

In General Motors, the *shora* ordered cuts in the salaries of overpaid administrators, while tripling the wages of the lowest paid workers. Company files were opened. Workers began to demand control of the GM plants when their contracts with their U.S. owners expired in late 1979. Oil workers resisted a decree that they had to work six days a week.

Divisions among Iran's new rulers about what to do in the face of these renewed struggles of the masses came sharply to the fore, along fault lines that had been there all along. It was later learned that the powerful Islamic Revolutionary Committee was initially composed of four "hats" and four "turbans"—the "hats" from the Bazargan wing of the old National Front, and the "turbans" obviously from the clergy. While others from each side were subsequently added, the divisions remained. Bazargan sought to maintain the old army in alliance with the US. In fact, he had proposed that U.S. military advisors be brought back, against opposition from Khomeini. Divisions arose over the imposition of the chador on women, which the clergy pushed.

Bazargan came from a tendency that wanted an Islamic government without the clergy; Khomeini wanted to safeguard the clergy as the leading power in the Islamic Republic. The stage was set for provocations, assassinations, bombings and executions at the top. One example early on was the assassination on May 1, 1979 of Khomeini acolyte Motahari, a young theologian on the original Islamic Revolutionary Committee, by a former political prisoner under the Shah.

Faced with the new upsurge in struggles, Bazargan and his allies resigned. Khomeini appointed Bani-Sadr as the new prime minister.

Thinking that these divisions could mean an opening to attack the revolution, Carter made a provocative move against the Iranian people. He brought the Shah into the United States from his exile in Mexico. When the Shah fled Iran he was under the protection of Washington, but Carter at that time thought it best that the despot be lodged elsewhere to deflect criticism of the U.S. role in installing and maintaining his brutal regime. Now, the Iranian people were outraged, and demanded that Carter turn over the Shah so he could stand trial for his crimes.

On November 4, a group of Islamic students held a sit-in at the U.S. embassy in Tehran, demanding the Shah's return. Initially, they had no intention of trying to occupy the embassy. But thousands of people came down to support the students, who were inspired to go further and occupy what they called the "nest of spies." Embassy personnel were held as hostages against any U.S. attempt to physically re-take the facility. The students did release the women and a Black marine. Khomeini came out in support of the students, a move that encouraged massive actions to demand the return of the Shah.

Carter used this event to begin to whip up anti-Iranian sentiment in the U.S. population in preparation for war. This became a crude racist campaign in the press, depicting all Iranians as bloodthirsty religious fanatics. Ugly cartoons appeared. Administration lies about alleged mistreatment of the embassy personnel became screaming headlines in the gutter press, while other media added a more "respectable" veneer to the campaign.

"An American intervention force probably would be drawn from what Secretary of Defense Harold Brown has designated the Rapid Deployment Forces—approximately 110,000 men and women drawn from all four services," a reporter for the *New York Times* wrote in its November 7 issue. "An airdrop to seize the embassy and Tehran's airport would be possible, qualified sources said."

On November 10, Carter ordered all Iranian students to report to the nearest Immigration and Naturalization Service office for possible deportation. On November 12 he ordered a halt to all oil imports from Iran, while the Pentagon mobilized 2,700 soldiers for "readiness maneuvers" at Fort Hood, Texas. On November 13, U.S. and British warships steamed into the Arabian Sea south of Iran and began rehearsals of simulated air-to-air combat, air-to-sea attacks, surveillance by patrol aircraft, and carrier landings.

Carter declared a state of emergency on November 14 and froze all Iranian government assets in the United States, seizing some $12 billion of Iranian property. TV stations showed clips of the Japanese attack on the U.S. military station in Pearl Harbor, Hawaii, in 1941— a ridiculous comparison. Democratic and Republican politicians fell over themselves to get on the war bandwagon. Andrew Pulley and Matilde Zimmermann, the SWP candidates for President and Vice-President, immediately issued a press release under the headline "Stop War Threat: Send Back Shah!"

Iran issued a statement on November 13 offering to negotiate, and proposing an international investigation into the crimes of the

Shah and the return of billions he stole from the country. This offer was brushed off by the administration.

The SWP did what it could to oppose the threat of war through its election campaigns, forums and sales of *The Militant*. Our task was to tell the truth about the history of U.S. imperialism's role in Iran and about the revolution. We were fighting against the stream, as Washington's chauvinist propaganda made headway among the American people. We knew, however, that in the wake of the Vietnam War the U.S. population was very leery of a new war and that if one was launched it would soon become unpopular. Opposition to the war began to appear in public statements.

Many others on the left were disoriented by the ruling class's campaign and were swept up in its wake. Another factor was that many had turned against the revolution, conflating the Khomeini leadership with the revolution itself in the belief that the Iranian masses were rightist religious fanatics. In this they echoed the propaganda that the Shah's regime was better than the revolution that overthrew it. They did not share the position of Marx and Lenin, who supported every struggle of the oppressed peoples against their imperialist oppressors unconditionally—that is, no matter what their leadership.

A few in the SWP and YSA were also affected by the jingoist pressure, and dropped out because of our uncompromising stand.

Struggles of the oppressed have often taken on religious garb in history, including in the United States—for example, among the Black leaders of slave revolts such as Nat Turner; the abolitionists including John Brown; Malcolm X and Martin Luther King. The HKS and the U.S. SWP supported every progressive step Khomeini made, and opposed every regressive thing his government did. Above all, we supported the fight of the Iranian masses against imperialism, including in the belly of the beast.

In Iran, the HKS reported that day after day tens of thousands of jubilant demonstrators assembled in the streets—contingents of construction workers, teachers, air force cadets, university and high school students, army troops, women, old men and children. HKS members were there every day with the masses, selling *Kagar*.

The new upsurge, as in the days of the insurrection, brought back solidarity of all the anti-Shah and anti-imperialist forces. The situation of the HKS prisoners was better, as demands began to be raised for the release of all political prisoners. The HKS 14 themselves sent a letter to the authorities asking for their release so they could join the struggle. On November 27, two of the prisoners were released. By mid-April 1980, all the prisoners had been released, including the two women.

On November 21, the day after Carter announced that the U.S. naval force in the Arabian Sea was on its way to the Iranian cost in the Persian Gulf, two million people massed in the streets of Tehran. Two days later, thousands of oil workers traveled to Tehran to express their support.

On November 26, Khomeini called on every young Iranian to take up arms to defend the country from a U.S. attack. Arms began to be distributed and training in their use began.

Kurdish leaders, who had defeated the government assault against the Kurdish people, called for a united stand against Washington. The other oppressed nationalities also joined the growing united front of resistance, while intensifying their struggle for their rights at the same time. *Kagar* carried a front-page headline calling for "unity in the trenches against imperialism."

The students occupying the U.S. embassy began to release documents they found proving their charge that the embassy was indeed a "nest of spies," and was plotting against the revolution. These documents were reprinted and widely circulated, deepening mass anti-imperialist sentiment, but were suppressed or given short shrift in the U.S. capitalist press.

The U.S. SWP, together with the National Emergency Civil Liberties Committee, filed a lawsuit on November 21 to stop the mass deportations of Iranian students rounded up by the Immigration authorities. The American Civil Liberties Union filed a separate lawsuit, which was merged with the SWP-ECLC suit. On December 11 a federal district judge ruled in favor of the suit. This was a big blow to the war drive.

We sent Cindy Jaquith back to Iran to report first-hand. She wrote:

"You can tell we are approaching the U.S. embassy as we drive along Ayatollah Taleghani Avenue as the walls are increasingly covered with banners, posters, and spray-painted slogans. As we get to the corner of the embassy compound a giant banner hangs from a pole, depicting U.S. imperialism as an octopus with its tentacles reaching out all over the world....

"The students are anxious to let the American people know they are fighting the U.S. war machine, not U.S. citizens. Thus another big sign reads: 'Our enemy is the Americans' government, not their nation.'...

"Through a translator I introduce myself to a woman running [the students' information] table and show her a *Militant*. She looks at the front-page story on growing U.S. opposition to Carter's war threats.

"'I am very pleased to meet you,' she says, shaking my hand. 'As the Imam has said we are not against the American people.'

"The women goes behind the table into a tent and returns with a new set of embassy files the students have just released. She gives me these and copies of all the students' statements to the media.

"We walk further down the street to look at the banners that workers, soldiers, peasants, and students have hung from the walls and trees to show solidarity with the fight against U.S. imperialism...."[22]

The Militant published an article by an HKS member in Tabriz, the largest city in Azerbaijan. On December 13 the largest demonstration the city of 1.3 million had ever seen drew people from all over Azerbaijan. The demonstrators' demands centered on their national rights, but also against government slanders that the Azerbaijanis did not support the anti-imperialist struggle. In fact, the U.S. consulate in Tabriz was occupied by students and renamed the Palestinian Consulate. The slanders stopped.

The government began to make conciliatory moves with the Azerbaijanis and the Kurds. Negotiations with the Kurdish leaders began in a quest to end the hostilities.

In November, I attended the World Congress of the Fourth International in Belgium. Some time earlier, a Swiss leader of the Fourth International, Charles-André Udry, had traveled to Iran with me. Gerry Foley also joined us. In consultation with the HKS, we had written a resolution on the Iranian revolution for submission to the sections of the International in preparation for the World Congress. The resolution was adopted by a large majority. The Congress also issued a statement in solidarity with Iran against Washington's war threats.

The huge mobilizations continued as 1979 drew to a close.

1 Asef Bayat, *Street Politics: Poor People's Movements in Iran* (Columbia University Press, 1997), pp. 29-49.

2 Quoted in *The Militant*, Nov. 17, 1978.

3 *The Militant*, Nov. 24, 1978.

4 *Pravda*, quoted in translation in *The Militant*, Dec. 15, 1978.

5 *The Militant*, Dec. 22, 1978.

6 Ibid., Feb. 9, 1979.

7 Ibid., March 9, 1979.

8 Ibid.

9 Ibid., March 16, 1979.

10 Ibid.
11 Kate Millett, *Going to Iran*, (Coward, McCann and Geoghegan, 1982), p. 165.
12 *The Militant*, March 23, 1979.
13 Ibid., April 6, 1979.
14 Ibid., April 27, 1979.
15 Ibid., May 18, 1979.
16 Ibid., June 15, 1979.
17 Ibid., June 29, 1979.
18 Ibid., Sept. 14, 1979.
19 Quoted in *The Militant*, July 27, 1979.
20 Ibid., Aug. 31, 1979.
21 Ibid., Nov. 2, 1979.
23 Ibid., Dec. 28, 1979.

CHAPTER SEVENTEEN: REVOLUTION IN NICARAGUA

In July 1979 there was another blow to U.S. imperialism. In the wake of the Iranian revolution the workers and peasants of Nicaragua, led by the Sandinista National Liberation Front (FSLN), overthrew the Somoza dictatorship. U.S. Marines had installed Anastasio Somoza as dictator in 1933. Power passed to his son Luiz and then to Anastasio, Jr., who was finally brought down by guerrilla warfare combined with urban insurrections in the country's cities. The FSLN's overthrow of Somoza was the lone victory by any of the many guerrilla movements throughout Latin America inspired by the Cuban Revolution of 1959.

The FSLN took its name from Augusto César Sandino, who led a six-year war against the U.S. Marines that, with a few interruptions, had occupied Nicaragua beginning in the early 20th century. Washington imposed governments of its choosing in this period. In 1927, Sandino, a general in the army, revolted when the United States imposed one of its client regimes. He came from plebian roots, and looked to the workers and peasants as the driving forces of the struggle for national liberation. Historian Matilde Zimmermann, who ran as the SWP candidate for Vice President in 1980, would later write, "The efforts of Sandino's peasant army, combined with growing opposition to the intervention inside the United States, led to the withdrawal of American troops in 1933. Sandino was assassinated in 1934 at the orders of Anastasio Somoza Garcia, the commander of a new US-trained military force called the Guardia Nacional [National Guard]."[1]

There were two bourgeois parties in the country, the Somocista Liberals and the tolerated opposition in the Conservative Party. Sometimes conflicts between these forces led to short-lived armed actions, but the National Guard ensured Somoza's tight grip on power and much of the economy. In the late 1950s there were attempts at armed struggles against the regime. A young student leader, Carlos Fonseca, took part in one of these armed initiatives. The Cuban Revolution of 1959 was having a profound impact throughout Latin America and Fonseca became a revolutionary socialist under the influence of the Revolution. He had first joined the Nicaraguan pro-Moscow party, but broke with the Stalinist conception that the anti-Somoza revolution had to be led by the nationalist bourgeoisie, and that revolutionists (and the workers and peasants) should therefore subordinate themselves to the bourgeois opposition.

Fonseca set out trying to duplicate the Cuban victory in his own country and in 1962 formed the FSLN as a guerrilla organization in the mountains of northern Nicaragua. Fonseca was the Front's central leader and wrote its main programmatic document, which became known as the "Historic Program." This program combined the struggle for national independence of Sandino with the lessons of the Cuban Revolution, recognizing that only the workers and peasants would lead a revolution that would not only overthrow the dictatorship, but open the way to a fundamental change in society in their interests.

The FSLN scored some victories and defeats in the coming years, mostly defeats. The National Guard killed and imprisoned many FSLN cadres, and at times the Front was reduced to a handful in Nicaragua with leaders in exile in Cuba or Costa Rica. In 1976, Fonseca himself was killed after he returned to Nicaragua from exile to join the guerrilla band. He and the FSLN had become well known in the country by this time as anti-Somoza fighters.

At the end of 1974, after a period of quiescence, the FSLN launched renewed armed struggle in the mountains. On Christmas day the FSLN launched a spectacular action in the capital of Managua. They "broke the silence" by invading a diplomatic reception and seizing many leading figures in the regime. They freed their hostages only when Somoza agreed to free political prisoners and provide the fighters with safe passage out of the country.

In response, Somoza launched a ferocious crackdown.

As Zimmermann explains in her excellent book, *Carlos Fonseca and the Nicaraguan Revolution,* "The government immediately declared a state of siege and launched a wave of repression that resulted in three thousand deaths. The first targets were radical students, workers, and Catholic activists in the cities, but the majority of victims were campesinos suspected of aiding the guerrillas. The massive counterinsurgency drive in the countryside that succeeded in killing Carlos Fonseca also involved dropping bombs and napalm on settlements, burning peasant homes and fields, and disappearances, rapes, and incarceration in concentration camps. As news of this terror reached the cities, the desire to rid the nation of Somoza acquired new urgency, especially among the lower classes...but also among middle-class Nicaraguans."

The Somozas had not ruled exclusively by violence, Zimmermann notes. They "had generally been able to convince significant sections of the population of their right to rule, through a combination of power sharing [with the Conservatives], economic policies that benefited the bourgeoisie as a whole, and populist appeals to workers. The repression of 1975 and 1976 seriously undermined the idea that Somoza had a moral right to govern Nicaragua or that he could continue to do so with any measure of stability. The increasing visibility of the FSLN, in spite of the repression, gave the bourgeois opposition yet another reason to hate Somoza. That government terror was spawning revolutionaries was as least as objectionable to them as Somoza's use of political power for unfair economic advantage."[2] Somoza's moral authority had already begun to be compromised after a severe earthquake destroyed much of Managua in 1972. The corrupt regime pilfered away most of the relief received from abroad and failed to reconstruct the capital.

The FSLN had been divided since 1972 into three factions, under the pressure of the difficult situation they operated in. These factions became hardened after Fonseca's death. They called themselves the Prolonged People's War Tendency (GPP), the Proletarian Tendency (TP), and the Insurrectionary Tendency (TI—also called the Third Tendency or *terceristas*). These factions of the FSLN claimed allegiance to the same organization, and to the programmatic positions of Carlos Fonseca contained in the "Historic Program." The discussions between the factions from 1972 to 1976 have largely been lost, and the differences remain somewhat murky. After 1976, the factions stopped discussing with each other.

However, some delineation can be made. The GPP, as its name implied, thought there would be a prolonged guerrilla struggle. This would be carried out in the countryside and eventually would become strong enough to surround the cities. This view was close to Maoist concepts. They stressed land reform, and worked only with students and intellectuals in the cities. The original central leaders of the GPP were killed in 1973, and then Henry Ruiz and Tomás Borge led this faction.

The TP agreed with the FSLN program that Nicaragua was a mainly agricultural society, but held that the peasantry had been proletarianized and needed unions more than land reform. They concentrated their work among the urban working-class communities. It was the only faction that never fielded its own rural guerrilla force. Their main leader was Jaime Wheelock.

The TI differed with the GPP in that it held that insurrection was not for a far-off future, but should be prepared in the current period. Its central leaders were Humberto and Daniel Ortega.

While he was alive, Fonseca criticized all three factions. Concerning the GPP he thought they were avoiding current struggles in the name of the "prolonged war." He thought the TP counterposed the cities to the countryside, did not understand the need for land reform that would include private peasant plots as well as collective agriculture where appropriate, and neglected the military struggle outside the big cities, where most Nicaraguans lived. He said the TI concentrated too much on armed actions to the detriment of political work.

All three tendencies were moving away from the Historic Program after Fonseca was killed. The TI carried this the furthest, envisioning an alliance with the bourgeois opposition whereby the FSLN would concentrate on the military struggle against the National Guard and the bourgeois opposition would dominate the post-Somoza government. The FSLN would be allowed some representation in the government. This went directly against the Historic Program, which viewed the exploited classes, the workers and peasants, as the driving force of the revolution, and who would take power under the leadership of the FSLN.

The harsh repression unleashed by Somoza led him to believe the FSLN was smashed, and he lifted the state of siege in September 1977. Indeed, 1977 was a dark year for the FSLN, but it survived. A women's organization linked to the FSLN was formed, concentrating on campaigns for political prisoners. The TP made gains in organizing a union of agricultural workers.

In January 1978 the country's best known bourgeois oppositionist, Pedro Chamorro, a leader of the Conservatives, was assassinated on his way to work at the *La Prensa* newspaper, known for its criticisms of Somoza. Protest demonstrations swept the country.

This was the beginning of a new wave of mass resistance to Somoza. As Zimmermann describes:

"New forms of popular struggle took shape, became generalized over the course of the next year, and came to symbolize the Nicaraguan insurrection: raging street bonfires of smelly rubber tires, homemade Molotov cocktails and contact bombs, and cobblestone barricades to protect poor neighborhoods from [National Guard] tanks. Hundreds and then thousands of walls sprouted revolutionary slogans, sometimes signed by the FSLN-GPP or FSLN-TP. In February 1978, an anti-Somoza uprising organized by none of the three tendencies erupted in the indigenous community of Monimbo, located in the city of Masaya, only twenty miles from Managua.

"In April a student strike closed Nicaragua's universities and 80 percent of its public and private high schools. In July crowds of cheering supporters gathered in several cities to greet members of Los Doce (The Twelve), a San-José-based group of pro-FSLN businessmen, intellectuals, and religious leaders, organized by the *terceristas.* The same month, popular Sandinista organizations, mostly influenced by the TP, coalesced to form the United People's Movement...."[3]

Then in August the TI organized a spectacular action that captured international attention, reminiscent of the 1974 raid. Disguised as guardsmen, two dozen guerrillas captured the National Palace in Managua, during a large gathering of Somoza supporters, holding hostage 3,500 politicians and businessmen until Somoza agreed to release all 59 FSLN political prisoners. Tens of thousands came out to cheer the freed prisoners as they passed through working-class neighborhoods on the way to the airport. At the end of the month 500 high school students supported by the population took control of the city of Matagalpa, fighting the National Guard for five days before the dictatorship retook control by sending in Special Forces units. The insurgents wore bandanas with the Sandinista colors of red and black, although there was not a single FSLN member in the city.

In September, the FSLN organized uprisings in six cities outside the capital. Somoza responded with aerial bombing and artillery. The TI had initiated the actions, but youth looking to all three tendencies took part in the fighting. The uprisings were crushed, and 50,000 people fled to Costa Rica, Honduras and El Salvador.

Caroline Lund and I were vacationing back from Paris in the United States, camping in New Hampshire, reading the reports in the newspapers and listening to Radio Havana on short wave. Caroline was so moved she wanted to go to Nicaragua to join the fighting. Of course, this was not practical, but indicated our excitement.

The SWP relied on reports from Carlos Fonseca's half-brother, Fausto Amador, through October of 1978. While he did cover the events, he downplayed the key role of the FSLN. Given the animosity between the FSLN leaders and himself, this was to be expected, but our reliance on his reports blinded us to the full picture of what was happening with the FSLN.

Some of the Nicaraguans who fled after the September uprising came to the United States, seeking political asylum. Immigration authorities told them bluntly "only people from Communist countries get asylum." The United States Committee for Justice to Latin American Political Prisoners (USLA), in which the SWP played a key role, launched a campaign demanding that these refugees be allowed to stay in the United States. On April 22, 1979, Norman Gonzalez and Selvia Nebbia from USLA were able to interview many of the detainees, who were being held under strict surveillance.

One of the detainees was Alfredo (last names weren't used in case they got deported back to Nicaragua, where they would face prison or worse), who had been held for five months. He said he had been a member of the FSLN since he was twelve years old. In the September uprising, he lost his father and mother, his wife and his two children. He had to leave Nicaragua in a hurry, without his papers, and hitched-hiked to Mexico and then to the United States.

Growing numbers of Nicaraguans came to see the FSLN as their organization. In response, U.S. President Carter formed a commission of the Organization of American States (OAS) to go to Nicaragua to bolster the bourgeois opposition, fearing it would be bypassed by the Sandinistas. But the OAS failed to negotiate a transfer of power from Somoza to the opposition. Repression increased, which only fueled the people's anger, and the ranks of the FSLN swelled. Armed clashes between FSLN guerrillas and the National Guard in the countryside increased. Strikes, demonstrations, land seizures, building occupations and attacks on the National Guard barracks mushroomed. Civil Defense Committees formed in many cities. Within a few months into 1979, a full-scale insurrection was underway.

The FSLN did not always initiate the actions, which grew spontaneously, but the fighters identified with the Front, wearing red and black kerchiefs. According to Zimmermann, "The tens of thousands of mostly young Nicaraguans who threw themselves into the fight against Somoza changed Nicaraguan politics, and they also changed the FSLN. The entry of these masses into action pushed the FSLN to the left, not only in terms of speeding up the war against Somoza but also in terms of the radicalization of the revolution's goals. This pushed all three tendencies back toward Carlos Fonseca, toward his vision of a Sandinista revolution that would indicate a process of radical social transformation."[4]

This led to a reunification of the three tendencies in March 1979. They formed a National Directorate of nine members, three from each tendency: Daniel and Humberto Ortega and Víctor Tirado from the TI; Tomás Borge, Bayardo Arce and Henry Ruiz from the GPP; Jaime Wheelock, Luis Carrión and Carlos Núñez from the TP. The reunification removed some confusion among the masses and united them behind the FSLN.

On June 4 the National Directorate issued a call for an insurrectionary general strike. A few days later it launched a full-scale uprising in Managua. The National Guard was forced to abandon León and Matagalpa, the next two largest cities, and many small towns.

"A massive uprising of workers and peasants, opposed to the bloody dictatorship of Gen. Anastasio Somoza is sweeping Nicaragua," wrote Suzanne Haig in *The Militant*. "Rebels from the Sandinista Liberation Front (FSLN) control León, the second largest city, and a general strike has shut down Managua, the capital."[5]

According to FSLN reports, Haig noted, the Carter administration was sending direct military aid to support Somoza's effort to defeat the revolt. As well, the U.S. backed regimes in Guatemala and El Salvador flew troops and war materials into Nicaragua with planes supplied by the United States. The rebels also announced the capture of a Guatemalan Army colonel, Oscar Ruben Castañeda, who was with Somoza's National Guard in León.

Demonstrations were held in U.S. cities, which of course SWP and YSA members participated in, demanding the Carter administration keep "Hands Off Nicaragua." The largest was in New York at the Nicaraguan Consulate, where a crowd of 500 demonstrated.

The urban insurrections Zimmermann notes were decidedly working class in character, as Fonseca had anticipated. According to almost all reports the uprisings were located in the urban slums. Consequently, Somoza bombed the working class neighborhoods in the cities, killing as many as 50,000 people. But as Zimmermann describes he could not defeat the fighters' firm resolve. "The FSLN had to scramble to catch up with the uprisings," she writes. "By the spring of 1979, committed and experienced FSLN cadres (who might have been in the organization only a few months) were leading the day-to-day activity of the revolution, distributing the limited number of weapons available, training milcianos, organizing community support, food supplies, and care of wounded, deciding when and where to strike and when to retreat, and in the process recruiting and training new leaders."[6]

Washington did all it could to prevent the Sandinistas from taking power, trying to put the bourgeois opposition in power instead. But the National Guard disintegrated in the face of the insurrection, Somoza fled to his imperialist masters in the United States, and on July 19 FSLN guerrilla columns marched into Managua, where they were greeted by cheering crowds underneath two large banners with the portraits of Sandino and Fonseca.

A new five-person coalition government was formed, with three Sandinistas and two bourgeois opposition figures, Violeta Chamorro, the widow of Pedro Chamorro, and industrialist Alfonso Robelo. But this was a figurehead government. The real power was in the hands of the FSLN National Directorate.

The Militant hailed the triumph of the workers and peasants as "a victory for working people throughout Latin America, in the United States and around the world." We sent *Militant* and *Intercontinental Press* reporter Fred Murphy and SWP National Committee member Peter Camejo to Nicaragua to cover the events. In Paris, the United Secretariat of the Fourth International, which Caroline Lund and I were members of, also issued a statement hailing the victory on July 4 and calling for an international campaign to defend the revolution. Around the world, supporters of the Fourth International threw themselves into this effort.

The new government immediately nationalized all the holdings of the Somoza clan in the cities and countryside. This was a major section of the economy, as the Somozas had utilized their dictatorial powers for decades to line their pockets. A new Nicaraguan Institute of Agrarian Reform (INRA) was formed, headed by Jaime Wheelock.

Fred Murphy reported for *The Militant*:

"Headed by a column of armed Sandinistas, more than 5,000 peasants and agricultural workers marched from Diramba to Jinotepe—two towns about 30 miles south of [Managua]—on July 29.

"More than twenty cooperatives of farmworkers from Carazo Province participated in the action, which was organized by the Field Workers Association (ATC). Their slogan was 'the lands of the assassins belong to the peasants.' According to an account published in the July 30 issue of the Sandinista daily *Barricada*, the peasants 'expressed their firm decision to expropriate the land of the *Somocistas* and administer them in a collective way to strengthen the process of agrarian reform in the area.' ....[the same issue reported that in León Provence] 'peasant militias are already in formation, since the peasants themselves have asked to be armed to defend their production in blood and fire—a display of enthusiasm for joining a revolutionary process in which they will be the first to benefit.'"[7]

Cuba immediately pledged aid and defense. Radio Havana, which previously said its was broadcasting from the "Free Territory of the Americas" now said it was coming from the "First Free Territory of the Americas." At the July 26 mass meeting in honor of the initial blow struck by the Cuban revolutionists on that date in 1953, Sandinista leaders and even the bourgeois figure Robelo traveled to Cuba to participate and were greeted by a tremendous reception. (Robelo didn't wear his usual business suit.)

Caroline and I came back from Paris to the United States to participate in the SWP convention held August 5-11 in Oberlin, Ohio. Peter Camejo and Fred Murphy arrived late from Nicaragua to the convention. Peter addressed the full convention, and told the cheering crowd of some 1,550 that "the socialist revolution has begun in Nicaragua!"

After the convention Camejo wrote about the political and social measures initiated by the new government, which went beyond the nationalization of Somoza's holdings and the beginning of the land reform:

"[The Sandinista government] has also nationalized all of Nicaragua's banks. This gives it control over the vast bulk of the country's industrial wealth.... The large number of buildings formerly owned by Somoza and the Somocistas will not be monopolized by private individuals or government administrators for personal use. Instead they are to be transformed into schools, child-care centers, sports centers, museums, and cultural centers.

"Government control has been established over all important exportable agricultural commodities, including cotton, coffee, sugar, and fish.... In the cities—especially in the working-class and poor districts—Sandinista Defense Committees are being formed on a block-by block-basis to oversee the distribution of food aid, organizing the reconstruction of housing and other buildings destroyed by Somoza's bombings, and work with the Sandinista militias.

"Workers in the factories, stores, banks, and other workplaces are also forming committees. These are usually elected by assemblies of all the workers. They are to form the basis of a new United Federation of Sandinista Workers, which integrate the trade unions that existed under the dictatorship with the new workers committees. It is to include the agricultural proletariat as well....

"The revolution's leaders have also announced some longer-range plans.... Chief among these is an ambitious campaign against illiteracy modeled on the example of what was done in Cuba after the 1959 revolution there. Some 60 percent of Nicaraguans do not know how to read and write.... Brigades of teachers—many of them high-school and college students—will soon begin being trained to carry out the literacy drive."[8]

In addition, plans were announced for the formation of a July 19 Sandinista Youth organization and a National Union of Nicaraguan Women.

Charles-André Udry, whom Caroline and I worked closely with in Paris, was among the over 200 international guests present at the convention. He stayed over, and at the end of August he and I along with Fred Halstead and others from the SWP and the Fourth International including Hugo Blanco went to Nicaragua. Charles-André was able to meet in private with a woman who was part of the broader FSLN leadership and sympathetic to the Fourth International. She had secretly attended the 1974 World Congress.

Charles-André and I stood shoulder-to-shoulder witnessing a parade of the just-formed army on September 1. It was somewhat rag-tag, having been hastily organized from the FSLN guerrillas and the militias who formed during the insurrection. They didn't all have the same arms as a regular army usually would have, but carried the weapons they had with them from the struggle. Included in the parade were a few captured National Guard tanks. We were impressed and greatly moved by the discipline and grim determination expressed on the faces of these young fighters, which included many women, as they passed by. They and the FSLN knew that their fight was not over—that Washington would swiftly organize to attempt to overthrow the revolution.

What we were witnessing were the first steps in the formation of a new armed power, the core of what could become a workers' state. I realized that the situation fit the concept we in the SWP had developed of a workers and farmers government. The old state power had been smashed. The new government rested on the mobilization of the workers and peasants. With the nationalization of the Somoza properties, a big section of the economy, the regime had shown the capacity to move against the rights, privileges, and property of the capitalist class. A new dynamic had been unleashed. When I returned to the United States, I reported my conclusion, which the rest of the leadership had tentatively held, waiting my report.

Peter Camejo, along with his companion Gloria Najar, moved to Managua to set up a bureau there to follow the revolution. I went back to Nicaragua and helped Peter to lease a house that would contain an office for the bureau as well as living quarters. Over the next years, there were a number of people who functioned as our representatives in the bureau.

Caroline and I returned to Paris. The United Secretariat had to deal with the question of Fausto Amador, who had held a news conference in 1969 reported in the Somoza press denouncing the FSLN and urging his brother Fonseca to turn himself in and work for social change in the legal framework set up by Somoza. Since it was we in the Leninist Trotskyist Faction who had insisted that Fausto Amador be accepted as part of the International in the process of the dissolution of the factions, as explained in Chapter Twelve, I wrote a letter to Fausto on behalf of the United Secretariat. In this letter I explained that Fausto should repudiate his 1969 statements and express his willingness to return to Nicaragua and place himself under the discipline of the FSLN in order to join the revolutionary process. Fausto rejected this proposal and he was subsequently expelled from the Fourth International.

We had another problem. Hugo Moreno had organized an armed detachment of his supporters called the Simon Bolivar Brigade from Columbia and some other countries to invade the Nicaraguan Atlantic coast during the insurrection. By and large the insurrection was confined to the Spanish-speaking majority areas of the country. The Atlantic coast communities were composed of English-speaking Blacks, descendants of slaves and workers brought there by the British in the 19th century, and indigenous dark-skinned people, including, importantly, the Miskito people, who spoke their own language.*

The Simon Bolivar Brigade tried to pass itself off as part of the FSLN, and set itself up as the government in sections of the Atlantic coast. Since the groups loyal to Moreno had been part of the Fourth International, we had to swiftly denounce this criminal adventure, and back the FSLN when it moved into the area to drive the Brigade out. The United Secretariat did so unanimously and publicly and also in person through Mexican and other comrades who had gone to Nicaragua to support the revolution. This adventure by the Morenistas echoed what they had done in the Portuguese revolution (see Chapter Nine). In both instances they tried to hijack a revolutionary process from the outside.

Notably, Peter Camejo in his memoir *North Star* makes a major error. In it he claims that Ernest Mandel and the majority of the Fourth International supported the Simon Bolivar Brigade. This assertion is false. Why Peter made this error is puzzling, since he publicly wrote the exact opposite at the time, when he was in Nicaragua.

•••

The Council of State the FSLN had agreed to in a compromise with bourgeois opponents of Somoza before the insurrection had become obsolete with the victory. Fred Murphy wrote, "It was disproportionally weighted toward the most conservative sectors of the anti-Somoza front. Out of 33 representatives on the Council the FSLN would have had only six or perhaps a few more."9 The government postponed the convening of the council until March 1980, and declared its composition would be changed to represent the "motor forces" of the revolution, the workers and peasants through their new organizations.

There were a few ultraleft groups that attacked the new government as bourgeois. These came from Maoist and Trotskyist backgrounds, although the latter did not represent and were opposed to the positions of the Fourth International. In general, they would "up the ante" on programs launched by the workers and peasants government, claiming they were not going fast enough or far enough. Some of their demands, such as for the immediate convening of a constituent assembly, were in fact if not in intent counter-revolutionary, as they implied the overthrow of the revolutionary government. The facts on the ground created by the insurrection had bypassed such demands.

The FSLN initially lumped these ultraleft groups with the remnants of the Somocistas and sought to repress them. This was an error, as the ultralefts had to be dealt with politically, through argument and discussion. The FSLN soon moved to correct this error. Tomás Borge said there were "honest people" in the ultraleft groups and the FSLN should open a dialogue with them. "Jail is not the best place for a dialogue," he pointed out in a speech. (Fred Murphy and Peter Camejo wrote a reasoned and pedagogical article on this subject that appeared in the November 16, 1979 issue of *The Militant.*)

...

Carlos Fonseca had been buried by the National Guard in the rural village of Waslala after they killed him. On November 5, his remains were brought to Matagalpa, where he was born. Some 30,000 to 50,000 people rallied in his honor there, including a contingent of volunteer doctors from Cuba. His coffin was carried through a series of villages on its way to Managua.

As Fred Murphy reported:

"More than 100,000 people poured into the streets [of Managua] on November 7 in a massive show of support for the gains of the revolution and to honor Carlos Fonseca Amador, founder of the Sandinista National Liberation Front. The demonstration and rally were the largest since the mobilization July 20 that greeted the FSLN fighters as they marched into Managua. The outpouring occurred against the background of border violations and harassment of Nicaraguan diplomatic officials by the rightist military dictatorship in Honduras. The Honduran government openly collaborates with officers of Somoza's National Guard who retreated into Honduras with their troops following the July insurrection....

"Interior Minister Tomás Borge addressed the rally and denounced these hostile acts. 'Pointing to the ominous character of these actions, Borge... [said] 'Could it be that this provocation by elements linked to the Honduran police and is part of a plan whose scope and content we are not yet fully aware?' [Indeed, they were part of the plan hatched in Washington to unleash the murderous

'Contra' war against Nicaragua that caused massive damage and casualties in the years to come.]"

In the three-day celebration from Matagalpa to Managua, Murphy further noted:

"The determination and spirit of commitment to the revolution that permeated these mobilizations was summed up by the quotation from Fonseca Amador repeated over and over through these three days and displayed on the front page of the Sandinista daily *Barricada* November 8: 'It is not simply a question of changing the men in power, but rather of changing the system, of overthrowing the exploiting classes and bringing the exploited classes to victory.'"[10]

Peter Camejo wrote an article in *The Militant* December 21, detailing the resistance being waged by those capitalists who hadn't fled against the revolution, including economic sabotage, as 1979 drew to a close.

•••

In the autumn of 1979 we began to take notice of a revolution that had occurred earlier in the year in the tiny Caribbean island nation of Grenada. Ernest Harsch went to Grenada for *Intercontinental Press,* where he reported: "Eight months after the March 13 insurrection that brought the New Jewel Movement (NJM) to power in this small eastern Caribbean island, support for the new government is widespread. If anything, it may even be deepening among the poorest layers of this impoverished country, as the People's Revolutionary Government (PRG) of Prime Minister Maurice Bishop drives ahead with a series of progressive measures aimed at improving the social position and living conditions of the vast majority of Grenada's 110,000 people—the workers and small farmers.

"While some sectors of Grenadan society—the conservative and wealthy—are reacting with concern, the general verdict among young people, workers, and the unemployed is that the government deserves support and that it appears committed to transforming society on their behalf."[11]

The Grenadian population is overwhelmingly Black, descendents of slaves brought by the British to their former colony. Maurice Bishop spoke in Harlem to a crowd of 1,200, a fact that brought to our attention that something significant was happening on the island that could speak directly to U.S. African Americans.

Cuba hailed the "Three Giants" rising up in the Caribbean—Cuba, Nicaragua and Grenada. It seemed to us that these interrelated revolutions were harbingers of a new period, posing new opportunities and new tasks for us.

* For more information about the formation of what became Nicaragua's Atlantic Coast, see Clifford D. Conner, *Colonel Despard: The Life and Times of an Anglo-Irish Rebel* (Combined Publishing, 2000).

1 Matilde Zimmermann, *Sandinista—Carlos Fonseca and the Nicaraguan Revolution*, (Duke University Press, 2000) p. 5.
2 Ibid., pp. 210-211.
3 Ibid., p. 212.
4 Ibid., p 215.
5 *The Militant*, June 15, 1975.
6 Ibid., Zimmermann, pp. 217-219.
7 *The Militant*, Aug. 10, 1979.
8 Ibid., Aug. 24, 1979.
9 Ibid., Nov. 9, 1979.
10 Ibid., Nov. 16, 1979.
11 Ibid., Nov. 30, 1979.

CHAPTER EIGHTEEN: THE 1979 WORLD CONGRESS

Throughout 1978 we were building a new international leadership team. This helped lay the groundwork for the preparations for the next World Congress of the Fourth International to be held in 1979. A part of this preparation included collaboration in writing proposed resolutions to be taken up in the United Secretariat, then the broader International Executive Committee, to be submitted to the membership of the sections in each country. The members would consider the proposed resolutions, together with any others written by opposition tendencies. On this basis, the discussions in each section would result in the election of delegates to the World Congress, the highest body of the International, for decision.

We knew we had to have a new resolution on Latin America that would revoke the 1969 guerrilla war resolution, and explain the new situation in the countries on the continent. The resolution would have to explain the openings and problems of party building in Latin America, without falling into the trap of proposing a single tactic on a continent-wide scale, which had been the fundamental error of the 1969 resolution. The strategic and tactical decisions for each country would be left up to the sections.

The United Secretariat asked two of its members, Gus Horowitz from the United States and Jean-Pierre Beauvais from France, to work with Manuel Aguilar of Mexico in drafting such a resolution. In preparation, they would have to make many trips to Latin America for discussions with the leaderships of the sections. It was also decided that Jack Barnes and Ernest Mandel would be tasked with writing a proposed world political resolution. The resolution would seek to analyze the world capitalist economy and the situation in the bureaucratically degenerated workers' states, the advanced imperialist countries, and the largely ex-colonial countries still exploited by imperialism. Based on our analysis, we would propose general guidelines the sections could utilize as they saw fit.

In the wake of the 1969 "turn," which resulted in an ultraleft bent expressed in majority-adopted reports and resolutions from the International Executive Committee and the 1974 World Congress on the International's tasks in Europe, it was decided that a new European resolution was needed. The two Charleses and I were to work on this resolution. Mary-Alice and Jacqueline also worked together to prepare a resolution on women's liberation.

In addition, there was a resolution on "socialist democracy" that had been held over for many years, to see if differences could be worked out. The SWP leadership thought the proposed draft was too much of a blueprint of how a healthy workers' state would function, and was unrealistic in glossing over steps that would have to be taken against counter-revolution. Ernest Mandel and I were assigned to see if these differences could now be worked out. I met with Ernest in the summer of 1979 in Boston, on one of my trips back to the United States. Ernest had been invited by Boston University to lecture. We amicably agreed to disagree.

The Congress was held in December 1979. There was wide agreement on the resolution on Latin America. Some minor changes had been made to the draft presented by Jean-Pierre Beauvais and Gus Horowitz in the International Executive Committee prior to the Congress, and it passed by a large majority. This was the final piece in overcoming the IMT-LTF faction fight, which had begun 10 years earlier.

The majority draft on "Socialist Democracy" was passed. But this was not a "hot" issue, as there was agreement on much of it, and besides, it referred to the future after successful socialist revolutions and not on what to do in the present. The SWP delegates presented the amended draft I had made, and the discussion was amicable, although the differences were made clear.

The resolution on Europe was also passed by a large margin, as it was edited after discussion in the United Secretariat and International Executive Committee. It was also agreed that the women's liberation resolution would be the basis for further discussion.

Before the Congress, it was clear we needed resolutions concerning the revolutions in Iran and Nicaragua. The resolution that Charles-André Udry, Gerry Foley and I had prepared on Iran passed. Some comrades voted against this resolution, along the lines of thinking that the Khomeini regime had already smashed the revolutionary upsurge. Of course, our resolution only covered up to November 1979. However, the revolution could not be tamed overnight, and was experiencing a new thrust forward with the occupation of the American Embassy. Part Two of this book will cover what happened in subsequent years in Iran.

The great majority of the International greeted the Nicaraguan revolution with enthusiasm. Many comrades had visited Nicaragua to experience it firsthand. There was broad agreement on supporting the revolution, the FSLN government, and the steps forward the Sandinistas had taken. There was also overwhelming agreement in defending the revolution against Washington's hostility towards the new regime. However, there were two resolutions presented.

Looking back, this situation was not only unnecessary, it introduced new tensions. One resolution was presented by the SWP and another by the European leaders. In fact, there were no major political differences between the resolutions. Both reflected the agreement referred to in the preceding paragraph. The difference was around a theoretical question, whether to characterize the Sandinista regime a workers and peasants government or not.

We in the SWP had come to the conclusion that a workers and peasants government had been formed in Nicaragua. We knew that the European comrades rejected the whole idea of a workers and peasants government as a possible distinct stage in a revolution, which could become either a workers' state or revert to a new capitalist regime.

This was how the SWP had analyzed the Chinese regime from 1949-1952, the Cuban regime before 1960, and the government that emerged from the Algerian Revolution in 1962. In our opinion, in China and Cuba the workers and peasants governments had gone on to establish workers' states, although going in very different directions. The Chinese workers' state was saddled from its inception with a privileged Stalinist bureaucracy, while Cuba's was a basically healthy workers' state with important deficiencies. In the Algerian example, the workers' and peasants' government withered on the vine until it was overthrown in a counter-revolutionary military coup.

Thus, we knew in advance that our position that a workers' and peasants' government had been established in Nicaragua would be a minority one in the International. A common resolution along the lines of our political agreement could have been passed, and the theoretical issue separated out, with agreement to have a leisurely and literary discussion of the workers' and peasants' government category. But we pressed ahead anyway, and forced the issue through two counter-posed resolutions. Actually, I should say that Jack Barnes forced the issue in the SWP leadership, and this was a factional move that tended to fissure in the International along the lines of the old dispute.

Jack and Ernest had come up with a world political resolution that was generally correct on its overview of world politics. But it contained a fundamentally flawed assertion that the working class in the capitalist countries worldwide, both imperialist and semi-colonial, was becoming radicalized. This radicalization would soon become a political radicalization, not just intensified trade union struggles. The conclusion was that in every capitalist country our sections should make a turn to colonize our members into industry.

It was my impression that Ernest did not actually agree with this analysis or conclusion, but was brow beaten by Jack into accepting it under the threat of there being two resolutions. What gave weight to this threat was the great prestige the SWP had gained as a result of being proved correct in the IMT-LTF faction fight.

The irony was that this perspective repeated the methodological errors of the 1969 IMT-led guerrilla turn in Latin America. The first error in 1969 was to make a sweeping generalization that in almost every country of the whole continent there could be no democratic openings in which our sections could work in the mass movement in a "normal" way. Any attempts to do so would be smashed by the military.

This generalization was not true. The political situation in each Latin American country had its own dynamic. Venezuela could not be put in the same boat as Bolivia, and so forth. Politics in each country had to be analyzed in its uniqueness. History soon proved the generalization was false, as the class struggle in the different countries did produce democratic and even pre-revolutionary openings, especially in Bolivia, which was singled out by the 1969 World Congress majority as the place to first launch rural guerrilla war.

The second error had been to conclude from this generalization that a possible tactic, rural guerrilla war, was elevated into a strategy that every section in Latin America had to begin carrying out or prepare to carry out.

Even under harsh military regimes it is not true that rural guerrilla war, which by its nature is based on the peasantry, is the preferred overall strategy. Such a strategy meant abandoning political work in the cities and the urban working class. If the concrete conditions in the peasantry indicated that rural guerrilla war was on the agenda, underground work in the cities would still have to be done in the actually existing situation in the countries of Latin America. Indeed, these countries had long histories of working-class struggle.

The generalization could be made that the struggles of the peasants had to be linked with the workers' movement. An alliance of the workers and peasants is obviously a strategic goal. But the tactics to reach that goal would be different in each country. Rural guerrilla war is only one tactic. The FSLN in Nicaragua had to learn that lesson the hard way.

The third error was not to take into account the actual reality of each section in the continent. How big was the section? What were its links with the workers? What were its links with the peasants? A party of thousands, with an implantation in the working class and in the peasantry can do things that a student group of 30 members cannot.

But the turn we foisted on the International in 1979 repeated every one of these errors. Our generalization that the political radicalization of the working class was on the agenda everywhere was ridiculous. The class struggle in each country has its own dynamic and timeline. While the 1969 turn to guerrilla war was based on a false generalization about a continent, we went that error one better by making our generalization cover the world. And it wasn't true. It did not happen in most countries, including in the United States.

Second, we drew from that generalization the proposal that all our sections had to make a tactic, colonization of the great majority of our members into industry, into a strategy applicable everywhere. A small propaganda group, such as our Israeli/Palestinian section of about 30 intellectuals, had to adopt this tactic as well as the far stronger American SWP.

Actually, many sections did try to do this, and it became disruptive. As an overall strategy, it failed. Jack then used this failure to divide some of the sections, into those who followed the SWP example and those who backed away from it. This factional move wrecked our attempts to rebuild the International.

---

* I will discuss the turn to industry in the United States, which could have had positive results if it was done correctly, in Part Two.

Part Two:
Decline and Collapse, 1980 - 1988

CHAPTER NINETEEN: THE DRAFT, THE PRDF SUIT, AND A NEW BLACK PARTY

Early in 1980, President Carter, hoping to capitalize on the anti-Iranian warmongering initiated by his administration and the press, raised the idea of reintroducing the military draft. The first step in this direction, Carter outlined in his State of the Union address, would be to reinstitute registration for a possible draft.

One of the retreats the ruling class was forced to make as a result of the youth radicalization and the antiwar movement was to abolish the compulsory draft in favor of an all-volunteer armed force.

Carter thought the time was right to try to reverse the "Vietnam Syndrome," as the media called it, the widespread opposition in the population to redoing anything like the Vietnam War. Calling this eminently rational view a "syndrome" made it seem like a temporary disease, like a fever, that would soon be overcome.

But Carter's trial balloon was immediately countered by massive opposition. "Just days after the specter of reinstituting the draft, thousands of young people took to the streets in angry protests," reported *The Militant*. "Twenty-five hundred rallied at the University of California at Berkeley; 1,800 at the University of Minnesota in Minneapolis; 1,000 at the University of Oregon at Eugene; 800 at Harvard; 800 at Colombia; and thousands more at campuses throughout the country."[1]

The fact that the Young Socialist Alliance (YSA) had made the decision to turn away from the campuses in order to have the large majority of its members go into industry meant that we were left largely on the outside of this movement. Of course, we still supported the fight against the draft, and did what we could to support it.

Registration was supposed to start in July. But there were demonstrators at the draft centers throughout the country, often many more than young people on the inside registering. But the *New York Daily News* reported that the Selective Service (the government draft organization) said that the turnout was "exceptionally light." In fact, it was a flop. Demonstrations against the draft continued into 1981, when Reagan took office, and the government was forced to retreat. While draft registration remained in place, efforts to reinstitute the draft itself were abandoned.

•••

Our civil liberties lawsuit against the government continued to expose dirty tricks, as the date for the opening of the trial in March 1981 approached. The suit had been filed in 1973, and the intervening years had been filled with what the courts call "discovery." For us, that meant prying from the FBI, CIA and many other government agencies their documents detailing their campaigns against the SWP and YSA. The government fought tooth and nail to keep these documents secret, but many were brought to light under order of Judge Thomas B. Griesa, who presided over the case.

What these documents revealed was a many-decades long record of break-ins of SWP offices and the homes of members, opening our mail, telephone taps, attempts to cause disruption of our election campaigns, attempts to sow discord on the left by issuing false leaflets in our name, and much other illegal activity. One of the latter was to get SWP members fired from their jobs. I myself was fired from a job in 1960 soon after I joined the SWP (see volume one of this work, pp. 41,42).

Two new cases of FBI-sponsored firings occurred in the final months of 1980. In November at the Brooklyn Navy Yard in New York five party members who had gotten jobs as pipefitters at Costal Dry Dock repairing Navy ships were marched out of the Yard after a months-long covert disruption effort by Naval Intelligence, the FBI, and the company. Their termination notices referred to a letter from the commanding officer of a ship in for repairs, which cited the notorious Smith Act, which had been declared unconstitutional years earlier.

The five reprinted the termination notice with their own statement on the back and passed out 500 copies to workers coming into the Yard the next day. They also contacted the lawyers for our suit, who immediately contacted the company. In two days the company reversed itself, and the workers were reinstated, with pay for time lost.

Then in December nine members were fired by Lockheed Aircraft in Georgia. At first, the company said they were fired for errors in their application forms for the jobs. But our lawyers subpoenaed Lockheed to give a deposition on the firings. Under oath, the company spokesman admitted that the workers were indeed fired for their memberships in the SWP or YSA and for handing out SWP campaign literature at a union meeting. Notably, the spokesman admitted the FBI was behind the firings. He also detailed how he and other company cops had followed the socialists after union meetings, and noted that some of them once drove to New York in a car driven by a "Negro male."

The company spokesman also said that under suspicion was anyone with a college degree, especially from California because campuses there were known as "a center for dissident and subversive activities during the Vietnam era." Anyone who gave as an emergency contact a person with a "foreign sounding" name was also suspect. Not surprisingly, this hit list included a number of workers who had nothing at all to do with the SWP or YSA.[2]

These two cases were proof that earlier FBI assertions that by 1976 it had stopped all disruption campaigns directed against the SWP and YSA were false.

While our discovery ventures unearthed hundreds of thousands of pages, although heavily redacted, of government crimes, the government was entitled to its own discovery probes. In the course of complying, we turned over thousands of discussion bulletins, minutes and other documents. Because of their dirty tricks, the government already had access to most.

The government attorney's also required party leaders and members to answer their questions in depositions, under oath. They especially wanted our named plaintiffs to so testify, and I was questioned as one. I was questioned about my positions in the party and Fourth International, as well as my international travels, and so forth. Many questions concerned the political views of the SWP and the Fourth International. Of course, all these things were public knowledge, and the government learned nothing new. They were trying to trip us up in the hopes of finding some inconsistencies, but they got little.

One person who sat in on my deposition was "my" FBI agent, the person assigned to follow my activities on a daily basis. He said nothing, but I guess he was there to check up on my memory.

Andy Rose described preparations for the trial in *The Militant*:

"A dramatic shift in Washington's public stance toward civil liberties and political rights has been exposed in trial preparations [for our suit]. The government now is putting forward the most sweeping claims it has ever made of a legal 'right' to spy on, harass, blacklist and deport those whose political views it disapproves of. It can undertake such secret-police actions, the government emphasizes, even against individuals and organizations whose political activities are completely legal and supposedly protected by the Bill of Rights.

"Federal attorneys representing the FBI, CIA and other government agencies and officials submitted court documents December 31 [1980] outlining the defense the United States government will present when the lawsuit comes to trial March 16. 'The issue in this case is not whether the SWP, the YSA or any of their members can be proved guilty of a crime beyond a reasonable doubt,' they assert. 'The issue is whether the government has the right to keep itself informed of activities of groups that openly advocate revolutionary change in the structure and leadership of the government of the United States, *even if such advocacy might be within the letter of the law*' (emphasis added). Furthermore, the document continues '...the Government may legally investigate individuals and organizations *regardless of their nature*' (emphasis added)."3

This admission, in fact an offensive move to have the judge rule that the government did have such sweeping powers, helped to squarely frame the issue. It was this and many other exposures that won our case wide and increasing support as the trial date approached.

For many weeks of the trial both the SWP and the government called witnesses. Our main witness to explain the party's program and activities in detail was Farrell Dobbs, former SWP National Secretary, and one of the party leaders sentenced to jail in the first Smith Act trial in 1941.

A surprise witness for the government was a paid FBI informant in the SWP, Edward Heisler. Heisler had joined the party in the 1960s and had been an active member for many years. He had been involved in an important union development as a railroad worker. The railroad unions were fractured into many separate craft unions, which weakened workers' bargaining power. Heisler had helped lead a movement among some of these unions to merge, a perspective which eventually won with the formation of the United Transportation Union. He also helped lead a successful effort to win the "right to vote" on union contracts. Eventually, Heisler was elected to the SWP National Committee, largely on the basis of his union work.

The government used his testimony to try to show that its informants were nice guys. Heisler even claimed on the stand that he had always been a dedicated Marxist-Leninist and loyal member of the SWP. (We didn't use the term "Marxist-Leninist" because it had become identified with Maoism.) He claimed that he became an informer for the FBI in 1966 because he became persuaded that at some point the government would try to victimize the SWP. If he "infiltrated" the FBI, he could then expose it in some future trial of the SWP.

Under cross-examination by our lawyers using documents we had obtained, this patently absurd tale fell apart. We had proof that in exchange for him becoming a fink, the FBI pressured the draft board to suddenly declare him unfit for the armed forces, so he escaped being drafted. Another motivation was the money. One of the women he had lived with told us that he spent a lot of money on things like massage parlors.

One of the reports Heisler made to the FBI contained a vicious lie, although on the stand he said he never falsified anything. In a report on a conference of the Student Mobilization Committee in 1969, Heisler said that SWP leader Andrew Pulley, in a public speech, talked about the antiwar movement reaching out to soldiers. He claimed, according to his report to the FBI, that Pulley went on to say, "GIs are not yet ready to take up arms against their officers or to overthrow capitalism, although this is the long term perspective."[4]

How was it possible for a person to be a union militant and a builder of the SWP, and also work for the FBI? Sometimes people have bifurcated minds. A famous example occurred in Russia. The leader of the Bolshevik Party fraction in the Duma, the truncated parliament sometimes allowed by the Tsar, a man named Roman Malinovsky had been exposed as a Tsarist agent. Yet he had done good work for the Bolsheviks. After the revolution Lenin argued that he should not be shot for his crimes, but imprisoned, in consideration of the positive work he did while a member of the Bolshevik Party. Lenin was outvoted in the new Soviet government, and Malinovsky was in fact shot.

I, along with other party members, also testified. My mother was in the courtroom, and the arrogant and vicious way I was cross-examined looked to her as if it was I who was on trial, not the government. After, she came up to Jack Barnes and told him that if I were sent to jail, she would bake me a cake with a hacksaw inside so I could escape. This bit of humor helped me relax.

Legal maneuvering by the government dragged the case on for a few more years. Finally, Judge Griesa found for us and against the government, a major victory for civil liberties for all Americans, and one which we were very proud of, and deservedly so.

•••

A major activity of the SWP in 1980 was supporting our Presidential election campaign of Andrew Pulley and Matilde Zimmermann. The candidates zigzagged the country for speaking engagements, press conferences, and radio interviews. An important part of this work was collecting signatures to put the party on the ballot in the face of very undemocratic election laws designed to preserve the dominance of the two capitalist parties, the Democratic and Republican parties.

One of the biggest efforts was in California. The election law required us to obtain 101,000 signatures of registered voters, while the capitalist parties had minimum requirements and were virtually automatically on the ballot. By July, our supporters had turned in 152,000 signatures. Unlike in the 1976 SWP ticket of Camejo and Reid, however, the Secretary of State for California ruled us off the ballot. She was a Democratic Party hack, who did what she was told by the Democratic bosses.

The SWP also ran candidates for many other offices around the country. One of these was Mark Friedman in the 43rd Congressional District in San Diego, California. His campaign drew notice since the Democrats had nominated Thomas Metzger, an open member of the Ku Klux Klan.

Nationally, Republican candidate Ronald Reagan, a former California governor, was making gains against the Democratic incumbent, President Jimmy Carter. While Reagan made a barely disguised appeal to racism, Carter made his own accommodation by spurning many Black Democrats seeking that party's nominations for state and local offices. This spurred a reaction among many African-Americans. Feeling betrayed, many of the more outspoken Black leaders began to discuss and organize around the idea of a more independent political stance.

In August 1980 there was a convention of the National Black Political Assembly in New Orleans. On a motion by the Rev. Ben Chavis, the convention voted to launch a movement to build an independent mass-based independent political party. Three months later, 1,500 Black activists met in Philadelphia to propose the formation of the National Black Independent Political Party (NBIPP). Among these activists were Black members of the SWP and YSA, who had joined local groups organizing to send delegates to Philadelphia. This meeting resolved to hold a founding convention in 1981.

Andrew Pulley and Matilde Zimmermann made supporting NBIPP a central part of their fall campaigns. As an African-American, Pulley was also active in the organizing efforts for the new party.

The SWP had long advocated that workers and Blacks and other oppressed nationalities break from the Democrats and Republicans and form their own mass parties. In particular, we supported the formation of an independent Black political party. The SWP and YSA as a whole jumped into publicizing and backing the formation of NBIPP. Our Black members in particular became active in organizing efforts on the local level in preparation for the founding convention.

One member in particular became a leader in this effort. He was Mel Mason, who had been elected in March 1980 to the city council in the small city of Seaside, California, on Monterey Bay south of San

Francisco. Unbeknownst to us, Mason had registered as a member of the SWP on his own, and it was as a socialist that he was elected with the support of Seaside's Black community and others.

The local newspaper, the *Seaside Post*, ran an article on Mason in August. He explained that it was after he had joined the Air Force in 1961 that he became politicized. As Mason told the newspaper, "The first time the plight of blacks really had an impact on me was when I was in Istanbul, Turkey, in the Air force. A Turkish officer asked me why blacks in America don't have a revolution because of the way they were being mistreated. I got angry with him and explained that things were getting better for blacks and they were waiting for changes to take place. The officer laughed at me and showed me a picture in a Turkish newspaper of dogs being set loose on Martin Luther King, Jr. and other civil rights demonstrators. Just seeing that picture in another country's newspaper was what woke me up. I was horrified and angry."

Mason's air force career was cut short in 1965 with a bad conduct discharge for assaults. "Partially, it was a reaction to the second-class treatment Black airman were getting, but mostly I was young and wild and rough," Mason explained.

Later, he became active in various struggles in Seaside, and also earned a degree from Golden Gate University. He joined the Black Panther Party in 1968, but by 1969 his affinity for the group had worn off. "Through its own ultraleft rhetoric, the Panthers had isolated themselves from the very people it was intending to help....I still feel the Black Panther Party was the forerunner for the kind of politically independent organization Black people need to have. The Panthers were beneficial in showing Blacks they could have an organization run and controlled by them, and not by the Ford foundation and other organizations dependent on the government for their existence."[5]

Mason became a member of the National Party Organizing Committee of NBIPP. Chapters were built in many areas of the country. These were formed on a democratic basis, and began to recruit in the Black communities where they were based. Vigorous discussions were held in these grassroots groups about the nature and program of the party, throughout the winter, spring and summer months following the Philadelphia meeting. Our Black members helped lead these discussions, which culminated in the election of delegates to the founding congress held in Gary, Indiana on August 21-23, 1981.

About 700 attended the congress, including delegates with vote from 33 chapters and 16 organizing committees, as well as guests. All participants were involved in the congress discussions.

"Commissions were set up on women, youth/students, prisoners, labor and the elderly to discuss the program of the party," reported Malik Miah for *The Militant*. "The [NBIPP] members who attended these meetings took their decisions to [the program commission] hearings to make sure their concerns were incorporated in the charter.

"State and local caucuses were also held during the congress. This allowed delegates to discuss the charter and other proposals for the party's platform. This lengthy, democratic process culminated with the vote on the charter, section-by-section.... Through this lively scenario—that went from 9 a.m. to as late as 2 or 3 a.m. in the morning of each day—the program and structure of the party was forged."[6]

The Militant reprinted the NBIPP platform in full. "The party must define our attitude toward the Democratic and Republican parties. We should observe both the Democrats and Republicans as serving the interests of the ruling class: therefore they are diametrically opposed to the interests of African and poor people," it stated.

However, ruling class pressure was brought to bear immediately. The Democrats moved to reverse Carter's course, and opened more space for Black participation in the party. (The Republicans had virtually written off the Black vote with their "Southern strategy.") In the context of both capitalist parties moving to the right, independent Black political action began to take a back seat to a move back toward "lesser evil" politics of "the Democrats aren't as bad as the Republicans for Black people" variety.

In spite of its auspicious beginning, NBIPP began to wither.

---

1 *The Militant*, Feb. 8, 1980.
2 Ibid., Dec. 19, 1980 and Jan. 16, 1981.
3 Ibid., Jan. 23, 1981.
4 Ibid., July 3, 1981.
5 *Seaside Post*, Aug. 13, 1980.
6 *The Militant*, Sept. 11, 1981.

CHAPTER TWENTY: THE EMERGENCE OF A CULT

The word "cult" has been used in different ways. A religious sect is sometimes referred to as a cult. The rites and ceremonies of worship in religions can be called the cult of said religions. In ancient Greece and Rome devotees of a particular god or goddess within the broader common religion, were, at least in English translations, referred to as cults of that deity. Another usage in my Webster dictionary is "devoted attachment to, or extravagant admiration for, a person, principle, etc." Religious sects sometimes have this characteristic.

Political cults revolve around individuals, in my use of the term. These are not all alike. The cults of Stalin and Mao grew out of the needs of a social layer, the ruling bureaucracy. It was not possible for this layer to practice democratic discussion and decision-making without it spilling over into the working classes and undermining bureaucratic rule. Totalitarianism was the result.

But there were different and conflicting self-interests involved in sections of the bureaucracy, for example over the allotment of state investments, salaries, promotions, fancy homes, educational opportunities for children, and the like. Internecine struggles went on behind the scenes. To decide among and settle these conflicting interests it became necessary to have arbiters, and finally an arbiter above the others, a supreme arbiter, in whom final authority in all matters rested.

Stalin and Mao were skilled maneuverers in the intra-bureaucratic struggles, and were adept at staying on top. They took care to maintain loyalty of decisive elements of the armed forces and secret police. When threatened, they utilized extreme brutality, including purges, imprisonment and executions. The different layers of the bureaucracy did not have personal devotion to Stalin and Mao, in the main. Their emotional tie to them was fundamentally fear.

Cults in small socialist groups are not based on such material interests. Although certain privileges can develop in the later stages, such groups play no role in the economy, or control vast resources.

To be specific about the cult that developed around Jack Barnes in the SWP, it should first be noted that it didn't occur all at once, but over a period of years. Jack was a talented leader of the SWP youth in the period of the radicalization of "The Sixties." He emerged from that period as the recognized central figure among the other younger leaders, including myself, as well as among the older leaders of the party. It was Jack's positive role in the previous period that earned his authority. Gradually, this authority was abused, until it turned into its opposite. From a positive force building the SWP, it became a negative and destructive force that wrecked the party.

One of Jack's strengths as a leader had been his ability to bring together the older and younger leaders. I do not mean that he physically brought them together, outside of party meetings, or that they became friends, although many did. His accomplishment was to include people from different generations in developing political policy.

Among the younger leaders he played the same role. He encouraged different comrades to bring their ideas into our discussions. We all felt we could freely raise our opinions, hash them out, and come to generally common positions. Different comrades had different strengths, and would contribute accordingly, as well as take on assignments where their strengths could be put to best use. Jack helped coordinate all this.

As many of the older leaders from the 1930s and 1940s retired from the Political Committee and National Committee, Jack continued to function in this mold. This was, in fact, how we were trained in the 1960s as younger members of the Political Committee. In the first volume of this work, I have a separate chapter, "Farrell Dobbs and the Political Committee," pages 217-224, which goes into this in more detail. It was a collective leadership, with no "star."

As I noted in Part One, there began an erosion of the collective leadership in the Political Committee in the mid-1970s. Jack began to become the "star." This took many years to develop. We didn't wake up one day to see the transformation. It arose incrementally, and so was hard to understand. By early 1978, I had come to the conclusion that something was amiss, which I described in my earlier reference to the Political Committee as a "one man band." By this time, it had in fact already developed into a cult around Barnes. Jack's threat to expel me if I pursued the question of his leadership style (as I at first thought of it when I broached the topic with him) was a demonstration of this fact. The Political Committee had turned into its opposite, from a collective leadership into a cult around an individual "star."

One characteristic of this cult was that all political initiative had become the sole prerogative of Jack Barnes. SWP organizational resolutions, including the updated resolution adopted in 1965, had analyzed the weakness of the "star" system of leadership: it is only as good (or bad) as the "star," and no one, no matter how talented, has all the answers, and if they go wrong the party itself is derailed.

Another characteristic was that Jack began functioning as the supreme arbiter when there were differences in the Political Committee. I will give one example.

When Caroline and I had returned from Paris in early 1980, President Carter had raised the issue of reinstating the draft for the armed forces. The question arose among antiwar forces that if there was a draft, should women be excluded on the basis of their sex and the supposed weaknesses of females. The National Organization for Women (NOW) at first opposed reinstating the draft, but also said women should be included if there was a draft, because not to do so solely on the basis of their sex was discriminatory and would reinforce the oppression of women in general by putting a government seal of approval on it.

The NOW leadership quickly compromised its position with the stance that including women would "strengthen the military."

The Political Committee held a discussion on the question shortly after I returned. I supported the position that NOW originally took, while the rest of the Political Committee opposed women being included in the draft even if it was reinstated. The reasoning of the majority was that since we were opposed to the draft and the imperialist military as an institution, we should be opposed to women being included.

Jack was not present at this discussion, but certainly had previously shaped the majority position. In the course of the meeting, it appeared to me from the discussion that the majority had abandoned our historical position concerning the draft in relation to our own members. In the Second World War, we had taken the position that if drafted, our members would accept being drafted and become part of the armed forces, in spite of our opposition to the imperialist aims of the United States in the war. In our view, Washington's primary goal in the war was to triumph over its imperialist rivals, both its "democratic" allies and fascist enemies, and emerge from the war as the dominant global imperialist power. This was in fact a major outcome of the war.

But we would go into the military if drafted, to be part of the large number of workers in a similar situation. We would go through the experience of the war with them, while maintaining our opposition to the war and fascism and the right to our socialist convictions while in the armed forces. Our name for this policy was the "proletarian military policy." At the end of the war, Washington hoped to use its deployed military presence in the Pacific to attack China, which was in revolutionary ferment. SWP members in the military in the Pacific became part of a massive movement in opposition, with the demand that the troops be brought home, which is what happened.

We took a similar position during the Vietnam War, as described in the first volume of this work. Our members who were drafted were open socialists and opponents of the war. As a result, when opposition to the war developed within the army, we were part of it. This policy was a success, and we helped the civilian antiwar movement to see the soldiers as potential allies.

At the early 1980 Political Committee meeting on women and the draft, the discussion veered toward abandoning the "proletarian military policy." I bluntly asked if this was what was being proposed, and both Mary-Alice Waters and Steve Clark responded, "yes." Another meeting was held a few days later, with Jack present. We all knew that Jack's position would decide the question. Like Alexander the Great, he cut the Gordian knot in two. He came down on one side, opposing women being included in the draft. On the other, he supported the continuation of the proletarian military policy.*

The nature of the cult around Jack Barnes was twofold. He became the sole initiator of policy, and the supreme arbiter in any discussion. The obvious result was a growing fear among other leaders of freely expressing their views, else they be deemed "wrong."

An aspect of this development was the increasing use of trials of members. Heretofore, trials were few and far between, and involved instances of violation of discipline, that is, of decisions taken democratically by the majority. But increasingly, minor violations of our drug policy were brought to trial, when the more sensible course would have been to discuss with the member involved.

One trial in the early 1980s was of two members, who were a couple, who held a private party and invited friends from the branch as well as co-workers they had become friendly with. The bizarre charge was that by so doing, they were forming an unauthorized grouping.

We had a principle against the formation of Black or women's caucuses in the party. We were for such formations in the unions and other organizations, to further the fight for equality within those groups, but the only basis for forming a caucus within the party had to be common political positions. Obviously, being Black or a woman did not imply holding any particular political positions. We did have a policy of furthering affirmative action in promoting oppressed minorities and women to leadership positions.

However, our opposition to Black or women caucuses in the party began to be twisted into prohibition of Black or women comrades getting together socially, even of going out for a drink or bite together after branch meetings. This broadened to frowning upon any informal get-togethers. Such a prohibition seems absurd, but there was a method to the madness—to instill fear among members of informal political discussion. Without such discussions, which previously had been the norm in the whole history of the SWP, the political life of the organization ossified.

To hold trials against comrades for such absurd "violations"—and I've only listed a few—was extremely destructive. Some members were expelled as a result, but over and above such losses, a climate of fear of "crossing" some arbitrary rule was fostered. This weakened membership control of the leadership and strengthened the cult.

As the years went by, the "star" system of leadership became more and more exacerbated and entrenched, including special treatment and perquisites for the top leader, special standards that applied to Jack Barnes and some around him, and not to the ordinary members.

---

* In retrospect, it is clear I was correct in this discussion. Until 1948, when President Truman issued an executive order to abolish it, racial segregation was official policy in the armed forces, which the SWP opposed. (It took until 1954 before the last segregated military unit was finally disbanded.) In recent years gays and lesbians have demanded that restrictions against their being included in the military be abolished. Revolutionary socialists should support them in this struggle, while maintaining opposition to the imperialist armed forces as an institution. The question is equal rights. Similarly, gays and lesbians have been demanding the right to marriage. We should support them in this struggle, while recognizing that the institution of the nuclear family perpetuates the oppression of women and of gays and lesbians.

CHAPTER TWENTY-ONE: AFGHANISTAN

In April 1978 the Afghan government of President Mohammed Daud was overthrown by forces in the military led by the pro-Moscow People's Democratic Party of Afghanistan (PDPA), with support from the populace in the capital, Kabul.

Daud himself had overthrown the monarchy of Zahir Shah in 1973. Shah was in a line installed by the British in 1929. Daud initially inspired hopes with promises to establish democracy and to carry out land reform. Peasants were under the exploitation of feudal landlords. The country was one of the poorest, with some of the highest rates of illiteracy and poor health in the world.

In the next five years Daud failed to carry out his promises. Instead of democracy, his regime became increasingly repressive and dictatorial. Land reform was a dead letter. Imperialist presence became more evident. A wing of the PDPA led by Babrak Karmal gave support to the Daud regime in expectation that he would carry out reforms. But the increasing repression led Karmal to unite in July 1977 with the PDFA wing led by Noor Mohammed Taraki in opposition to the government. Karmal's faction was called "Parcham" and Taraki's, "Khalq."

The PDPA's influence grew, including among troops and officers in the military. In April 1978 Daud launched a new wave of repression aimed at beheading the PDPA. Taraki, Karmal and Hafizulla Amin—who headed the party's work in the army—were imprisoned. Large crowds organized by the PDPA gathered in Kabul, and military units under PDPA command revolted. Insurgent tanks knocked down the walls of the prison, and the prisoners released.

The new regime went on the radio to announce "the last remnants of monarchy, tyranny, despotism and the power of the dynasty [installed by the British] ... has ended, and all powers of the state are in the hands of the people of Afghanistan." Daud held out briefly in the presidential palace, but he and his relatives were killed.

The May 6 *New York Times* reported "Soldiers who distributed the [new] Government newspaper from army buses were besieged at every corner by crowds of eager buyers. Even people who are illiterate—as nine out of tens Afghans are—seemed eager to study the photographs, which showed the extensive damage done during the coup and scenes of 'citizens welcoming the elimination of the despotic sultanate' of President Daud. The paper also carried accounts or photographs of 'citizens happily welcoming the revolution in every region of the country.... " Foreign journalists, the *Times* reported, said that nearly every Afghan they interviewed was delighted at the coup.

Taraki was named President and Prime Minister, and Karmal and Amin became deputy Prime Ministers. At a May 6 news conference, Taraki said, "Our main objective is to secure the welfare of the workers and the peasants." A few days later he outlined the regime's program, including the abolition of feudal property relations in the countryside, agrarian reform, national rights for the country's national minorities, universal primary education for both girls and boys, and equality between men and women.

The SWP leadership supported these objectives, while noting that the PDPA was Stalinist, as the "opening of the Afghan revolution." It could spread to neighboring Iran and Pakistan, we thought. Ferment in Iran was already beginning, as explained in Chapter Sixteen in Part One.

On May 5, 1978, The New York Times ran an editorial entitled "Communist Coup in Afghanistan." It advocated giving sanctuary and other aid to opponents of the revolution, asserting that "Countries in the region should be prepared to lend a hand, and the wealthier nations should help them carry the burden."

Ernest Harsch wrote in *The Militant* that the Afghan events "spread alarm in reactionary circles far and wide. Immediately after the April insurrection, the Iranian and Pakistani regimes closed their borders with Afghanistan and placed their armies on alert." Washington set in motion what would eventually become a massive counter-revolutionary guerrilla war aimed to topple the new regime. The reactionary theocratic monarchy in Saudi Arabia was mobilized to provide massive financial backing, while the Pakistani military dictatorship of General Zia ul-Haq provided the guerrillas with training and sanctuary, and arms supplied by the US. The counter-revolutionary forces gradually built up during 1978.

Moscow became increasingly involved, providing military advisors and arms to the government. The primary reason it did so was not to advance the revolution, but to prevent the creation of an imperialist puppet regime on its borders. The Kremlin wanted to preserve Afghanistan as a buffer state against the pro-US Pakistani dictatorship. The USSR and Afghanistan signed many agreements, whereby Moscow would provide help in industrial development, energy, exploitation of natural resources, and military cooperation.

There were enormous objective obstacles facing the government. The country was one of the poorest in the world. The working class was very small, reflecting undeveloped industry. Over 90 percent of the country was illiterate. Women were excluded from public life except partly in the cities. Most of the population was rural, peasants in feudal relations with landlords. Religious obscurantism was especially prevalent in the rural areas. There were many different national groups that made true unification of the country difficult. The heel of British imperialism imposed the continuation of this backwardness in the 19th and much of the 20th centuries. Moreover, the British had artificially drawn the border between Afghanistan and the part of British-controlled India that became Pakistan, so that there were people in some of the national groupings who were on both sides of the border.

A revolutionary Marxist leadership would have had a difficult time in the context of the imperialist-backed counter-revolution. But there was no such leadership. Instead, there was the hardened Stalinist PDPA, whose policies made matters much worse. In much of 1978 and 1979, we didn't report on the shortcomings of the PDPA. This was largely due to lack of information, but there was also wishful thinking involved. We did begin to take notice as solid information became available.

In an article in April 1980, Ernest Harsch wrote:

"Under both the monarchy and the Daud regime, the party [PDPA] put its approach into practice by seeking alliances with 'patriotic' merchants and 'national' capitalists. One wing...initially supported Mohammad Daud and was rewarded with four posts in his regime. It was caught unawares when the 'progressive' Daud turned against the party, as well as against the toiling population. When the PDPA did finally carry out the insurrection against Daud, the choice was not entirely its own. It had been compelled to act partly out of self-defense ... and partly under pressure from its supporters in the streets.

"Since coming to power, the PDPA has sought to control and limit the revolutionary process. Although the PDPA had to allow—and even to encourage—a certain amount of mass organization and mobilization to carry through the reforms, it did so carefully, under strict party supervision, for fear that the actions might develop their own momentum and escape control. As a consequence, the initiative of the masses was kept at a minimum. The trade unions and women's and youth organizations grew only moderately. The Committees for the Defense of the Revolution—the armed militia units set up to fight the counter-revolution—played only a secondary role. This limited level of mass mobilization—resulting from the PDPA's bureaucratic constraints—was one of the greatest weaknesses of the Afghan revolution.

"Coupled with the Afghan leadership's hesitancy to call out the masses was its over-reliance on the state apparatus to try to carry through the reform program. Since the civil service, police, and army had only been purged following Daud's overthrow—not dissolved and replaced with new mass-based, revolutionary institutions—they were far from reliable instruments. Under the pressures of the counterrevolution and the sharpening class struggle, fissures developed. Some army units mutinied and some defected to the enemy....

"The party's bureaucratic approach—without the self-correcting feedback from mass participation in decision-making—also left the leadership more prone to error and misjudgment. Under the literacy campaign, for example, the PDPA activists who went out into the villages to organize classes immediately attempted to introduce coeducation, without regard to the problems of doing so in areas where women were still commonly segregated from men in public life. Rather than carefully and patiently trying to overcome conservative prejudices against women's emancipation, they sought to force the process....

"Similarly in carrying out the land reform, insufficient attention was paid to organizing the provision of agricultural assistance to the new peasant proprietors, who had previously relied on the landlords for seed, fertilizer, farm implements, and access to sources of water. An effective land reform requires careful organization and political preparation. Its results must be immediately tangible, easing the burdens on the peasantry; otherwise, the disposed landlords can play on discontent.

"In dealing with the counterrevolution, the regime's response was likewise bureaucratic and arbitrary. Its basic answer to all opposition was repressive force. Since it was carried out with an army that had been formed under the monarchy, there were undoubtedly excesses, tarnishing the revolution's image in the countryside and making it more difficult to defeat the counterrevolution politically.

"Repression, moreover, was not just used against the right. Any political dissent, even from supporters of the revolution and party members, was met with dismissal, imprisonment, or execution. The Aqsa (Agency for the Preservation of the Interests of Afghanistan), a secret police force assisted by Soviet advisors, was set up to deal with such opposition....

"The political weaknesses of the Afghan leadership were further magnified by sharp factional disputes. The reunification of the PDPA's Khalq ... and Parcham factions in 1977 had been an uneasy one. Within months of the PDPA's coming to power, the old disputes and rivalries erupted once again, with renewed vigor. If there were clear political disagreements involved, they were not made public....

"Parcham lost the first round. In June and July 1978, Karmal, Anahita Ratebzad, and other Parcham leaders were removed from key positions of authority and 'reassigned' as ambassadors abroad. In August, Abdul Qadir and two Parcham members of the cabinet were arrested and accused of plotting to overthrow the Taraki regime. Qadir was a popular military figure who had played a key role in the April insurrection (as well as the overthrow of King Zahir Shah in 1973); although he was originally a Parcham member, he was not now closely identified with either faction.... Taraki claimed that Karmal and other Parcham leaders were also implicated in the alleged plot and expelled them from the party. When he called them back from their ambassadorial post abroad, they prudently declined to return.

"A few Parcham leaders survived the purge, but the bulk—accounting for a sizeable minority of the party leadership—ended up in prison or in exile.... In 1979, as the growth of the imperialist-backed counterrevolution put greater strains on the regime, new rifts appeared within the Khalq faction itself. As the year progressed, Hafizulla Amin steadily consolidated his position within the regime and party. In March he took over as prime minister from Taraki (who retained the post of president). In July he acquired the Defense Ministry.... On September 24, after a shoot-out at the presidential palace, Amin emerged as the head of state. Radio Kabul later announced that Takari was dead.... The change in government did not result in any basic shifts in policy, although Amin did put greater emphasis on the use of military force and repression. Aqsa ... was disbanded and replaced by the KAM (Workers Intelligence Institute), headed by Amin's cousin..."

In October a major offensive by the government in one section of the country along the Pakistan border inflicted heavy casualties on the guerrillas, but within weeks the rightists began to filter back. Troops mutinied at Kabul's largest infantry garrison. Amin managed to put it down, but a nearby tank corps refused to come to Amin's aid.

The regime was collapsing. In this situation, the Kremlin decided to directly intervene, sending tens of thousands of troops, which initially set back the rightists. At the same time, the Soviet command arrested and executed Amin and his cousin, claiming they were "CIA agents," and set up a new government under Karmal, who had been in the Soviet Union.

The assessment contained in the above quoted article, was in fact in contradiction to its conclusion, which supported the Soviet invasion. This was in line with a report adopted by the National Committee at its meeting of January 5-9, 1980. That report said, "The presence of Soviet troops, by barring the road to the counterrevolution, creates a new and more favorable situation.... If Soviet troops help the new regime score victories over the reactionaries, this takes pressure off the Afghan revolution and encourages and inspires the struggle for social revolution in that country."

The report also said that the entry of Soviet troops "strengthens the hand of the anti-imperialist fighters in Iran. And it even buys more time for the revolutionary government in Nicaragua, halfway around the world. Needless to say, the impact will be great in Pakistan, India, Bangladesh, and Turkey."

At that NC meeting was a member of the International Executive Committee of the Fourth International, Daniel Bensaïd, who was also a leader of the French LCR. He spoke against the line we adopted. Flush from our "victory" at the World Congress in November 1979, we smugly dismissed him. Also involved was our "triumphalism" at the time. The Iranian revolution had struck a blow against US imperialism, as had the Nicaraguan and Grenadian revolutions. Revolutionists in El Salvador had united in the Farabundo Marti National Liberation Front (FMLN), named after a Communist Party martyr in an uprising in the 1930s, and were making progress.   We believed we were on the threshold of a political radicalization of the working class on an international scale, including in the US and the other imperialist countries.

At a meeting of the United Secretariat soon after, I, along with Australian and British comrades, argued along the same line. In our press and Presidential election campaign of Pulley and Zimmerman we continued to present this erroneous position. For example, Fred Feldman wrote an article entitled, "Afghanistan – Russia's Vietnam?" claiming the opposite was the case. "Far from being a 'Russian Vietnam,' the dispatching of Soviet troops to Afghanistan placed a new big obstacle in the way of Washington's drive to prepare a new Vietnam in the Middle East and Southwest Asia." Of course it did become "Russia's Vietnam" in the sense it became a quagmire in the years to come. The Soviet Union was eventually defeated, and the U.S.-backed rightists were able to roll back the gains the revolution had initially made. These rightists themselves were fractured along national and regional lines. The corrupt "warlords" beholden to their own landlords waged a war among themselves that practically destroyed the country, and paved the way for the emergence of another extreme rightist group, the Taliban, who promised to end the internal wars and corruption. Such was the legacy of the U.S.-organized counter-revolution.

In August 1980, we held an Activist and Educational Conference at Oberlin College in Ohio. Caroline Lund gave a class on Afghanistan, in which she explained our position supporting the Soviet invasion.

Following the conference a special meeting of the Political Committee was called, to which were invited the members of the National Committee and leaders of other FI sections who had been present at the conference. Without previous discussion on the PC, Doug Jenness proposed a change in line. The real report was given by Jack Barnes rejecting the position on Soviet troops the NC had adopted in January. He had not only sandbagged Caroline, but most of the PC including myself, and the whole NC. In Part One I explained how I had become uneasy with how Jack Barnes had begun to do this in the Political Committee as the 1970s wore on, leading me to conclude that the leadership had become a "one man band" as I explained it to Mary-Alice Waters early in 1978, who agreed with me at that time. But in this action, Jack had demonstrated that the "one man band" was indeed a fully formed cult around him.

One factor Jack cited in his own rethinking was the position of the Cuban leadership, which, while supporting the Soviet invasion, had done so with misgivings. Cuban Ambassador to the United Nations, Raul Roa, strongly condemned the U.S. proxy war but referred to the "historical dilemma" the Cubans found themselves in concerning the Soviet invasion. In this instance the Cuban's influence on the SWP was positive.

Barnes had been responsible for formulating both the January position and its reversal in August, without a single NC member, including myself, expressing disagreement, with one exception. That was Andrew Pulley, who had been defending the Soviet invasion in campaign appearances all spring and summer, but he supported the new line in the end.

Peter Camejo asked for a meeting of the Political Committee after the expanded PC meeting was over. Peter explained that he agreed with the new position (it had become obvious that the Soviet invasion was a disaster), but he strongly rejected how it was done. Mary-Alice agreed with him. I was quiet, although I also agreed with Peter and Mary-Alice, because I had become frightened that I might be expelled, given Jack's threat to me in 1978. Jack backed off, and agreed to a full discussion in the NC before any public correction was made. That was done at an NC meeting in November.

Looking back, it is clear that Jack's initial support of the Soviet invasion was an adaptation to the Soviet bureaucracy, which he then pulled back from. His unilateral reversal at the August 1980 expanded PC meeting was a shock to our Australian cothinkers, and resulted in a break between our organizations. The Australians were not about to jump at Jack's command. Unfortunately, they held fast to the wrong position of supporting the ill-fated Soviet invasion.

CHAPTER TWENTY-TWO: IRAN

The students who occupied the huge U.S. Embassy in Tehran in November 1979 began releasing confidential documents naming names of CIA operatives in the embassy. These included the cover stories they used to further U.S. plots against the revolution. Some of the revelations included documentation of U.S. collusion with the more pro-imperialist elements within the Iranian regime itself. Prime Minister Medhi Bazargan was implicated, leading to his dismissal and replacement by Abolhassan Bani-Sadr.

On December 23 there was a demonstration of tens of thousands of workers in front of the Embassy. The Islamic Workers Shora (committee) representing 128 factory committees in the Tehran area, called the action. Workers from many auto factories were present, including General Motors, British Leyland, Mercedes Benz, Renault and Iran National Car. Among other contingents were textile workers and workers from the Kian Tire Company and Phillips Electronics. A delegation of students inside the Embassy hailed the workers as "the arm of the revolution."

The decision by Khomeini to support the occupation not only served his interests in the faction fights at the top by raising his prestige among the masses, it also opened the door to renewed intervention by them. A statement adopted by the Islamic Workers Shora at the December 23 demonstration illustrated this. "We declare our hatred for imperialism," the statement began, promising that if there were an invasion by Washington, "we will make Iran the graveyard of the American troops." The statement called for the return of the Shah to face trial, and for the spies to be brought before "open, revolutionary trials, which will also be trials of U.S. imperialism for its crimes." This latter demand contrasted sharply with the Khomeini regime's secret trials.

Iranian landlords and capitalists began hording raw materials in expectation that a U.S. blockade would cause shortages and higher prices. They held back new investment, refused to make needed repairs in workplaces, closed factories and were sending money out of the country. Merchants and capitalists used government subsidies for imports such as steel to reap super profits by reselling them on the black market.

"We condemn the shameless conspiracies of the comprador capitalists and looters here in Iran," the statement said. "Cut off the hands of the capitalists who are sabotaging production! Abolish capitalism and plunder! The government should take complete control of industrial planning, and run industry in the interests of national growth. The government should run all the factories in collaboration with the shora in each plant." The Islamic Workers Shora called for land to the peasants. Other demands against imperialism and for independent economic development were included, as well as a call for "all the oppressed of the world to join with us in struggle against the colonial system headed by U.S. imperialism."[1]

The pressures of the mobilization against Washington, and the struggle between revolution and counter-revolution, led to a split in the HKS (Iranian Socialist Workers Party). The minority, composed mainly of comrades who had come back from Europe, had come to the conclusion that the revolution was in fact a fascist movement. They formed a grouping called the HKS Militant Wing. To avoid confusion, the majority changed its name to the HKE (Revolutionary Workers Party), and continued to publish *Kargar*. In early January 1980 the HKE announced that Mahmoud Sayrafiezadeh was its candidate for President in the upcoming elections. The HKS Militant Wing went underground, and some time after its members returned to Europe.

In April 1980, U.S. President Carter ordered a clandestine raid to attempt to free the hostages held in the Embassy, as a first strike to be followed up by a wider invasion. The raid was a complete fiasco, and these plans had to be aborted.

One week after the failed raid, there were big demonstrations on May Day throughout Iran.

Reporting for *The Militant*, Fred Feldman described Washington's threats and the growing conflict within the country:

"Factories and workplaces were shut down so that workers could participate.... The Tehran march was organized by the Islamic Workers Shora.... An estimated 250,000 people turned out, with contingents of workers carrying banners from their factory committees. At a May Day rally in Isfahan, President Bani-Sadr denounced an 'American plot' to overthrow the government. He repeated the same theme in a letter to United Nations Secretary General Kurt Waldheim, charging that Washington's actions were 'carried out with the aim of toppling the revolutionary regime and reestablishing U.S. domination over Iran.' Recent bombings in Tehran, including the placing of bombs along the route of the Tehran May Day march, are widely regarded in Iran as part of a U.S. effort to destabilize the regime....

"There is mounting evidence that Carter is backing counterrevolutionary armed gangs seeking to crush the revolution. The April 30 *Christian Science Monitor* cited the case of General

Gholam Ali Oveisi, leader of a rightist group called Azadegan. Oveisi was head of the shah's ground forces before the monarchy was toppled in February 1979. He was responsible for the deaths of thousands of peaceful anti-shah demonstrators. He lived in the United States until recently, and is now said to be based in [U.S. ally] Iraq. 'General Oveisi,' reports *Strategy Week*, a newsletter with close Pentagon ties, 'has moved quietly...to develop a strong military team and the bases from which to prepare. His funding position is known to be sound.'....

"But the capitalist government of Abolhassan Bani-Sadr has not responded to Washington's threats by strengthening the workers' committees. Nor has it forged unity between the oppressed nationalities and the rest of Iran's working people. Instead Bani-Sadr has attempted to launch attacks on these revolutionary forces. The Islamic Workers Shora of Tehran distributed a leaflet at its May 1 rally protesting the arrest of four Abadan workers active in the Islamic Shora of Oil Workers."

The leaflet by the Tehran Shora denounced the head of the oil ministry as a remnant of the old regime who "could not accept the concept of shora," who had the four arrested when they attempted to discuss bad conditions and the continued dominance of the old oil industry administration. The workers asked how it was possible that agents of the old regime were still in the administration while these Islamic fighters were in prison?

The Militant also described Bani-Sadr's collusion with rightist forces:

"Bani-Sadr also gave a green light to ultraright gangs that attacked the campuses in several cities in mid-April. They were attempting to back up the government's call for an end to political activity on campus. The attackers wanted to block the moves by the Islamic Students Organizations [ISOs]...to transform the universities into a base for arming the masses, spreading literacy, and deepening the revolution.... The rightists centered their attacks on organizations which have a following at the universities but are less popular than the ISOs among the Iranian masses—the Fedayeen and the Mujahadeen. Dozens were reported killed in heavy street fighting. But the attempt to crush the campus-based political activity did not have the desired result. On May Day, the Fedayeen and Mujahadeen were able to stage rallies of their own with tens of thousands of participants. (These groups have taken a sectarian stance toward the mass workers movement; they abstained from the May Day demonstrations organized by the factory committees.) And the ferment on the campuses continued. In the aftermath of May Day, meetings were held at Tehran University where members of the

ISOs, Fedayeen, Mujahadeen, Tudeh Party (the pro-Moscow Stalinist Party), Revolutionary Workers Party, and others freely debated proposals on how to put the universities at the service of the revolution.

"The regime's most brutal attacks are being carried out in Kurdistan, where the Kurdish minority has been fighting for autonomy. A general military drive was apparently launched April 24 against most of the main Kurdish towns and cities.... Helicopter gunships and tanks are being used against civilians protesting the new attacks, and many casualties have been reported."[2]

On July 10, Bani-Sadr announced that a coup attempt had been squashed. Feldman wrote:

"The Iranian government appears to have succeeded in breaking up a large-scale U.S.-backed coup attempt by army officers, the Iraqi government, and followers of Shapur Bakhtiar. Bakhtiar was the shah's last premier, who has been attempting to organize counterrevolutionary forces from Paris.... A detailed version of the coup plans appeared in the July 14 *Christian Science Monitor.* 'The plotters planned to set up a military junta in Iran,' stated correspondent Leslie Keith. 'They would then have installed former Premier Shapur Bakhtiar as President.'

"Their blueprint called for even more initial bloodshed than the 1953 coup which Washington engineered to bring the shah back to the throne. After capturing Hamadan air base, some 200 miles southwest of Tehran, 'about 30 American-made Phantom aircraft were to have taken off to bomb various sensitive targets.... The most important of these was the home of Ayatollah Khomeini.... About 15 Phantoms were given the job of bombing this target.... Another was President Bani-Sadr's office in Tehran.... Ten of the Phantoms were to head for Qum, about 80 miles south of Tehran. They were to have bombed the Faizieh school and important institutions of religious learning.... The Phantoms were also to have bombed and totally destroyed the Park Hotel in Tehran and a teacher's club where most of the deputies in Iran's new parliament are staying, thus wiping out in a stroke the majority of members. One of the first acts of the new junta,' Keith claimed, 'was to have been the release of the [hostages at the Embassy]. They were then to have rounded up about 70 of the top leaders, put them against walls wherever they were found, and shot them.'....

"According to Keith, the Iraqi government was to stage a diversion: 'The night the coup was to have been staged, Iraqi aircraft were to have entered Iran to bomb a number of unimportant targets. This, say the Iranian authorities, was the excuse the plotters were to have had to take off from Hamadan.'"[3]

Following the breaking up of the coup, Carter and Saddam Hussein launched their buildup for an all-out attack. Iraqi forces began skirmishes on the border with Iran. "The events on the western border are a serious warning, signaling the need to defend the Iranian revolution," warned an editorial in *Kargar*. "There are sufficient facts to show the serious and extraordinary significance of these events:

• A week has passed since the right-wing coup in Turkey.
• The mobilization of the U.S. military strike force continues.
• Movements by the U.S. strike force in Egypt have been reported.
• Activities of elements associated with the Pahlavi autocracy, such as [Gen. Gholam] Oveisi, [Gen. Ahmed] Palizban and Bakhtiar in Iraq—both in the field of news propaganda and of military mobilizations—have continued and expanded."

Kargar explained that it was the bastions of the workers, the women, the peasants and the oppressed nationalities that must be mobilized to defeat the counterrevolution. "What is on the agenda of the Iranian revolution is: achieving total and genuine independence from imperialism; solving the land problem; emancipating the masses of peasants and farmers from poverty and oppression; and expropriating power and wealth from landowners, millionaire capitalists, the rich, and other indigenous agents of imperialism." The shoras and other mass organizations should be armed, Kargar declared. "Now, for the defense of the revolution, it is necessary for the toiling masses of Iran to mobilize for war against imperialism as one united family, to close ranks, and to strike as one fist."4

Less than a week after the *Kargar* editorial was printed, Iraq launched a full-scale invasion of Iran on September 22, 1980, accompanied by intense bombing of heavily populated cities by U.S.-supplied aircraft. The U.S. obtained agreement from Britain, France, West Germany, Italy and Japan to assemble an international naval force should it become necessary to counter Iran if it attempted to close the narrow Strait of Hormuz at the mouth of the Persian Gulf to oil tankers from Iraq. Washington also sent four radar and command aircraft to Saudi Arabia to provide intelligence to the Iraqi invasion forces.

The U.S. counted on a quick Iraqi victory. Washington's optimism was based on the fact that the Iranian army was weakened in the course of the insurrection. But the warmongers didn't take into account the response of the Iranian masses.

As Janice Lynn wrote in *The Militant:*

"Reports from socialists in Tehran indicate that throughout the country there have been massive demonstrations and rallies in defense of the revolution. At first the Iranian government thought it could depend solely on the armed forces to counter the assault by the Iraqi regime. But it soon became clear that this would not be possible.

"Workers in factories throughout Tehran began to sign up through their factory shoras ... to volunteer to fight.... Iranian president Abolhassan Bani-Sadr asked every mosque throughout the country to sign up twenty-two people to fight the Iraqi military attacks. In Tehran, this request was fulfilled within hours. On September 23, the day after the Iraqi attack on Tehran's Mehrabad international airport, a million-strong demonstration ... took place at Tehran University.... A *Reuter's* dispatch reporting on the rally said, 'All the leftist groups have offered to send men to the front.'

"The September 30 [*New York Times*] ran a dispatch from [the Paris daily] *Le Monde*.... 'Random conversations with Iranians indicate that the people are less politically divided than before the war. They still criticize politicians and mullahs, and sometimes even Ayatollah Ruhollah Khomeini himself, but most seem to throw their support behind the Government.... Despite their differences on domestic issues, all political parties, nationalists, centrists, leftists, Marxist and Moslems, legal or illegal, are calling for support to the war effort. Signing up for the armed forces has become so popular that authorities have had to turn many men down.'"5

The Washington-Baghdad planners calculated that the Iranian regime's attacks on the oppressed nationalities would cause them to support the invasion. They chose to first attack with ground forces the predominantly Arab province of Khuzestan expecting sympathy from fellow Arabs.

Feldman wrote:

"The Tehran government in Iran encouraged such assessments by falsely branding Arabs and Kurds who demanded national rights as Iraqi and imperialist agents. In the first days of fighting, U.S. journalists did what they could to bolster the 'intelligence' estimates. In the September 28 *New York Times*, John Kifner reported meeting with three soldiers, purporting to be Iranian Arabs, who were fighting with Iraqi forces. He passed along their claim that 'the Arab population had risen to fight the Persians.' But the uprising never got off the printed page....

"In the October 6 *Christian Science Monitor*, Geoffrey Godsell pointed to predictions of Arab and Kurdish support to Iraq as another miscalculation. 'This more diverse patchwork [of nationalities] within Iran suggests to an outsider that under pressure Iran would more readily disintegrate than Iraq. Yet the rallying within hitherto debilitated Iran against the Iraqi attacks of the past two weeks points in the opposite direction.... According to Iranian socialists, the army and revolutionary guards are distributing arms to many Arab civilians. Others are fighting bare-handed or with whatever comes to hand.

"The October 1 issue of the Paris daily *Le Monde* confirmed that Khuzestan's Arabs responded to President Abolhassan Bani-Sadr's call for a mobilization against the counterrevolutionary drive by the Iraqi regime. 'The authorities of Khuzestan have admitted today what was unimaginable hardly a week ago,' wrote Eric Ropuleau. 'They are cooperating with leftist groups in the organization of resistance fighters to whom arms are being distributed.'.... The Iraqi rulers have acknowledged the stand of the Arabs in their own way, with brutal shelling of the civilian population and looting of occupied segments of Khorramshar [in Khuzestan].

"The Kurdish people, who were close to full scale war with the Tehran government at times in recent months because of government attempts to block demands for autonomy appear to be centering their fire on the Iraqi regime."[6]

The Arabs, Kurds, Azerbaijanis and other oppressed groups rallied to repel the invasion. Volunteers from across Iran poured into Khuzestan to join the Arab masses in battle. The invasion of Khuzestan was smashed, but Iraq continued to hold Iranian territory near the border. Driven back to their border with Iran, the Hussein regime continued the attack against Iran for many years with massive bombing and shelling of Tehran and other cities, and fighting along the border, in a bloody war that caused millions of deaths on both sides.

Washington continued to back Iraq in this bloodbath to weaken and debilitate Iran. The other Western powers joined in. Germany provided Iraq with poison gas, used against Iran and Iraqi Kurds. Hussein accused Iraqi Kurds of supporting Iranian Kurds in their defense of the revolution. The Kremlin, which had trained the Iraqi army, joined Washington's war by pouring arms into Iraq. France also armed Iraq.*

The government used the war as a pretext to clamp down, in what became a turning point in the revolution. In June 1982, members of the Mujahadeen, which presented itself as a left Islamic group and had played a role in opposition to the Shah, were executed. The group responded by declaring it was taking up arms against the government. Then, on June 22, Bani-Sadr was ousted as president by a vote in Parliament. "None of the fundamental issues of concern to the masses of Iranian workers—the struggle against imperialist threats, the Iraqi invasion, or the economic and social problems—

were debated or discussed in this power struggle," observed *The Militant*. "Bani-Sadr's ouster was not comparable to the fall of the government headed by former Prime Minister Mehdi Bazargan in November 1979. That fall was based on the anti-imperialist mass mobilizations surrounding the occupation of the U.S. embassy (Spy Den). It was an expression of the masses' opposition to the complicity of the capitalist politicians such as Bazargan with U.S. imperialism. And during this process workers and peasants raised their own demands and the workers' independent organizations were strengthened. There was an expansion of democratic rights such as freedom of the press and assembly. In contrast, Bani-Sadr's ouster in a vote by Parliament has been accompanied by repressive measures—the banning of newspapers, attacks on activists, arrests and executions."[7]

On June 28, there was a huge bomb attack on the headquarters of the Islamic Republican Party (IRP) that killed at least 72 top party leaders. *The Militant* denounced the attack as "a serious blow to the Iranian revolution." Among those killed in the blast were IRP leader Ayatollah Mohammad Mantazeri, son of Tehran's main religious leader; four cabinet ministers; six deputy ministers; and 27 elected members of parliament. As *The Militant* reported, "This action strengthens the hand of U.S. imperialism against the Iranian revolution. It facilitates Washington's campaign to disrupt Iran's war effort against Iraqi invaders, to demoralize and wear down the working masses, and to open the door to outright intervention by U.S.-supported counterrevolutionary forces. The Iranian masses immediately responded to the attack on their revolution. More than one million people poured into the streets of Tehran on June 30 to attend the funeral for the IRP leaders. They gathered in front of the parliament building and marched to the...cemetery tens miles away. The major chants throughout the march were 'America is the enemy' and 'death to America.'"[8]

Whether more sinister forces were involved, or if this was the sole handiwork of the Mujahadeen, didn't really matter. The former left group joined forces with the capitalist politician Bani-Sadr to wage a terror campaign of bombings and murder for over a year, and openly went over to the side of Iraq and the counterrevolution, mounting attacks on Iran from within Iraqi territory. On September 21 Bani-Sadr called on the imperialists to tighten the economic blockade.

The overwhelming support the masses gave the Khomeini regime, which still was able to project itself as the leader of the revolution, impelled them to vehemently reject the Mujahadeen terror campaign. That this group and supporters of Bani-Sadr went over to Iraq which was still carrying out massive bombing of Iranian cities, inflicting death and destruction, put them on the side of imperialism in the eyes of most Iranians. The regime was able to utilize the "leftism" of the Mujahadeen and Bani-Sadr too, who had cultivated that image, to begin a campaign against socialists of all types. The Soviet bureaucracy's support of Iraq, while clandestine, was also known and utilized by the regime in this campaign.

The first arrests and executions were of Mujahadeen fighters, and other armed groups taking up arms against the regime such as a wing of the Fedayeen, but there were arrests of others, too. Two women members of the HKE were arrested and charged with being members of one of the other armed groups. "On July 9, a reporter for the HKE newspaper *Kargar* attended a press conference at Evin Prison held by Tehran's Revolutionary Prosecutor General [Assadollah] Lajverdi. The *Kargar* reporter asked Lajverdi why in the context of imperialism's stepped-up campaign of terror against the Iranian revolution have two such staunch anti-imperialist fighters been arrested? The two women have played an important part in the military mobilizations in their factory against the Iraqi invasion and in anti-imperialist struggles. Lajverdi's response was that all Marxists are enemies of the Islamic revolution."9

In 1982 the terror campaign and the regime's repression escalated. The government attempted to introduce a new labor law aimed at restricting workers' rights and social gains. This attempt met with resistance in the workplaces, strong enough to compel the leaders of the workplace shoras on a national level to protest, and the proposed law was withdrawn. The attacks on democratic rights centered on the left. Workers' newspapers were banned, with *Kargar* being the last such in March 1982. In all, 127 issues of *Kargar* had been published. This was an important achievement in the face of the growing hostility and repression of the Khomeini government.

But in the course of 1982 the repression extended beyond the left, and sparked opposition. Khomeini felt compelled to issue a statement on December 15 against arbitrary arrests, although "subversives" were specifically exempted from such arrests.

On January 17, 1983, HKE central leader Babak Zahraie was arrested. No one, including his wife Kateh Vafadari, knew where he was being held or if he was alive. When Kateh gave birth to a son six months later, she used an Iranian Islamic custom to find out if he was alive and where he was being held. The father was supposed to name his son, so Kateh went to the authorities so that Babak could be notified of the birth. They came to Babak's cell to get him to name his son, which he refused to do. News of this came back to Kateh, so she knew he was alive and being held at the Evin prison. Kateh had begun to organize a civil liberties defense campaign since his arrest.

The campaign lasted for years to alleviate Babak's conditions and for his release. Babak was held in solitary confinement for the first years (1,075 days) of his imprisonment, without any outside contact and reading material for the first 600 days.

In February 1983, central leaders of the Tudeh Party (the pro-Moscow Stalinist party) were also arrested. Then, on May 4, the Tudeh Party itself was banned.

The Militant editorialized:

"In a blow to the Iranian revolution and the right of workers to form political parties to advance their struggles, the Iranian government banned the Tudeh Party...the largest and oldest workers' party in Iran. The same day, Iranian officials expelled 18 Soviet diplomats from the country. About a week later, the Iranian government announced it had arrested 1,000 Tudeh members around the country, in addition to party leaders arrested in February.

"These moves are a serious setback for the Iranian people's struggle against the ongoing attacks of U.S. imperialism and the continued aggression from the Iraqi regime, and battles of workers and peasants for land reform, labor rights, and the new society they overthrew the shah in order to build.... This came in the context of tightening restrictions on other workers parties, including the Revolutionary Workers Party (HKE), several of whose leaders are in jail. There has been stepped-up harassment of militant Islamic currents in mass organizations like the *Jihad*, the Reconstruction Crusade which has been active in the countryside among peasants.... The banning of the Tudeh Party came after Iranian television and radio broadcast three days of fake confessions by leading Tudeh figures. The purpose of these statements, clearly false and extracted under coercion, was to promote anti-Soviet, anti-Marxist views and to pressure workers' organizations to dissolve and cease functioning in any manner independent from the ruling Islamic Republican Party....

"The Iranian regime remains in bitter conflict with U.S. imperialism and has recently established important trade and diplomatic relations with countries like Nicaragua. Nonetheless, Iranian officials have at the same time intensified their polemics against Marxism and the idea of class struggle, through the media, at prayer meetings, and in the factories and mass organizations. These attacks are not mainly aimed at the Tudeh and other workers parties, which remain relatively small, but at the broader working-class movement."[10]

Subsequently, the left was completely crushed, with thousands of executions. This was accompanied by the smashing of the shoras as independent working class organizations. The revolutionary aspirations of the masses were defeated in the consolidation of the capitalist regime.

Imperialism, however, continued its attempts to overthrow Iran and reestablish the complete control it enjoyed under the Shah. Iraq continued its attack, but by 1982 Iran did push Iraq back from most of the country.**

The war dragged on. The defeat of the left and the demobilization of the masses took its toll on the war effort, until Iran was finally forced to accept a "peace" acceptable to Iraq and its imperialist masters in 1988. Perhaps the major gain of the Iranian revolution which has lasted was its conquering of independence, and the anti-imperialist consciousness of the Iranian people, which makes Iran, still as I write in 2011, a thorn in Washington's side.

Kateh launched, at first with cadres of the HKE and a few intellectuals like the revered Shams Al-Ahmad, the defense campaign to improve the conditions of Babak's imprisonment. Like the other socialist groups, the HKE gradually disintegrated. Under severe pressure and threats, some capitulated. Most were driven out of the country. Kateh persisted in her efforts and Babak's conditions gradually improved, although he came to the brink of execution a number of times. It was harder for the regime to execute HKE members because of their revolutionary record. Babak believes they would have executed him if he had capitulated and made a public "confession," since he would no longer have been of use to them alive. This was the fate of the leaders of the other left groups. Babak was released in 1988 and forced into exile. In the end, no HKE members were killed in the repression, although a few died in defending the revolution from the imperialist-backed Iraqi assault.

I would draw attention to Kateh's defense campaign. This effort took courage especially in the face of the increasingly anti-women regime. Her efforts in the end undoubtedly helped save Babak's life, demonstrating the importance of defense efforts on behalf of working class fighters even under repressive regimes.

Babak Zahraie and Kateh Vafadari take their place among the many unsung heroes of the struggles of the world working class.

---

* During the U.S. wars against Iraq beginning in 1991, Washington cynically pointed to Saddam Hussein's use of poison gas against Iraqi Kurds as a pretext, while avoiding mentioning its use against Iran. The full extent of the West's (and Soviet) backing of Iraq against Iran is not known. When, in the lead-up to the 2003 invasion the Iraqi regime compiled a full dossier on everything provided it during the Iranian war for presentation to the United Nations and the public,

U.S. Secretary of State Colin Powell demanded to see it first, and it was expunged of all references to such backing.

** After the Iranians beat back Iraq to the border in 1982, some socialists, including in the Fourth International, denounced Iran for not declaring peace, adopting a neutral stance in the war. But this was not a border dispute between semi-colonial countries under capitalist governments, which we would oppose. It was an imperialist assault carried out by a proxy targeting the gains the Iranian masses won in the revolution.

1 *The Militant,* Jan. 18, 1980.
2 Ibid., May 23, 1980.
3 Ibid., July 15, 1980.
4 Ibid., Oct. 3, 1980.
5 Ibid., Oct. 10, 1980.
6 Ibid., Oct. 17, 1980.
7 Ibid., July 10, 1981.
8 Ibid.
9 Ibid., July 17, 1981.
10 Ibid., June 3, 1983.

CHAPTER TWENTY-THREE: POLAND

The summer of 1980 saw Poland's biggest strike wave in a decade. It was a major challenge to the Stalinist government of President Edward Gierek.

The SWP followed the events in Poland closely, providing extensive coverage in *The Militant*. Fred Feldman described the background to the strikes in an August 1980 report:

"Tens of thousands of workers have shut down some 170 factories in the Baltic Sea port cities of Gdansk, Gdynia, and Sopot. The driving force in the struggle was the 17,000 workers at the Lenin shipyard in Gdansk, who have taken over the yard and turned it into an organizing center for the struggle.

"Strikes are also reported in other parts of Poland, part of a tide of protest that began welling up on July 1 [1980] when the government imposed a sharp increase in meat prices. The Lenin shipyard workers halted work on August 13. Their action was sparked by the firing of a woman worker who had played a role in leading earlier struggles [at the beginning of the year].

"Their demands initially centered on a $66 a month wage increase to match price rises and recognition of their right to form a union independent of the Gierek government. But the demands have included a wide range of democratic and economic rights. The shipyard workers have elected a strike committee to represent them. It is headed by Lech Walesa, a shipyard worker fired in 1976 for protest activities.

"The August 18 *New York Times* reported Jack [Jacek] Kuron, a representative of the Committee for Social Self-Defense [KOR in its Polish initials] saying that an inter-factory strike committee had been formed when representatives of the shipyard strikers visited 20 other factories in Gdnya and Sopot to express solidarity. Support for the strikers grew steadily. 'Throughout the day,' wrote John Darton in the August 20 *Times*, 'factory delegates continued to arrive at the shipyard in vans flying the red and white Polish flag. As they strode into the grimy, red-brick conference building serving as strike headquarters, they were given a rousing welcome by delegates already there, seated at long tables with makeshift placards identifying their plants.'"[1]

The Gdansk shipyard workers continued to galvanize workers across the country. Then the regime caved in.

Andy Rose wrote in *The Militant*:

"Polish workers have won an historic victory: the right to organize independent, democratic trade unions, free from the control of the Stalinist bureaucracy. The Warsaw regime buckled August 30 on this key issue—the strikers' 'Demand No. 1'—as tens of thousands of coal miners and steelworkers in Silesia joined the mass workers' revolt.

"The strikers evidently scored major gains on all of their twenty-one demands, including:

• wage increases,
• automatic cost-of-living adjustments,
• release of political prisoners,
• wider civil liberties,
• more food supplies,
• better health service,
• more day-care centers,
• liberalized maternity leaves for working women, and
• the right to a big say in all aspects of national planning.

"While shipyard workers and other strikers on the Baltic Coast returned to work September 1, the coal miners' walkout spread explosively in response to the deaths of eight miners in an underground accident that day. In addition to demanding assurance they would be covered by the government's settlement with the Gdansk and Szczecin strike committee, the miners raised their own grievances around safety and working conditions. They called for an end to Saturday work, abolition of a round-the-clock shift system, 'repair of worn-out mining equipment,' and 'an end to the robbery-like coal extraction policy.'

"By September 2 more than 200,000 workers were on strike in Silesia, Poland's industrial heartland, shutting down nineteen coal mines and thirteen other facilities. The Silesian strikers set up a coordinating committee, as the Baltic Coast workers had earlier done.... Meanwhile, the agreement between the government and the Gdansk committee was broadcast in full on radio and television throughout Poland. The full text, including all the strikers' demands and settlement terms, was also published in major newspapers.... 'We have not won everything that we hoped and dreamed about,' said Lech Walesa, head of the Gdansk Interfactory Strike Committee. 'But we have achieved as much as we could under the circumstances, including respect for certain civil rights.'"[2]

The movement gained steam. "In the few weeks since the victorious strikes of August and early September, the free trade union movement has swelled into a flood sweeping Poland," Gerry Foley reported. "At the first national conference of these unions in Gdansk on September 17, organizers announced that 3 million workers from about 3,500 plants and institutions have signed up as many members as the official Polish Communist Party [Polish United Workers' Party], which for thirty years has served as the representative of the social caste that holds a near monopoly on material privileges and possibilities of advancement."3

The power and spread of the workers' upsurge put the Kremlin and world Stalinism on the defensive. The U.S. Communist Party (CP) initially had raised a howl about "anti-socialist elements" involved in the strikes. But after the first workers' victories the CP's *Daily World* wrote: "A notable feature of the Polish developments is that no anti-socialist or anti-Soviet slogans were raised. It was not socialism which came under attack in Poland, but the failure to carry it out." Even Soviet leader Leonid Brezhnev chimed in that "socialism and democracy are inseparable." But in the course of the struggle the Stalinists would prove once again their fidelity to neither democracy nor socialism.

The union movement spread across Poland and soon centralized itself under the name "Solidarity." The bureaucratic caste, a parasite on the workers' state, fought back. It tried to divide the movement, and found an ally in this endeavor in the reactionary and anti-Semitic Catholic Church hierarchy. Both targeted the most left wing of the movement, KOR, and played on the fear of a Soviet invasion. During the strikes the Church called on the workers to go back to work, a call that went unheeded. Then, in December, the Council of Bishops issued a statement, warning, "It is forbidden to undertake actions that could raise the danger of a threat to the freedom and statehood of the fatherland." A spokesperson for the Bishops, Father Orszulik, made clear who the target was. In a dispatch to the December 13 *New York Times,* he "mentioned a statement attributed to the spokesman for KOR, Jacek Kuroń, that said opposition elements would try to gain power gradually, not immediately, out of fear of provoking Soviet intervention. Father Orszulik said the statement had 'irritated the whole [Soviet] bloc.'"

The same day that the Bishops issued their statement, the Polish military newspaper wrote, "His [Kuroń's] directions, aimed at sabotaging the authority and crushing state structures, are particularly dangerous." The German *Der Spiegel* published a circular sent out to local party propagandists advising them to stress the atheism and Jewish backgrounds of leading KOR members. The Church had suffered repression at the hands of the bureaucracy, and was held in high regard by many Poles as a result. But the Bishops feared the emergence of a socialist democracy more than they did the Stalinists, and played on the historic anti-Semitism in Poland, which, while weakened by the Soviet defeat of the Nazis, still existed.

"The KOR and independent union leaders confronted the problem of the conservatism of the forces grouped around the Catholic hierarchy in an effective way," noted Gerry Foley in *The Militant*. "They did not give an inch to the cardinal's appeals for giving in to the regime. But they strove to safeguard unity and avoid offending the religious sentiments of the Polish masses.... The deepening radicalization of the Polish working class is inspiring criticism and opposition within the ranks of the governing Polish United Workers Party, Poland's Stalinist party. According to *Le Monde's* Polish correspondent Bernard Guetta, 60 percent of the working-class members of the CP have joined Solidarity. In the December 2 issue of the Paris daily Guetta reported that 'a strong radicalization of party activists emerged in the regional meetings in early November, which were attended by members of the national leadership. From that time on violent attacks began to be launched at the lack of democracy in the party and the isolation of the CP that resulted from this.'"4

The regime sought to renege on promises it had made to the workers. Millions of workers responded in a massive strike on January 24, 1981, and Solidarity called a general strike for February 3. Two days before the scheduled general strike, the Stalinists backed down. The agreement signed by the government and Solidarity was described by union spokesman Karol Modzelewski as "an initial stage in the fulfillment of the Gdansk agreement." A *Militant* report by William Gottlieb described the list of concessions offered to the workers. "The government agreed to give workers three Saturdays a month off during 1981 instead of only two. It was agreed that a five-day forty-hour workweek will be established in 1982.... The government also backed down from a threat to dock workers' pay for the massive January 24 walkout.... The government conceded the right of the union to publish its own weekly newspaper. Solidarity is also to have access at regular intervals to radio and television."5

The rise of the workers' struggle in Poland and the formation of Solidarity electrified the SWP. This was true of the whole of the Fourth International and most Trotskyists outside it. Many from our movement began to visit Poland. Of course, this was easier for European comrades. But SWP members went, too, and because of our turn to industry most were blue-collar workers.

A new prime minister, General Wojciech Jaruzelski, was installed to try to ameliorate the situation for the bureaucracy. His appointment was at first viewed by Solidarity as a conciliatory measure. He was less unpopular because as defense minister he is thought to have refused to use the army to put down workers' strikes in 1970 and 1976. But, as Gottlieb reported, on "March 19 leaders of

Solidarity and representatives of the farmers were evicted from the headquarters of the local assembly in Bydgoszcz by club-swinging cops. Several workers and farmers were injured, including Jan Rulewski, a member of Solidarity's national commission. This was the first such use of force by the government since Solidarity was born out of the mass strikes last August."[6] In response, Solidarity threatened a general strike, and the government backed down again.

The anti-bureaucratic infection spread in the ruling party. In a play on the ruling party's official name, Polish United Workers' Party (PUWP), one party member at the Gdansk shipyard was quoted in a Warsaw daily: "We must do everything to ensure that our party becomes truly Polish, truly united, and truly of the workers and truly a party," the last referring to the fact that the PUWP was not a political party at all but an instrument of bureaucratic rule. One worker member of the PUWP at his plant had led the strikes, and was elected secretary of his factory party organization. He was expelled by party higher ups when he called for a "thorough housecleaning throughout Poland," insisting "the factories must have greater autonomy and the workers must be able to make the decisions." But the defiant party workers instead reelected him in his plant.[7]

The Kremlin became alarmed and decided to directly intervene in the PUWP.

Suzanne Haig reported for *The Militant*:

"As the July 14-18 [1981] congress of [the PUWP] approaches, Moscow is applying maximum pressure.... On June 5, the Central Committee of the Soviet Communist Party sent a letter to the Central Committee of the PUWP, criticizing the Kania leadership of its 'constant concessions' to 'anti-socialist' and 'counterrevolutionary elements (code words for workers fighting for democratic rights).' It attacked the openness of the press and the weakness of security forces, and called for a change of line before the congress.

"Why is Moscow so worried?

"The Polish Communist Party is in the midst of a deep discussion. Demands have been raised for more democracy within the party, more access to information, the expulsion of corrupt and inept leaders, and the separation of party and government. Some 60 percent of factory delegates to the congress are members of the independent union, Solidarity. As a result of pressure from the ranks, the new Politbureau will be elected at the congress by secret ballot....

"The Soviet letter expressed alarm that 'It is no longer unusual for casual people who overtly espouse opportunistic points of view to lead local party organizations or figure among delegates to conferences and to the congress.... It cannot be excluded,' the letter continued, 'that during the congress itself an attempt could be made to strike a decisive blow against Marxist-Leninists forces in the party in order to liquidate it.' In other words the congress could codify more democratic policies."[8]

The PUWP was becoming much weaker as a reliable instrument of the bureaucracy. Consequently, the regime turned more to Prime Minister Jaruzelski and the repressive apparatus. But Solidarity continued to make gains, and a direct assault on the workers was not yet feasible.

Earlier in the year a commission of Solidarity was charged with drafting a program for the union. It was then taken up by the National Coordinating Committee for approval, printed in Solidarity's newspaper, and widely discussed among the union's ten million members in preparation for the first national convention of Solidarity.

Our accomplished linguist, Gerry Foley, translated the long document for *Intercontinental Press*. There were three parts to the document, each of which was also printed as an installment in *The Militant*.

In the first part, the principles of the union were set out:

"Our union was formed barely a half year ago [from when the draft was written] as a result of the struggle of the workers, supported by the whole country. Today we are a powerful social force. Thanks to this, all working people in Poland can at last advance their common aims with dignity and effectiveness. We were born out of the protest against injustice, humiliation, and abuse. We are an independent and self-governing union of working people of all regions and occupations. We defend the rights, dignity, and interests of all workers.

"We want to peacefully shape the life of our country in accordance with patriotic ideals, social justice, and democratic rights. As a trade union, we do not aim to replace the government in performing its tasks, but we do want to represent the interests of working people in relation to the state. We thus defend the rights of the individual, the citizen, and the worker. At the same time, we do not shirk our responsibility for the destiny of our people and country. The best national traditions, the ethical principles of Christianity, the political banner of democracy, and the social thought of socialism—those are the four main sources of our inspiration."[9]

In fighting for economic democracy, the union found it had to go further and fight for democracy in the rest of society. The lack of democracy inherent in the bureaucracy's totalitarian control over the economic plan had resulted in grossly unequal distribution of goods, corruption, mismanagement and sabotage of the plan itself. In

Poland this had led to a generalized economic crises.* In the second part, the draft program explained in detail how the economic crisis developed out of the bureaucratic system, and proposed immediate steps to be taken, as well as longer range goals. The thrust was the self-management by the workers in their enterprises and in the economic plan as a whole.

The third part of the program dealt with the lack of democracy in the system. It called for the rule of law to replace the arbitrary police-state rule, election of judges and the independence of the judiciary with powers to protect basic freedoms, and the establishment of a special tribunal "to judge people in high positions who have committed abuses, endangered the nation, or caused great harm." Consequently, the trade union freedoms won in Solidarity's battle should be codified in law. "It is crucial that the authorities function out in the open, and not keep covering up behind a screen of secrecy decisions that are harmful, self-serving, illegal or even criminal," the program declared. The program explained in detail how free and democratic elections were to be held at the local, regional and national levels.

The program ended with a long section on how Solidarity should function as a united, democratic and fighting union based on worker solidarity. This was appropriate for Poland at the time, but its proposals read like what all unions throughout the world should be like today.

The Solidarity convention was held in Gdansk early September. *The Militant* sent Martin Koppel to cover it:

"To the thunderous applause Lech Walesa proclaimed: 'I hereby open our Congress—the First National Congress of the Independent Self-Governing Trade Union. We are here,' continued the president of Solidarity, 'at the will of those who elected us—the working people of all Poland. Each of us separately does not count for much. Taken together, we all count for as much as the strength of those millions of people who constitute Solidarity. It is they, they alone, whom we want to remain faithful to during the present debates.'

"As Walesa uttered these words, 100,000 Soviet troops accompanied by tanks, planes, and warships were beginning an eight day series of military maneuvers near the Polish border and in the Baltic Sea. Even more ominously, the Soviet authorities began to stage gatherings in Leningrad and other cities to denounce Solidarity, accusing it of plotting 'counter-revolution.' Such 'spontaneous' rallies are designed to turn Soviet workers against their brothers and sisters in Poland and could help serve as political cover for a possible intervention.

"The 892 delegates, elected during the preceding three months of discussion at the local union level, received stacks of documents and countless other congress materials. A special congress newspaper *Glos Wolny* (Free Voice) appeared daily, along with an English edition.... The first part of the Solidarity congress, originally scheduled from September 5-7, and extended another three days, discussed amendments to the union's charter, heard initial discussion on proposals for a program of activities and demands, and elected commissions and working groups to lay the groundwork for the second part, to be held from September 28 to October 3. At this second session the delegates will adopt a program, as well as a plan for national economic reform and for workers' self-management. They will also elect a new leadership body."[10]

The next months saw rising tensions, with the threat of Soviet invasion clamoring, and continued threats by the Prime Minister Jaruzelski. Then, on December 13, Jaruzelski declared martial law and unleashed a brutal suppression of the Polish workers and farmers. Under the military junta he established to run the country all strikes and political gatherings were outlawed, and a nightly curfew was imposed. Troops patrolled the streets, and everyone had to carry identification papers. Gasoline sales were halted. Distribution of unauthorized leaflets and newspapers was forbidden. All international telephone and telex communications were cut.

The Militant ran a front page editorial under the headline "Defend Polish Workers!" It stated that the "brutal suppression of the Polish workers and farmers by the Polish regime, backed up by the Kremlin, must be condemned and opposed by everyone fighting for workers' rights and socialism. The suspension of all democratic rights, the arrests of leaders of Solidarity, and the use of force to evict strikers from factories and break up demonstrations are criminal acts, indefensible before the workers of the world."[11] The editorial also denounced the Reagan administration for using the crackdown as a cover to announce "military contingency plans" against Cuba, Nicaragua and El Salvador.

Solidarity was not prepared to effectively oppose the counter-revolutionary onslaught. It did not call for a general strike. Within the country, it had the support of the overwhelming majority of the population, including the PUWP ranks, but failed to mobilize that support. Of course, there was the Soviet threat, and the workers faced grave danger. It is not for me to say what could have been done. But it is better to fight and lose, and set an example for the workers of the world, than to avoid the battle and lose anyway. The result was gradual demoralization of the workers, to the extent that when the Berlin Wall came down eight years later, they had come to see the restoration of capitalism as the lesser evil. And under the new capitalist regime, Solidarity and its program of socialist democracy was a thing of the past. Lech Walesa himself became head of the new capitalist government.

The uprising of the Polish workers in 1980-81 was the last of the attempts in Eastern Europe to overthrow the Stalinist bureaucracy, from the workers' rising in East Germany in 1953 to the Hungarian Revolution of 1956, the Prague Spring of 1968, and the Polish events of 1970 and 1976. A chapter had been closed, leading to the collapse of the Soviet bloc at the hands of the bureaucracy itself.

Two minority tendencies had developed in the SWP, and the atmosphere in the party had become factionalized by the time of the 1981 party convention (these differences will be discussed in later chapters). But there were no major differences in the SWP over Poland before the imposition of martial law. George Shriver, a supporter of one of the minority tendencies gave the report on Poland at the 1981 convention, which was adopted unanimously. But after the crackdown, a difference did emerge, not over our position, but how to participate in the demonstrations and meetings that sprang up in response. The party leadership majority, over the objections of the minorities, said that we could not join with social democrats, or groupings that emerged from the splits in the International Socialists organization, in protesting martial law and in support of Solidarity. The specious argument of the majority was that it was impermissible to join any protest with these groups present because they did not defend the Polish workers' state. But we could have joined with them on what we agreed with, and at the same time made clear we were against the overthrow by capitalist reaction of the workers' state.

What was underneath this wrong-headed position was another instance of the majority pulling back from contact with other groups, and abstention from action. The SWP's increasing abstentionism was the telling thing, and whatever arguments used to justify it were irrelevant.

---

* For a thorough explanation of how the lack of workers' democracy leads to crisis for a planned economy, see *The Revolution Betrayed* by Leon Trotsky, (Dover Publications, 2004).

1 *The Militant,* Aug. 29, 1980.
2 Ibid., Sept. 12, 1980.
3 Ibid., Sept. 20, 1980.
4 Ibid., Dec. 26, 1980.
5 Ibid., Feb. 13, 1981.

6 Ibid., April 3, 1981.
7 Ibid., May 29, 1981.
8 Ibid., July 24, 1981.
9 Ibid.
10 Ibid., Sept. 25, 1981.
11 Ibid., Dec. 25, 1981.

CHAPTER TWENTY-FOUR: GRENADA

"At the end of the Windward Islands in the Caribbean lies Grenada, a country of 110,000 people whose revolution a year ago is having a political impact throughout the region. On March 13, 1979, a popular insurrection led by the New Jewel Movement toppled the repressive regime of Eric Gairy and established the People's Revolutionary Government.

"Almost immediately, the new government instituted social measures that provided jobs, increased wages, improved and expanded health care, and implemented a literacy program. The government eliminated taxes for the lowest-income people and increased taxes on big companies. More than a fifth of the 1980 budget will be allocated for health and education. Mobilizing workers and small farmers, the PRG has greatly expanded their rights. The Trade Union Recognition Act compels employers to recognize any union that has the support of 50 percent of the workers they employ. Unionization of urban workers has increased from 30 percent under the Gairy dictatorship to 80 percent today. Agricultural Workers Councils have been organized on government and private estates across the island.

"Although a small country, Grenada's revolutionary developments are affecting the rest of the Caribbean islands and are of special significance here [in the U.S.]. Grenadians are Black and English-speaking. Thousands of Grenadians—as well as other West Indians—live and work in the United States.[1]

Grenada had been a British colony. London had forcibly imported Africans as slaves to work on its plantations on the islands. The descendants of these slaves became the Grenadian people, and this history explains why it was Black and English-speaking. Britain "granted" Grenada formal independence in 1974, installing Gairy.

African Americans began to take notice. At the end of 1979 the new Grenadian Prime Minister, Maurice Bishop, spoke to a large meeting in Harlem. We saw the potential for the revolution to inspire Blacks as well as others and draw them to the "Three Giants"— Nicaragua, Grenada and Cuba—rising up in the Caribbean. These three forged close ties, and opened new possibilities for the world revolution.

The new government completely dismantled Gairy's army, building a new army and militia. It was independent of the imperialist and local capitalist classes. Our analysis was that a workers and peasants government had been formed. Bishop would later explain, "With the working people we made our popular, anti-imperialist and democratic revolution. With them we will build and advance to socialism and final victory."

We joined with others to build Grenada solidarity committees. In the San Francisco Bay Area, our comrades Jeff and Gretchen Mackler spearheaded this effort. In the next years such committees collected material aid for the poor country, as well as popularized the revolution. In the summer of 1980, the SWP Presidential candidate, Andrew Pulley, along with Steve Clark and Diane Wang, toured the island. They obtained a long interview with Maurice Bishop. From day one of the revolution, the Carter administration began to beat the war drums. It gave asylum to Gairy, and launched a propaganda offensive that reached new lows in lies, including fantasies. Among these were that Cuban workers who came to Grenada to expand and modernize its small airport were creating a Soviet military base. Supposedly, the PRG cut down the forests in the center of the island to build an underground Soviet missile-launching site. The country was portrayed as a police state terrorizing and suppressing the population. U.S. citizens were advised that it was unsafe to travel to Grenada.

One of the points Bishop made in the interview was that Americans should come down and see for themselves that these were lies. "We would certainly see it as important for Black Americans to come down to Grenada, for the rest of America generally to come, members of the American working class, American working people to our country *to see for themselves*. We feel that in the final analysis that is the best proof. Don't wait and listen to the propaganda. Come down and see."[2] Many SWP members did so.

Caroline Lund and I had moved to the San Francisco Bay Area in 1980. As the organizer of the San Francisco branch, I worked with Jeff and Gretchen on the Grenada defense effort. In March 1981 the Grenada Friendship Society organized a tour of the Bay Area by Joseph Burke, Consul General to North America for Grenada. He had many speaking engagements, and was given an official city welcome by San Francisco supervisors. Among the sponsors of the tour were Representative Ron Dellums, Geraldine Johnson of the Coalition of Black Trade unionists, State Assemblyman Elihu Harris and Alameda County supervisor John George. Jeff and I visited Angela Davis, a leading Communist Party (CP) member in the area, to sponsor the tour, but she coldly refused.[*]

In 1981 and 1982, important steps forward were made. In this period of international recession, "the economies of the Caribbean region were plagued by lack of growth and unemployment [but] Grenada made solid gains," wrote Sue Hagen. In August 1982 the World Bank reported a nine percent growth over the three years of the revolution. The unemployment rate dropped from 49 percent to 14.2 percent. "In agriculture, the 'motor of our economy,' Bishop reported that the People's Revolutionary Government was spending 54 times more money for development than Gairy ever spent. Grenada continued to be plagued, however, by falling export revenues for nutmeg and cocoa. To deal with the crisis, the government moved to put more land into production. With the aid of the Canadian government, it began a cocoa rehabilitation project that will bring 10,000 acres under cultivation over eight years."[3]

Crop diversification was promoted, and other measures to support local farmers to provide food for the population were taken. Food imports fell from 40 percent of total imports in 1979 to 28 percent. Many other steps were taken to improve the lives of the people, from new housing to education. "In January 1982, delegates from the mass organizations began the process of formulating what Bishop called 'a genuine people's budget.' Zonal and workers parish councils in every corner of the island met to draw up proposals. The process culminated in a mass public meeting in March that produced 'a virtual treasure chest of valuable and creative ideas coming out of the concrete experiences ... of our people,' Bishop reported."[4]

In a major address to the nation on January 3, 1983, Bishop announced that 1983 would be the Year of Political and Academic Education. "Our overall objective is to make our country and revolution a big popular school.... Let us put into full practice that great principle of the revolution that education never stops—that it is the fundamental right of all our people.... Without education, no genuine people's democracy can be built, since real democracy always assumes the informed, conscious, and educated participation of the people. Without education, there can be no real worker participation, no substantial increase in production and productivity ... no true dignity, no genuine independence."[5]

Like the Cuban and Nicaraguan, the Grenadian revolution was a deeply humanistic one in its methods and objectives. Unlike the Stalinist regimes, it put the basic needs of the people for education, health, food and shelter in the forefront. It based its power on the mobilization of the workers and farmers in direct participation in their own struggle for emancipation.

Washington stepped up its threats. In speeches on March 10 and 23, 1983 U.S. President Reagan accused Grenada, along with Cuba and Nicaragua, of posing a threat to U.S. national security. On March 28, at a packed news conference at the United Nations in New York, Grenadian Foreign Minister Unison Whiteman, responded. Those speeches, he said, signaled a "heightening of preparations" for a military attack, either directly or indirectly. He pointed to "all kinds of fabrications, distortions, lies and deceptions about Grenada" coming from the White House. "They are hoping in such a way to create a climate of hysteria such that public opinion [in the U.S.] would accept an aggression against Grenada. The present propaganda campaign against Grenada is classic in that it uses methods that were used by the CIA before military aggression in Guatemala in 1954 and Chile in 1973." Reagan made similar charges to a joint session of Congress on April 27.

In this atmosphere of increasing tensions, TransAfrica, an African American foreign affairs lobby group based in Washington, and the Congressional Black Caucus (CBC) invited Bishop to visit the U.S. It took pressure from Black Congressmen George Crockett, John Conyers, Ronald Dellums and Mervin Dymally to get the State Department to grant him a visa.

At the end of his 10-day visit, Bishop announced at a news conference at the United Nations on June 9 that he together with other leaders had achieved three objectives with the visit: "to deepen and further develop closer people-to-people contacts with Grenadian and Caribbean nationals living in the United States, with the Afro-American community, and with our many friends and supporters here; to speak to different strata and sectors of the American society with the hope of providing a better understanding of the Grenadian revolution; and to initiate dialogue with officials of the U.S. administration with a view towards normalizing relations between our two governments."

Reporting on the press conference, Malik Miah wrote, "At present, Washington has refused to recognize Grenada's ambassador to the United States. Initially, Bishop explained, the Reagan administration only offered a secondary official to meet with him and his delegation. The Grenadians turned it down as inappropriate. Finally on June 7 the White House proposed William Clarke, Reagan's National Security Council advisor, and Deputy Secretary of State Kenneth Dam meet with Bishop and Grenada's Foreign Minister Unison Whiteman. Bishop said that meeting 'constituted a useful first step between our governments.' The beginning of the dialogue, Bishop said, did not mean 'the threat has been entirely removed' of a CIA-coordinated invasion of the island. But he added, it is possible the time-table for such an attack has been pushed back by the discussions."[6]

The visit included Bishop speaking before 1,200 at the TransAfrica annual dinner and to a breakfast organized by the Detroit City Council which passed a motion, reading in part, "Detroit, with its large Black population, recognizes the importance of the growth and development of other Black countries, joining them in a united common spirit; and the Detroit City council gives utmost respect to Prime Minister Maurice Bishop for the vast improvements he has overseen in his country since taking office in 1979...."

Bishop also spoke to a session of the Organization of American States. He and Whiteman met with the UN Secretary General, with more than 40 members of the Council on Foreign Relations and 20 members of the House of Representatives.

The highlight of his visit was a mass meeting at Hunter College in New York City, with an enthusiastic overflow crowd of 2,500 on June 5. Many more had to be turned away at the door. "In its large majority the crowd was Black, including many Grenadian nationals, others from the Caribbean, and many Afro-Americans. In addition, many whites and some Latinos also attended," wrote Geoff Mirelowitz. Bishop was interrupted with standing ovations many times, including when he introduced liberation fighters from Palestine and South Africa in the audience. He spoke for two hours, explaining the revolution, its desire to have normal relations with the U.S., but also its determination to continue and deepen the revolution and maintain close relations with any country it chooses, including Cuba. He singled out Cuba for its internationalism and many internal achievements.

One point in his talk was "that Grenada had taken new steps to move forward on the road to institutionalize the process of participation of the working people in running the country. The previous day, in the capital city of St. Georges, a commission was established to draw up a new constitution. Bishop promised that the new document 'won't be like that the Queen [of England] gave us in 1974. 'Grenada's sole participation in that process consisted of Gairy's receiving the constitution from Buckingham Palace in the mail. This constitution,' he pledged, 'will come out of the bones of our people and out of our earth. Democracy is much more than just an election. It is more than putting an "x" next to Tweedledee or Tweedledum.'"[7]

In Mid-July, 1983, Thomas Burke, the Grenadian Consul General to the United States (not recognized by Washington) made another tour of California. He spoke to public meetings around the state, as well as on radio, TV and was interviewed in newspapers. In the San Francisco Bay Area, where I was, he was featured on the major Black radio stations. During a call-in show on a jazz station, many were inspired to offer to move to Grenada to help out.

In Seaside, a town south of the Bay Area, Burke's visit, which was announced a few weeks before, caused a stir. Mel Mason was a city councilman, a leader of the Black community, and a member of the Socialist Workers Party. As Bay Area SWP organizer, I had helped build a branch in Seaside after Mel joined the party. The branch, together with other members of the community, had publicized Burke's visit. The American Legion and Veterans of Foreign Wars went on a campaign against Burke. Death threats, especially against Mason, who had visited Grenada in 1981, were made. A right-wing columnist wrote that since he was "a trained Green Beret, as many of us are in this area, we know from where Mel Mason speaks and we have a solution for this!!!!" Organizers of the tour went house to house explaining the Grenadian revolution, distributed leaflets throughout the city, and held a well-attended news conference demanding the city council ensure the safety of Burke.

His public meeting was held without incident on July 12, with the Mayor, the head of the Chamber of Commerce, the City Clerk, and the editor of the Black *Seaside Post* in attendance. To a standing ovation, Burke opened his talk saying, "Despite all the slanders, intimidation, and threats, I am here with you. And whenever the black and working people of Seaside request our presence, no amount of threats will keep us away."

While the immediate threat of an attack by Washington receded, a fatal blow was being prepared within the revolution itself. A grouping around New Jewel leader Bernard Coard began "organizing a secret faction in the NJM, the army and the government apparatus for some time. This included pushing aside some central NJM leaders and then finally began to raise false charges against Bishop himself—that Bishop was 'petty-bourgeois': that he was a social democrat, not a real communist, and that he was building up a personality cult around himself. Coard's faction blamed the objective problems facing the Grenadian revolution on Bishop, and put forward Coard as the 'real Marxist.'.... At the end of September, when Bishop was out of the country, Coard's secret faction had reached such dimensions that it was able to begin systematically disarming the people's militias," wrote Margaret Jayko.[8]

Bishop had been visiting Hungary and Czechoslovakia, and stopped over in Cuba October 6, and returned to Grenada October 8. Coard struck his *coup d'etat* on October 12, placing Bishop under house arrest and installing a military regime.

A slogan began to appear on walls: "No Bishop, no revo," demonstrating that many Grenadians understood that the revolutionary power had been overthrown. On October 19, a massive street demonstration freed Bishop from house arrest. The new regime struck back, using the army to fire on the massed people. Then and there they executed Maurice Bishop; Unison Whiteman; Jacqueline Creft, minister of education; Vincent Noel, first vice-president of the trade union federation; Norris Bain, minister of housing; and Fitzroy Bain, general secretary of the agricultural workers union.

Malik Miah and I were in Paris for a meeting of the United Secretariat, and were following the news. Before this, we in the SWP were unaware of the Coard group and its foul plot. Neither were the Cubans. We talked over the horrendous developments in our apartment that night, and came to the conclusion that the workers and farmers government had been overthrown. The next day, we informed the United Secretariat of our conclusion. Ernest Mandel (who didn't accept the category of a workers and farmers government which had not yet established a workers state) asked me if we thought if the class character of the Grenadian government had changed, and agreed with us it had. We learned by telephone that the SWP leadership in New York had come to the same conclusion.

The Cuban government denounced the overthrow. In a statement for the government issued October 20, Fidel Castro said, "Bishop was among the political leaders who most enjoyed sympathy and respect among our people, for his talent, his simplicity, his revolutionary sincerity and honesty, and his proven friendship for our country. Beside that, he enjoyed great international prestige. The news of his death stirred the leadership of our party, and we render deepest tribute to his memory.

"It is most unfortunate that the differences among the Grenadian revolutionaries climaxed in this bloody drama. No doctrine, no principle or position held up as revolutionary, and no internal division justifies atrocious proceedings like the physical elimination of Bishop and the outstanding group of honest and worthy leaders killed yesterday. The death of Bishop and his comrades must be clarified, and if they were executed in cold blood the guilty ones deserve to be punished in an exemplary way.

"Imperialism will now try to make use of this tragedy and the grave errors committed by Grenadian revolutionaries in order to sweep away the revolutionary process in Grenada and subject it once again to neocolonial and imperial domination." The statement concluded, "Let it be hoped that the painful events that have taken place cause all the revolutionaries of Grenada and the world to reflect deeply, and that the concept prevail that no crime must be committed in the name of the revolution and freedom."⁹ The Nicaraguan government made a similar forceful statement.

The Cuban government ordered three days of official mourning for Bishop. The Nicaraguan government did likewise.

Castro was right. In Paris, Malik and I heard on the radio that Reagan, upon being informed of the overthrow, immediately ordered warships in the Caribbean to set course for Grenada. A massive imperialist invasion was launched. Six thousand U.S. troops landed on the island, with another 10,000 just offshore. This against a country of 110,000. The Grenadian people were stunned and demoralized by the overthrow of their government. They no longer had their people's militias, and for leadership had only traitors. What resistance there was to the invasion was quickly overcome.

Cuban workers helping to build the airport did fight back when they were attacked by U.S. troops. Twenty-four were killed.

On November 4, there was a rally of over one million people in Havana to honor the Cuban workers killed in the invasion. Castro made a speech that refuted one by one the lies coming out of Washington in justification of the invasion. He added, "Unfortunately, the Grenadian revolutionaries themselves unleashed the events that opened the door to imperialist aggression. Hyenas emerged from the revolutionary ranks. Today no one can yet say whether those who used the dagger of divisionism and internal confrontation did so for their own ends or were inspired and egged on by imperialism. It is something that could have been done by the CIA—and, if somebody else was responsible, the CIA could not have done it any better."

In his speech Castro explained that Coard's group never had the close relations with the Cubans that Bishop had. "This group of Coard's expressed serious reservations toward Cuba from the very beginning because of our well-known and unquestionable friendship with Bishop.... Our relations [with Coard's government] were actually cold and tense...." He likened the Coard group to Pol Pot in Cambodia. "Aren't Pol Pot and Ieng Sary—the ones responsible for the genocide in Kampuchea—the most loyal allies of Yankee imperialism has in Southeast Asia at present? In Cuba, ever since the Grenadian crisis began, we have called Coard's group—to give it a name—the Pol Potist group."¹⁰

We came to the conclusion that the Coard group represented a nascent bureaucratic formation that used Stalinist methods to wrest power from the revolutionists around Bishop. To carry through their project they not only assassinated those leaders, but opened fire on the masses of revolutionary peopled gathered to protect their revolution. We noted the similarity between it and the secret faction around Annibal Escalante in Cuba in the 1960s that (unsuccessfully) sought to take power from the Cuban revolutionists (see Volume One of this work, p. 80). In that case there were direct ties to Moscow through the Czechoslovak embassy, but there was no evidence of such ties in Coard's case. But we did learn later that there were some relations between Coard and members of the CP in the United States. After Bishop's murder, for a few days some CPers taunted our members about the loss of "your guy" in Grenada. These stopped after the U.S. invasion and Castro's strong statements became known.

The overthrow of the Grenadian revolution was a severe blow to Cuba and Nicaragua. Washington was emboldened to step up its campaign against both.

---

* Ten years later, as the Soviet Union collapsed, Angela Davis left the CP with many others to form the Committees of Correspondence.

1 *The Militant*, Sept. 5, 1980
2 Ibid.
3 *The Militant*, March 18, 1983.
4 Ibid.
5 Ibid.
6 Ibid., June 24, 1983
7 Ibid., June 17, 1983
8 Ibid., Dec. 9, 1983
9 See the full text in *The Militant*, Nov. 4, 1983.
10 See the full text in *The Militant*, Nov. 25, 1983.

CHAPTER TWENTY-FIVE: WAR IN NICARAGUA

The new workers' and peasants' government that came to power in July 1979 as a result of the insurrectionary overthrow of the Somoza dictatorship faced enormous problems. Nicaragua was one of the poorest countries in Latin America.

Reporting from Managua for *The Militant*, Anibal Yanez wrote:

"The Nicaraguan workers and peasants, led by the Sandinista National Liberation Front (FSLN), are entering a new phase of their struggle. During the last weeks of 1979, the Sandinistas took further steps, including important changes in the government, to defend, deepen and consolidate the revolution.

"As Commander of the Revolution Víctor Manuel Tirado López explained during a public meeting in Managua on December 27, the main goals of the revolutionary government for 1980 are the literary crusade and planning for economic reconstruction.... The vast majority of Nicaraguans have lived in poverty. This is the result of the voracious capitalist system maintained by Somoza and his U.S. imperialist backers. The situation was worsened by the dictator's deliberate destruction of the country's industry during the war of liberation and the accompanying disruption of the planting season. Today, unemployment, hunger, disease, and child malnutrition are among the tremendous problems that the Sandinista government must begin to solve if the revolution is to march forward.

"Its proposed solution is the 1980 Plan for Economic Reactivation. According to Tirado, this plan is aimed at benefiting 'mainly the poorest, most backward sectors of the population, those who have always had to bear the weight of the crisis, of social or natural catastrophes. It is not a question...of only raising production, but at the same time of distributing it in a just way, to progressively close the social chasms that the *Somozaist* regime deepened every day,' Tirado explained.

"The plan will place emphasis on reactivating the production of basic goods such as food, clothing, shoes, and medicine. It also projects creating 90,000 jobs to help reduce unemployment and underemployment; raising the minimum wage; and protecting the real wages of the poorest sectors through government-supplied basic goods, price controls, and state spending on education, health and social welfare."[1]

Important changes were made to the government. The FSLN forced the cabinet to resign, and announced a thoroughgoing reorganization. Roberto Mayorga, a bourgeois technocrat, was removed as minister of planning, and FSLN Commander of the Revolution Henry Ruiz replaced him. Bernardino Larios, a former officer of the Somoza National Guard who had defected from the dictator, was replaced as minister of defense by Humberto Ortega, commander in chief of the new Sandinista People's Army.

Capitalists still held important sections of the economy, especially in big agriculture. Ruiz warned them that if the private sector "takes a wait and see attitude" with regard to reactivating production, "the revolution will take measures, and here the unproductive latifundio will disappear. If the private enterprise does not understand that the secret of harmony consists of all of us working for the benefit of the people, they will have made an enormous mistake."[2]

Commander of the Revolution Jaime Wheelock replaced an anti-Somoza landowner as head of the ministry of agricultural development. Agricultural production, primarily cotton and coffee, made up 56 percent of Nicaragua's exports in 1978.

The bourgeoisie, organized into the Superior Council of Private Enterprise (COSEP), attacked these measures in a statement printed in the anti-Somoza bourgeois newspaper, *La Prensa*. COSEP demanded that the Sandinistas abandon their policy of placing the interests of the workers and peasants in the forefront, and instead promote "private enterprise." The new Sandinista Workers Federation (CST) roundly denounced them in the pages of *Barricada*, the FSLN newspaper. The CST incorporated some of the older unions under the former regime and was busy organizing workers in new unions. The CST called COSEP the "traitorous bourgeoisie" and warned that the only way they could be part of the political process was to join in the economic reactivation effort. The revolutionary process must go forward, the CST said, "until it culminates in the victory of the working class." Other mass organizations were growing, including a new women's federation and the Sandinista Defense Committees. The latter worked at the local level overseeing distribution of food and services.

The victory in Nicaragua gave an impetus to revolutionary forces in other Central American countries, especially in El Salvador. A number of groups had been fighting the military rulers of that country. In early January, they began a process of cooperation, which culminated some months later with the formation of the Faribundo Martí National Liberation Front (FMLN).

Matilde Zimmermann, the SWP candidate for vice president, together with four SWP senatorial candidates, visited Nicaragua in

February to learn firsthand about the revolution. Defense of the revolution was a central aspect of our election campaigns in 1980.

Peter Camejo and Gloria Najar, who were part of our bureau in Managua, visited a mine 160 miles northeast of the capital. They wrote:

"The Neptune mine in Bananza is a big one, producing several different metals. In 1976 it produced 23,340 ounces of gold, along with 15,796 tons of zinc, 696 tons of copper, 1,393 tons of lead, and 94,634 ounces of silver. Neptune had been owned by the big U.S. mining company, ASARCO, until it, along with all other Nicaraguan mines was nationalized in early November [1979] by the revolutionary government.... Wages at Neptune averaged only twenty-eight dollars per week for its 1,022 employees. (The figure for most workers was even lower when one accounts for the high salaries paid to the Canadian and U.S. managers; these range as high as $45,000 per year.)....

"But low wages tell only part of the story of extreme exploitation that has been carried out by the North American mining corporations in their effort to drain out every dollar possible from Nicaragua. Traditionally, only Misquito Indians have been given jobs as miners. In this manner the corporations kept the local population divided between mill workers and miners, always reserving the hardest and lowest-paid jobs for the Misquito. The local unit of the Somoza's National Guard was paid for and run by the mining company itself.

"Unions never existed in these mines until October 1979, after the triumph of the revolution that overthrew Somoza. An organizing effort some twenty-five years ago was crushed. Ernesto Povedo Rodriguiz, a leader of the new Revolutionary Miners Workers Union...described to us the conditions miners suffered before the revolution: 'We had no protection, anyone could be fired at any time. If you tried to protest, the National Guard...would arrest you. We had no coffee breaks. No real retirement plan. A weak social security program was started in 1967, which provided for pensions from 140 to 250 cordobas ($14 to $25) per month. But it often would not be paid. You needed documents to apply, and many Misquitos have no papers.... If a miner died in an accident, they would give the widow 2,000 cordobas ($200)—in a pile of small bills to make it look like a lot of money. If you lost an eye, leg, or hand, you got nothing; you were fired."[3]

Peter and Gloria went down the mine, and saw that there was no ventilation, no place to eat, and no lighting other than the miners' headlamps. Eighty five percent of the miners suffered from silicosis.

With the nationalization of the mine and the new union giving voice to the workers, these conditions began to change for the better.

In the next months and years, many SWP members visited Nicaragua and wrote articles, in addition to those who did stints living in the party apartment in Managua as part of *The Militant's* bureau.

•••

On February 22, 1980, the government brought charges against a Stalinist group, the People's Action Movement (PAM). Among other charges, the group was found to have been organizing its own clandestine armed wing, in violation of a law prohibiting such formations outside of the mass militias being organized. This group was opposed to the revolutionary government, and having its own armed wing may have implied it was keeping open the possibility of moving against it at some point. The main danger the revolution faced was continued attacks by armed Somocista groups against Sandinista mass organizations and projects. Against these attacks the FSLN outlawed any armed groups not under the control of the revolution. Having armed units of organizations such as the PAM cut across the defense of the revolution and got in the way of disarming the Somocistas. After the government confronted them, the PAM agreed to disband its armed units. The charges against it were dropped and the disruption activities of this group ceased.

One target of the counterrevolution were the 70,000 young people mobilized to fan out over the country in a great literacy campaign to teach basic reading and writing skills to 900,000 people, one half of the entire population over 10 years of age. Some of these selfless young people were murdered.

Lorraine Thiebaud wrote in *The Militant*:

"Celebrating International Women's Day for the first time in a country free from tyranny, thousands of Nicaraguan women marched through the streets of Managua March 9. The demonstration was the culmination of a week of activities. Women of all ages came from every corner of Nicaragua and marched in provisional contingents, frequently led by all-women militia units. With raised fists they entered the Plaza of the Workers, shouting the main slogan of the women's movement here—'Building a new country, we build the new woman!.'.... Special emphasis during the week's events was placed on the upcoming literacy campaign, which has such fundamental significance in improving the lives of Nicaraguan women. More than 60 percent of urban women and 90 percent of rural women can neither read nor write their own names. Illiterate women in every city and town organized meetings to honor the mothers of the teenaged men and women who will live in the countryside for six months."4

The successful completion of the literacy campaign was a major achievement of the revolution's first year.

But capitalist sabotage continued. Fred Murphy reported from Managua:

"In an impressive display of the growing strength of the FSLN-led mass organizations in Nicaragua, more than 30,000 peasants and agricultural laborers from across the country marched and rallied here February 17. [The Rural Workers Association (ATC) organized the march.] At the rally in the Plaza of the Revolution, ATC general secretary Eduardo Garcia explained...'we demand that the lands intervened by INRA [National Institute of Agrarian Reform] that could not be confiscated now pass over to the People's Property Sector and that not a single inch of land be returned' to the big owners.

"Garcia was referring to the growing number of big farms that have been placed under INRA administration owing to the refusal of their private owners to put them into production or to meet the new government's standards on wages, working conditions, and social benefits for farm laborers. Other demands included in the ATC's Plan of Struggle include a total revision of the old regime's Labor Code...with the participation of the ATC and the trade unions; a halt to firings and harassment of ATC organizers on private estates; greater participation by farm workers in the administration of INRA's state farms with full knowledge and discussion of production plans, income, and expenses; and further improvements in food, housing, health care, and education on both state and private farms."5

In one example, Thiebaud described how union members at El Caracol Industries, a food-processing factory, took over their plant in February 1980, but kept up full production. The unionists prohibited owners Magelda and Oscar Campos from entering the factory. They also demanded the government investigate their charge that the Campos family was trying to bankrupt the company by reducing production and decapitalizing.

"When I visited El Caracol," wrote Thiebaud, "the workers displayed storerooms and warehouses which have been kept almost empty of raw materials in recent months, well below the minimum required to keep up the productive pace. Ten delivery trucks had been idled because the owners would not buy repair parts. Many of the machines in the factory now run only because the workers themselves have found ways to fix them."6

On March 2, 1980, the government issued a strong decree against capitalist sabotage, including removing "from the country the fixed or circulating assets of enterprises (that is, the capital of such enterprises). Violators of the new decree face the penalty of intervention of their enterprises (that is, putting them under state administration) plus fines of up to three times the value of the capital removed from Nicaragua. Individuals convicted under the decree may be jailed for one to three years." It should be noted that intervention was not expropriation—the capitalists would remain owners, accruing profit, but would not run intervened enterprises.

"The experience at El Caracol Industries is clear," the decree noted, "the owners have been aiming to clear out and take huge profits. Will the revolutionary government permit such actions? Will the workers permit the destruction of their source of employment? El Caracol Industries; Nicatex; Hurtado Cannery in Granada; Lacayo Supermarket, also in Granada—these mark the beginning of an anti-patriotic campaign that can only be halted by direct control over production by the workers and due attention by the state to such problems. Can we reactivate our economy with historical characters like the anti-patriotic businessmen? Obviously not."

The struggle in neighboring El Salvador against the military junta was also heating up. When the dictatorship murdered Archbishop Óscar Romero, who had taken the side of the El Salvadoran people, there was a big demonstration of protest in Managua in solidarity. Another big demonstration welcomed Grenadian Prime Minister Maurice Bishop. These expressions of internationalism were matched by enthusiasm in thanking Cuban doctors and other workers helping Nicaragua to rebuild.

Nancy Cole reported for *The Militant:*

"The Sandinista-led government of Nicaragua has taken another step toward establishing the right of the workers and peasants to a decisive say in how their country is run. On April 21, the government junta announced that a majority of delegates to the Council of State set to convene May 4 will represent the mass organizations. This altered the original balance weighted heavily in favor of capitalist forces....

"The restructured council will still provide seats to the capitalist organizations and parties that were originally included. But it has been expanded.... Nine of the council's members are to be chosen on a regional basis by the Sandinista Defense Committees. Eight will come from Nicaragua's five trade union federations, including three representatives from the Sandinista Workers Federation. Three delegates will represent the Rural Workers Association and one each will be chosen from the teachers union, health workers union, and journalists union. The Association of Nicaraguan Women and the July 19 Sandinista Youth will each have a delegate. And for the first time on any Nicaraguan government body, the Indian minorities of the Atlantic Coast region will be represented with one delegate. The FSLN will have six representatives, and six other smaller [leftist] political parties will have one delegate each."7

Even though the Sandinista Workers Federation was growing rapidly, it had only three of the eight spots reserved for the union federations. Two delegates were allotted to the Independent General Workers Federation, led by the pro-Moscow Nicaraguan Socialist Party and based primarily among construction workers; one representative to the Confederation of Trade Union Action, led by the ultra-left Stalinist Communist Party and based mainly among Managua textile workers; one to the Confederation of Trade Union Unification tied to the U.S. AFL-CIO; and one to the Confederation of Nicaraguan Workers controlled by an anti-communist Christian Democratic current.

The three capitalist parties had one delegate each, as did the six organizations of industrialists, landlords, merchants and big farmers making up COSEP. The capitalists raised a howl at being put in the minority. Two of the original five-member ruling junta (the other three were FSLN), Alfonso Robelo and Violeta Chamorro, resigned in protest. The U.S. press also screamed against this "totalitarian" takeover by the representatives of the great majority.

Robelo and COSEP launched a campaign of anticommunist demagoguery in the capitalist press, especially in *La Prensa*, which was increasingly the voice of the bourgeoisie. After a young *brigadista* in the literacy campaign was murdered, there was a big demonstration of protest in Managua. FSLN leader Tomás Borge spoke, and outlined steps to fight the growing counterrevolution. One was to counter the anticommunist demagoguery. The political work and vigilance of the Sandinista Defense Committees in each neighborhood would be stepped up. There would be a major push to organize militias in the cities and countryside. Borge listed 32 Somozaist encampments in Honduras along the border, and said defenses along the border would be stepped up.

Behind the scenes, Washington was arming and organizing the counterrevolutionary groups in Honduras. Later referred to as the "contras," these groups were forming an army to carry out forays into Nicaragua, which would develop into a major counterrevolutionary war in the following years. The United States also stepped up arming the military junta in El Salvador in its war against the growing guerilla movement, including sending "advisors." As well, the dictatorships in Honduras and Guatemala received increased imperialist aid.

Plots for armed actions organized by capitalist forces in Nicaragua were discovered and broken up. One of these was led by Col. Bernardino Larios, the first defense minister of the new government after the overthrow of Somoza. Another plot consisted of the formation of nine squads of 25 men each to assassinate the nine FSLN commanders, who held ultimate power. The unmasking of one plot led to a shootout that resulted in the death of the main conspirator, Jorge Salazar, a coffee plantation owner. *La Prensa* hailed him as a "hero" and COSEP denounced his death as a "political crime," notwithstanding that the facts of his arsenal of guns and money were exposed. On November 19, 1980, there was a rally of 100,000 workers and peasants in Managua denouncing these counterrevolutionary crimes.*

"Open class conflict affects every aspect of daily life," Matilde Zimmermann wrote about the situation developing in the country. She pointed to the conflict of ideas between the bourgeois press, especially *La Prensa* and those of the workers' organizations including the FSLN's *Barricada*. Counter rallies were another expression. From Managua, Zimmermann and Arnold Weissberg reported, "An estimated half million Nicaraguans shouted their approval of stiff new laws establishing greater government control over the economy at a rally here July 19. The demonstration marked the second anniversary of the Nicaraguan revolution as well as the twentieth of the founding of the Sandinista National Liberation Front (FSLN). The new laws were adopted in response to a series of demonstrations by the trade unions and other mass organizations. They make it easier for the government to halt 'decapitalization' (removal of capital from the country by industrialists and wealthy farmers). The new laws will also make more land available to landless peasants."[8]

A deep recession in the United States was hitting Central America hard. Austerity measures that made the workers and peasants pay for the crisis were the norm for the region. Nicaragua also was forced to take such measures, but these were different from those of the other Central American countries.

Zimmermann wrote:

"On September 10, the Government of National Reconstruction [as it was now named] invoked a 'state of economic and social emergency,' during which various activities are banned, such as price speculation and hoarding, the publication of false information designed to generate economic panic, the sabotage of production, illegal strikes and land occupations outside the framework of the agrarian reform law.

"A series of austerity measures were announced, including a 5 percent cut in the current budget, a freeze on hiring in the state agencies, and a 10 percent cut in certain government subsidies. Not affected are subsidies for milk (which costs thirty [US] cents a liter), public transportation (ten cents a ride) or any of the basic foodstuffs sold below cost because of government price support. Nor will gas, water, or electricity rates be allowed to rise.

"Three new laws are designed to tighten control over the economy and save or generate foreign exchange. One imposes stiff penalties for various types of business—tax evasion, double bookkeeping, corruption. The second raises import taxes on several categories of luxury goods manufactured outside Central America. A third decree has temporarily closed the so-called parallel market, that is, the buying and selling of U.S. dollars on the street at more than the official rate of exchange. The parallel market will be allowed to reopen in a few weeks, but only in authorized offices and under tight control by the central banks. The uncontrolled parallel market has contributed to decapitalization or capital flight, by giving the rich a way to obtain dollars they can stash in foreign bank accounts."9

The worsening economic situation came in the context of the intensifying U.S.-backed contra war. A month-long mobilization of the army and militias as well as of the trade unions was launched October 3 to counter U.S.-Honduran naval maneuvers taking place just off the Nicaraguan coast. The war against the contras began to eat into the economy. Four top capitalists, leaders of COSEP, were arrested October 21 for violations of the September 9 decrees. Nevertheless, the revolution continued to make progress in rebuilding the devastated country.

Some years later, in 1985-1986, the FSLN acknowledged it had made two serious errors in the first years of the revolution. One was its emphasis on state farms and cooperatives in the agrarian reform, to the detriment of providing land to the landless peasants. In part this was to avoid the nationalization of the large capitalist farms, in what turned out to be a vain hope of winning the support of these farmers. While there was participation in production by the capitalist farmers, it was grudging, and was accompanied by behind-the-scenes decapitalization.

More important, the failure to carry through a sweeping land reform including a massive program to provide land to all peasants who wanted individual farms played into the contras' propaganda. In particular, peasants in the north, along the border with Honduras, who had their own farms since the days of the Somoza dynasty, were told that the Sandinistas wanted to take away their land and force them into state farms. Peasants in the north had been a source of troops for the Somoza National Guard, and now began to provide some mass support for the contras.

Of course, if the Sandinistas had nationalized the capitalist farms early on to carry through a far-reaching agrarian reform that included land to the peasants, such as was carried out in the Russian and Cuban revolutions, that would have meant a major showdown with the capitalist class, which the FSLN leaders were trying to avoid. But I believe that if they had taken this step early on, it would have put the revolution on a firmer footing economically, politically and militarily. Of course it would have also infuriated the U.S.-backed counter-revolution, but that happened in any case.

The second big error the Sandinistas later pointed to was their high-handed treatment of the peoples of the Atlantic Coast. These included Indians, mainly Miskitos, and English-speaking Blacks, descendents of slaves brought there by the British. The Atlantic Coast was geographically and linguistically separated from the Spanish-speaking majority. The revolution bypassed this important part of the country. The Sandinistas sent in Spanish speakers to take control of these areas, and, although they brought in some reforms, were resented. The result was the Atlantic Coast became another source for a mass base for the contras.

It should be noted that these two errors were in contradiction to the FSLN's "Historic Program" written by FSLN founding leader Carlos Fonseca. That program called for land to the peasants and for self-determination for the Atlantic Coast, both key democratic demands.

We, along with the rest of the movement in solidarity with the Central American revolutions did not take notice of these errors at the time. Weissberg did note that in late 1981 and early 1982 there had been "a virtual invasion" of the northern part of the Nicaraguan Atlantic Coast by counterrevolutionary terrorists operating out of Honduras. To generate support in the coastal area, former Miskito leader turned contra, Steadman Fagoth, claimed his goal was establishment of a Miskito state. These contra forces operated at least one base within Nicaragua.[10]

We continued to maintain that the contras consisted only of U.S.-paid mercenaries. Washington was the force behind the contras, to be sure, and they wouldn't have existed without its financial and military backing. But they were also gaining something of a mass base inside the country. The war drained scarce resources and inflicted heavy casualties among the most selfless and devoted cadres as it dragged on for the next several years.

One of the reporters in our Managua Bureau was Jose Perez. Like Mike Bauman and Jane Harris who had preceded Jose in the assignment, he came into conflict with the party leadership in New York. Years later he wrote to me about the "consistent difference with how *The Militant* presented the situation in Nicaragua, which was to hail every real and even imagined step forward no matter how slight as world historic while depicting the difficulties, contradictions and above all the toll being exacted by the war in the faintest pastels." The leadership in New York thought it knew better what was happening in Nicaragua than the people on the ground.

Under the pressure of the war, a leading Sandinista, Eden Pastora, the former defense minister for Nicaragua, broke with the revolution at a press conference April 15, 1982 in Costa Rica. "Now Washington has a new and 'attractive' ally in its campaign to draw the noose more tightly around the Nicaraguan revolution," wrote Will Reissner for *The Militant*. "What makes Pastora so valuable to Washington is that he was an active participant in the struggle...that overthrew the hated dictator Anastasio Somoza in July 1979.... Since his break with the FSLN, Pastora has traveled to Western Europe to try to win social-democratic parties there to his anti-Sandinista positions. He is reportedly planning a trip to Washington to meet with liberals in Congress. Pastora has also been the subject of sympathetic articles in leading U.S. newspapers."[11]

Despite the pressures the revolution was facing, both politically and militarily, there was considerable public sympathy for the Sandinista cause in the United States and internationally. On June 12, 1982, nearly one million people rallied in New York's Central Park for peace and nuclear disarmament. Contingents calling for the United States to get out of Central America were well received.

•••

In 1981, the ATC broke into two organizations with the formation of UNAG (National Union of Farmers and Ranchers). The latter became the organization of small peasants.

A pro-Sandinista academic, Ilja A. Luciak, who favored the policy of "national unity"—that is, "unity" with the capitalist farmers—wrote:

"Until 1983 UNAG organized the peasantry around an agrarian reform, centered on building agricultural cooperatives.... The bias against big producers [sic] was mainly a function of the view of former ATC cadres, who had joined UNAG in 1981 when the rural workers movement broke apart. These officials belonged to the rural proletariat and shared a history of struggle against the agrarian bourgeoisie. Having suffered years of exploitation at the hands of rich landowners, they perceived any farmer with a sizeable landholding as the class enemy.... Wilberto Lara, UNAG's second president (1982-1984), represented a good example of someone holding this position. A committed revolutionary, he could not transcend his proletarian background. During his tenure, UNAG was scorned by even those members of the rural bourgeoisie who, though open to the changes brought about by the revolution, rejected UNAG leadership's antibourgeois rhetoric. This class bias, in many cases unwarranted, limited the development of the revolutionary process. Large landowners, crucial to a viable alliance between FSLN and the bourgeoisie under the policy of national unity, felt alienated, and many turned against the Sandinista revolution....

"In an effort to reinvigorate the policy of national unity in Nicaragua's rural sector, the UNAG leadership began a discussion in October 1983 concerning the active recruitment of 'influential producers.' This important redirection of policy that ended the exclusion of the agrarian bourgeoisie was consolidated with the election of a new leader [Daniel Nunez].... Nunez ushered in a new era, beginning UNAG's rise to become the mostly important Sandinista grassroots movement. The second major development...was the participation of large producers in the July 1984 assembly. Whereas the recruitment of the [capitalist farmers] was essential from the perspective of forging national unity, UNAG's focus on the recruitment of rich peasants was not without consequences. Most significantly [they] came to dominate the decision-making structures of UNAG....

"Further, it has been argued...that the incorporation of the [capitalist farmers] strengthened their political power in the *comarca*, the rural hamlets of their origin, vis-à-vis the poor peasantry. This reality was in conflict with the Sandinista goal of strengthening grassroots democracy and resurrected power structures from the days of the Somoza regime ...."[12]

This shift marked the erosion of the workers and peasants government. The Sandinista government began to turn its face toward accommodating the key sector of the capitalist class, the agricultural bourgeoisie. Accelerating this process was the big blow of the overthrow of the Grenadian revolution in October 1983. This negatively affected the revolutionary morale of a sector of the Nicaraguan masses.

Another weight holding back the revolution was the failure of the Soviet Union to provide adequate military aid while the United States was pouring tens of millions into the contra forces.

It was in 1983 that I raised at a meeting of the SWP National Committee the question of the length of time since the revolution without a decisive blow being struck against the still-dominant economic power of the capitalist class. Our view of workers and farmers governments was that they were highly unstable, and either had to go forward with the establishment of a full workers' state through the expropriation of the bourgeoisie in a relatively short time, or they would be rolled back and a capitalist state re-stabilized. I raised this as a question, not for a vote.

In the summer of 1983, at a party national educational conference, Mary-Alice Waters gave a talk on the workers and farmers government where she appeared to answer me by revising our former conception. The new view she put forth was that the workers and farmers government was the first stage of the dictatorship of the proletariat, a workers state. This implied that a workers state had already been achieved in Nicaragua, so the delay in the expropriation of the capitalists was of no great matter. She later developed this new concept in a written article in the *New International* in 1984. By this time Jack Barnes had begun to equate the concept of "workers and peasants government" with Lenin's pre-1917 idea of a "democratic dictatorship of the workers and peasants" as the likely outcome of the future Russian Revolution. Waters' speech did not address the question of whether Lenin's formulation amounted to the first stage of a workers' state, a concept which Lenin explicitly rejected.

This new concept of "workers and peasants government" was thus a muddle. In the course of the slow decline of the Nicaraguan revolution in the next years under the blows of the imperialist offensive, the majority leadership quietly dropped the concept, and rejected that a workers' state had been established in Nicaragua.

In Nicaragua new elections were held in November 1984. The new government which took power in January 1985 was no longer a workers and peasants government, but a coalition government with the capitalist class. Much later, in July 1989 (after I had left the SWP), the National Committee adopted a resolution that observed, "By the time the newly elected Nicaraguan government took office in early 1985, those leaders of the revolution least attracted to a socialist course had become dominant in the government's executive branch and the FSLN leadership." Nevertheless, the National Committee maintained in 1989 that a workers and peasants government still existed. This was given the lie the following year when openly bourgeois forces swept the FSLN from power like so much ash in a bourgeois-style election.

Looking back on his experience in Nicaragua, Jose Perez wrote:

"Beginning in 1984 or so, as the war deepened, throwing the country into a deep economic and social crisis, the contra's social base grew to encompass a big fraction of the peasantry of the 'agricultural frontier.' They also had significant support in the major cities and towns of the agricultural zones, as was evident from their attack on Ocotal in mid-1984, which they overran and occupied briefly, something they were able to do even though there was a big government military base on the opposite side of the highway from the town with the aid of supporters inside the town.

"The resentment of the peasants towards the revolution came from a couple of sources. One was the FSLN took apart the traditional financial networks in the countryside after taking power, but was unable to effectively replace them. The state established a monopoly in basic grains, buying from the peasants at fixed prices, but at the same time it made a decision to finance the war by printing money, which made inflation unstoppable. This meant that the countryside was subsidizing the FSLN's social programs in the cities, and getting ruined economically, making it dependent on state credits and handouts, which many hated.

"Nor were the peasants getting as much back in terms of social change as you might imagine. The agrarian reform prioritized collectivization, state farms and cooperatives in which people worked the land together. This was something which peasants in this agricultural frontier were slow to warm to, to say the least. Even many who joined cooperatives would have preferred to work individually. Yet in the four years I lived in Nicaragua, I did not meet a single peasant who had ever received an individual plot of land and title to work it on his own from the revolution....

"The social advances that the revolution had initially brought were largely or completely reversed by 1986 or 1987, or had been dwarfed by the crisis. Most of the rural schools had closed because they did not have teachers. The hospitals were in terrible shape, medical posts had been closed or abandoned, the rationing system had broken down and Sandinista Defense Committees and other mass organizations had largely ceased to function, or soon would. The big majority of the population was pushed into a grinding, demoralizing day-to-day struggle for existence....

"Tied into all this was a process of bureaucratization of the revolution, both the use of administrative methods instead of political methods and the granting or taking of privileges that while, in many cases small, rubbed salt in the wounds of a population being suffocated by an incredible economic crisis."

Because of their social base, the contras could not be militarily defeated by the FSLN. Finally, the FSLN signed a peace agreement with them in 1987. This was facilitated by changes in the contra leadership, where the original leaders who came from the Somocista

National Guard were replaced. The accord reflected the military situation on the ground. Perez reports, "The National Resistance [the contras' official name] was allowed to concentrate its forces in certain areas and remained armed pending the holding of elections, which were moved up from the end of 1990 to the beginning of the year. Press censorship and other similar measures were lifted; and it was stipulated that after the elections, the former members of the National Resistance would receive individual plots of land to farm if they wanted them."

The mistakes of the FSLN were important. But I agree with Perez that the "main cause of the defeat of the revolution was the pressure of imperialism, the revolution was beat to a bloody pulp by the contra war." It was the colossus to the north, which bore down on the small, poor country in a campaign of mass murder and economic strangulation that finally crushed this valiant and heroic people. But like the Paris Communards, they and the FSLN will be remembered and cherished in spite of their defeat for their powerful example.

•••

The SWP did support the Nicaraguan revolution from day one. It provided on the ground reporting from its bureau in Managua and from SWP members who visited the country. We actively promoted the antiwar demonstrations in defense of the Central American and Caribbean revolutions, and joined them. But in this whole period, we never attempted to lead the antiwar movement itself, in stark contrast to our exemplary role during the anti-Vietnam-War movement. This was another expression of the SWP's growing abstentionism from mass movements, as well as increasing unwillingness to promote united front work with other organized forces and drawing back from polemicizing with such forces.

---

* Rightist violence also flared in El Salvador. Thugs allied with the government murdered five leaders of the revolutionary forces. Four American women, three Catholic nuns and a missionary, were also murdered on their way to attend the funeral of the slain FDR [Revolutionary Democratic Front—soon to become the FMLN] leaders. "The bodies of Ita Ford, Maura Clarke, Dorothy Kazel and Jean Donovan were found buried in a common grave near the village of San Juan Nonualco, twenty-five miles east of San Salvador," wrote Fred Murphy in a Dec. 19, 1980 report for *The Militant* from Managua. "All had been tortured and shot in the neck.... Members of the Canadian delegation to the FDR funeral reported that they last saw the American women when the latter's car was halted at a

National Guard roadblock. The roadblock site was not far from the area where the bodies and the burned-out remains of the vehicle were later discovered." These nuns were selflessly devoted to helping the poor. They were part of a movement within the Catholic Church in Latin America at the time known as "liberation theology." This movement was later denounced as pro-Marxist and disbanded by Pope John Paul II.

When the nuns' disappearance became known on December 3, Washington was embarrassed, and tried to distance itself from the crime. But U.S. backing of the rightist dictatorship soon was back to normal.

On May 3, 1981, there was a demonstration in Washington, D.C., demanding the United States get out of El Salvador. Various anti-war groups, and the Committee in Solidarity with the People of El Salvador (CISPES) organized the march.

** See http://bit.ly/w4BqnL and http://bit.ly/vZoRkJ For a more complete selection of Jose Perez' views.

1 *The Militant,* Jan. 18, 1980.
2 *Barricada* (newspaper of the FSLN), December 30, 1979. Translation by *The Militant.*
3 *The Militant,* Feb. 22, 1980.
4 Ibid., March 28, 1980.
5 Ibid., March 14, 1980.
6 Ibid., March 28,1980.
7 Ibid., May 9, 1980.
8 Ibid., July 24 and July 31, 1981.
9 Ibid., Sept. 25, 1981.
10 Ibid., Feb. 19, 1982.
11 Ibid., Aug. 6, 1982.
12 Ilja A. Luciak, *The Sandinista Legacy: Lessons from a Political Economy Transition* (University Press of Florida, 1993), Ch. 4.

CHAPTER TWENTY-SIX: THE TURN DERAILS

In 1980, the turn to industry began to turn on itself. Part of the reasoning behind the drive to get a majority of our members into industry was to break out of what we called our "semi-sectarian" existence. What we meant was that due to the fact that the bulk of our members recruited in the period of the youth radicalization of "The Sixties" came from the campuses, they naturally tended as they graduated to get white-collar jobs, such as teaching, social services and so forth.

We did have people in industry, of course, but we were lopsided toward white-collar jobs. This meant we were by and large not among the industrial proletariat, the socially most important sector of the working class. The fading of anti-communism meant that we could get such jobs, and we thought that the struggles of the miners and steelworkers at the end of the 1970s augured a new political radicalization of the working class.

However, in the report on the turn adopted in 1978 we projected also maintaining an orientation toward the campuses, and explicitly rejected that YSA members on campuses would join the turn to industry. But in August 1979 the YSA National Committee decided that as many YSA members as possible would also make the turn. Six months later, the YSA convention projected that the youth organization would "increasingly become an organization of young industrial workers."[1] This was a serious error.

Even in periods of working class retreat, as in the 1950s, there has always been a layer of students attracted to various progressive issues, and some to socialism. While the student radicalization of "The Sixties" was over, the campuses did not revert to a period like the witchhunt. There was still openness to socialist ideas among many students. By turning away from the campuses, we turned our backs on this important arena to recruit youth.

This self-isolation from the students reflected a retreat from including white-collar workers in our membership and their unions as areas of our political work. Soon our teachers' unions and AFSCME fractions were dissolved, dissipating years of constructive efforts by those fractions, directly in contradiction to the 1978 "turn" report on this question. To paraphrase from that report, "we were out of our minds" to demand that Jeff Mackler and Ray Markey, leaders of those respective factions, go into industry. This blunder sealed the SWP off from the many struggles by teachers and other government workers that have become important in the decades since.

In the 1978 report and discussion we projected that comrades who got jobs in industry would wear "three hats." One was to become part of the workforce. Another was to be trade union activists. The third was to be seen as socialists, and draw people around the party.

The first, to become part of the workforce, became more and more undermined by a policy of transferring members from the branches and industries they were in to other branches and industries. Such transfers are needed from time to time to help solve problems that can develop in branches, including loss of branch leadership, personal conflicts, and the like. In the 1970s we began to greatly expand into new cities, which necessitated the transfer of many members to those cities. That expansion slowed down and reversed in the 1980s.

But such transfers come at a cost, especially when members new to an industry are striving to become "part of the workforce."

It takes time to get to know fellow workers, and for them to get to know you. Skills have to be learned. It takes time to understand the politics of the local union, and to get a feel of the range of views on broader social and political questions that exist in every workplace. It is important to know who your potential allies, enemies, and neutrals are to help guide your activity.

A rationalization began to be developed among the party leadership that such concerns were not that important, because it was the fraction of party members in a plant that would develop and maintain this needed sense of connection and continuity. Individuals could be "plugged into" a fraction to replace a member transferred out, without much or any loss. A key idea was thus lost, that to be effective, comrades had to sink roots in their places of work and unions. In fact, Jack Barnes began to ridicule the idea of sinking such roots, and this was picked up and repeated in the leadership and membership.

There began to be a pullback from trade union politics, the second "hat." A story told to me many years later by Linda Loew indicated the first steps. Linda was a member of the Dallas branch, and had gotten a job as a steelworker at a plant in the area, Gardner Denver, with about 1,100 workers. The local union was somewhat unique, with elected leaders who worked full time in the plant. In January 1980, the local went on strike, rejecting a company proposal for a 10 cent an hour raise amidst high inflation, a $100,000 lifetime cap on health insurance coverage, and no relief for very long hours, up to 80 a week, with forced overtime.

"All this was happening with me just a few hours off probation," Linda wrote to me. "I was the only comrade in the plant from a branch of about 15. At that stage my main acquaintance was the supervisor who trained me. I had to quickly move beyond him...." Linda drove down to the trailer that was the strike headquarters, and began discussing ideas about how to strengthen the strike, which were greeted with enthusiasm. In the next two weeks Linda became part of the strike leadership. "Working in the trailer around the clock, we were running on adrenaline. I went home to sleep no more than two-three hours a day."

Linda's suggestions involved basic organizing, such as compiling a phone list of members, signing members up for picket duty, picket lines to be up 24 hours daily, putting out press releases, calling a press conference on the picket line, calling on unionists in the area to come down to the picket lines in support, and similar ideas. She recalls that she had quite a time convincing workers "*not* to put nails under the tires of clerical workers or threaten them as they went into the plant. These workers had no union, no protection if they walked off the job."

Linda saw a newfound solidarity developing in the union. "White and Black workers talked with each other, often for the first time, about their jobs, their families, their lives. Workers saw their story being told in the newspapers, and on TV and radio.... After the first week over 800 workers turned out at a meeting to discuss the company's latest offer (barely different from the first). Debate was animated and the offer soundly rejected."

She was also able to make several new contacts for the party, and be an open socialist. When an issue of *The Militant* carried a story by her on the strike, "it was well received. Strikers bought single copies and subscriptions right on the picket line. The union treasurer, a Black co-worker, agreed to speak at the Militant Forum on the strike."

After two weeks, the workers won a significantly better contract.

At first, Linda had the support of the branch leadership, and consulted with people in the national office. But then, in the middle of the strike, others in the branch leadership met with her and proposed that she leave the job and become branch organizer. She "strenuously disagreed with the proposal." Later, another comrade got a job in the plant. The local union leadership proposed that the two "help to launch a union newsletter. We declined. Party members were not generally encouraged to get involved in day-to-day responsibilities."

Linda wrote, "In retrospect, it seems that the party elsewhere was becoming preoccupied with internal organization questions.... But turning our face outward seemed always to have energizing and healthy ramifications, a sound posture in any period.... I sensed a shift that would not be good for the life and health of the party."

Informally, Jack Barnes began to express the view that comrades who had come to the fore as leaders in the movements of "The Sixties," would be bypassed as a result of the turn to industry. His argument was that lessons learned in these previous movements had no application to the unions. Many of Linda's proposals to the union in this battle did in fact come from what she learned in the women's and antiwar movements, and her education in the party generally. Of course, the politics of the unions are different, and other skills are applicable, but much of what we had learned in "The Sixties" did carry over. Barnes' aim in putting forth this silly point was to put down those who had become SWP leaders in the previous period. Ironically, Jack fit his own category, but of course he didn't apply his conclusion to himself.

We had many talented comrades like Linda. While she stumbled on a particularly favorable situation, our participation in the affairs of the unions could have stood us in good stead in the months and years to come. But a different direction was charted.

Members began to be discouraged from accepting any positions in the unions, including those with such close ties to the membership as union stewards. Our members' general knowledge and competence often caused workers to propose us for such posts. Participation in union politics was similarly increasingly forbidden. The danger of becoming drawn into the union bureaucracy was cited. This danger is always there, but can be countered by the branch and fraction.

But fear of getting your hands dirty leads to sitting back, abstaining from union affairs and from the immediate concerns of the workers.

We did continue to build women's committees in the unions, and were involved in strike support work. Our main focus, however, was in being socialists on the job, codified as "talking socialism." Comrades were pressured to "come out" as socialists soon after being hired. By 1980 this orientation meant concentrating on socialist propaganda, selling *The Militant* and books. Increasingly, our socialist propaganda on the job centered on explaining Cuba as a model of socialism.

Of course, defense of Cuba, Nicaragua and Grenada from imperialism's attack was an important task, as was explaining their steps forward in health care, education and so forth. But these poor countries could not be models for what socialism would mean for the

United States, or the other industrialized countries, leaving aside the important political weaknesses in these revolutions.

"Talking socialism" took on an aspect of self-isolation, making party members appear to many workers like proselytizing Jehovah's Witnesses. It also took on a broadside approach to everybody, without common sense discrimination between those more open to socialist ideas, those downright hostile, and the majority somewhere in between. This, too, cut across our task of becoming integrated in the workforce. The effort to break out of our semi-sectarian existence by becoming more integrated in the industrial workforce was instead beginning to look like a self-imposed isolation.

What began to be developed was abstention from participating in the labor movement as it was, however limited such work in the given situation. This did not happen all at once, and took years to fully develop. But it began in 1980.

We had also originally projected that the fractions in industry would organize themselves democratically in their local unions and nationally. The fraction members would elect their leaders locally on up to the national level. We said this would result in another leadership structure next to the branches and any city or state organizations and the national political structures. The result would be to strengthen the party as a whole, and bring new leaders to the fore. But in 1981 this process was cut short.

Members of a number of fractions were preparing to elect their national leaderships while attending the August 1981 national SWP convention. At a meeting of the Political Committee before the convention, Jack proposed that the fractions not be allowed to do this. The reason given was that they "weren't ready" for this step. In subsequent years it became apparent that the actual reason was to squash any leaders emerging from the fractions who were not under Barnes' control.

Political Committee member Malik Miah had been one of the leaders of the turn nationally, and had been functioning as the national organizer of the steel fraction. He objected to this proposal, and voted against it. Subsequently, he was pressured not to have his vote recorded in the minutes, which is why it doesn't appear in the record. Barnes did not want the members of the National Committee to know that there was a difference in the Political Committee, which could lead others to question the decision.

The background to all this was that we had made a larger error of judgment in 1978 and 1979, as capsulized in our projection that a "political radicalization" of the working class was taking place. We mistook struggles that had occurred in the late 1970s, above all the great 1978 strike of the coal miners, and the development of

Steelworkers Fight Back, as signaling the beginning of similar, broader battles. In fact, these were exceptions to the general trend. What had begun to occur was a retreat of the labor movement in the face of assaults by the capitalist class and its government on working people, whereas we had expected a surge forward in response to those attacks.

We had projected not only increased struggles by the unions and within the unions for more militant actions on the economic front. We thought that there would be a leap forward *politically* by the working class. In the new political radicalization of workers, socialists in the industrial workplaces and unions would recruit, and their influence would grow.

But not only did this radicalization on the economic and political fronts fail to materialize, things began to go in the opposite direction. In the 1980 Presidential elections, the reactionary Ronald Reagan launched a barely disguised racist campaign. One of his first speaking engagements was in Philadelphia, Mississippi, where 16 years before three civil rights workers were brutally tortured and murdered in a case that became famous throughout the country and world. Reagan chose to make this the venue to speak out for "states' rights"—code words that had been used for decades by those practicing legal apartheid in the South. Reagan's message was understood not only in the South.

From the mid-1970s both the Democrats and Republicans began to chip away at the gains won in the radicalization of 1960-1973. Laws and court rulings pushed back against a woman's right to abortion, and affirmative action for women, Blacks and other oppressed nationalities.

Early in 1980, then President Carter attempted to re-impose the military draft, playing on the chauvinism whipped up against the Iranian revolution. His hope was to reverse the "Vietnam syndrome": the opposition of most Americans to repeat anything like the Vietnam War. Carter failed in this effort, but it was another push toward the right.

Reagan won the election, appealing to the racist fears of a section of white workers, who became known as "Reagan Democrats." This was an indication that workers in general were not moving politically to the left, but were disoriented, with some attracted to the right. We dismissed this development, asserting that only capitalist politics was moving to the right, while underneath, workers were actually becoming politically radicalized.

It was a mistake on our part to project a political radicalization and then base our policy as if it had happened. In politics, mistakes are bound to happen. But it is important for mistakes to be corrected in a timely fashion, or the mistake will more and more distort policy. We were guilty of wishful thinking, and all in the leadership, including two minority groups discussed in a later chapter, clung to the myth of a developing political radicalization of the working class, while evidence to the contrary continued to mount in the years ahead.

I believe the distortions in our policy in the workplace and unions described above were the result of Jack Barnes' reaction to the reality as he personally saw it. With some exceptions, the unions were in retreat. His response was to pull away from participation in union politics. But believing that a political radicalization of the working class was nevertheless developing, our central focus was to be socialist propaganda. In that way we would tap into this supposed radicalization. And to do this, it was not necessary for our members to develop roots in the workplace or the unions, since one member was as good as another in "talking socialism," selling *The Militant*, and so forth.

A correction was needed. First of all, in our analysis of the political reality, and flowing from that our policy. But Jack Barnes had so identified his own personal prestige with this analysis and policy that he could not pull back.

---

1 *The Militant*, Feb. 1, 1980.

CHAPTER TWENTY-SEVEN: AN ALTERNATIVE PATH FOR THE TURN

The turn to industry could have been a big step forward for the party, instead of the disaster it became. In the 1978 report proposing the turn, there was a note of do or die, which developed over the next year or two into a forced march, riding roughshod over a continued campus orientation for the YSA and the maintaining of our teachers, health care workers, and social service workers fractions, as was noted in the previous chapter.

The error of projecting a political radicalization of the working class just about to happen would have to have been corrected in a timely fashion, as the evidence to the contrary began to mount.

Of course, such a projection was an error from the start. Strategy and tactics have to be based on what actually is and becoming, not on projections of what might be. Banking on the most favorable immediate future developments can blind one from seeing what is actually occurring. If a political radicalization of the working class had developed, it couldn't have happened all at once. It would be a process that would become apparent in real life, and policy could be adjusted accordingly. But many "most favorable" scenarios often do not work out in this world, and this one did not.

Errors are also made in politics, and no one has all the answers, even someone as talented as Jack Barnes. Correcting the errors in time could have led to taking a different path. A forced march to build our industrial fractions, based on the erroneous projection that dictated we had to immediately turn the party upside down or be left behind, would have been relaxed. Patience in building our presence in industry would have replaced the forced march.

There were important reasons to make a turn toward building industrial fractions, aside from this political projection. Our composition was lopsided. And there were openings to do political work in the industrial unions. Anti-communism, while still existing in the backward sections of the working class in both blue- and white-collar occupations, had diminished to where we could effectively function. Racism among white workers had diminished as a result of the victories of the Black struggle, although it still existed among more backward sections of the white working class.

Our teachers' fraction had become our largest fraction, with about 110 comrades. It should have been cut back through inspiring many teachers to get industrial jobs. The key word is inspiring, not creating an atmosphere where such comrades began to feel like second-class citizens—which is what happened. The teachers fraction should have been maintained, even at half its size or so. Past work and subsequent developments over the next years and decades show the continued importance of these workers. The same was true about other government workers in our AFSCME (American Federation of State, County and Municipal Employees) fraction.

While there was no political radicalization of the working class, there are always battles occurring in every workplace. The class struggle never ceases, even under fascism. We should have been participants in such struggles, even though they were more modest than we had projected. Through such participation we could have become known as union fighters.

Likewise, we should have participated in union politics. In many unions there were divisions between the increasingly class collaborationist bureaucracy and the ranks. These presented opportunities to raise our proposals. In certain cases there were reform caucuses, often reflecting merely the "outs" versus the "ins," but some times critical support to one side or another could help us concretely further our class struggle approach. Accepting positions such as stewards or working on the union newspaper, or helping to put out independent plant newsletters would advance our work in certain situations. The blanket rejection of such was an abstentionist error. It also blocked thinking through tactics on the ground, diminishing our comrades' development as working-class leaders. No need to think about tactics in the unions when all that was required was to "talk socialism."

Historically, the SWP's tactics in the unions were centered in opposition to the class enemy, not the union bureaucracy. In this way our opposition to the class-collaborationist policies of the bureaucracy would be understandable to the workers in the context of real struggles. But this never was meant to be a blanket rejection of criticizing the bureaucracy—quite the opposite.

An important development we missed was the formation of Teamsters for a Democratic Union (TDU), a caucus initiated by socialists from another tendency, which had its origins in the International Socialists. The TDU waged a heroic battle against the gangster-ridden Teamster bureaucracy. They often faced severe violence from the leadership's goons, but persevered in opposition, raising not only the centrally important issue of union democracy but also the need to fight the bosses. We could have been part of TDU, which would have enhanced our work in other unions.

We didn't even target the Teamsters as one of the unions we were hoping to colonize, despite the fact that the Teamsters were one of the largest industrial unions. In retrospect, I am convinced that our failure to do so was to avoid having to take a position on TDU, reflecting our growing abstentionism in the labor movement. Another reason was that individuals from the International Socialists initiated the TDU, and we were retreating from any common work with other socialist tendencies. For the same reason we abstained from the development of *Labor Notes,* a magazine that began to regroup union militants from many unions nationally, important people to get to know and collaborate with.

We had comrades who had worked for many years in the construction trades, including painters, electricians, ironworkers and others. While these members were in highly corrupt unions, we could have collaborated with these comrades instead of ignoring them, which is what we did. There were openings for work in these unions, as we had proven in our fraction in the International Union of Painters and Allied Trades (IUPAT) in the Bay Area and New York. My brother Roland was able to do important work in the IUPAT in the Bay Area. The same was true for my brother Roger in the International Brotherhood of Electrical Workers (IBEW) in Boston. There were other examples.

Being open socialists on the job would have been developed more in tune with the situations comrades found themselves in. When to "come out" as a socialist would have been based on each comrade's situation, not on a party-ordered command to do so right away. Becoming known as union participants and fighters would have encouraged workers to consider our broader ideas. Knowing which workers would be most interested in aspects of our political work outside of the unions and plants, such as women's liberation, the struggles of Blacks and other oppressed nationalities, the revolutions in Central America and the Caribbean, the danger of war against Iran, our election campaigns and so on could only be furthered by becoming rooted in our places of work. It is also always useful to know who is hostile to our views, to avoid unnecessary conflict.

When the turn to industry was first proposed, we projected that we would build fractions of members in particular plants and in the unions nationally. Such fractions would discuss our tactics and policies in the concrete situations we found ourselves in. Over time, the fractions would elect their own leaderships, and would parallel our political units from the branches to our national structures. Of course, the fractions would work within the guidelines set politically, but would require a large leeway in making their own decisions based on their concrete experiences. In this way, we hoped, the fractions would develop new leaders, strengthening our national leadership generally.

The turn toward abstentionism blocked this development, as did the policy of needless transfers. On a national level, discussion in the fractions became more and more rehashes of our political policies developed by our political bodies—useless repetitions of what everyone already knew. Concrete, productive discussion of the problems facing our union work became less and less.

A related development was that the fractions did not elect their national leaderships. I believe Jack blocked the development of fraction leaders because they would have had independent bases of support, and threatened the cult.

Recognizing that there had been a political retreat of the radicalization of "The Sixties," and that there was a retreat politically of the working class in the 1980s, would have dictated a course opposite to the forced march into industry and tightening of discipline that occurred. A more relaxed atmosphere in the party was called for, in keeping with the slower pace of developments.

In the period of retreat in the 1950s, the party leadership took the lead in relaxing norms. When the student and Black movements arose in the 1960s, we began to ask more of our members, for more discipline and membership commitment. This was in keeping with our growing needs to participate in outside work, and was seen throughout the party as natural and necessary. Being attuned to such rhythms is an important aspect of responsible leadership.

This tentative sketch of how the turn could have developed in a rational way indicates, I believe, that it could have become an important step forward for the SWP, instead of the disaster it became.

The critical perspective I have outlined here isn't something new. It is rooted in how the SWP and its forerunners operated in the unions for decades. Led by Jack Barnes, the overthrow of this accumulated experience amounted to a break with this rich history.

CHAPTER TWENTY-EIGHT: FACTION FIGHT AND SPLIT

I use the word "split" in this chapter in a neutral way, meaning there was a division in the SWP in the early 1980s leading to four organizations: the SWP, Socialist Action, the Fourth Internationalist Tendency, and North Star. As will become clear, I believe that the majority leadership of the SWP was responsible for these splits.

In 1978 there was a discussion in leading bodies of the party concerning Cuba. It was begun in the Political Committee in August, and then in the National Committee in December. It should be noted that National Committee members could follow the Political Committee discussion through minutes and reports circulated within the National Committee.

One result of this discussion was that National Committee members who had been leaders of the Revolutionary Marxist Committee (RMC) that fused with the SWP in 1977 were won to the position that Cuba was a workers' state, with bureaucratic deformations, but not Stalinist. The RMC had held that the Soviet bloc, China, Vietnam and Cuba were "state capitalist," a position they continued to hold after they joined the SWP. The ex-RMC comrades not only came to support our basic views on Cuba, which included the decisive turning point when the Cuban capitalist class and U.S. capitalist holdings were expropriated and a nationalized and planned economy was set up, as marking the creation of a workers' state in October 1960. They also abandoned their "state capitalist" views on the USSR and the other countries.

But there was another development that emerged from the discussion. Long-time leader of the SWP, George Breitman, raised the position that we should abandon our characterization of the Castro leadership as revolutionary, and instead call it centrist. By centrist, George meant that it vacillated between reformism and revolution. The reformism he referred to was Stalinism.

During the 1978 discussion, the majority held that our positions developed in the 1960s remained valid. In 1978, we published a book of our major resolutions and reports on Cuba from the 1960s, which had been authored by Joseph Hansen. We called it the "yellow book" because of the color of its cover, and urged members to study it. The majority position was adopted almost unanimously at the 1979 convention of the party.

Looking back, I think Breitman had a valid point. While he dropped his arguments about the terminology of "centrism," he correctly pointed out that there had been internal changes in Cuba in a Stalinist direction in the 1970s. This was true even while Cuba maintained a revolutionary and internationalist foreign policy as evidenced by its sending of troops to help beat back the U.S.-sponsored South African invasion of Angola in 1975.

The most important of these internal developments was the adoption of Soviet-style bureaucratic economic planning. There were others. In the mid-1970s, I worked for a few months on *Intercontinental Press*, to help its editor, Joseph Hansen, whose health was deteriorating. Joe discussed with me his view that there were negative developments in Cuba, in addition to the character of economic planning. One was the recent introduction of ranks into the army, which from the days of the July 26 movement had *commandantes,* but not the hierarchy of generals on down to privates of capitalist armies. Such ranks serve to separate the mass of soldiers from their officers, elevate the officers above them, promote rigid discipline that stifles input from below, and separates the army from the population. While none of these tendencies went as far as in capitalist or Stalinist armies, the danger was there.

Another important development occurred in 1975. The founding congress of the Cuban Communist Party that year prohibited internal party tendencies and factions. Cuba was declared a one-party state. Again, these features have never gone as far as in Stalinist parties. In fact, there has always been vigorous discussion in the Cuban party, but these were negative developments.[*]

But when Joe and I collaborated in writing an article along these lines, Jack Barnes intervened and demanded that there be no further articles like this one. At a subsequent party convention, I was singled out by Larry Seigle (under Jack's orders) publicly for denunciation because of the article.

Breitman didn't go enough into detail about these negative developments in Cuba. But the differences in the party deepened. With the victory of the Nicaraguan and Grenadian revolutions, and their enthusiastic embrace by Cuba, a new factor had entered world politics. The morale of Cuban workers and peasants was given a shot in the arm by these extensions of the Cuban revolution. The development of the Nicaraguan and Grenadian revolutions followed their unique courses, as is true in every revolution. In particular, urban insurrections had played a decisive role in the overthrow of the old powers, and more democratic forms emerged, which had the potential to influence Cuba itself. A big impulse was also given to the prospects for the left in Latin America, and immediately for El

Salvador. In El Salvador, five different groups had been battling the U.S.-imposed dictatorship, and they united into the Farabundo Martí National Liberation Front (FMLN).

We saw the potential for new international collaboration to develop from these revolutions, which the Fourth International and the SWP could participate in. Such an opening could lead over time to the formation of a new, expanded International. This dynamic was later cut short by the overthrow of the Grenadian revolution by a Stalinist faction and the disintegration of the Nicaraguan revolution. But we were absolutely correct to jump into this new opening, while it lasted.

The majority leadership lurched beyond this, however, and quickly adopted an uncritical attitude toward the Cuban leadership. One indication of this was the shoving into the background of the "yellow book." We dropped the criticisms of the Cuban Revolution we had adopted in the 1960s. These included the lack of proletarian organs of democratic rule, such as the workers, peasants, and soldiers councils (soviets) that developed in the Russian Revolution. (These new positions of the majority leadership, for the reasons discussed previously, were formulated by a single person, Jack Barnes.)

We also turned a blind eye to the Soviet-style bureaucratic economic planning. Ironically, some years later, in 1986, Fidel Castro himself denounced this system, which had created a bloated bureaucracy and the blunders and inefficiency endemic to such bureaucratic planning. One of many examples Castro cited was of a bridge that had been completed, but the roads connecting it had not been built (a "bridge to nowhere"). Castro's speech in fact countered our new position that nothing much had changed in Cuba in the 1970s.

Notably, a "rectification" campaign, as the Cubans called it, was launched in 1986. This campaign re-raised some ideas of Che Guevara, including promoting volunteer labor. Communities would develop their own projects, built by volunteer labor, with materials provided by the state. In this way things like plans for new schools, recreation centers and other community projects, would be proposed and executed by the grass roots, outside of the economic plan and bureaucratic control. There was greater participation by the working people in the economic plan, although still restricted largely to questions of production in the workplace. The bureaucracy was drastically slashed.

The concept of voluntary labor in such projects, outside of the regular employment of the volunteers, had been raised in the early days of the Russian Revolution, but was truncated by the severe economic situation and the civil war. In the early days of the Cuban Revolution, Che had raised the idea as a small step toward the voluntary labor that would replace compulsory labor in a free communist society. He linked it to using moral incentives and not only material ones to increase production, and emphasized the importance of developing socialist consciousness and morals.

•••

In 1979, one good initiative made by Jack was to re-launch the party school, where a group of comrades on the National Committee would spend about five months living and studying in a secluded facility. Freed from day-to-day party tasks, reading, studying and discussing aspects of Marxist theory would be their only assignment. Earlier, this school was called the "Trotsky school." It had been abandoned when we were forced to sell "Mountain Spring Camp," some land and buildings where the school and other functions were held, in the 1960s.

The new party school was held in a large former farmhouse in upstate New York. The first session was held in the spring and early summer of 1980, with a curriculum centered on the writings of Marx and Engels. Moscow, after all the intervening decades, had begun finally to publish in serial fashion English translations of their works, and these volumes were the basis of the readings at the school. Since the volumes were being published in chronological order, the school began with their early writings, but also included readings in *Capital* and other works already in English.

Jack selected the student body as well as a "teacher" who coordinated the discussions, as he did in the subsequent sessions over the next few years. The "graduates" of the first session were a big hit at the August 1980 educational conference, wearing T-shirts with the name in German of the newspaper Marx and Engels published during the revolutions of 1848, *Neue Rheinische Zeitung*.

It was at the 1980 conference that the switch in line on Afghanistan was made. The new view of Cuba began to be discussed there, as part of the emphasis on the revolutions in Nicaragua and Grenada, and the struggle in El Salvador. As the person primarily in charge of the conference, I helped arrange for speakers from the Grenadian New Jewel Movement, the Nicaraguan FSLN, and one group in the FMLN, the Peoples Revolutionary Bloc, to attend.

But as the new line on Cuba began to be elaborated in our press in 1980, even if in a way new ideas are often worked out, with some confusion and contradictions, Breitman and those who agreed with him opposed the direction the leadership was taking on Cuba.

By the time preparations began for the 1981 party convention, Breitman presented a series of amendments to the political resolution drafted by the majority leadership. One aspect of Breitman's amendments was to reject a downplaying of the Fourth International evident in the majority draft. The main amendments were to reassert our criticisms of the Cuban Revolution, including our analysis (contained in the "yellow book") of the development of the Cuban leadership, which were dropped from the majority political resolution.

A Breitman amendment reasserted that the Castro leadership "evolved through combat from a petty-bourgeois grouping into the leadership of the Cuban social revolution...." The majority instead was moving toward the new position, later made explicit, that the Castro team had always been "revolutionary Marxist," a blatant falsification of history. In fact, we had never before used such a designation, which we had reserved for Leninists—which in the concrete real world meant "Trotskyists," however small a current we were on the world scene. The distinction was important, since it referred to our full political program, including support to the political revolution to overthrow the Stalinist bureaucracies, a position the Cubans opposed.

There was enough support in the party for the Breitman amendments to win five delegates to the 1981 convention.

•••

Another tendency had formed in the National Committee, led by Nat Weinstein and Lynn Henderson. At a January 1980 meeting of the National Committee, Weinstein had disagreed with and voted against the position on Nicaragua the leadership had put forward at the recently concluded World Congress of the Fourth International. Later, in April 1981, he would write, "In the resolution adopted at that time [January 1980], the 'workers and farmers government' characterization was stamped on the FSLN-led regime in Nicaragua. And using this label as license, a series of adaptations to the positions and policies of the FSLN was initiated."[1] Lynn Henderson then joined with Nat in the formation of a tendency on the National Committee, which became a tendency in the party for the purposes of electing delegates to the 1981 convention.

In a subsequent resolution submitted for the 1981 convention, Weinstein and Henderson clarified their position on Nicaragua, accepting the designation of the FSLN government as a workers' and peasants' government. However, they maintained their criticism of the majority position, which had evolved over the course of 1980. The position the majority put forward for the 1981 convention was that the Nicaraguan workers, under the leadership of the FSLN, was "driving forward the class struggle on the road toward consolidating a new workers state." The Weinstein-Henderson tendency rejected this optimistic projection, which they characterized as tantamount to saying that a workers' state had already been established.

A correct point Weinstein and Henderson made was that the FSLN government had failed to carry out a thorough-going land reform, mobilizing the peasants to take the land. (I discussed this crucial question in a previous chapter.)

At the 1981 convention the Weinstein-Henderson tendency had proposed a resolution, voted down, that corrected the abstentionist and propagandist position on the unions. Weinstein-Henderson reaffirmed our historic orientation toward the unions. The Lovell-Bloom tendency followed suit early in 1982. Given the centrality of the turn to industry in the life of the party, the majority's failure to make this correction as proposed by the minorities marked the gathering degeneration.

At the convention, Weinstein asked point blank whether the majority was abandoning the Trotskyist theory of "permanent revolution." The answer was "no."

This answer, in my view, did reflect the position at the time of most in the majority leadership, including me. But events soon disclosed that Jack Barnes was moving toward rejecting Trotsky's theory.

•••

After the 1981 convention, the national office proposed a series of classes be held throughout the party on Lenin's writings from the period after the Russian Revolution of 1905 (which the Tsar was able to crush) up to the successful revolution of 1917. That was well and good. We had tended to ignore these writings except the major works, such as *What Is To Be Done; Imperialism, the Highest Stage of Capitalism; State and Revolution* and others. But these classes introduced a pernicious novel practice. Any mention of Trotsky's views was forbidden, and any attempt to do so was subject to disciplinary action. In this way the classes became an indoctrination of the view that Lenin's conception was superior to Trotsky's of the same period. Hitherto, we had the reverse view.

Then an article appeared in the party's theoretical journal, *International Socialist Review*, written by Doug Jenness, on the anniversary of the Russian Revolution. Jenness wrote that Lenin's pre-1917 conception of the revolution was the sole correct one, without mentioning Trotsky's theory of permanent revolution or Trotsky's central role in the 1917 revolution.

In fact, the differences between Lenin and Trotsky were overcome in the crucible of tremendous events, the slaughter of World War One and the unfolding of the Russian Revolution itself, including the peasant war against the landlords that emerged from the disintegration of the largely peasant Tsarist army.** The peasant war engulfed the huge Russian countryside, while in the cities the working class moved toward revolution. These developments overcame any differences between Lenin and Trotsky concerning the revolutionary potential of the peasantry and the necessity for the proletariat to take power.

Why, then, was it so important to revise our views on the positions of Lenin and Trotsky before the war and revolution, and how they developed, changed and converged in these world-shaking events? I believe there were two reasons.

The first involved our attempt to reach out to the new international current emerging from the Cuban, Nicaraguan and Grenadian revolutions. The leaderships of these revolutions had prejudices against Trotskyism that Stalinism had introduced in the workers' movement on a world scale. But they did have a favorable view of Lenin.

This reason for revising a fundamental aspect of our program was blatantly opportunistic. It was also completely unnecessary. We did face a problem in differentiating from many groups in the world claiming to be Trotskyist who were hostile to the Cuban, Nicaraguan and Grenadian leaderships and combined this hostility with a sectarian interpretation of permanent revolution.

This sectarian interpretation of permanent revolution was to equate it with socialist revolution. If that was Trotsky's concept of the Russian revolution before 1917 he would have said so, and not have proposed the concept of permanent revolution but plainly said that Russia faced socialist revolution. Trotsky agreed with Lenin that the coming Russian revolution would be a bourgeois-democratic one to overthrow the Tsarist semi-feudalist landlord-based autocracy, carry out land reform, and the other democratic tasks facing Russia. He also agreed with Lenin that the capitalist class could not and would not carry out the bourgeois democratic revolution, but the workers and peasants, with the workers in the lead, were the only class forces that could.

Trotsky went further than Lenin before 1917, and said that the workers once in power would not stop at carrying through the bourgeois-democratic tasks, but would be compelled to begin the socialist revolution. Permanent revolution was thus conceived as a bridge between the democratic and socialist revolutions, not as an over-leaping of the democratic revolution and jumping at once to the socialist revolution.

The Cuban revolution itself followed the path of permanent revolution. We only had to champion the path the Cuban revolution took to explain the correct interpretation of permanent revolution against the sectarian Trotskyists. Our concept of permanent revolution was not an obstacle at all in making strong links with the Nicaraguan and Grenadian revolutions, as explained in pervious chapters, links far stronger than those made by the U.S. Communist Party.

The second reason was a need for Barnes to break with the past history of the SWP in all aspects. He was on a messianic mission to remake the SWP from top to bottom, under his exclusive control and leadership. Earlier I discussed his break with the whole history of the SWP's participation in the labor movement. His hell-bent drive now to break with the SWP's theoretical past was another expression of the developing cult around Barnes.

In line with these developments, a statement by Jack for the majority following the 1981 convention introduced a new organizational concept. Responding to the announcement by Weinstein and Henderson that they would maintain their tendency, the majority statement took them to task for doing so. The statement quoted from the party's organizational principles, "When the party has made its decision on the issues in dispute, groupings formed during the polemical struggle should dissolve into the party as a whole." But our organizational principles never stated that such groupings *must* so dissolve. For our common work as a party, as decided by majority vote, it would be better if they didn't feel the need to continue. But if a tendency felt the need to do so, they had that right, within the bounds of carrying out majority decisions. Subsequently, this new norm of party functioning was expanded to claim that people supporting a tendency could not communicate with each other except during a pre-convention discussion.

Such was not how we functioned when we had helped form the Leninist-Trotskyist Tendency (LTF) in the Fourth International. Of course we communicated with others in the LTF about developments in the class struggle and the International. How else could we draw up resolutions for the discussion? How else could we make the later decision to transform the tendency into a faction? To outlaw such discussion is utopian—it could never be enforced—and went against actual practice in the workers' movement historically.

•••

At the 1981 convention, Frank Lovell and Steve Bloom were elected to the National Committee, representing the viewpoint that had been expressed in the Breitman amendments. George Breitman's health was deteriorating, and Lovell and Bloom began to speak for their caucus. In view of the Lenin classes, one of the things they proposed was that there be a written discussion open to all party members on Lenin's views. This was rejected at a National Committee meeting in November 1981.

Around this time, Les Evans wrote an article for the *International Socialist Review* polemicizing with Jenness's article. It was rejected for publication. It was now clear that the majority had blocked any discussion public or internal of its new line *introduced after, not before, the recently concluded convention.*

In 1982 the differences only deepened. Early in the year, at a meeting of the National Committee, Jack Barnes introduced the concept that Lenin's early view of a "democratic dictatorship of the proletariat and peasantry" was the same as our view of a workers' and peasants' government as we had developed it in relation to the Chinese, Cuban, Nicaraguan and Grenadian revolutions, along the lines of Joseph Hansen's contributions.

At a convention of the YSA held over the New Years week of 1982-83, Jack gave a public speech entitled "Their Trotsky and Ours." In this somewhat garbled and self-contradictory speech he broke with Trotsky's pre-1917 theory of "permanent revolution." The speech wasn't printed until the fall 1983 issue of our re-named theoretical journal, *New International*. In this speech Barnes seemed at one point to say that Trotsky's application of permanent revolution after he became a Bolshevik was correct. Trotsky had broadened the scope of permanent revolution to apply to the countries oppressed by imperialism, where the democratic revolution was on the agenda. As in Russia, Trotsky held that the bourgeoisie in these countries would not be able to carry through the democratic revolution for actual national independence from imperialism, land reform, and so forth, but the working class in alliance with and leading the peasantry were the class forces that could do so. If they were victorious, this would begin the socialist revolution. Barnes, however, whatever his initial formulations in "Their Trotsky and Ours," soon rejected permanent revolution *in toto.*

Theory must be tested against reality. Those colonial countries that did in fact carry through permanent revolution, whatever the leadership of these revolutions thought of the theory, such as China, Vietnam and Cuba, have been the only such countries that achieved real independence from imperialism, carried through land reform, and established workers' states. Many other colonial countries (for example, India) did achieve formal independence from imperialism, but did not break imperialism's economic dominance or carry out the other democratic tasks. In fact, Trotsky's theory has held up quite well to the test of history. [This book is not the place to discuss China's subsequent re-establishment of capitalism.]

•••

In 1983, a major rift involving our organizational principles and practices occurred. A convention had been scheduled for that summer. But before pre-convention discussion was opened, the majority leadership decided to call it off. Given that the differences within the party had widened, and that questions of our program were involved, this was a profoundly undemocratic decision. The ridiculous rationalization for canceling the convention was that the issues involved were completely settled at the 1981 convention, and therefore we didn't need another one.

Looking back, I believe that Jack Barnes cancelled the convention because he was not sure how to answer the minorities' arguments concerning permanent revolution, especially the suppressed article by Les Evans. The minorities had been told over and over that their views would get a full airing in the 1983 pre-convention discussion and at the convention itself. Suddenly, they were confronted with the *fait accompli* that their views would not be presented before the membership, but would continue to be suppressed. The majority had broken with democratic centralism.

This violation of our norms was compounded at the National Committee meeting immediately following the 1983 educational conference. The Weinstein-Henderson and Lovell-Bloom tendencies formed a bloc at this meeting. For this, these four comrades were suspended for forming an "unauthorized faction." (National Committee members could not be expelled by the National Committee under the SWP Constitution, but only suspended pending final decision of the convention. But this action was a virtual expulsion.)

In the course of 1981-83, the kinds of trials referred to earlier were stepped up. More and more, they became directed at members of the minority tendencies. Most of these trials were spurious. Whatever infractions of our rules may have been broken, it was within the context of the destruction of democracy by the majority, and thus were moot.

In the wake of the suspensions of the four comrades from the National Committee, the denial of their democratic rights to present their views before the party membership, and the trials, some in the Weinstein-Henderson grouping had decided that they had to leave the SWP, a completely understandable position. One of their supporters in the San Francisco branch expressed as much.

Then the Barnes leadership executed a maneuver to get rid of all supporters of the minorities. Comrades were assigned to question each of them, demanding that they repudiate the statement of the San Francisco branch member. The Lovell-Bloom grouping had wanted to remain inside the SWP, but was caught up in the trap. As they were principled comrades, they too refused to repudiate the statement, along with the Weinstein-Henderson members. In this way supporters of both groupings were expelled. Two new organizations soon emerged, Socialist Action and the Fourth Internationalist Tendency, generally lining up along the lines of the two previous tendencies.

The membership of the SWP had been dwindling during the course of the faction fight. Together with the expelled members, the membership figures had gone down by over five hundred.

This act marked the death-knell of the SWP. No tendencies or factions have ever again appeared in the party in the decades since. Internal life became monolithic and top-down commandism became the norm.

•••

The expulsion of Peter Camejo came earlier. At a meeting of the National Committee in 1981, Olga Rodriguez, the New York branch organizer, reported that Camejo had resigned from the SWP. Years later I learned that this was a lie. What had actually happened was that Peter had asked for a leave of absence from the branch, something that was routinely granted in every case I ever knew of. But it was not in this case. Peter took a bit of a vacation anyway in Venezuela. The fact that he did so was then the basis, not for accusing him of indiscipline, but of claiming he had resigned. There is no question in my mind that Rodriguez did not invent this blatant lie—she would never have done so on her own. It came from Jack Barnes.

Peter had growing doubts about the SWP, although from quite a different stance than the criticisms of the Weinstein and Breitman minorities, which were from the left. Peter had raised questions that indicated he thought the SWP was sometimes too leftist. He had also been subject to personal slights from a section of the leadership around Barnes that I wasn't privy to, which I described earlier concerning the 1976 Presidential campaign. These contributed to his wanting a leave of absence to think things over, but I have recently learned that there was a more immediate reason. I was living in California at the time and was unaware of this development.

Sometime after he returned from Nicaragua in 1980, Peter and his companion Gloria got jobs in New York's large garment industry, to be part of the turn. The decision to build a fraction in the garment unions was new. David Walters was a member of the New York SWP at the time, working in the Brooklyn Navy Yard as a pipefitter. "There were many young Central Americans working in New York's garment district," Walters wrote to me in 2011. "Peter joined this fraction and soon recruited a number of young garment workers."

Peter was an enthusiastic supporter of the Nicaraguan revolution, and of the reorientation of the party toward the "Three Giants." His work in garment put him in contact with radical supporters of the revolutionary struggles in Central America and Puerto Rico. "He proposed that the New York SWP should initiate a 'United Socialist Slate' in upcoming municipal elections to be held, I believe, in the fall of 1981. Peter articulated the view that we should act like the Cubans to further trying to bring together all who stood, in their own way, for independent working class political action," Walters wrote.

"His focus was that the common points of unity would be: No support to the capitalist parties, including the Democrats; Community control over schools in racially oppressed communities; Bi-lingual/bi-cultural education; against cutbacks of social services occurring in New York; and support to the revolutions in Cuba, Nicaragua, Grenada and El Salvador.

"The groups Peter and many of us who supported this creative proposal had in mind was the large Puerto Rican Socialist Party, a group called *El Comité*, the Black United Front and a few other organizations that had survived from the anti-Vietnam War movement and had roots in the communities of the oppressed.

"Barnes didn't like this idea at all. Peter warned me that the leadership would pull out all stops to smash this proposal, and 'run me through the mud.' I was at first skeptical this would be the case, but at the meeting where this came to a head, the comrades working in the national headquarters, who were not generally active in the city organization, were mobilized to attend and speak and vote against the proposal. [The] New York SWP organizer was lined up to lead the attack.

"They accused Peter on the one hand of 'proposing to split the Puerto Rican Socialist Party' and we'd be seen as splitters and sectarian. On the other hand, they argued that Peter was proposing a 'popular front' or a class collaborationist alliance with a section of the capitalist parties."

Both arguments were patently bogus. In my view, this was another example of Barnes' abstentionism and recoiling from having anything to do with other radical groups.

Walters said, "We managed, after an hour or so of debate to garner about 30 percent of the vote. But the debate against Peter was so harsh, so terrible, that this was the last meeting for many members, especially the young ones including the garment workers Peter had recruited."

It was subsequent to this assault that Peter asked for a leave of absence. No wonder Peter wanted some time off!*** After he was out of the SWP, Peter helped form, for a time, a new organization called North Star, after the newspaper of that name founded by the great abolitionist Frederick Douglas.

Camejo subsequently come to the conclusion that in light of the Nicaraguan revolution, and in hindsight the Cuban revolution, the U.S. SWP's program was sectarian, among other things that Trotsky's analysis of Stalinism was sectarian and an obstacle. He became swept up in the enthusiasm for Gorbachev's reforms in the mid-1980s. After Caroline and I left the SWP, Peter told Caroline and I he thought the SWP program in general was sectarian.

After the collapse of the Soviet bloc, and then the 1991 collapse of the Soviet Union itself, it was clear that Gorbachev's road was not toward a renewal of Soviet democracy, but of accommodation to imperialism. The Soviet bureaucracy became more and more the organ of world imperialism within the USSR, and was the instrument that overthrew the remaining gains of the Russian Revolution and reestablished capitalism, as Trotsky had predicted would happen if the Soviet workers did not overthrow the bureaucracy first. Peter began to reread Trotsky's *The Revolution Betrayed*, and held long telephone discussions with me about how right Trotsky was concerning Stalinism and the USSR.

•••

In 1981 there was another factional move by Barnes, and that was to drive out another party leader, Lew Jones. Lew had been the Bay Area District organizer before me. At the 1981 convention, without my knowledge Barnes maneuvered with some of the delegates from the Bay Area to launch a vicious personal attack on Lew before the convention's nominating commission. This resulted in his not being reelected to the new National Committee.

When I got back to the Bay Area, I met with Lew and explained I had not been aware of this attack against him and that I didn't agree with it. He was in tears, at a total loss to understand what had happened, which he had no inkling of before. I knew that what happened to Lew could happen to me at any time. Demoralized, Lew dropped out of the party, and for a time joined Peter Camejo in North Star.

Just as in Camejo's case, Barnes was over time systematically driving out all the younger leaders of the party, with the exception of a dwindling number of toadies.

What was done to Lew Jones at the 1981 convention was an expression of a new and pernicious policy of Barnes to intervene in the deliberations of the nominating commission. Our strict policy from the 1940s when the nominating commission process was first adopted was that the central leaders should keep hands off. The whole idea of the nominating commission for election to the National Committee was to break as far as possible with the horse-trading and behind-the-scenes maneuvering of capitalist politics, including the tendency for the outgoing central leadership to perpetuate itself.

The process we had put in place allowed each branch delegation to the convention to select its representatives to the nominating commission at the beginning of the convention. The commission then met at off-times throughout the convention. These rank-and-file delegates discussed the various proposals coming from the branches for nominations to the election of the National Committee. Through a process of discussion and voting, the nominating commission then came up with a slate of nominations to be presented to the convention. Delegates then made further nominations. Finally, the delegates voted in secret ballot on all the proposed nominations to elect the National Committee.

A leader of the SWP at the time, Jose Perez, writing on an email list in November 2002, years after he left the SWP, said, "a very important component of Cannon's method was abandoned.... There was increasing intervention by the outgoing central leadership in guiding and shaping the slate."

Perez was right about Cannon, who in writing about the idea of the nominating commission in 1944, said, "It would be grossly improper for individual central leaders to intrude themselves upon the commission and seek to dominate its proceedings. That would amount to circumvention of the democratic process aimed at in the proposal [for the nominating commission]. It is part of wisdom for the central leaders to leave the nominating commission to its own devices, respecting the essence of party democracy as well as the form.... Room must be left for competition and rivalry and differences of opinion to operate without artificial restraints. Members of the outgoing NC [National Committee] should be placed in exactly the same status as new aspirants—as *candidates* for election."[2]

At the 1985 convention, Perez noted, "on Jack's initiative the outgoing central leadership *did* intervene in the election of the new NC. Reports were given to the PC [Political Committee], and then conveyed in one form or another to the nominating commission.... I became aware of at least a couple of meetings of the nominating commission that Jack went to. What I was told is the commission had asked him to come to describe the various roles of various people in the central leadership. As a result, there was an extremely high turnover of the NC in those years, and the *majority* of the [National Committee] that initiated the turn to industry was gone a few years later."

This new practice smashed the democratic deliberations of the nominating commission—one more step in junking the "old" SWP and turning it into its opposite.

•••

The factionalism of Jack Barnes that wrecked the SWP had its counterpart in the Fourth International. After the World Congress at the end of 1979, the SWP majority began to build factions in sections of the International where it could. One aspect of the political basis of these groupings was agreement with the forced march character of the turn to industry increasingly championed by the SWP, irrespective of the concrete situations sections faced politically in their countries or the size and strength of the sections. The leaderships in most sections pulled back from this forced march, and the pro-SWP groups were small opposition currents. In Canada, there was a split on this basis.

The second political aspect of these pro-SWP groups was initially agreement on the character of the Nicaraguan government. This rapidly expanded to include Barnes' revisionism on Cuba, permanent revolution, and Trotskyism.

These pro-SWP groups would attend meetings of the SWP National Committee and its conventions, where they were expected to adopt whatever positions the SWP came up with. Representatives of the groups were given speaking rights at these gatherings, but they did not have voting rights. They were expected to toe the line. One thing that stuck in my mind was Jack explaining at a National Committee meeting that these groups had to "give their souls to the SWP." I was disquieted, but said nothing.

By 1986, this process had developed to the point where members of these groupings sold *The Militant* as their paper, whatever the language of the country they were in. In those cases where these groups were the section in their country, such as in Iceland and New Zealand, or were in separate groups as in Canada, they stopped publishing their own papers. The small section in New Zealand had developed their own newspaper—now they sold *The Militant* as their organ. The Canadian comrades had built up two good newspapers, one in English and the other in French. Now they were reduced to selling *The Militant*.

The SWP had succeeded in forming its own "international" of satellite groups, which did not determine their own positions but followed the line as laid down by the SWP, which they had no say in. This toy international was far more centralized than anything the old International Majority Tendency (IMT) had ever supported. In this aspect as in many others, the SWP had turned into its opposite.

---

* The Cuban Communist Party has many differences with Stalinist parties. Communist Party membership in Cuba has to be approved by secret ballot by workers in their workplaces. Nor has there ever been in Cuba the settling of differences in the party by imprisonment and executions, as under Stalin and Mao. In foreign policy the Cuban party is internationalist and revolutionary, while Stalinist parties are counter-revolutionary and nationalist.

** It is beyond the scope of this book to completely explain the polemic that occurred in the party. I have only lightly sketched it. Similarly, this is not the place to make a thorough analysis of the pre-1917 differences between Lenin and Trotsky. I will only outline them and make a comment of my own.

Within the Russian Social Democratic Labor Party (RSDLP), two major tendencies arose concerning the nature of the coming Russian Revolution. One was labeled the "majority" (Bolshevik in Russian) and the other the "minority" (Menshevik) because of a chance division in the early history of the party. In fact, the Bolsheviks were a minority most of the time. The whole of the RSDLP recognized that the main task of the revolution would be to overthrow Tsarist absolutism and the feudal remnants on which it was based, especially the class of landlords, and establish democracy. Historically, Marxists have described such objectives as "bourgeois-democratic" because they were raised by the great bourgeois-led revolutions, especially the French and American, and because in and of themselves they are not incompatible with capitalist rule. Thus all groupings in the RSDLP saw the coming revolution as a bourgeois-democratic one.

But there was a fundamental disagreement between the Bolsheviks and Mensheviks on the social forces that could carry out the revolution. In the failed bourgeois-democratic revolutions of 1848 in Europe, Marx and Engels thought, the bourgeoisie turned on its own revolutions out of fear of the working class, which by that time had become strong enough to begin to assert its own demands, which terrified the capitalists. Utilizing these insights and through his own independent study of the growth of capitalism and the working class in Russia, Lenin, the foremost leader of the Bolsheviks, concluded that the liberal bourgeoisie could not carry out the bourgeois-democratic revolution. The only classes that could do this were the proletariat and the peasantry. Lenin formulated this idea as the "democratic dictatorship of the proletariat and peasantry."

The Mensheviks, on the other hand, reasoned from formal logic, not on study of the real class forces in Russia. Since the revolution was bourgeois-democratic, they derived, the liberal bourgeoisie would have to lead it and the socialists would support this class and wait until a later time to raise the need for socialism, after the bourgeoisie had built up a capitalist society.

Trotsky, basing himself on the experience of the failed 1905 revolution, presented a different view. He agreed with Lenin that the bourgeoisie had shown it could not lead the revolution against Tsarism. He also agreed that there had to be an alliance between the peasantry and the working class to win the revolution. The proletariat would have to lead the peasantry, and play the dominant role in the revolutionary government. The peasantry as a whole had an interest in overthrowing the landlords and carrying out the agrarian reform, but the peasantry was stratified from very poor to better off, was decentralized across the great expanse of rural Russia, had a small-capitalist mentality (they wanted to become free owners of their own land), and were not capable of formulating an independent policy from either the proletariat or the bourgeoisie. But Trotsky went further and said the revolution would have to be carried out by the working class through its own party taking power, with the support of the peasantry as a whole as the working class led the fight against the landlords. Once in power, however, the proletariat would be compelled to go beyond the bourgeois-democratic phase because it would have to defend the basic interests of the workers against the capitalists. The democratic revolution would grow over into a socialist one, and as this happened, the differentiations in the peasantry would grow. It would be the poor peasants and agricultural workers who would rally around the government in struggle against the richer peasants.

Both Lenin and Trotsky believed that in overwhelmingly peasant Russia the revolution could only hold power if it spread to the socialist revolution in the European advanced capitalist countries.

Both Lenin and Trotsky's views also changed and deepened in the crucible of the horrors of the First World War and the revolution that emerged from it in February 1917. Both opposed the imperialist war and the capitulation of most socialist parties to support "their own" capitalist classes in the war. Lenin saw more clearly that these socialist parties had ceased to be revolutionists, while Trotsky hoped that some could still be won to a revolutionary position. The course of the war impelled Trotsky to Lenin's view.

War weariness and suffering were key elements in the beginning of the revolution that overthrew Tsarism in February 1917. The largely peasant armies of the Tsar disintegrated, and the peasants returned home to wage an insurrectionary war against the landlords that swept the vast spaces of rural Russia. At the same time, the workers in the cities increasingly became opposed to the weak bourgeois government. This government continued the hated war, opposed the economic demands of the workers, and opposed the peasant war. In April 1917, Lenin said the "democratic dictatorship of the proletariat and the peasantry" had already been achieved with the formation of the soviets of the workers, peasants, and soldiers that sprung up during the first days of the revolution. But, said Lenin, the reformist leaders of the soviets, the Mensheviks and Socialist Revolutionaries, had ceded power to a bourgeois provisional government that the first soviet leaders had set up. The former dominant class under the Tsar, the landlords, had been overthrown, and the capitalist class now had power.

Based on this analysis, Lenin charted a course toward proletarian power supported by the peasantry through a government of the workers', soldiers', and peasants' soviets. In essential agreement, Trotsky's smaller forces now joined the Bolsheviks. Under this orientation, and the slogans of "peace, bread and land," the Bolsheviks won the leadership of the soviets against the Mensheviks and Socialist Revolutionaries. The soviets did take power, under the leadership of the Bolsheviks, in November 1917, establishing the dictatorship of the proletariat. [Under the old Julian calendar, the workers' seizure of power took place on October 25. In early 1918, the Gregorian calendar replaced it, moving the date of the revolution to November 7.] In the revolution itself Trotsky emerged as a Bolshevik leader second only to Lenin. It was Trotsky who led the actual insurrection. The new government carried through the bourgeois-democratic revolution, above all by supporting the peasant war that smashed landlordism. It was compelled to begin anti-capitalist measures, and in the summer of 1918 the peasantry split as the civil war heated up. The poor peasants and agricultural workers supported the Red Army and the richer peasants the counterrevolutionary Whites.

There is no question that on the main outlines of the Russian Revolution, Trotsky was right. Trotsky did make some wrong formulations on the peasantry before 1917 (but not in 1906). The peasant war put those to rest. The pre-1917 differences between

Lenin and Trotsky were then forgotten. Stalin dragged them up again only later, when Trotsky fought the counterrevolution led by Stalin.

I personally found that reading Lenin more thoroughly during the "Lenin classes" did convince me that Lenin understood the role of the peasantry better than Trotsky did. But I am also reminded of something my first teacher said after I joined the SWP. Larry Trainor told me, "Trotsky saw further, and Lenin saw deeper."

*** In Peter Camejo's memoir, *North Star*, this whole episode is missing. There he says nothing about the positive political work he did while in the garment industry. Nothing about the recruits he made. In his memoir he paints a picture of his time in garment as a political waste of time, and he doesn't mention his proposal for the New York elections. One can only speculate why. Perhaps he thought this story would get in the way of the political points he was making in his memoir. There are other important errors, even untruths, in the latter part of *North Star*, which his editor, Les Evans, should have caught. I was in contact with Peter as he was dying while rushing to finish his memoir. I noticed uncharacteristic outbursts of anger, and I suspect that he was under terrific stress connected with his incurable cancer. I should emphasize that Peter's memoir contains much valuable material relating to the history of the SWP, and is overall a positive contribution and should be read.

1 Nat Weinstein, A Criticism of the March 26, 1981 Draft Political Resolution, SWP Discussion Bulletin (Vol. 37, No. 2), May 1981.
2 James P. Cannon, *Letters From Prison* (Merit Publishers, 1968), pp. 211-212.

CHAPTER TWENTY-NINE: MY CULPABILITY

I knew from the incident I described in 1978, when Jack Barnes threatened me unless I desisted from pursuing my conviction at the time that the SWP central leadership was becoming "a one-man band" under his leadership, that my days in the SWP were numbered. In spite of this I was fully responsible for and complicit with the course of the SWP from 1979 through the expulsions of 1983, and for a time beyond. I include both the political and organizational aspects.

I'll take up the political side first, which consisted of two new developments, the turn to industry and important anti-imperialist revolutions—the revolutions in Iran, Grenada, and Nicaragua, and the impact these had on Cuba. Another important development was the anti-bureaucratic uprising in Poland, which I have already dealt with. Here I will present my thinking, looking back, about these political developments.

My assignments at the time the turn to industry was formulated were mainly concerned with international work. I was not part of thinking through the turn, but I accepted the reasoning and factual experience on which it was based, in the report given by Jack Barnes in 1978, and in subsequent documents. I edited the resolutions and reports after 1978, and agreed with them, including the projection that a political radicalization of the working class in the United States and around the world was in the offing. My criticism of the turn is contained in an earlier chapter and there is no need to repeat it here. Suffice it to say that it took my own experience in industry in Pittsburgh in the latter part of 1985 and in 1986 for my position crystallized, and I'll take this up in a subsequent chapter.

Concerning Iran, I believe our position was fundamentally correct. We supported the revolution that overthrew the Shah and the domination of the country by U.S. imperialism. At the same time, we supported the attempt by our Iranian co-thinkers to build an independent working class party to fight for workers rights, the peasantry, women, the oppressed nationalities and for a workers' and peasants' government. We saw those two tasks as inseparately interlinked.

In this regard we gave no political support to the clerical-capitalist regime that emerged from the revolution in the absence of a mass workers' party capable of presenting a governmental alternative. Unlike many other socialist groups, however, we supported the regime in its conflict with imperialism.

We saw the war launched by Iraq's Saddam Hussein against Iran in 1980 as a cat's paw for U.S. imperialism in its attempt to regain its lost position in Iran and reverse the revolution. Consequently, we and our Iranian co-thinkers defended the Iranian side. Iranian comrades participated heroically and actively in the resistance. This remained our position, correctly, throughout the war. I've already taken up how the regime's attack on and annihilation of the socialist left greatly undermined the fight against Iraq and its imperialist backers.

Both minorities in the party began to oppose our position on the war, and I think they were wrong.

The 1979 revolutions in Nicaragua and Grenada broke the isolation of the Cuban revolution, with the establishment of workers' and peasants' governments. We and the Cuban leadership hailed these advances, expressed by the Cubans as "three giants arising in the Caribbean." From the beginning, the three revolutions reinforced each other and developed close ties, much to the alarm of Washington, which immediately began to take steps against Nicaragua and Grenada (and to tighten the blockade of Cuba). The three leaderships had common roots, and could be seen broadly speaking as an emerging "Castroist" current.

I think we were correct to orient toward this current. The potential existed for a qualitative step forward in rebuilding a revolutionary socialist international. We thought that the SWP and the Fourth International should embrace this perspective, and seek to build ties to this breakthrough.

The Weinstein tendency rejected this orientation, mocking the whole concept of the "three giants." The Breitman group was closer to our view, but didn't see the potential for the advance of the Nicaraguan and Grenadian revolutions to positively affect Cuba. Both tendencies were not enthusiastic about the opportunities these developments opened for the SWP and the Fourth International.

However, a disturbing element crept into our view of the potential for a rebuilt international to emerge. In 1980 and 1981 the SWP leadership began to make formulations that counterposed the existing Fourth International to the "new international," which was still a potential but not actual reality.

By 1983, the long contra war against Nicaragua was taking its toll in lives and treasure, bleeding the country, one of the poorest in Latin America. When our representatives in Managua reported back on these facts they were discounted. Once, Jose Perez, coming back from Nicaragua, said in his opinion the government should no longer be considered a workers' and peasants' government. In one meeting (I don't recall whether it was of the National Committee or Political Committee) when I was present, Jack Barnes berated the reporters on the scene for not getting out and talking to workers and peasants in the field. As a result of this admonishment, our press continued to paint a rosy picture of defeat after defeat of the contras, and steps forward in deepening the revolution.

The overthrow of the Grenadian revolution and the turn toward the capitalist class in Nicaragua in 1983 meant the "new international" was now a dead letter. Yet the SWP persisted, against the evidence of the real situation in Nicaragua and Grenada, in projecting it as a realistic perspective. This furthered the isolation of the SWP and the grouplets that looked to it in other countries from the rest of the Fourth International.

I was a willing participant and supporter of every destructive organizational measure taken against the minority currents in the SWP from 1980 through the mass expulsions of 1983. These included the many trials against individuals that extended beyond the minority members. Some of these were for supposed violations of discipline, but increasingly were moralistic in tone and nature. Minor violations of our policy against the use of illegal drugs were dealt with the same harsh penalty of expulsion those truly dangerous violations, such as the case of Sudie-Geb discussed in an earlier chapter, merited. Harsh words between comrades or the throwing of a pillow were put on the same level as spouse beating. A sense of proportion was abandoned. The result was the introduction of an atmosphere of terrorization of the membership.

One especially shameful incident I was involved in concerned George Breitman. Jack assigned Tom Leonard, Wendy Lyons, and myself to confront Breitman and George Weissman and challenge them to repudiate the alleged split sentiment expressed by a member of the San Francisco branch referred to previously. Breitman had been in poor health for some time. I can still see him virtually wilting in front of us, holding his head, barely able to speak, never thinking he could be expelled from the SWP, the party he had been a founding member and central leader of for decades. Weissman was different— when he saw us at his door he told us to "go to hell" and slammed it shut. After, we three went to a bar and drank a number of martinis, ostensibly to celebrate but in reality to numb ourselves to the disgraceful thing we had done.

I had continued to support the majority political positions. But even so, I should have fought against the organizational degeneration. I ought to have made a bloc with the minorities in defense of party democracy while holding my own political positions.

I also should have opposed the cult by supporting Peter Camejo's objection to the manner in which the correction on Afghanistan was made in 1980, and then I ought to have directly raised the question in the National Committee and proposed the removal of Jack Barnes as National Secretary.

I believe it is important to explore why I became complicit in the political and organizational degeneration of this period. There are lessons for future generations who will rebuild the socialist movement. I said earlier that I did this in spite of knowing since 1978 that I was being driven out of the party. But in reality it was this knowledge itself that compelled me in this direction. Jack's initial threat against me was made in 1978, as I reported. But he made sure I knew in the following years that being driven out hung over me like the sword of Damocles. He did this by his cold demeanor every time we met, averting his face, giving me a limp handshake, and barely speaking.

I had devoted my life to building and leading the SWP. The prospect of being out of it was terrifying and almost inconceivable. I knew I would be shunned by my former comrades and closest friends, as well as by the membership at large that had looked up to me as a central leader and teacher for decades. Under this pressure, I now see, I did everything I could to please Jack in the (vain) hope I would be spared the axe.

Ostracism, shunning, has been an important tool for maintaining conformity and obedience by many religious organizations such as the Catholic Church, Jehovah's Witnesses and others. The Stalinists used it against Trotskyists in the Communist and labor movements internationally and we were educated that this was a reprehensible practice inimical to workers' democracy and socialism. In his *History of American Trotskyism*, SWP leader James P. Cannon explained how the original Trotskyists were subjected to it after they were expelled from the Communist Party:

"A wall of ostracism separated us from the [Communist Party] members. People whom we had known and worked with for years became strangers to us overnight. Our whole lives, you must remember, had been in the Communist movement and its periphery. We were professional party workers. We had no interests, no associations of a social nature outside the party and its periphery. All our friends, all our associates, all our collaborators in daily work for years had been in this milieu. Then, overnight, this was closed to us....

"We lived in those first days under a form of pressure which is in many respects the most terrific that can be brought to bear against a human being—social ostracism from people of one's own kind....

Many comrades who sympathized with us personally, who had been our friends, and many who sympathized at least in part with our ideas were terrorized against coming with us or associating with us because of that terrible penalty of ostracism."[1]

A related factor came out of my discussions with Caroline, whom I confided in about my conviction that the party was becoming a cult. She raised the question we had been taught that political questions were paramount, and my criticism was organizational. What were my political differences? In 1978, 1979 and a few years beyond, I thought I had no political differences with Jack or the majority. It took time for me to gradually understand that the party was heading in the wrong direction politically. But in this case, the organizational question was paramount. The formation of a cult in the party leadership blocked correction of political errors in the turn to industry, the assessment of the change in the objective situation in the Caribbean, the question of permanent revolution, and then other theoretical and political errors. The cult prevented correction of the degeneration of the party's organizational practice.

I offer this explanation not to avoid my responsibility and culpability, which I fully acknowledge. But to warn against practices that led to the destruction of an organization that once stood head and shoulders above any other on the U.S. socialist left.

---

1 James P. Cannon, *The History of American Trotskyism* (Pathfinder Press,1972), pp. 64-65.

CHAPTER THIRTY: I LEAVE THE LEADERSHIP

In March 1983, Caroline was asked by Jack to attend the party school in Roscoe, New York. In August the party school let out, and Caroline and I attended the SWP educational conference at Oberlin, Ohio I've referred to. After the conference, we drove back to New York from the Bay Area, camping along the way. Once there, Caroline got a job in the garment industry, and then was re-hired at the General Motors plant north of the city. I was asked to become the organizer of the New York branch, replacing Olga Rodriguez. I accepted the proposal, although I knew that it was in part intended to keep me out of the National Office, as was the previous assignment to San Francisco.

I found the New York branch to be in bad shape, desultory and demoralized. Wendy Lyons was the Newark branch organizer, which had been in a common district with the New York branch shortly before I got there. Wendy and Olga were both upset. They felt they had been under attack from Ken Shilman, the previous district organizer. Shilman had moved to the Bay Area, and subsequently resigned from the SWP. After Caroline and I left the party in 1988, I visited the Bay Area and talked to Ken, who told me he had been under attack by Craig Gannon in the National Office. At the time (1983), it appeared to me that the pressure against Wendy and Olga was that they were not being aggressive enough in driving out members who failed to get industrial jobs. The pressure was obviously coming from Jack Barnes through both Gannon and Shilman.

I sought to reverse all of this, an indication I was becoming critical of the way the turn was being carried out. I quickly established good relations with Lyons and Rodriguez. I began to resist the forced-march character of the turn to industry, and both branches started to breath easier. The spirit of the Newark branch was pretty good. I met with the New York branch executive committee to discuss the malaise in the branch, which was still our largest with nearly 100 members. The nine members of the executive committee including myself divided up the branch membership, with the task of personally discussing one on one with each member how they viewed the branch and their role.

We found indeed dissatisfaction and demoralization. We halted the pressure on members to go into industry who were not in a position to do so. The branch began to rally and do more outside work, including public forums, sales, and participation in antiwar actions.

But this period was also when we carried through the mass expulsions of the minorities, which demonstrated my uneven consciousness of the process occurring in the party.

At the time of the expulsions, Barnes made the decision that members of the former minorities would not be allowed into public meetings organized by the party. The rationale, specious of course, was to prevent any possibility of violence, as feelings were running high. At a National Committee meeting some months later, I argued that there was no longer any such danger, and the ban should be ended. I was overruled, and the ban in fact became permanent. Also, Jack indicated at one meeting that the members of the former minorities should be personally shunned. He said, "Whenever I sight one of them, I look right through them." It was clear that his example was to be rigorously followed.

Caroline was working at the GM plant in Tarrytown as part of our fraction there.* An opening appeared for hiring at the factory among skilled workers. We proposed to some comrades who because of their personal situations needed higher salaries, and had the skills, to take such jobs. They did. This greatly strengthened the fraction and put us in direct contact with an important section of the workforce.

There were some plants where we had no comrades and the branch had carried out *Militant* plant gate sales. These plants were mostly in New Jersey. I would get up early to make the drive out with a team at one of these plants. By this time in the political retreat of the working class we were selling zero copies of our paper each week. Similar results were happening at other plants. I noticed that no one beside myself on the Political Committee ever participated in the plant gate sales, so they were not experiencing on the ground this reflection of where workers actually were at. The Political Committee resolved the situation by passing a motion that its members were exempted from plant gate sales, further isolating it. The reality was slowly sinking into my consciousness.

While contending with these difficulties, there were small successes. In the summer of 1983, while Ken Shilman was still the district organizer, the party had organized a public meeting featuring speakers from the Vietnamese United Nations (UN) delegation, to commemorate the anniversary of the victory over the United States and its puppet government in 1975. Counterrevolutionary Vietnamese groups organized to try to break up the meeting, and Ken organized a strong defense guard. There was a physical confrontation, but the meeting was held.

In 1984, we decided to repeat the anniversary meeting again. It was a bit peculiar that it was the SWP and not the Communist Party (CP) that organized these meetings. After all, the U.S. CP was supposed to be the "sister" party of the Vietnamese. The CP wanted no part of such confrontations or close identification with the Vietnamese, as they were following the Soviet line of attempting to accommodate U.S. imperialism. In addition, the Vietnamese knew quite well the leading role we had played in the antiwar movement. We were able to wage a public campaign for the police to defend the meeting, and garnered enough support that the city government decided to do so. The city was responsible for the security of the UN delegations, after all.

The day of the meeting, the police did show up in force. We also had a strong defense guard outside and inside the meeting. A tough woman cop relied on me outside the meeting to tell her who to allow in. The counterrevolutionaries were kept out. We wanted to keep the area in front clear of any disruption or loitering these elements could use to try to get in. Then the Spartacist League decided to make a provocation, attempting to assert their "right" to sell their press directly in front of the door. They refused to leave when I asked them to. The policewoman in charge looked over at me, and I signaled that the Spartacists should be moved aside. The cops pushed them one block over, and they did this brutally, as is their standard operating procedure. The Spartacists continued to sell their paper to the people coming into the meeting.

The meeting was a big success, with an audience of hundreds and coverage in the press. After, the Vietnamese delegation invited a few of us for a lunch in appreciation, where they served us tea and Vietnamese delicacies.

•••

Our branch headquarters was in the Soho district in lower Manhattan. Comrades in the National Office raised with me the idea of expanding our small bookstore in the headquarters to house a real public store stocked with a wide variety of books on the labor, women's, Black, Chicano and other movements, international struggles and Marxist works. The titles would include much more than our own publications. This was a good idea. To do it, we would have to expand into loft space to the rear, and rebuild the whole place. Our rent would go up considerably and we would have to put another comrade on full time to run the bookstore. The finances were beyond the reach of the branch to cover, I explained after drawing up a budget, and it was agreed that the national party would pay us the difference on a monthly basis.

We went ahead and built with our members' labor a beautiful bookstore, with a new meeting place in the back for our internal meetings and public forums.

•••

In March 1985, I went to the party school. Jack chose the students, which included some from pro-SWP groups from other countries.

The school was held in an old farmhouse with enough rooms to house the dozen or so students. There was a suite reserved for Jack or Mary-Alice when they should happen to be present. It was furnished with an extensive library for their use, and was empty for most of the time I was at the school. This special perquisite of theirs was small, but it was a precursor of larger examples of corruption that developed later on. Another large suite, comprised of two rooms connected by a lounge area, was reserved for Craig Gannon who was appointed to run the organizational aspect of the school. The other students occupied single rooms. The one assigned to me was the smallest, about 10 by 20 feet. The different students were given various assignments concerning the running of the school. My task was to change the oil in the van we used to buy groceries, ferry people to and from the school to the bus stop, and similar uses. Since this assignment hardly took much time, it was clear to the other students that my responsibilities were nil.

The school was surrounded by grassy property; on which was a pond where we could swim. There was an adjacent structure we used as a gym. Beyond were woods. All in all, a very pleasant rural setting about a mile or two from the small town of Roscoe.

We shared cooking duties in a large kitchen, with teams of two cooking for a week, on a rotating schedule. My partner was my old friend, Mel Mason. We also split up into teams for weekly cleanup.

Most of the day was spent reading through the collected works of Marx and Engels, that is, those volumes Moscow had finally gotten out in English after decades, and some other editions of their works, including *Capital*. The syllabus for each day's reading had been originally drawn up by Jack and Mary-Alice, and had been modified based on the experience of each session. It was a good syllabus.

Every other day I would run in the hilly countryside for many miles. On alternating days I would lift weights in our little gym. I liked the other students, and we would have some social times together as a student body, as well as at meals.

If this session were like others, I, as the most experienced person present, would have been assigned as "teacher"—that is, the discussion leader in our seminars held a few times a week after we had completed reading assignments. But Jack appointed himself as the "teacher." He told me two years later that I was not qualified. However, since Jack was almost never at the school, but mostly stayed in New York City, I functioned as the seminar leader as a matter of course. And when he was there, my participation was on a par with his.

In spite of these deliberate slights, I threw myself into Marx and Engels. Having this nearly five months of uninterrupted study was a pleasure. I learned a great deal. My awareness that I was being driven out of the leadership was secondary.

We took two breaks during the school session for a few days each. On one of these, Caroline informed me that the decision was made to pull those comrades who had taken skilled jobs at GM out of the plant. This brainchild of Jack's was stupid, but it was also cruel. These comrades had given up higher paying jobs to be part of our auto fraction. Now they were left high and dry. One comrade affected, Jerry, needed the higher wage to help care for his disabled son. The spurious reason given was that we didn't want to be part of the better paid "labor aristocracy." What the real reason was I don't know.

At the end of the school session I was told Caroline and I would be transferred to the Pittsburgh branch. This was the final action in removing me from the central party leadership.

The economic situation in Pittsburgh was dire. While most of the country had emerged from the 1981-82 recession, Pittsburgh had not. Unemployment remained high and wages were low as a result of structural changes in the economy. The most important of these was the closing of the big steel mills that had made Pittsburgh famous. Young people were leaving the city. Getting jobs was hard. We scoured the listings at the unemployment offices, but there were slim pickings. Our applications were ignored where we did apply.

We had no unemployment benefits, and soon depleted the small savings Caroline had put aside from her GM wages. We began to go to government food banks, where we could pick up rice, cooking oil, American cheese and some other basic foodstuffs. Caroline, without telling me, once sold her blood at $10 a pint. She then found some work cleaning homes. Luckily, because of the population exodus, rent was cheap. In addition, I was 48 years old and had worked full time for the SWP or YSA for 24 years. I had no other work history. I did get a job at minimum wage at an envelope factory for a few weeks. My fingers weren't nimble enough, and I was fired when a customer complained that blood (mine) was on their envelopes. For a short time, Caroline got a job in a garment factory at minimum wage quite a drive down near West Virginia where the workforce was largely made up of white women wives of coal miners. Her wages scarcely covered the cost of gas for her commute, and she gave it up.

She then got a job for about $6 per hour at a small factory in Pittsburgh that made welding equipment, which is what we lived on. To save money, the factory hired some deaf people, because the government subsidized their wages. Caroline made friends with these workers, and began to learn sign language. Also working at this plant was an ex-member of the SWP, Ginny Hildebrand. Ginny had been National Secretary of the YSA in the early 1970s. She had been a victim of one of the moralistic trials concerning marijuana use by another member, and had resigned as a result. Caroline, with support from Ginny in political discussions, recruited to the party a young woman worker, who became good friends with us.

It may seem that Barnes' driving us into poverty was a simple expression of cruelty to punish me because of my view that the SWP was becoming a cult around him. I think that was true, but more was involved. It had always been party policy that people who had worked for many years as party full-time workers at subsistence wages would be guaranteed by the party a stipend to keep body and soul together if they left full time work for whatever reason.

I remember Farrell Dobbs explaining this policy to me when I was new to the leadership. How could we expect to ask comrades to make the sacrifice financially to work full time for the party for most of their active lives if when they could no longer do so we tossed them on the trash heap?, he explained.

Barnes began to jettison this policy. He did keep up support help to retired older comrades, such as George Novack, Harry Ring and others who were still alive. But he began to stop this practice for anyone younger. I think his main reason was to save money, like any good CEO.

In my case, I was still able-bodied, and could eventually find a job. Caroline and I went through many difficult months, with some help from relatives, but eventually did obtain jobs to support ourselves. But we should have been given some support to get us through the transition.

I enrolled in a school run by the city for free, where I began to learn how to weld. After some months this helped me to get a job at a small factory that made railroad equipment. The place was unionized by the Machinists, and the starting wage was $6.85 per hour. We were part of an amalgamated local that never held meetings. Our contracts were negotiated by the union "leaders" and we never even voted on them.

It was at this job that I came face to face with racism in the workforce. An aspect of the party's wrong view that the working class was radicalizing on a political level was that racism among white workers, while still present, was no longer a major factor. It is true that the victory over Jim Crow in the 1960s had dealt a major blow to white racism throughout the country. Blacks were hired in industries that had previously been largely closed to them, and were able to move into job categories that had better wages and conditions in many industries. These victories of affirmative action were won in the struggle.

It is also true that racism among white workers is to this day more pronounced in places like Western Pennsylvania. In fact, the Ku Klux Klan was active in the area, and the SWP branch participated in rallies to oppose them. At my Machinist job there were no Blacks, and casual racist remarks were not uncommon. But we were all intimidated by one particularly virulent racist, a belligerent man well over six feet tall and about 230 pounds. This experience caused me to further question our belief that there was a political radicalization of the working class. Later, I got a job in one of the remaining steel mills, where there were Blacks, and I found deep racism among some white workers there, too.

•••

In 1985, there began an important strike among meatpacking workers at the Hormel plant in the small city of Austin, Minnesota. The union had been formed there in 1933. That year the workers staged a "sit-down" strike (factory occupation), the first such in the country in what became the great labor upsurge of the 1930s. The most famous sit-down strike occurred in the creation of the United Automobile Workers (UAW) in Flint, Michigan in 1936.

The meatpackers' union nationally had become part of the United Food and Commercial Workers (UFCW). The Austin local was called "P-9." Since the recession of 1974-75, the capitalist class had been on the offensive against the workers, and Hormel and the other big meatpacking companies were no exception. The UFCW national leaders adopted the same strategy as the large majority of the union bureaucracies in the face of the capitalist offensive—concessions. The UFCW tops were open about it, publicly declaring that was their policy.

The P-9 local had gone along with these givebacks, starting in 1978. Wages and benefits were cut, and the large measure of workers' control over conditions in the plant won in past struggle was gutted. As a result of speedup, injuries to workers in this hard and dangerous job done with very sharp knives soared. Anger among the workers also rose. In the early 1980s, a new local leadership was elected that included people who had opposed the concessions.

In 1984, the company imposed a new contract that included even more draconian attacks on the workers. The new president of P-9, Jim Guyette, and his team discovered they were legally prevented from striking, due to a seven-year no-strike pledge the UFCW tops had foisted on the Austin local in 1978. So the local made preparations for a future strike, which included forming support groups of worker's spouses and people from the Austin community. All decisions of the local were made by democratic vote at mass meetings of members and their families. When it became legal to do so, the P-9 members struck against the new contract in August 1985.

The mobilization of the membership and the community in Austin was only the beginning. P-9 reached out to unions and other groups across the country. They discovered that Hormel had ties to South Africa, and were able to win support among anti-apartheid activists on campuses. Teams of P-9 members spread out across the country to speak about the struggle. Demonstrations were held, and supporters began to donate food, clothing and money to the strike.**

Roving picket lines at other Hormel plants cut into the company's production. The battle was winning support among workers nationally, and became a bright spot in an otherwise dismal picture of the labor movement overall.

The SWP and other socialist groups, including Socialist Action and the Fourth Internationalist Tendency, mobilized to help the strikers on arranging their speaking tours and to win local union support. Many union fighters were inspired to come to Austin to attend big solidarity meetings and demonstrations. The SWP sent reporters, and many members went to these events.

Hormel had opened the plant to scabs in January 1986. But the mass picketing and demonstrations made this largely ineffective. Then Hormel got the Minnesota governor to send in the National Guard. Caroline found time to drive out to Austin with a few other Pittsburgh SWPers to join one of the demonstrations in February. There were 3,000 strikers and supporters there and she saw the military vehicles and soldiers herding the scabs.

From the beginning, the UFCW bureaucracy sabotaged the strike. They correctly saw it as running dead against their concessions policy. In January they issued a "fact book" defending Hormel and slandering P-9. In March the UFCW International Executive Committee ordered the strikers back to work. Strike benefits were cut off. The P-9 members immediately voted to continue the strike, and in April a demonstration of 5,000 was held in Austin in defiance of the National Guard and the UFCW's treachery.

In the spring, two P-9 members came to Pittsburgh. I helped drive them to various meetings arranged by the SWP and other

310 INTERREGNUM, DECLINE AND COLLAPSE, 1973-1988

organizations in the area, including in eastern Ohio. They spoke to students who had built a tent city at the University of Pittsburgh in solidarity with the anti-apartheid struggle in South Africa. Most of the P-9 workers were white, and one of them I helped ferry around had never heard of the NAACP before he spoke at its Pittsburgh chapter and received a warm welcome. Struggle brings the exploited and oppressed together.

In May, the UFCW put P-9 into receivership, suspended its leadership and imposed a one-man dictatorship over the local on the grounds that it had not gone back to work on the company's terms as ordered.

P-9 President Guyette and some other strikers attended the August 1986 educational conference the SWP held in Oberlin, Ohio. They received a hero's welcome.

Unfortunately, the smashing of P-9 by the UFCW tops had taken its toll, and the struggle wound down. At a subsequent meeting of the SWP National Committee, however, the leadership refused to recognize this reality. One member, Joel Britton, even made the claim that not only was the strike winning, but that it marked the "1934" of a new labor upsurge. The reference was to the three strikes in 1934 that augured the explosion of the subsequent Depression-era labor upsurge. I objected to this characterization, but was a lone voice.

The P-9 fight stands to be remembered. It was an example of what could have been done under a class struggle leadership nationally in face of the employer offensive. I recommend a pamphlet by Fred Halstead we published on the battle, *The 1985-86 Hormel Meat-Packers Strike*. One positive note is that in this instance the SWP did take on the UFCW bureaucracy, one of the most corrupt in the country in its accommodation to the employers. Another comment is in order—the CP came down on the side of the bureaucracy and against P-9.

•••

The Machinist-organized small factory I was in was susceptible to the vagaries of the economy, and minor downturns led to layoffs. I was able to get work in other places during these times. One was as an assembler in a large Westinghouse plant that made controls for subway trains. I was hired through Manpower, the staffing agency, at $5.79 per hour, which placed me in this factory.

Another job was at a steel fabrication plant. I was hired to work on a big project building a system of many large, room-sized steel tanks to be used for certain painting jobs at a Honda plant being constructed somewhere in the South. This shop was organized by the

Sheet Metal Workers. This union was a job trust—you had to be someone's relative to get in with membership rights. There were many others hired for the project, workers who paid dues to the union but had no speaking or voting rights. At the time full members of the union received about $16 per hour, and the rest of us $4.50. The foreman, who did the hiring and firing, was in the pro-company union.

The skilled jobs, aside from welders, were at the $16 level. The foreman knew I could read blueprints and had used such to build things at Westinghouse, and he put me on the job of putting together the large and complicated tanks from steel sheets, struts and tubing, using a small overhead crane to hold things up. A welder worked with me "tacking" these materials together, and then a final welder would stitch together all the seams. All the other workers who did this job were $16 men. I was $4.50 per hour, so as the job wound down in a few months, the others were laid off by their union brother and I finished the project.

I really enjoyed this work. My sub-foreman would give me the blueprints for the next tank to be assembled. He generally did not know exactly how to proceed, and left me to figure it out. "Barry's thinking," he would say, as I looked over the prints and decided what to do. I was able to use my knowledge of plain geometry and trigonometry to help with the measurements, squaring, and so forth. At the same time the job was physical, wrestling with the steel components with the help of the crane and my welder helper. We wore fire-retardant "greens" because of the welding sparks, which I had to be in the middle of holding things together to be tack welded.

I would come home tired and dirty, but Caroline would notice when I walked in that I was happy.

•••

In August 1986, Judge Griesa handed down his decision in the SWP lawsuit against the government. It was a complete victory for us and the fight for democratic rights. I was interviewed by the *Pittsburgh Post Gazette* on the meaning of the decision, as I had been one of the named plaintiffs in the suit. I went down to the newspaper office after work at the Machinist-organized plant, accompanied by a young worker I had befriended.[1]

The local Pittsburg branch also held a public meeting on the victory, at which the famous South African poet and anti-apartheid fighter, Dennis Brutus, spoke. He had been forced into exile by the racist regime, and was living in Pittsburgh. "We have forced the courts to restate the basic values of this country," he said. "This ruling condemns COINTELPRO, the informers, the dossiers, the black-bag jobs. These things attacked people at the point where they are organizing to defend themselves. It defends the rights of all Americans."[2] The victory was widely hailed.

---

* After Caroline was rehired at the GM plant, a leaflet was passed out by the Workers League accusing Caroline of being an FBI agent.

** The Twin Cities P-9 Support Committee organized impressive motorcades to deliver many truckloads of food and supplies to the strikers and their families in Austin. A founding member of the SWP, Jake Cooper, played a notable role in these strike support efforts and was a popular figure among the Hormel strikers. Cooper was a veteran of the 1934 Minneapolis Teamster strikes, a bodyguard to Leon Trotsky in Mexico, and one of 18 party defendants in the Smith Act trial of 1941. He was expelled from the SWP in 1982 as part of the purge of those with minority views, although he was not part of the two main minorities.

1 The full text of Judge Griesa's decision is in the book, *FBI on Trial: The Victory in the Socialist Workers Party Suit Against Government Spying*, edited by Margaret Jayko (Pathfinder Press, 1988).
2 *The Militant*, Oct. 10, 1986.

CHAPTER THIRTY-ONE: CAROLINE AND I LEAVE THE SWP

Both Caroline and I continued to be active in the Pittsburgh branch. In addition to branch meetings we held weekly public forums, as did all our branches. The branch organizer was Chris H. When he was asked to transfer to another city, for a time a young comrade, Mark E., stepped in, but he soon decided to move to the West Coast. I had collaborated with both Chris and Mark, and then I became the organizer. I didn't know it at the time, but was informed later that before Caroline and I moved to Pittsburgh, Mac Warren from the National Office had met with the branch executive committee to inform them that we were coming. He also told the executive committee that under no circumstances was I to become the organizer, and that I had "fucked up" as organizer in New York. I surmise that what he was referring to was my putting a halt to the forced march into industry. In addition, I had been aware that Barnes had been waging an underground campaign charging I had misled the National Office about the finances of establishing and operating the new bookstore in New York, falsely claiming I had agreed that the branch would take over these costs and relieve the party's national office of its share.

However, while I wanted a younger person to be branch organizer, when both Chris and Mark left, I took over the job temporarily because there was no one else to do it at the time. This led to a confrontation with the National Office. I happened to walk in on a meeting in our headquarters with members of our United Mineworkers Union fraction from different parts of the country. Mac Warren was making a report. I sat in on the meeting, as would be normal for a branch organizer to do. The substance of Mac's report was to propose to the fraction that it designate the Pittsburgh branch as a "coal branch." The branch was to become the political center overseeing the Morgantown and Charleston West Virginia branches, which had members in the United Mine Workers (UMWA). The focus of the branch's activity would now center on the mine workers.

Without consulting the Pittsburgh branch, the coal fraction was to be used in this way to dictate our branch priorities. The proposal itself was preposterous. The West Virginia branches were quite some distance away. We had two women comrades in the Pittsburgh branch in mines in southern Pennsylvania, an hour's drive for them each way. These two comrades, Kipp Dawson and Claire Franzel, had been very active in the union and had helped organize the women's group inside it. But the industry was shrinking from the days of its expansion in the 1970s, and these Pennsylvania mines closed soon after this proposal was made. The most important union in Pittsburgh still was the United Steelworkers, which had branched out to organize other industries. If we were going to be a one-union branch, the steelworkers would be it. But our national orientation for the branches was not to concentrate on one union, but to have diverse work fractions in each city.

I objected vigorously to the proposal, both concerning its content and to the way it was to be carried out behind the backs of the branch membership. Some in the fraction were swayed in my favor. Mac went to the phone and called New York. The result was that Jack called a special National Committee meeting to hear me out.

This was a strange meeting. By this time, I was ready to expand my report to include that the whole analysis we had made in 1978-79 that a political radicalization of the working class was beginning was wrong. Things had gone in the opposite direction. The retreat of the UMWA was just part of this overall process. I minced no words, and Jack, who was sitting in the front row, became livid, red in the face and shaking. He then answered me, and made a concession. He said that the last years had seen a "rout" of the labor movement in the face of the capitalist offensive, but maintained the proposal that the Pittsburgh branch become a "coal branch."

This was the first time anyone on the National Committee had heard of this "rout." The whole National Committee was quiet. Finally, Susan Lamont took the floor to ask Jack, "Why have you capitulated to Barry?" No one else spoke. I abstained on the vote on Jack's report, because he had come closer to my position, but I didn't believe it was sincere, and I was still opposed to the "coal branch" proposal. The rest of the National Committee voted for his report and against mine. A part of Jack's report was to propose that there be a party active workers conference in Pittsburgh of members of branches with mineworker comrades. Obviously pre-arranged, Wendy Lyons took the floor to make a motion that all members of the National Committee were under discipline to present the majority National Committee position at the active workers conference.

This was first time in the history of the SWP that such a motion for "committee discipline" was ever adopted. We did have a practice of not taking every difference in the National Committee to the membership even during preconvention discussion. But major differences on the National Committee were always brought before the party membership to decide. Cannon wrote forcefully on this subject, explaining that the membership had the right to know where elected leaders stood. Indeed, without knowing this, members are deprived of all the information they need to make up their own minds, and party democracy is compromised.

Another dirty trick was perpetrated. Unbeknownst to the Pittsburgh branch, the National Office sent out leaders to speak before the branches whose members were coming to the active workers conference on the issues in dispute. With one exception: the Pittsburgh branch. In fact, we were told *not* to have a discussion on these issues before the conference even though we were the branch most affected. Thus the active workers conference was rigged. I was surprised when miner comrades who had expressed initial agreement with me at the fraction meeting I had walked into earlier were now lined up against my position.

The active workers conference was chaired by Andrea Morell for the National Committee. She opened the conference with an appeal to all present to freely express their opinions in the discussion. She didn't mention that I was bound by the National Committee vote not to voice my opinions (unless I were to lie and support the majority line). Caroline did raise objections to the report, but the conference had already been rigged and the outcome was a foregone conclusion. Shortly after, an article appeared in *The Militant* claiming the "rout" of the labor movement was over.

In the wake of the conference, Jack Barnes began to express the view that such active workers' conferences were in fact more important and democratic than party conventions. (Indeed, the party would hold no conventions centered on U.S. politics from 1981 until 1990.) He decided that since the Pittsburgh conference was such a success, it should be duplicated around the country. Since the leadership was learning so much from all these conferences, it was decided to hold another conference in the Pittsburgh region (actually held in Morgantown, West Virginia) to share with us these insights. The leadership, had, it is true, used the conferences to whip itself into a frenzy. At the last one, in our region, the leadership went wild with optimism. John Gage gave one of the reports, which centered on the assertion that plant gate sales would now become a major source of recruitment. We would recruit workers going into their plants by virtue of their seeing *The Militant!* I was trying to be quiet, but at this astounding good news I burst into a guffaw of laughter.

Following the conference the National Office transferred into the Pittsburgh branch six or seven people to lead the turn to establishing it as a "coal branch." I welcomed these transfers, since Caroline and I were not the people to carry out this orientation. Jim Little became the new organizer, and we got along fine. However, all we did in relation to the UMWA was to sell subscriptions in some mining areas in West Virginia and outlying areas in Pennsylvania. More accurately, we *tried* to sell subscriptions, because overall we got a hostile response, including from people who had previously bought subscriptions during the upsurge of the UMWA at the end of the 1970s and early 1980s.

In fact, we never became a "coal branch."

•••

One of the younger comrades who had been transferred to Pittsburgh was Greg Jackson, an African American whom we had recruited from prison. I knew him in New York when I was the organizer there. In August 1987, there was a vicious racist attack in Pittsburgh's Morningside district, which some residents considered a "whites only" enclave. A Black woman bus driver had gone into a store in Morningside with her daughter and nine-month old nephew and some of her daughter's friends. They were attacked by a group of white thugs, wielding sticks. One had an ice pick. She and her nephew got away, but her daughter and friends were beaten and robbed.

In reaction to the racist incident, a Coalition Against Racist Violence was formed. Greg quickly became a leader of the coalition, and appeared on TV as a spokesperson. The coalition won wide support from Black and religious groups and figures, as well as from trade unionists, and peace groups. The Coalition Against Racist Violence organized a mass, integrated march of 500 through Morningside in September. The public campaign forced the city to provide police protection for the march in the face of racist threats to attack it. While there were some racist taunts along the march, there were also white residents who came out to applaud the marchers and assert their own rights to resist the racists.

I had worked closely with Greg in his work as a coalition leader. Together, we wrote the article about the march for *The Militant*.[1] The whole branch had enthusiastically helped widen the coalition and build the demonstration. The coalition decided to continue organizing, to be able to counter any renewed racist attacks. But then a peculiar thing happened. Jim Little reported to the branch that Greg was to leave the coalition, and that we would not favor the coalition continuing. The reason given was that the Coalition Against Racist Violence had not been organized through the unions, but community groups! This was not only a repudiation of our work in building the march, but another example of the SWP's abstentionism from real struggle, and pulling back from working with others in united coalitions in the name of the turn to the industrial unions.

Greg was stunned. He and his companion Sue S. (who had been with Caroline at the party school) came over to our house to discuss the issue. Greg and Sue thought that the fault lay with Jim Little. We pointed out that Jim had helped mobilize the whole branch behind Greg's work. His reversal must have been the result of orders from above. This began a long period of discussions with Greg and Sue about what was happening to the party on a national level, and began to include other comrades. One of these reported back to the branch leadership that a group hostile to the national leadership was being formed.

In the spring of 1987, Caroline and three other comrades got jobs in one of the remaining steel mills, Allegheny-Ludlum. This mill survived because it was not basic steel, but produced specialty steels such as various types of stainless and other materials with special magnetic and electrical properties. The market for these products was strong. The branch was becoming more of a steel branch, but not exclusively so.

During the summer, another educational conference was held at Oberlin College in Ohio. I was asked to give two classes, one on Iran and the other on Palestine. I had worked the second shift the night before, and drove the two hours to Oberlin in the morning, and gave the two classes one after the other. I was a bit tired, and went to bed early. About 10 p.m. I got up to use the restroom. I had noticed that one near my room was ordinarily a men's room, as I had glanced a urinal inside during the day. As was often the case, the conference organizers had designated it as a temporary women's room, and had put up a sign to that effect. But at this hour, a conference party was scheduled, and no one was around the dormitory, it seemed. So I slipped in to use the urinal. Then a woman came into the facility, and was startled to see me, and ran out. So I was wrong about the dorm being empty.

I was brought up on charges, and tried by the Political Committee. There was no dispute about the facts: I had violated conference rules. The Political Committee began in the early morning, when I testified. After I left, the committee debated the question all day. I later learned from a member of the Political Committee that Jack had initially argued for my suspension from the party, the most severe sentence that could be made against a member of the National Committee. Twice during the day Mac Warren came out of the meeting, and found me to ask if I was staying for the meeting of the National Committee to be held after the conference. I told him yes. Finally, I was told that my punishment was to be censured. Probably the reason I was censured and not suspended, was that the upcoming National Committee meeting would have had to take up the question in the case of suspension, and Jack was not prepared to spring this on the National Committee at that time.

I should relate that the offense of using the wrong restroom was rather common, as might be expected at any such large gathering. In fact, over the course of many years at Oberlin, my dormitory room was often next to Jack's. Across the hall was a designated women's restroom. It was not unusual for Jack or I to go into this women's room to get water for our drinks at the end of the day. We could have been charged and censured for this casual behavior.

A month later, the Political Committee report on the case was mailed out to the members of the National Committee. The lengthy report did not only cover the fact that I had broken a conference rule, but charged I had intentionally sought to harm the woman who had come upon me. I wrote a reply to refute this incredible charge, and asked that it be sent to the National Committee members, who had received the report. My reply was not sent out. Greg Jackson had been on conference security, and the security detail had all been informed of the event. Greg raised the topic with me. Under the present climate in the party, he was not surprised about the attack on me.

I tried to raise the issue at the next National Committee meeting in November, but was ruled out of order. I did so again at a spring 1988 meeting, with the same result. The National Committee members never saw my side of the story. At both of these National Committee meetings I was shunned by most, especially by the women comrades. This was to be expected as a result of the Political Committee portraying me as deliberately trying to harm a woman. The scuttlebutt, which went beyond the National Committee, had me as some kind of monster who hung around women's rooms to terrify them. Under Barnes' lead the stage was now set for my departure from the party.

•••

In June, Allegheny-Ludlum was again hiring. There were many applicants, as there were the year before when Caroline was hired. As then, the company was looking for more educated workers, and put us all through a rigorous series of tests of general aptitude, mechanical reasoning, and so forth. Greg and I were hired. Then the branch received word from the National Office that Greg and I were not to be allowed to accept the jobs. The "reasoning" was that we had a rule that no more than four comrades could work at the same plant, and four were already there. This rule was not only blatantly stupid and weakened our work, its justification was that if we had too many comrades in one plant, we would get a false sense of our influence. What was really behind this, I believe, was to keep our industrial fractions from becoming too strong, and slip out from total control of the party "center," i.e., Jack Barnes.

The branch meeting took up the matter when Jim Little and I were at the National Committee meeting in New York in the spring of 1988. Caroline proposed at the branch meeting that consideration of the matter should be delayed until I, as one of those directly involved, and Jim, as the branch organizer, could be present. She was voted down. The branch decision was that Greg could not accept the job, but I could, since I was "a national leader," even though my doing so would "hurt the fraction." I kid the reader not.

I knew I was going to accept the job no matter what the branch voted. I would break discipline if I had to, and therefore I knew I could not remain a member. After the last National Committee meeting I knew my counter-report on the restroom incident would never be heard. With all this in mind, Caroline and I took a weekend camping trip. On the way back, she turned to me in the car and said we should both resign, and we did, on July 4, 1988, Independence Day.

I took the job. Greg made the decision that he would, too. The branch brought him up on charges for violating the branch decision. He asked to see me. His companion, Sue, was on the branch executive committee, which was the trial body. She told him that he would be expelled unless he claimed that I had convinced him to take the job. I laughed, and told him to tell the trial committee whatever he wanted. The executive committee's reasoning was implicitly racist, with its assumption that a Black comrade wasn't capable of making his own decisions. Greg and Sue left Pittsburgh, and Caroline and I gave them $300 to help them do so. I don't know what happened to them.

•••

Some six months later, another party leader, Malik Miah was suspended from the party (virtually expelled). He had been in the San Francisco Bay Area working as a mechanic at the large maintenance base for United Airlines at the San Francisco airport. We had a fraction there (ironically, more than four members) and Malik was the elected fraction head. Eastern Airlines had been on strike by the International Association of Machinists, the same union as at United, as well as by the pilots and flight attendants unions. It was a bitter, long, strike.

At one point the pilots voted to go back to work. At a meeting of the National Committee the majority put forward the line that it didn't matter if the pilots went back to work, because they weren't workers, but small bourgeois. The strike wasn't affected, it was claimed. Malik made a counter-report, giving his opinion that the pilots were indeed workers, if many were highly paid. But, he said, whatever class analysis was made of them, their defection was a serious blow to the strike, which was in danger of being lost. Malik was soon proved to be correct, and the always "up, up and away" optimism of the majority view of the state of the working class was proved false.

Upon returning to San Francisco, Malik reported to the members of the fraction at United the position of the majority, as well as his own position. He was charged with violating "committee discipline" in expressing his own minority view. Malik had also convinced the fraction not to sell *The Militant* issue with the National Committee line in the plant, since it countered what the fraction had been saying. John Gage was delegated to report to the United fraction the decision of the National Committee to suspend Malik. Gage told the fraction that he was reporting for the National Committee, and that the fraction members would not be told what Gage himself thought, to emphasize the need for "committee discipline."

In addition to Malik, myself and Caroline, by this time Peter Camejo, Lew Jones and Gus Horowitz among the young central leaders of the party who had emerged as leaders in the 1960s and 1970s were gone. This was in addition, of course, to the many minority supporters expelled in 1983. Others were pushed out or marginalized over the next several years, including Larry Seigle, Linda Jenness, Doug Jenness, Mac Warren, Andrew Pulley, John Gage, Fred Feldman and many others. As Jose Perez pointed out, the majority of National Committee members who had supported the 1978 turn to industry were gone. Former leaders like Wendy Lyons, Betsy Stone, and Joel Britton were put out to pasture in branches. The only national leaders from that time playing central roles today are Jack Barnes, Mary-Alice Waters, and Steve Clark. Clark himself only emerged as a national leader in the latter 1970s, and mainly as a writer.

---

1 *The Militant*, Oct. 2, 1987.

CHAPTER THIRTY-TWO:
CONCLUSIONS

The two volumes of this book cover my time in the Socialist Workers Party (SWP) from November 1959 to July 1988. They ought to be read as a single whole. I included in the first volume some details with an eye to the second. Of course, the SWP of the first volume was quite different from the party I have outlined in this one. My central theme is that over the course of the period 1960--1988 the SWP was transformed into its opposite in key aspects, a thesis which is not intelligible without reference to the first volume.

Before I do that, I want to explain the reasons, in my view, for the degeneration of the party.

The objective context for this development was the political retreat of the American working class beginning at the end of the 1970s. In the three decades since, this retreat has continued. The politics of the two capitalist parties has by and large shifted sharply to the right. This rightward shift at the top has not been countered by a renewed radicalization from below. The youth and Black radicalization of "The Sixties" is now far behind us. The rhythm of radicalization and relatively conservative periods seen earlier in the twentieth century has been altered. In the first decades of the 1900s, the formation of the Socialist Party and the Industrial Workers of the World marked a working class upsurge. It was accompanied by a renewed struggle of African Americans signified by the creation of the National Association for the Advancement of Colored People and the Black Nationalist movement led by Marcus Garvey, and the rise of the women's fight for the right to vote.

A period of relative prosperity and conservatism set in during the 1920s, which, however, did see the formation of the Communist Party inspired by the Russian Revolution. This was followed by the great labor upsurge in the 1930s during the Great Depression, marked principally by the formation of the industrial unions in massive battles. The Second World War saw the increasing bureaucratization of the unions and political confusion among the workers, although there was an upsurge in strike activity at the end of the war.

The Cold War and witchhunt marked a period of retreat, which began to be broken in 1956 with the Montgomery Bus Boycott. In the 1960s the Black civil rights movement in the South took off, and the Black struggle encompassed the whole country. The youth radicalization, which centered on the anti-Vietnam War movement, exploded. In this fresh wave of radicalization a new women's movement was born, as well as movements among Chicanos and other Latinos, and the gay liberation movement.

The periods between these radicalizations were relatively short compared to what we have experienced since the winding down of "The Sixties." This long period without a new radicalization has weighed down on all socialist organizations, including the SWP. It would have been tough sledding for the party even with the best leadership.

The international situation also has been largely negative. I have taken some time to discuss five revolutions in Afghanistan, Iran, Poland, Grenada and Nicaragua, which raised great hopes in the SWP. But from the period of 1978 through 1983, these revolutions were defeated. The Soviet bureaucracy moved more and more toward imperialism, a process that finally resulted in the collapse of the Soviet bloc in 1989--91, and the restoration of capitalism. A similar road has been taken in China.

These objective developments in the United States and internationally would have in any case made it more difficult for the SWP. But compounding the picture was the SWP's reaction to them. As has been explained, the SWP leadership refused to adjust its view of the objective situation nationally and internationally as reality demonstrated we had been wrong in our political assessment. As the years have gone by, the disconnect with reality has widened.

The fundamental cause of the degeneration was the rise of the Barnes cult in the mid-1970s, which predates the political degeneration. The "star" method of leadership has the drawback of being dependent upon one individual. Moreover, the cult dynamic makes it very difficult for the "star" to admit any mistakes, lest his position be undermined. The cult is therefore prone to persist in errors, as I have attempted to demonstrate, with the result of compounding them.

I believe it was James P. Cannon who made the observation that the question of whether or not the working class will rise to its historical challenge and take power is the question of the revolutionary vanguard party, whether it will be up to snuff and built in time—and, the question of the party is the question of the leadership the party creates, whether it is healthy and capable.

The formation of the Barnes cult began first in the Political Committee. As I have noted, I became aware of this in 1978. The reader will recall when I first raised my concerns with Jack Barnes privately, he threatened me, demonstrating his concept that the leadership must be loyal to him personally and centered on him personally—one of the hallmarks of a cult leader. This concept was gradually accepted, at least implicitly, within the Political Committee. From there it spread to the National Committee and the broader leadership in the branches. Consequently, the party leadership was destroyed. The destruction of the party as a whole followed suit.

It would be naïve to think that the membership itself could resist this juggernaut. It could only have been stopped in the Political Committee itself. Jack couldn't do it—he didn't understand what he was fashioning. It was up to the rest of us on the Political Committee, but we failed. The responsibility is primarily mine, since I was the first to understand it, and next to Jack I had the greatest leadership authority.

The die was caste in the early 1980s. Since then, the negative features that came to characterize the SWP have only become more pronounced. This book is not the place to chronicle the evolution of the SWP after 1988. A few examples will suffice.

In the years after Caroline and I left, the behavior of the cult became more grotesque. A comrade I did not know named John Cox was a member of the Political Committee in the 1990s. Many newer comrades became members of the National Committee and Political Committee as most from Jack's generation were pushed out. Sometime after Cox himself was out of the SWP, he posted comments about his experience on the Internet in 2001, including the following:

"While I was in New York, Political Committee [PC] meetings would be called for a given time, maybe 1 p.m. Wednesday. Half the PC was also on *The Militant* staff, so the editor, also a PC member, tries to organize around this meeting time. Wednesday afternoon arrives, and Barnes is nowhere to be seen; no one knows if they can go to lunch, the editor doesn't know what's going on and is not going to ask, etc. Barnes appears at 4:30, and we meet until 9:00, three hours devoted to unprepared and rambling ruminations of the Helmsman. [Mao Zedung was referred to as the "Great Helmsman" – B.S.]

"This was the rule, rather than the exception, and needless to say no one ever complained about this highly abusive routine. Further, no one on the PC, with the possible exception of Waters and/or [Steve] Clark, has any idea how Barnes passes his time, outside of the 15-20 hours a week when he is in the Pathfinder building. Nor is he held to account for any self-imposed deadlines."

When I was on the Political Committee they always started on time, on the dot. Farrell Dobbs recounted to me that when he was with Trotsky in Mexico, the Old Man would shut and lock the door the second a meeting was to begin. Anyone late had to knock, and Trotsky himself would go to the door to let the person in. They were never late again. Being respectful of other people's time who have big work responsibilities is necessary not only for efficiency, but for comradely relations. Malcolm X made the same point, and he was always punctual.

The cavalier attitude toward others Cox describes is characteristic of the narcissism that had overtaken Barnes' personality.

Another young comrade told Caroline and I in the 1990s, after she had been expelled, that she was in meetings where Jack was present where comrades would openly refer to him as the "Lenin of our time."

The collapse of the Soviet bloc offered more evidence of the political and theoretical degeneration of the SWP leadership. Barnes declared that this momentous event indicated that the United States had "lost the Cold War."[1] A corollary was the assertion that the former republics of the U.S.S.R. remained workers' states, as did the countries of Eastern Europe. The most bizarre assertion was that East Germany was still a workers' state after its incorporation into the really existing capitalist state of Germany. Is there a single person among the hundreds of millions of people in Russia or Eastern Europe that believes anything like this? Only a few hundred people in the world believe these outlandish assertions.

Moreover, this position put the SWP in sharp disagreement with the Cuban leadership. The Cubans, after all, live in the real world and suffered greatly from the collapse of their major trading partners. It was at this time that Barnes began in private to tell leaders of his grouping worldwide that after all, the Castroists were not revolutionary Marxists. The only people in the world who fit that designation were the members of the SWP and the various Communist League groups in the party's orbit.

A central characteristic defining what the SWP became is abstention from the mass movements. It turned increasingly inward, circling the wagons, walling itself off from contact with other organizations. One aspect of how the party now functions is to take positions opposite from what the broader left movement holds. The dwindling membership is then forced to jump through the hoop of accepting the leadership's view upon pain of being classified as part of the "petty bourgeois left," as all outside the SWP are stigmatized.

One example concerned a famous international incident. A young Cuban boy, Elián González, was kidnapped by counter-revolutionary relatives in Miami. His father in Cuba demanded that the U.S. government return him to Cuba to be with his family there. The rest of the left and a majority of the American people supported the father. The Cuban people united as one against this outrage, as hundreds of thousands marched to demand Elian's safe return. Under this pressure the U.S. government, after initially resisting, did finally return Elian. The SWP denounced the government for doing so—a sharp break with not only the rest of the left and basic humanitarian values, but also with the Cuban leadership and people.

Another example involved the anti-Iraq War movement. A year after the invasion and occupation of Iraq, there were demonstrations worldwide in March 2004 in opposition to the occupation. The SWP denounced the demonstrations outside the United States as manifestations of "anti-Americanism" and support to the U.S.'s imperialist competitors. The demonstrations inside the United States were denounced as being pro-Democratic Party. I won't dignify these arguments with a reply. In any case, how the SWP publicly defends its positions isn't the point—the positions themselves are. In this case, the position to attack demonstrations against the occupation went even further than mere abstentionism to outright reactionary pro-imperialism.

This position against the anti-occupation demonstrations was accompanied by Jack Barnes asserting in public speeches that the occupation had a positive side, providing "political space" for the Iraqi workers' movement. The rightist content of his views couldn't be clearer.

Some supporters of the Canadian Communist League, the SWP satellite there, were expelled for supporting the Canadian anti-occupation demonstrations.

Early in 2009 *The Militant* also ran a series of articles repudiating the SWP's long-standing position on Israel, embracing instead a number of arguments put forward by apologists for the Zionist state. They asserted that 1) There is no Zionist movement today; 2) Anti-Zionism is a cover for anti-Semitism; 3) Israel's rulers plan to give back to the Palestinians most of the West Bank and Gaza; 4) Israel is not an apartheid state; 5) the democratic, secular Palestine that the SWP envisages must grant a special right of return for Jews worldwide; 6) The Boycott, Divestment and Sanctions (BDS) campaign is not only wrong, it is anti-Semitic.[2]

Actually living, breathing Zionists do think they themselves exist, but they agree with the SWP that anti-Zionism is anti-Semitism.

In July 2005, more than 170 Palestinian organizations, including trade unions, political and social organizations, and women's and youth groups issued an appeal for international solidarity. They asked supporters of their struggle to organize an international campaign to focus attention on Israel's violation of Palestinian human rights, based on a boycott, divestment and sanctions strategy broadly similar to the one developed in the struggle against apartheid South Africa. This appeal has won wide support, including from Jewish organizations. The international BDS movement has become today, in 2011, one of the most dynamic and fastest-growing components of the Palestinian solidarity movement.

Apologists for Israel's policies have attacked the BDS movement with particular virulence. By echoing these attacks the SWP leadership finds itself in the same camp on this question as the Israeli lobby led by AIPAC (the American Israel Public Affairs Committee.)

In its opposition to the anti-Iraqi-occupation demonstrations in 2004, and in its new positions on Israel and Palestine, the SWP adopted openly right-wing positions. The increasing abstentionism from mass movements involved a more subtle shift to the right from the SWP's historic positions, beginning in 1980. Most often, the stated reasons for adopting abstentionist positions are super-revolutionary, ultraleft reasons, which can mask their actual content.

An example of leftist rhetoric justifying an abstentionist position masking a *de facto* shift to the right was the pulling back from taking any responsibilities in the union movement. The reason given was that otherwise comrades would be sucked into the labor bureaucracy. But the actual result was the party pulled back, with some exceptions, from confronting the anti-working-class actions of the bureaucracy in fact. This was a shift to the right compared with the SWP's historic practice (actually from the practice not only of the SWP, but its antecedents in the Industrial Workers of the World, the Socialist Party, and the early Communist Party). Such is the logic of abstentionism from the living class struggle. This "hands off" policy does, it is true, keep one from getting "dirty hands," and makes it easier to "work with" the bureaucracy on limited questions because the bureaucrats don't view the SWP as a threat.

The conclusion is clear. The generalization of abstentionism to the antiwar and other mass movements has resulted in a general shift to the right compared with the SWP of the first volume of this book.

The increasing political degeneration has been accompanied by further stifling of internal life. Trials continue to keep the membership in line. In one instance Caroline and I learned about in the late 1990s, a young woman recruit was charged in her branch with underage drinking of an alcoholic beverage. Then she was charged with using a swearword in an argument with another comrade. She was suspended from membership for a short time in both cases. She was finally expelled for discussing an internal party matter with a member of the National Committee.

Since Caroline and I left the SWP in 1988, public information has come to light that raises questions about possible financial corruption involving Jack Barnes and Mary-Alice Waters. By financial corruption I do not mean anything illegal, but violation of proletarian morality.

In the 1970s, Jack would sometimes hold meetings at a restaurant near our headquarters, called the Sazerac, with the party picking up the tab for the dinners. On some occasions this was perfectly legitimate, such as when we invited international guests to an informal discussion and dinner with a few comrades. One instance I remember was a dinner I was at with the Irish revolutionary Bernadette Devlin McAliskey. There also were times when holding such a dinner with a comrade was the best way to deal with a difficult personal problem, when a more formal meeting would not be appropriate.

But little by little, Jack would hold political meetings over such dinners that could just as well been held at the headquarters or in one of our homes. Those comrades invited would partake of this small perk. I myself did so when I was present. Our full-time subsistence didn't allow us much leeway for eating in restaurants. But Jack was always present at these dinners, and they became more frequent. In this way, Jack lived just a little bit better than the rest of us. Of course, this was a small deviation, nothing like the extravagant expense accounts of capitalist politicians or union bureaucrats.

The small scratch of dining at the Sazerac has festered and grown in the intervening decades. The special rooms at the party school, being housed at hotels when traveling rather than at comrade's homes, not being expected to attend the many meetings and perform the many duties required of other comrades, these and other special privileges are examples of the type of moral corruption that set in.

Recently public information seems to indicate that more is involved. This concerns a tax-exemption foundation, Anchor, which the party helped establish to publish books and other materials.

Anchor functions with scrupulous legality. As such, it is required by law to make its tax returns public. These must record all significant assets and expenses, all contributions over $5,000 and the salaries of its officers. There are only two officers of the Anchor foundation, Jack Barnes and Mary-Alice Waters.

Anchor owned the building at 410 West Street in New York City that housed our headquarters, printing press, *The Militant* and Pathfinder offices and other national departments. In 2003, this building was sold. The tax returns for 2003 and 2004 showed that Barnes received $475,000 for finder's fees and supervisory services in connection with the sale and acquisition of new premises. Mary-

Alice Waters received $363,730 for the same services. Prior to 2003, both Barnes and Mary-Alice contributed back to Anchor substantial sums. In 2001 and 2002, the net from their incomes minus their contributions was about $15,000 yearly, commensurate with what one would expect for full-timers.

This changed in 2003, with their net incomes from Anchor growing. By 2007, their net income was $77,700 each. In 2008, their net income was $86,000 each and in 2009, $73,000 each. Salaries like these, while not comparable to those of top-level union bureaucrats, are still far, far above the standard other full time SWP workers receive.

It is not known how much Barnes and Waters have donated to the SWP from these salaries.

In July 2007, an article published in *The New York Observer* reported that "a two-bedroom loft at 380 West 12th Street...was sold by American socialist leaders Jack Barnes and Mary-Alice Waters." The price they got was $1,872,500.

"It isn't clear," the article said, "when Mr. Barnes and Ms. Waters bought the place or how much they paid, but city records date back to 1993, when apartments were massively cheaper." It also isn't known where the money came from for Barnes and Waters to make the original purchase. Possibly it came from an inheritance or some other personal source. Nor is it known what they did with the substantial profit, after capital-gains taxes.

However, a series of photos of the interior of the apartment that accompanied the article show a beautiful, spacious six-room apartment with modern décor. It would appear that Jack and Mary-Alice lived well above the level of most other SWP full time workers.

Whatever the full truth, which we may never know, it is not the case that financial perks led to the degeneration of the SWP. Rather, it's the other way around.

•••

How has the SWP turned into its opposite in the course of 1960 up to 1988 and beyond? This two-volume book goes back to the 1960s, and so doesn't include the earlier history of the SWP, but even with this limitation, I believe I have demonstrated the following partial list:

- The method of collective leadership was transformed into its opposite, the leadership of a single individual, the "star."
- The Trotskyist (revolutionary Marxist) character of the SWP was transformed in an anti-Trotskyist direction.
- The leadership role of the SWP in the anti-Vietnam War movement in the 1960s and 1970s became an abstentionist stance in the antiwar movements of the 1980s and after.

- The historic interventionist practice of the SWP in the internal life of the labor movement, in relation to union elections, taking leadership posts when warranted, fighting the bureaucracy, participation in union caucuses, leading class battles and more, became abstentionist and tail-endist relative to the bureaucracy.

- Our opposition to an over-centralized International, and our position that each section in each country must be free to develop its own political positions and leadership and publish its own press became a grotesque caricature of a super-centralized toy International.

- From being the most important section in the founding of the Fourth International on up to its positive role in the International Majority Tendency/Leninist-Trotskyist Faction debate, the SWP in the 1980s launched a destructive factional attack on the Fourth International and finally left it in 1990.

- Party democracy and full discussion was transformed into monolithic functioning. Comradely relations were scuttled by numerous trials and threats of trials of rank and file members.

- The respect the SWP had earned on the left (although feared and despised by some) has degenerated to the point where it is now considered irrelevant, even a joke.

A reading of both volumes outlines the transformation of Jack Barnes himself, from the foremost young party leader to emerge in "The Sixties," helping to build a collective team leadership aggressively intervening in the mass movements, into becoming the cult leader of the degeneration of the SWP. Besides the erroneous political positions taken beginning in 1979 was Barnes' break with Trotsky. In this he joined Max Shachtman, Tony Cliff, Sam Marcy and others. As a revolutionary leader, Trotsky, of course, towers in every way above Barnes and these others. Whatever Barnes' narcissistic view of himself, he has become a fool. He turned into his opposite, a truly tragic figure worthy of a Greek or Shakespearian play. I mourn the demise of my once comrade and friend.

The degeneration of the SWP was not inevitable. A correct orientation in the labor movement, among both industrial and white-collar workers, would have secured an important place for us there, and led to some growth among workers. This would have meant we would have been situated to make an important impact in the working class in the massive crisis of the capitalist system that began in 2007--2008.

A correct orientation internationally would have led us to gain respect and influence in the left. One example could have been providing the only coherent explanation of the collapse of the Soviet Union, which would have mitigated the resulting demoralization on the socialist left.

If we had played a leading role in the movements against the U.S. wars in Nicaragua, El Salvador, in Iraq in 1991 and 2003, and Afghanistan, we would have grown as we did during the Vietnam era.

If we had maintained our orientation to campus youth, no doubt we would have recruited there in large numbers. The proof is that the International Socialist Organization (ISO), which did have such an orientation, recruited thousands on campus in the 1980s and 1990s. The ISO has its own weaknesses, but nevertheless is the largest and youngest among the revolutionary socialist groups in the United States. We would have done better than the ISO, because campus recruits would have been attracted to our greater implantation in the labor movement, and our interventionist leadership in the antiwar struggles, something that the ISO has also failed to do.

Finally, I want to emphasize that I have never regretted joining the SWP. Whatever constructive leadership role I was able to play I am proud of. These two volumes will help preserve what was positive in that experience and warn against what was negative. I hope this book will help in rebuilding the revolutionary socialist party that is so needed today in the midst of the present catastrophe of wars and capitalist economic collapse.

—September 2011

---

1 "U.S. Imperialism Has Lost the Cold War," by Jack Barnes, *New International* (No. 11, 1998.)

2 "Why We Boycott Israel: A reply to the U.S. Socialist Workers Party," by Art Young. http://www.socialistvoice.ca/?p=1289.

APPENDIX: AN EXAMPLE OF WORK IN THE UNIONS

This volume is dedicated to Caroline Lund. In part to honor her and in part to show that the decline and death of the Socialist Workers Party (SWP) was not inevitable, and to demonstrate by example that another path for the turn to industry was possible, here is a brief outline of the work Caroline was able to do as an auto worker for 14 years. In singling her out, I know there are other examples just as worthy.

Partially because she and I moved around the country for political reasons, but also because of the SWP's wrongheaded policy of moving people from industry to industry, Caroline worked in the following industries from 1980 through 1992: automobile, telephone, oil refinery, garment, auto again, garment again, steel, and oil again.

In 1992 she became employed at the New United Motor Manufacturing, Inc. (NUMMI) plant in Fremont, California. NUMMI was a joint venture of Toyota and General Motors (GM).* Caroline worked there until her illness prevented her from doing so in early 2006. So she was able to sink roots in the plant and union, Local 2244 of the United Auto Workers (UAW).

During these years she worked in two areas, the door line and then in the plastics department. She formed friendships with coworkers in both. She soon became known as a union militant, and attended and spoke up at Local meetings. The UAW still had many democratic traditions, one of which was the right of rank and file members to observe meetings of the Local Executive Committee, which she took advantage of. She discussed the meetings of the Local and the Executive Committee with her coworkers, as well as broader political issues in the International union, the country and the world, becoming known as a socialist.

For the first years she was active in the union, the Administration Caucus held the majority of Local officers and the Executive Committee. The Administration Caucus was part of the national machine of the same name that was the organ of the UAW bureaucracy in Detroit. There was an opposition grouping called the People's Caucus in Local 2244, which attempted to counter the pro-company bias of the Administration Caucus, and promote union democracy against its heavy-handed methods. For a time, Caroline joined the People's Caucus. She also became active in a national grouping in the UAW, New Directions. New Directions sought to fight against the policy of giving concessions to the auto companies championed by the national UAW leadership since 1979. New Directions later went under, but Caroline joined subsequent national class struggle groupings in the UAW, the most recent being Soldiers of Solidarity.

When Caroline was hired, there were a few SWP members in the plant. These were barred by the SWP from participating in any caucus or intervening in internal union affairs. In the mid 1990s, the SWP pulled its members from the plant, as part of the elimination of its entire auto fraction. Eventually the SWP shut down its rail and oil fractions, too.

In contract negotiations in 1994, NUMMI management tried to cut health care benefits. Although the Administration Caucus held the majority of positions, Richard Aguilar, who was from the People's Caucus, had been elected chairman of the Local's bargaining committee. He was also the only other member of New Directions in the plant. Caroline worked closely with Aguilar, and although she was a "mere" rank and filer, became his right hand, drafting his leaflets and providing advice. Against the wishes of the Administration Caucus, Aguilar led a strike when the contract expired at midnight. The night shift, which normally worked until 1 a.m. or longer, streamed out of the plant to the union headquarters across the street. Within two hours management capitulated. This was the only strike in NUMMI's history.

Caroline began to see that the People's Caucus had many features of the "outs" versus the "ins" dynamic in the union movement; that is, its leaders were interested in union posts to get ahead personally. She decided then to become an independent in the plant. She still supported the People's Caucus in opposition to the Administration Caucus because of its more militant stance toward the company.

The official newspaper of Local 2244 kept the workers in the dark concerning the Local's functioning and relations with the company, concentrating on fluff. In 1998, Caroline decided to step into this vacuum by publishing her own plant newsletter. She called it *The Barking Dog*, naming it after a plant newsletter published by a Black militant worker in the 1970s and early 1980s, when the factory was a GM plant. (GM shut the plant down, and then it reopened as the joint venture with Toyota in 1984.) Caroline had discussed with old timers the union's relations with GM, before the era of concessions, and that is how she came across the original *Barking Dog* and obtained a set of its issues.

Besides reporting on decisions of the Local, *The Barking Dog* reported on struggles in the plant and in the UAW nationally. She also wrote opinion pieces, and opened its pages to any workers who had something to say. Her newsletter quickly became popular in the plant, except among the Administration Caucus leaders. *The Barking Dog* exposed management abuses, but also criticized the Local and national union leadership when they failed to defend the workers.

One fight Caroline took on was that of mainly women workers who had been punished for taking days off to attend to family medical emergencies. This company policy was in violation of the law, specifically the Family Medical Leave Act. Caroline helped explain the issue to the workers throughout the plant, and helped these workers to bring their case before the National Labor Relations Board (NLRB). The NLRB ruled in favor of the workers and forced NUMMI management to change its policy, something they didn't like and blamed Caroline for.

Top management in NUMMI, who mainly came from Toyota and were used to labor laws in Japan, first tried to ban *The Barking Dog*. They were taken aback when the Local leadership, including the Administration Caucus, informed them they could not ban such material. The whole leadership saw that allowing management to ban *The Barking Dog* would cripple the union's ability generally to produce newsletters, leaflets, and other materials.

Caroline was not only a critic, but also a politician. She won both caucuses' support to a major labor battle of the mid-1990s. Three unions in Decatur, Illinois waged a long struggle that captured the imagination of labor militants across the country, a story told by Steve Ashby and C. J. Hawking in their book, *Staley: The Fight for a New American Labor Movement*.** Caroline also helped build a Bay Area support committee for the Decatur strikes. Two strikers on separate occasions, part of teams sent out nationally, stayed at our house when they came through the Bay Area, and they spoke at a number of union meetings. His wife accompanied one of these road warriors, and Caroline and I took them on an excursion to see the redwoods at Muir Woods National Park. Caroline also got the Local to support Toyota workers in the South who were attempting to win union recognition. There were other national battles Caroline helped get the Local to support.

At one point the Local leadership tried to suppress *The Barking Dog* when Caroline criticized them. A lawyer paid by the Administration Caucus sent Caroline a blistering letter threatening her with a libel suit. Anonymous threatening letters were sent, one enclosing a picture of our house. She and I found a capable young pro-labor lawyer, who drew up a reply that proved labor law and the First Amendment were on Caroline's side. Caroline printed both letters in *The Barking Dog*, and flooded the plant with them. Workers were furious that their "leaders" would threaten a rank-and-file worker for criticizing them. Our lawyer also pointed out that those who filed frivolous lawsuits were liable for all legal costs in California, and the threatened libel suit was hastily withdrawn.

The Barking Dog was also distributed nationally through the nation-wide militant caucuses Caroline was a member of. It also caught the attention of fighters abroad. One group of German autoworkers invited her to attend and speak at a conference in Germany they organized.

Caroline became well known throughout the plant as a result of her activities and newsletter. She earned the admiration of many of her co-workers for fighting and winning against the Administration Caucus leadership. In 2000, she decided to run for Trustee in the Local's elections. She ran as an independent against the candidates of both the Administration and People's caucuses, and won. She supported the People's Caucus candidates for other posts. This election put her on the Executive Committee of the Local, which changed the balance of forces.

Some of the Administration Caucus leaders, mainly those who had some connection to the Local in the old GM days, united in a new caucus with the People's Caucus. In elections held in 2003, this new caucus threw out the Administration Caucus. Caroline was re-elected as an independent, and was able to work with the new leadership. In fact, she was asked to become the editor of the Local's newspaper. She decided not to accept this post, but worked on the newspaper's staff with the new editor, a young woman. The newspaper was transformed. There were now regular reports from the new Local leaders, as well as information about management's maneuvers against the workers, and other reports of relevance to NUMMI workers and about struggles nationally.

One thing Caroline reprinted in the Local newspaper was an article written in the 1980s by Genora Johnson (Dollinger) concerning the failure of the UAW to fight for things like universal health care for all and adequate social security, instead of what became the UAW leadership's strategy of winning benefits company by company—a strategy that has shown its utter bankruptcy in the Great Recession. This has relevance to this book also in the fact that Genora was a leader of the Women's Auxiliary in the great Flint sit-down strike of 1936--1937 that was key to the formation of the UAW. Genora was a founding member of the SWP in 1938, and she left with the Cochran group in 1953.

Caroline kept up *The Barking Dog*, which supplemented the Local newspaper from the left, and helped keep the leadership honest. Or more honest. Once, she was invited as a member of the Executive Committee to a regional conference of the UAW leadership. She reported in *The Barking Dog* that not much of substance happened, but each night the invitees were treated to lavish meals, with a free bar, bowls of shrimp throughout the room, large roasts on spits carved to order, and so forth. Caroline wrote that she wouldn't ever again attend such a gathering. The new leadership wasn't pleased.

All in all, *The Barking Dog* published about once a month or two for over 60 issues.

There were three elected Trustees. Caroline in fact ran this committee, which oversaw the Local's finances. She found some irregularities, especially on the part of the Local treasurer, who was a supporter of the Administration Caucus. This treasurer also treated the Local's secretary staff in a high-handed and obnoxious manner, and Caroline became their defender. The upshot was that the treasurer was brought up on charges in the Local, and was removed with even the concurrence of the Administration Caucus.

In contract talks in 2005, the company again tried to attack health care and other benefits. Caroline and the other leaders launched a drive to mobilize the membership to fight back. They organized demonstrations in front of the plant with a big banner spread on a bridge crossing a major freeway, covered by TV news. Management's ploy had been to project a "labor friendly" image, and they didn't like this publicity or the fact that the workers were appealing to public opinion.

Both the Local newspaper and *The Barking Dog* talked up in the plant the need to be ready to strike. As the deadline for the contract's expiration approached in July, a couple of thousand workers signed up for picket duty. At midnight when the contract expired, Caroline and I were at the union hall, and there were still hundreds signing up. The contract was extended hour-by-hour as negotiations continued. Then it was announced that the company had capitulated, to cheers in the hall.

Shortly thereafter, in August 2005, Caroline experienced the first symptoms of Lou Gehrig's disease (ALS), which would take her life a little more than a year later.

With the exception of strike support work and her discussing socialist politics with her coworkers, all of the above activities Caroline carried out were strictly forbidden to SWP members in industry. And, she did this work as an individual in the plant, without the support of a party. She had no newspaper like *The Militant* behind her. She did have the support of myself and Malik Miah, who played a leading role in the union at his job as a mechanic at United Airlines. We formed a kind of mini party, and got together to discuss strategy and tactics at both NUMMI and United. She also had support from her friends in the national militant groups in the UAW, as well as from Erwin Baur, a retired autoworker in the Bay Area who had once played a central role in the SWP's auto fraction (he left the SWP in the 1953 split).

With a little imagination one can picture what could have been accomplished by over a thousand SWPers in both industrial and white-collar unions, organized into self-confident fractions, collaborating in the plants and nationally with a correct orientation. We could not only have survived, but become well known as fighters who had broader ideas about how capitalism functions, and the socialist alternative. Together with an independent youth organization focused on campuses, we could have been an important pole for the fightback as the massive crisis of finance capital plunged the United States and much of the world into the Great Recession in 2007.

---

* The New United Motor Manufacturing, Inc. (NUMMI) plant in Fremont closed in 2010 during the Great Recession.

** Steven K. Ashby & C. J. Hawking, *Staley: The Fight for a New American Labor Movement* (University of Illinois Press, 2009). 384 pages.

Index

Table of Acronyms

AFSCME	American Federation of State, County and Municipal Emplo
ATC	Rural Workers Association (Nicaragua)
FI	Fourth International
FMLN	Farabundo Marti National Liberation Front (El Salvador)
FSLN	Sandinista National Liberation Front (Nicaragua)
FUR	United Revolutionary Front (Portugal)
HKE	Revolutionary Workers Party (Iran)
HKS	Socialist Workers Party (Iran)
IEC	International Executive Committee (Fourth International)
IMG	International Marxist Group (England)
IMT	International Majority Tendency (Fourth International)
ISO	International Socialist Organization
IS	International Socialists
IT	Internationalist Tendency
KOR	Committee for Social Self-Defense (Poland)
LC	Communist League (France) (Spain)
LCI	International Communist League (Portugal)
LCR	Revolutionary Communist League (France, Spain)
LS	Socialist League (Mexico)
LSA/LSO	League for Socialist Action/Socialist Workers League (Can
LTF/LTT	Leninist-Trotskyist Faction (Tendency)
MIR	Movement of the Revolutionary Left (Chile)
NAACP	National Association for the Advancement of Colored Peo
NBIPP	National Black Independent Political Party
NLF	National Liberation Front (Vietnam)
NSCAR	National Student Committee Against Racism
OCI	Internationalist Communist Organization (France)

OCRFI	Organizing Committee for the Reconstruction of the Fourth International (France)
PAM	People's Action Movement (Nicaragua)
PDPA	People's Democratic Party of Afghanistan
PL	Progressive Labor (Party)
POR	Revolutionary Workers Party (Bolivia)
POT	Proletarian Orientation Tendency
PRDF	Political Rights Defense Fund
PRT	Revolutionary Workers Party (Argentina, Mexico, Portugal)
RMC	Revolutionary Marxist Committee
RMG	Revolutionary Marxist Group (Canada)
ROAR	Restore Our Alienated Rights
SDS	Students for a Democratic Society
SLA	Symbionese Liberation Army
SMC	Student Mobilization Committee
SWP	Socialist Workers Party (USA, Australia)
TDU	Teamsters for a Democratic Union
UAW	United Auto Workers
UFCW	United Food and Commercial Workers
UFT	United Federation of Teachers
UFW	United Farm Workers
UMWA	United Mine Workers of America
UNAG	National Union of Farmers and Ranchers (Nicaragua)
USLA	United States Committee on Latin American Political Prisoner
YAWF	Youth Against War and Fascism
YSA	Young Socialist Alliance

About Resistance Books

Resistance Books is the publishing arm of Socialist Resistance, a revolutionary Marxist organisation which is the British section of the Fourth International. We publish books jointly with the International Institute for Research and Education in Amsterdam and independently under the name of Resistance books. Socialist Resistance also publishes a bi-monthly magazine of the same name and occasional pamphlets.

Socialist Resistance is an organisation active in the trade union movement and in many campaigns against the war, in solidarity with Palestine and with anti-capitalist movements across the globe. We are ecosocialist – we argue that much of what is produced under capitalism is socially useless and either redundant or directly harmful. Capitalism's drive for profit is creating environmental disaster – and it is the poor, the working class and the global south that are paying the highest price for this.

We have been long standing supporters of women's liberation and the struggles of lesbians, gay people bisexuals and transgender people. We believe those struggles must be led by those directly affected – none so fit to break the chains as those who wear them. We work in antiracist and anti-fascist networks, including campaigns for the rights of immigrants and asylum seekers.

Socialist Resistance believes that democracy is an essential component of any successful movement of resistance and struggle. With Britain and the western imperialist countries moving into a long period of capitalist austerity and crisis, deeper than any since the Second World War, Socialist Resistance stands together with all those who are organising to make another world is possible.

Further information about Resistance Books and Socialist Resistance can be obtained at www.socialistresistance.org.

International Viewpoint is the English language on-line magazine of the Fourth International, which can be read at www.internationalviewpoint.org.

New and notable

Militant years - car workers' struggles in Britain in the 60s and 70s, Alan Thornett, February 2011 (£12, €14, $19).

The Global Fight for Climate Justice – Anti-capitalist responses to global warming and environmental destruction, Ian Angus ed., June 2009 (£10, €14, $18).

Ireland's Credit Crunch, Kearing, Morrison & Corrigan, October 2010 (£6, €8, $10).

Foundations of Christianity: a study in Christian origins, Karl Kautsky (£12, €18, $25).

The Permanent Revolution & Results and Prospects, Leon Trotsky (£9, €15, $18).

My Life Under White Supremacy and in Exile, Leonard Nikani, February 2009 (£10, €12, $15).

Cuba at Sea, Ron Ridenour, May 2008 (£8, €12, $15).

Ecosocialism or Barbarism (new expanded edition), Jane Kelly ed., February 2008 (£6, €9, $12).

Cuba: Beyond the Crossroads (new expanded edition), Ron Ridenour, April 2007 (£10, €15, $20).

Middle East: war, imperialism, and ecology – sixty years of resistance, Roland Rance & Terry Conway eds. and Gilbert Achcar (contributor) et al., March 2007 (£12, €14, $19).

It's never too late to love or rebel, Celia Hart, August 2006 (£8, €15, $20).

Notebooks for study and research

New Parties of the Left – Experiences from Europe, Daniel Bensaïd , Alain Krivine, Alda Sousa, Alan Thornett et al., May 2011 (€8, £7, $11).

Revolution and Counter-revolution in Europe from 1918 to 1968, Pierre Frank, May 2011 (€10, £9, $14), NSR 49.

Women's Liberation & Socialist Revolution: Documents of the Fourth International, Penelope Duggan ed., October 2010 (€8, £7, $11) NSR 48, IIRE pub.

The Long March of the Trotskyists: Contributions to the history of the International, Pierre Frank, Daniel Bensaïd, Ernest Mandel, October 2010 (€8, £5, $8), NSR 47, IIRE and Resistance books pub.

October Readings: The development of the concept of Permanent Revolution, D. R. O'Connor Lysaght ed., October 2010 (£5, €6, $8), NSR 46, IIRE and Resistance books pub.

Building Unity Against Fascism: Classic Marxist Writings, Leon Trotsky, Daniel Guérin, Ted Grant et al., October 2010 (€6, £5, $8), NSR 44/45, IIRE and Resistance books pub.

Strategies of Resistance & 'Who Are the Trotskyists', Daniel Bensaïd, November 2009 (€8, £6, $10), NSR 42/43, IIRE and Resistance books pub.

Living Internationalism: the IIRE's history, Murray Smith and Joost Kircz eds., January 2011 (€5, £4, $7), NSR 41, IIRE pub.

Socialists and the Capitalist Recession (with Ernest Mandel's 'Basic Theories of Karl Marx'), Raphie De Santos, Michel Husson, Claudio Katz et al., March 2009 (€9, £6, $12), NSR 39/40, IIRE and Resistance books pub.

Take the Power to Change the World, Phil Hearse ed., June 2007 (€9, £6, $12), NSR 37/38, IIRE and Resistance books pub.

The Porto Alegre Alternative: Direct Democracy in Action, Iain Bruce ed. (€19, £13, $23.50), NSR 35/36.

The Clash of Barbarisms: September 11 & the Making of the New World Disorder, Gilbert Achcar (€15, £10, $16), NSR 33/34.

Globalization: Neoliberal Challenge, Radical Responses, Robert Went (€21, £14, $21), NSR 31/32.

Understanding the Nazi Genocide: Marxism after Auschwitz, Enzo Traverso (€19.20, £13, $19.) NSR 29/30.

Fatherland or Mother Earth? Essays on the National Question, Michael Löwy (€16, £10.99, $16), NSR 27

Forthcoming books

Capitalism - Crisis and Alternatives, Ozlem Onaran, Michel Husson, John Rees, Claudio Katz et al., July 2011 (€8, £7, $11).

Marxism and Anarchism, Karl Marx, Frederick Engels, Leon Trotsky, September 2011 (€8, £7, $11).

Fascism and the far right in Europe, September 2011

Introduction to Marxist Economic Theory (Third Edition), Ernest Mandel, Özlem Onaran, Raphie de Santos, November 2011.

The thought of Leon Trotsky, Denise Avenas, Michael Löwy, Jean-Michel Krivine.

The united front & the Transitional Programme, Leon Trotsky, Daniel Bensaïd, John Riddell.

Dangerous relationships: marriage and divorces between Marxism and feminism, Cinzia Arruzza.

Lightning Source UK Ltd.
Milton Keynes UK
UKOW05f0253051114

241122UK00004B/456/P